How Far Can a Piano Fly?

And Other Tales from Column One in the Los Angeles Times

Los Angeles Times
BOOKS

Editors: Roxane Arnold, Marc Duvoisin,
Simon K.C. Li, Roger Smith
Designer: Catherine Vandecasteele
Cover Design: Tom Trapnell
Copy Editor: Stephanie Goodman

ISBN: 1-883792-74-6
Copyright 2003 Los Angeles Times
202 W. 1st St., Los Angeles, CA 90012

First printing August 2003
Printed in the U.S.A.

Los Angeles Times

Publisher: John P. Puerner
Editor: John S. Carroll
Book Development General Manager: Carla Lazzareschi

❖

How Far Can a Piano Fly?
And Other Tales from the Los Angeles Times

Los Angeles Times
BOOKS

CONTENTS

. . .

❖

FOREWORD

BY PATT MORRISON

It's the sweetest piece of real estate in all the hulking bulk of the Los Angeles Times, and it has been for 35 years.

Up there, near the top left of the front page, shouldered under the Gothic letters of the nameplate, it's the headline that meets your gaze each morning, the place where your eye slews instinctively — Column One.

Seven days each week, for those 3 1/2 decades, Column One has provided a dozen Scheherazades' worth of prime storytelling. Whatever mayhem the day's news brings, Column One is an oasis, a leisurely, considered account, nothing like the hurried, Gatling gun rat-a-tat of news stories.

To follow the verbs and nouns and adjectives down that long, deep well of type is to embark on a singular word-excursion, from shivering among the penguins on Inaccessible Island in the Antarctic to a virtual visit to the rings of Saturn … from whisking Gobi desert sand off fossils 70,000 millennia old, into the tantalizing, not-so-far-off future, where nanotechnology dangles before us the promise of life everlasting.

Since the first Column One appeared many thousands of days ago, it's become the newspaper's showcase and showplace — for readers, a brisk daily plunge into the engrossing and unconventional, and for writers, an opportunity to unshackle their talents from confining notions of what a newspaper story is and isn't.

Column One made an implicit pact with readers: We will give you something you will not find anywhere else. The day's news comes and goes. But Column One is the yarn that stays with you. A Times foreign correspondent once told his editor that he'd

1

rather have one of his stories appear in Column One than have it splashed as the lead story on Page 1.

The competition to make Column One is the newspaper world's version of the struggles of millions of sperm to become the one to reach the egg first.

Here's the math:

The Times employs hundreds of reporters. They write hundreds of stories every day, for hundreds of days per annum.

The front page carries at least a half-dozen stories every day. But there's only one Column One per diem, and while The Times is a polite and collegial place, it was known to happen on a very rare occasion that an editor may have oh-so-subtly critiqued another editor's Column One offering, to the benefit of his or her own. One editor used to keep a running tally of how many Column Ones his reporters had scored — a measure, he believed, of how good he and they were.

As varied as Column Ones are, one thing they definitely are not is "news you can use," except as fuel for the imagination. These stories are quests — into minds, into places, into past and future. For the two bits you spent for the newspaper — four bits now, but that's what 35 years of inflation will do — you met the Nebraska man who supplies young racist Germans with forbidden Nazi literature. You learned the history of the paper clip. You trod the earth of a pristine, primeval 2,000-year-old Polish forest, survivor of war and ax and chainsaw.

It began, as so many experiments did, in the 1960s. What came to be called "literary journalism," the stylishness of fiction paired with the authenticity of news, was then just pecking its way out of the hard shell of old-fashioned who-what-when journalism — "the stiff-necked approach to news," as Times former editor William F. Thomas put it, the attitude that "some very interesting stories and social phenomena simply 'did not belong in a newspaper.' "

The precise chemistry that conjured up Column One, no one now remembers exactly. Was it one part city editor Thomas, and three parts editor Nick Williams, the man who once wrote in a memorandum, "Being serious in purpose does not mean being drab"?

That was Column One in a sentence: storyteller prose with substance at its heart.

In September 1968, the Beatles were still together, but the nation was coming apart — Vietnam, black power and flower power, women's lib and the Pill, and drugs and sex and rock 'n' roll.

John Foley had just come back from assignment at the police batting practice melee that was the Democratic convention in Chicago, to be told that he had a new job. He would be in charge of something radically new for The Times — and he would not be merely running it, but, by his choices and decisions, defining it.

Foley was offered two stories to choose between for the inaugural Column One: the hard truths in the making of a beauty queen, or the rise of the Christian Democratic movement in Latin America, from one of The Times' new foreign bureaus. "I thought this was going to be something like the Atlantic Monthly or Harper's, so I went with the big time." Politics trumped sex, and Column One was launched. Of that first one, Foley says, "I don't think anybody ever read it."

If that's the case, it was the first and probably the last time. (The beauty queen story ran the next day, and whatever allure the first Column One may have lacked, the word "blonde" in headline type guaranteed that the second made up for it.)

The gold standard for Column One was that it had to elicit some variant of that magic phrase, "Gee, that's interesting. I didn't know that."

In short order, Column One became the premium "play" in the newspaper. It acquired the name Column One in October 1989, under managing editor George Cotliar. But for the longest time, it didn't have any formal name at all. The managing editor when the feature began was Frank Haven, who kept trying to pin it with the label "non-duplicative," a cumbersome way of saying the story wouldn't be found in any other newspaper. His staff sensibly clipped it to "non-dupe." To this day, you can figure out which Times staffers are veterans and which are the newcomers by what they call it. Old-timers call it "the non-dupe"; the new guys call it Column One.

Not every writer was Column One material, nor every editor. "Many fine and intelligent editors," Thomas recalls, "simply had tunnel vision when it came to a column without borders."

That's because the breadth and range of Column One flattened the century-old walls that had divvied up newspapers by subject sections like sports, by "hard news" versus "soft news," by "writerly pieces" versus "reported pieces."

There was no foolproof recipe for writing a Column One, but, like Supreme Court Justice Potter Stewart's definition of porn, editors knew one when they saw one: original in subject, engaging in writing, perhaps a slightly canted take on a familiar topic.

Retired Timesman Rudy Abramson, who bagged his share of Column Ones, says the beauty of it was that very thing: There was no formula. The real test of a good Column One, he thinks, is the test of time: Can it stand up to being read a year, five, 10 years on?

While 1,800 words was suggested as an ideal Column One length, there was in fact no hard and fast limit.

Some of them ran to several thousand encyclopedic words — an account of one man enmeshed in the dilemmas of Oregon's assisted suicide law weighed in at 13,518

— and some were a paltry few hundred. Foley remembers his dentist pausing above his mouth once to tell him what a great story that was — a trifling 800-word postcard from The Times' correspondent in Cairo.

Try to classify Column Ones by category, and you find that many match several categories, and some elude pigeonholing altogether. But here are some broad classifications, and a sampling of Column Ones that you won't necessarily find within this book, but which illustrate the breadth and reach of the Column One experience.

— Process or, in hardware-store language, the how-to: how Time magazine selects its Person of the Year; the search to find the annual Easter Seal poster child; how it took 16 years, 6,700 authors and 32,600 pages to assembly the definitive art history compendium; how a dozen anonymous men and women decide on movie ratings; how Nazi scientific research is putting a match to medical ethics debates.

— Profiles: France's most feared lawyer, defender of Nazis and terrorists; the last American Commie left standing; the San Andreas fault; a Times journalist's account of being a non-practicing Jew reporting in Israel.

— Anniversary and history revisited: the legend of skyjacker D.B. Cooper, 25 years after he leaped from a plane and vanished; "the Bomb" at 40; Arthur Miller and the half-century since "Death of a Salesman" hit the boards; Peary and the Pole — did he make it or fake it?

— Snapshots from abroad: Russian mobsters hiding in plain sight by getting elected to the Duma, where they can't be arrested; Japan's obsession with the toilet, computerized, Web-sited, even rendered in 24-karat-gold; Colombia's Romeo-and-Juliet romance between a guerrilla girl and an Army conscript; Brazilians' fondness for quirky first names like Waterloo, Xerox and Skylab; France ending its near-century-old ban on artificial sweeteners; Germans mourning as European Union speed limits slow them down on the Autobahn.

— "Well, I'll be damned": an anti-gay-marriage political crusader whose gay son campaigns against him; the Mojave Phone Booth, the only pay phone for miles, with fans and Web sites dedicated to it; a South Carolina town's annual tobacco-spitting contest; the war for the credit and the bucks among some Nobel Peace Prize winners

— "I never thought about that": gang members paralyzed by bullets and stuck in wheelchairs who keep trying to gangbang; Americans who live without television; the homeless who surf the Internet; obsolete tombstones, pre-cut with 19 — death dates, and here it is the millennium and you're still alive.

— The American cultural laboratory: political correctness changing language, like the Crayola color known as Indian red and a plant called the wandering Jew; heroin going upscale; the Midwest's new crops, frijoles and tortilla corn; black migration from the inner city to the suburbs; L.A.'s language lab, from a Latino restaurant worker who picks up Hebrew from the boss to the black mailman who learns Armenian on his Glendale route.

— A moment in time: dateless and desperate for the biggest night of the year, New Year's Eve 1999; sob stories, students' pathetic essays to get into UC schools; Hawaii's Peter Pans, its eternal beach boys; the last of the rail-riding hoboes; colleges trying to, like, stamp out "Mallspeak," you know?; a day in the life of a 14-year-old boy, the elusive target audience for moviemakers; 50 years of L.A. freeway spills, from brassieres to ketchup.

Sometimes this sweet spot on Page 1 launched a series, like "The Hunger Wars," "The California Century," "Space, Time and Strings" — about new theories of physics — and "TV's Diversity Dilemma." Some Column Ones were team efforts, some were bravura solo performances.

"My feeling," Thomas says, "always has been that if it's interesting, it belongs."

So here, from the choicest place in the paper, the thousands have been winnowed to hundreds, and the hundreds to a few dozen. Open these pages and sample the selections; some you'll revisit, and some will be new to you (you must have been on vacation, of course).

These were not necessarily chosen as the best — editors would be wearing slings and bloodied bandages if they'd had to fight it out over what "the best" means. Instead, think of them as a Column One smorgasbord, as fresh and original today as they were 35 years ago.

This Rich Life

❖

The Sage of Fortune Cookies

A quest to discover why the ubiquitous little messages so rarely predict the future anymore leads through a byzantine world of secrecy and suspicion to an unlikely oracle.

By Terry McDermott · November 4, 2000

SAN FRANCISCO — On Mendell Street, down among the low warehouses, apartment blocks and alfresco drug bazaars of Hunter's Point, sits a small, shabby building with a front door that never opens. Locked behind it, Steven Yang sits with a secret he does not wish to share.

We arrived here seeking enlightenment — true enlightenment, not some guru's pale imitation but genuine illumination, the real thing, the easy thing, the wished-for, dreamed-of blinding flash of unearned knowledge, the stunning insight that knocks us, all Pauls en route to Damascus, clean out of the saddle.

We speak, in other words, of fortune cookies, the slight, curvy sugar wafers enfolding the wisdom of the ages.

Maybe that's a stretch. Truth be told, fortune cookies were never the font of much wisdom: mere after-dinner entertainments. Who, after all, could ever take seriously an anonymous message tucked inside a sugar cookie?

Quite a few people, as it turns out, which leads to our current mystery: Something dreadful has happened to fortune cookies — they almost never contain fortunes.

Think of the last time you opened a cookie. What did the message inside say? Think of the last 10, 50, 100 times. They weren't real fortunes, were they? They were aphorisms, or silly cliches, or small pieces of lame advice. Or, more recently, perhaps a veiled threat. One recent fortune received in Los Angeles warned: "Choose your enemies wisely."

What happened? Who took the fortunes out of fortune cookies?

We think Steven Yang knows. We have come to his locked door to find out.

The sun shines from its perfect sky. Mendell Street is fogless in the early morning light. The circumstances couldn't be more clouded.

· · ·

The path to fortune cookie knowledge winds through weird places, most notably a machine shop in a Boston suburb and Bob's Typing Service in San Francisco. It begins with the history and subsequent nature of the business.

As ancient institutions go, the fortune cookie is not all that ancient. The Chinese fortune cookie was invented in the United States sometime in the early part of the 20th century, probably by either a Japanese American gardener in San Francisco or a Chinese American cook in Los Angeles.

There are suggestions that it has antecedents among Chinese moon cakes, which carried hidden messages in the 14th century. Given the 600-odd-year gap, these seem like feeble attempts at undeserved authenticity. Even if they are true, the similarities between the moon cakes, made from lotus nut paste and used to plan an insurrection against Mongol occupiers, and the little gold cracker that arrives on your tip tray are slight enough to melt beneath the dimmest of lights.

Whoever invented the cookies, they remained regional California oddities until 1948, when a San Francisco truck driver, Edward Louie, devised a machine that partly automated the labor-intensive process of making the flour-egg-sugar-and-water confection. Louie then partnered with a local restaurant that began the tradition of serving the cookies as complimentary desserts.

Others improved Louie's design, and the more automated cookie production became, the greater the distribution of the cookie. The machine now sold most widely throughout the United States was invented by Yong Lee, a Korean-born engineer in Massachusetts, who complains that it was the single worst thing that ever happened to him.

"Wasted all my productive years on it," he said.

Up through the 1970s, most of the cookies sold in the United States came from California. With the introduction of Lee's machines, production spread throughout the country and into Canada, Mexico — even China. At one point, more than two-thirds of the fortune cookies baked in the United States were made on Yong Lee machines, which have a "Babes in Toyland" quality to them.

A spigot squeezes dough onto round metal griddles. A turntable passes the dough through a gas oven. The cookies bake in about 30 seconds and remain pliable enough to be folded for another 15.

When a cookie comes out of the oven, an arm drops a fortune into the middle of the warm wafer, then presses the cookie down through a slot, which has the effect of folding it in half. Two more arms then press the cookie over a metal rod set at right angles to the slot, folding it again in the other direction. By the time the cookie tumbles down a conveyor into a box, it has hardened with the message inside.

Today, most large American cities have at least one and sometimes as many as a dozen fortune-cookie makers, most of them small, family businesses. With some exceptions, most cater to local markets. "The low margin has kept bigger companies out of the business," said Donna Tong of Peking Noodle Co. in Los Angeles, the largest California producer and one of the biggest in the country.

Lee estimates the national output at a billion cookies a month. This seems exaggerated, for the simple reason that fortune cookies are mainly an American item, and in order to consume a billion of them a month, every man, woman and child in the country would have to eat Chinese food once a week.

It is not a get-rich-quick business, although it has grown steadily as people continue to eat out more and the use of cookies for promotional purposes accelerates. (Al Gore and George Bush both bought more than a million of them for their conventions this summer, and McDonald's once ordered 55 million for a special promotion.) The result is an industry with dozens of small businesses competing fiercely, almost solely on price.

It's a cutthroat industry, said Greg Louie, Edward's grandson, in which "nobody trusts anybody." Research for this article supports the notion.

Told that a reporter had visited Peking Noodle, a competitor expressed surprise. "Peking let you walk through? I'm shocked. They never let anyone in," he said. He paused, lowered his voice and asked, "What's it like?"

Conversations with other fortune-cookie people tended to go like this: Cookie? Big secret.

Various people tried to explain what exactly was being kept secret.

The machines, they said.

But doesn't everybody have the machines?

The recipe, they said.

But aren't they all basically the same recipe?

The messages, they said.

Well, how can messages be secret when they're read by the thousands every day?

Big secret. Goodbye.

As invariably happens when industries grow, specialization occurs. When inventor Lee began shipping his machines all over North America — later followed by a Japanese-made machine that increases production sixfold — many of the mom-and-pop bakers who bought them had little knowledge of what to put inside the cookies. They were businesspeople, not soothsayers.

Many cookie makers simply stole fortunes from one another, accumulating what amounted to an almost universal stock of fortunes written by early cookie pioneers.

These were lifted from sources as diverse as the Bible and Poor Richard's Almanac, and translated into a kind of mock "Confucius say" language.

"In those days, they were all farmer phrases," Greg Louie said. "We changed over the years, borrowing from Bartlett's, Yiddish sayings, wherever."

Lee built a stock of thousands of the traditional fortunes and began selling them very cheaply to the people who bought his machines. That's when the problems started. Fortunes that seemed perfectly acceptable in one part of the country suddenly became offensive in, say, Decatur, Georgia.

"Message says: 'A handsome young man is in your future,'" Lee said. "Southern old lady take it very seriously and complain. They're afraid of young man. It's a joke. Still they complain. They don't take it as a joke."

It wasn't just Southerners. Everybody complained: feminists, grammarians, Asian Americans.

"Had to get rid of a bunch of messages," Lee said. "It all became nonsense."

. . .

Clearly, a wholesale rewriting of fortunes was needed, which brings us back to Steven Yang, a young Shanghai-born engineer whom Lee hired to sell his machines. Yang said he had no trouble selling the machines but was having great trouble getting paid what he considered adequate commissions.

"Yong Lee has no money," Yang said. "He say, 'Next time, Steven. Next time.'"

So, in 1993, Yang quit and went into business for himself. He bought Chinese Yellow Pages for the entire United States and started calling cookie makers. Then he got in his car and went to see them.

He sold them fortunes. He didn't have the wherewithal to start manufacturing cookie machines, but he spied an opportunity in the message business, which was little more than a sideline for Lee. Yang made copies of all the messages he could get his hands on and went to work taking Lee's message customers away from him.

He set up a printing operation in San Francisco and started cranking out fortunes by the millions. Today, this little shop in a bad part of San Francisco is by far the nation's biggest content provider for cookies.

Yang is very reluctant to discuss his business. He never unlocks his front door. He and his wife, Linda Qiu, work alone, seven days a week, up to 14 hours a day, printing, cutting and shipping messages all over the country. Sometimes, they sleep in the shop. He almost never lets anyone else in and, to preserve secrecy, doesn't hire help.

"No one knows how we do this. Chinese are smart. They're working for you, after one or two years, they leave, taking my business with him."

Just like you?

He laughed. "Just like me."

Yang consented to a telephone interview and, later, a meeting on neutral ground, but never a visit to his shop. The key to his success, he said, is a method he has devised to cut labor costs.

"Over seven years in business, I never show to anyone. It is secret. No one knows how to pack the paper. We do very beautiful packing. I got a very special machine. I saw some company — one people cutting messages, five people packing. Make no money. I have one people cutting. One people packing."

That's the big secret, how the paper is packed? This is the reason you won't answer your door?

"I'm very scared. Too many questions. You going to steal my business," Yang said.

After Yang figured out the economic key to success, his secret packing machine, he still faced the same dilemma that had perplexed Lee — the messages themselves.

"I copy all of Yong Lee's messages," Yang said. "It doesn't work. Everything is so stupid. That's no good. I don't know how to write a message. So one time one lady call me from San Diego. I think she is a schoolteacher. She goes to Chinese restaurant. Opens cookie…. Very bad. Message really is for fun, isn't supposed to make people angry."

Yang, tired of the criticism, hired the complaining woman to rewrite the messages he had taken from Lee.

So a San Diego schoolteacher writes all the messages? Who is she?

"Lola, I think. I can't remember. She doesn't do it anymore. I lost her number."

Yang eventually recovered Lola's number. Except she isn't Lola, and she isn't a schoolteacher. Her name is Donna Jackson, and she's a speech pathologist. Jackson said her principal complaint wasn't the content of the messages, but their form — a singsong Charlie Chan English she found offensive.

"I didn't know if they wanted them to sound that way or what. Some were incomprehensible. 'One foot on the moon will be green,' stuff like that," she said. So she agreed to edit Yang's messages. When she couldn't even figure out what many of them were intended to say, she wrote new ones. Those she mainly lifted from a library book on astrology. She didn't much care what they said, just that they be grammatical. This accounts for many of the messages you read that ascribe personal qualities to the reader. For example, "You are kindhearted, hospitable, cheerful and well-liked."

The grammar corrections did little to slow the pace of complaints, Yang said, and after he lost "Lola's" number, he grew desperate, asking everybody he knew to write new messages.

One day, driving in San Francisco, he saw a place advertising small-business services — copying, printing, proofreading. He stopped and asked the owner if he would like to write fortunes. The man said, no, he wasn't really in that business, but he had a writer friend who might. The friend called, met Steven and initially agreed, for a dime apiece, to write 1,000 messages, a deal that would make him the most prolific fortune-cookie fortune writer in history.

Yang thinks we want to steal his packing machine. All we really want to know is who this guy, the sage of San Francisco, is. Yang can't remember.

How about the name of the business that referred him?

"It's an English name," Yang said.

Maybe it had the word "Printing" in it, he said. Calls to more than 100 printers yielded nothing.

Then Yang helpfully said that maybe it's not listed as a printer, but a copy place. They had copy machines. More calls, more puzzled people who knew nothing.

This went on for weeks.

One day, Yang, by now eager to help find the fortune writer as a way to throw us off the scent of his precious packing machine, remembered that the business was on Geary, a street that cuts through almost all of San Francisco, from the Pacific Ocean to the bay. No matter, this was progress.

More calls. Nothing.

Finally, Yang remembered that the shop was near a particular hospital. A quick check of the neighborhood turned up a place called Bob's Typing Service.

That's it, Yang said. Bob is the man who knows the man who wrote the fortunes. We called.

"Bob's Typing Service," said the woman on the telephone.

Bob, please.

"Bob sold the business. He doesn't work here anymore."

That's what she said. She might as well have added: It's not Chinatown, Jake. It's fortune cookies.

. . .

Yang's messages come in four broad categories: a few genuine fortunes, aphorisms, advice and those zodiacal descriptions of personal attributes.

A true fortune is one that predicts the future. Here's one of Yang's, for example:

"A financial investment will yield returns beyond your dreams." Although, in this dot-com age, it might be hard to imagine what could conceivably qualify as being "beyond" one's dreams, this is undeniably a fortune.

"You possess a rare beauty," more typical of Yang's current offerings, is not.

It's a nice thing to say. It might even be true, but it is not a fortune.

Neither is this: "Pay less attention to your living conditions and more attention to your life."

This grim admonition was among the fortunes written by the great and elusive sage of San Francisco, the man we finally tracked to Bob's Typing Service, now absent Bob.

The people at Bob's, amused, called the original Bob, Bob Cristoph, and relayed our ridiculous question. Unlike everyone else connected to the fortune-writing business, Cristoph actually keeps track of names and phone numbers. He remembered Yang and the man he referred to him. The sage was revealed — a bookkeeper named Russell Rowland.

Rowland was eager to talk.

Rowland's day job is in accounts receivable at an advertising agency. At night he writes novels, four of them to date, one of which — a Montana ranch saga — is scheduled to be published next year.

A couple of years ago, Rowland was moonlighting as a proofreader for Bob's Typing Service. The ad agency job was only part time. So when Bob called and asked if he'd be interested in some extra money writing fortune-cookie fortunes, he said yes.

Yang offered him a dime a message: a hundred dollars for a thousand fortunes. Rowland later countered with a quarter, and Yang preemptively raised it to 30 cents.

"I suspected I was in trouble when he was so eager to go higher," Rowland said. "So after the first 200, I called him and told him we needed to renegotiate, and he jumped all the way to 70 cents!"

Rowland eventually wrote 700 new messages, quite possibly the highest output in contemporary fortune-cookie history. Given the distribution of Yang's fortunes, Rowland is probably America's best read and worst paid novelist. If it were his novels people were reading, he wouldn't care about the lousy pay.

Rowland is tall — tall enough to be a sage — and kindly looking enough too, with a soft, round face, glasses and a high, wise forehead. He lacks the self-importance we might want in our oracles, substituting a disconcerting Montana prairie aw-shucksness.

Rowland's been around — in the Navy, where he learned to type, in Montana, where he learned to sell shoes, and in Massachusetts, where he started to write. He's had a rough couple of decades. Even the one unqualified success, the acceptance of his novel for publication, dwindled into ambiguity when his publisher was bought by another, his editor fired and his book stuck in limbo for a year. The new publisher eventually agreed to bring the book out, but not until next fall, which will be three years after it was purchased.

Rowland is not a grudge-bearing man, but his difficulties have expressed themselves in the fortunes he wrote for Yang.

He said he tried in his fortune-writing career to give people a sense of hope. Perhaps, but his particular brand of hope can come across as fatalism. For example, one of his fortunes says: "Be confident enough to dance badly."

Another reads: "Pain indicates injury, while a painful sensation indicates growth; learn to distinguish between them."

Still another warns: "After today, you shall have a deeper understanding of both good and evil."

Nobody's complained about that one yet, maybe because they don't really want to contemplate what it means.

The list goes on in the same vein. At times, Rowland's fortunes read like themes for novels — tragic novels. Rowland tried to be funny, he said, but discovered he didn't know how and in the end wrote what he felt.

He said he had not set out to eliminate fortunes from fortune cookies, but realized what he was doing as he did it.

Reflecting, perhaps, the role that change has played in his own life, he said: "I don't like telling people things are going to change their lives."

Yang, for his part, doesn't really care what the fortunes say so long as nobody complains. He doesn't even read the messages. He has about 2,000 of them now. They're rotated periodically, with about a quarter in circulation at any one time. He is always on the lookout for more.

"I pay 30 cents," he said. "Can you write some?"

It's a measure of the economic velocity of our world that a two-person operation in a cubbyhole office in San Francisco cranks out most of the fortunes read across the continent. It's a measure of the strangeness of that same world that the principal criterion of those fortunes be that they not offend a single person anywhere in it.

Instead, with cosmic irony, the fortune-writing business has been turned over to a man who, despite kind intentions, is apt to end up unnerving everyone.

Where's Confucius when you need him?

❖❖

A Medium-Rare Dare in Amarillo

Big Texan Steak Ranch offers a beefy challenge — a 72-ouncer, with sides, free if you finish. Many have been called, by signs along Route 66, but few have forked it down and not forked over.

BY JESSE KATZ • SEPTEMBER 27, 1997

AMARILLO, Texas — "Oh, man," said Luis Rodriguez, eyeing the steak dinner headed his way. It was the voice of dread more than desire. He rubbed his belly, a condolence to his own innards. What on earth could have possessed him to attempt such a gluttonous feat?

In front of this slim, mild-mannered, 31-year-old data analyst was now the mightiest cut of meat he had ever seen: the Big Texan Steak Ranch's 72-ounce top sirloin, a slab of beef the size of the Yellow Pages, so colossal that McDonald's could turn it into 18 Quarter Pounders. You can only get two of these steaks out of a single cow. Each one weighs more than six times the human heart.

"Oh, man," Rodriguez said again.

Just finding room for it inside his 130-pound frame would have been a sizable achievement. But Rodriguez was after something even grander, driven by a Texas-size challenge that lures hundreds of cross-country travelers to this Panhandle eatery each year: Consume all 72 ounces in an hour and the meal would be his free. Lest that appear insufficiently Herculean, he would also have to wolf down a baked potato, shrimp cocktail, salad and roll. The price of failure is $50 — payable in advance, given that most contestants are too indisposed afterward to be reaching for their wallets.

"Oh, man."

The Big Texan is the carnivore's Everest, a gamble for glory that mocks the rational mind. Dozens of billboards along old Route 66 whet appetites from Missouri to New Mexico. "Why do people do it?" said general manager Dan Lee, repeating a question that has been asked of his family-run restaurant for nearly four decades. The answer is well rehearsed: "Because it's there."

The 72-ounce sweepstakes date to the Big Texan's inaugural year, 1959, when (according to legend) a real-life cowboy sauntered in off the range and told Lee's father, the late R.J. "Bob" Lee, that he was hungry enough to eat a whole dadgum

17

horse. The elder Lee served him up a steak, then another and another. By the time the cowboy said stop, he'd devoured 72 ounces — a big enough pile of bull, as the Lee family delights in noting, to make anybody a genuine Texan.

Since then, about 27,000 people have tried to scale that summit; only 4,600 have succeeded. No one has died (at least not inside the restaurant), but more than a few have spewed up their steak dinner (yes, right there at the table). The youngest to get it all down was an 11-year-old boy. The oldest was a 63-year-old grandmother. Klondike Bill, a professional wrestler, ate two dinners (that's 9 pounds of beef) in the allotted time. Frank Pastore, a pitcher for the Cincinnati Reds, set a speed record by inhaling his meal in 9 1/2 minutes. "It's all in the wrist," he explained afterward.

Going *mano a mano* with gastronomic history was not exactly on Rodriguez's mind when he stepped into the Big Texan's faux 19th-century yellow-and-blue gingerbread dining hall on a recent September night.

As far as he knew, he and his girlfriend were simply having dinner with two German tourists, one of whom worked for the international oil pipeline company that employed Rodriguez in Houston. Thomas Meinzer and Hans Binkele, both 30, had a better idea of what they were in for, the Big Texan being one of the must-sees on their three-week trek through the heart of Americana.

"Do you understand what we have to eat?" Rodriguez asked them incredulously upon reading the contest rules.

"Hans says it's no problem," said Meinzer, his Pipetronix colleague, who helped translate for Binkele, a police officer whose chiseled face and rippled 188-pound physique bore a striking resemblance to Arnold Schwarzenegger.

"I think you're all insane," said Rodriguez's girlfriend, a 24-year-old psychology major named Kristen Watrous. Her perspective was somewhat colored, however; she's a vegetarian.

After waiting an hour — that's how long it takes to grill a 72-ouncer — the three men were led to a small stage, where they were seated side by side and introduced to the Big Texan crowd by Hody Porterfield, an adopted member of the Cree Indian Nation who wears buckskin britches and lives in a teepee on the restaurant's gravel parking lot. He went over the rules with them, explaining that they would have to eat everything but the gristle and the potato skin. Nobody could help them cut or chew. They couldn't stand up or leave the table. And one last thing:

"If you get sick," Porterfield cautioned, "the contest is over."

He looked at his gold pocket watch. It was 9 p.m. "Let's give these gentlemen some applause, a little encouragement," Porterfield implored, egging on the crowd like a circus barker. People whooped and hollered. Flashbulbs popped. Some diners walked up to the stage and gawked, picking favorites and placing bets.

"I always wanted to be famous," Rodriguez said.

"This is your 15 minutes, baby," his girlfriend told him.

Then it was time to eat. Binkele lived up to his image by slicing into his 2-inch-thick, 9-inch-wide and 11-inch-long steak as if it were a wedge of cheesecake. There was no wasted motion, no ironic banter, just the ceaseless swing of elbow and jaw, cutting and chewing, chewing and cutting, like the silent arc of an oil pump. "Go, Hans, go," someone at another table shouted.

Meinzer's first move was to unfasten the top button of his size 33 jeans, a tactic that did not inspire great confidence. After a few bites, he had spattered steak juices all over his shirt, then squandered several minutes draining the broth from his plate into a butter dish.

Rodriguez asked for a bottle of A1 and emptied it onto his meat. But even with the puddle of sauce, his chewing soon began to look labored, head rocking, eyebrows arched, cheeks bulging like Don Corleone.

"Oh, man," he managed to mumble.

It takes more than hunger to make good on the Big Texan's dare. Strategy is as important as a rumbling gut. The restaurant recommends ordering your steak medium-rare and slicing it into thin bites, the better to conserve those all-important mandibular muscles. Many folks make the mistake of ordering it well-done — thinking that the extra cook time will shrink the corpulence of the meat — only to end up with lockjaw. A few have even asked for their steak chilled and raw, with the idea that it might slip down the gullet more readily, but the potential benefits of that technique remain unconfirmed.

"You can usually tell within the first 10 minutes," said Lee, adding that some contestants have been caught trying to slip strips of beef down their boots. "If they're going to finish it, there'll be just something about the way they attack it, the rhythm, like a machine."

Binkele proved that theory true, effortlessly shifting gears between his steak and the side dishes; meat to salad, salad to potato, potato to meat, meat to roll, shrimp cocktail in three spoonfuls. He finished it all in 37 minutes, then momentarily dropped his head to his chest — his only acknowledgment the entire night that this had been anything but a normal meal. As he got up and walked to the bathroom, the dining room burst into applause.

"Damn, I don't believe it," Rodriguez said. He and Meinzer still had huge piles of beef in front of them, getting colder and tougher by the minute. They were picking at it, stalling. Every bite was painful.

"You only got 12 minutes left, now shovel it in!" commanded Watrous, who had made a rather easy transition from critic to cheerleader. She was eating a strawberry shortcake, sharing it with Binkele, who seemed pleased to be getting his $50 back.

Rodriguez hugged his middle and moaned. "I think I'm pregnant," he said. "I think I'm going to have a cow."

Mercifully, the hour expired without a birth. Rodriguez's plate was weighed, revealing that he had left 16 ounces of meat. Meinzer, who had left 16 1/2 ounces, took one more bite to lock them in a tie. They were offered a doggy bag. Both declined.

In the lobby of the restaurant, Binkele was asked to add his name and address to the Big Texan roster, making him a member of America's "most exclusive" steak-eating club. For a moment, it actually seemed heroic, a chance for one man to leave his mark, no matter how insignificant, on the world.

Outside, in the car, as the four of them headed toward a motel, Rodriguez asked Binkele to pull over to the side of the road. There, on Interstate 40, doubled over under the endless Texas sky, he too left a mark of his own.

❖

How Far Can a Piano Fly?

Catapult devotees get high on hurling coffins, commodes, even small cars. 'Every once in a while,' one aficionado says, 'you really want to do something that is ... really stupid.'

By Richard E. Meyer · June 9, 1996

NORTH BEND, Washington — The big arm began to move. The sling tightened.

The coffin, gunmetal gray with gold-painted handles, shot straight up, so fast that John Wayne could hardly see it.

The arm and the sling tugged the coffin into an arc, then flung it into the blinding blue sky over Rattlesnake Lake. It climbed 200 feet, end over end, tumbling and flashing like quicksilver.

John Wayne heard the hint of a whistle. Otherwise there was no sound. The coffin traced a graceful curve against hemlocks and firs that marched 1,500 feet up the side of Rattlesnake Ledge. In a haunting frieze, it lingered for a moment at an outcropping of volcanic rock near the top.

Then slowly it began to fall. Plastic flowers and an American flag tore from the coffin and hung in the air like a rainbow. The coffin hit the lake with a crystal splash. It sank. John Wayne could see it on the bottom, among the ruins of a village called Cedar Falls, flooded by a water project after the turn of the century. "Awesome," he muttered to himself.

Finally, however, the lunacy overwhelmed him. "A force of 20 Gs," he chuckled. Then he laughed. When that coffin came out of the catapult, any dearly departed would have been squashed like a comma. "Kind of uncomfortable in there for eternity." To this day, he laughs aloud when he remembers what he thought. "If that guy had rigor mortis, he was going to be 2 feet tall forever."

But the truth is that none of it was for real. He had staged the whole thing for television. The coffin was, in fact, empty. What John Wayne Cyra did, however, has made a big difference. At the moment when he first fired his catapult, John Wayne, as he prefers to be called in honor of his hero, entered an exclusive, even distinguished, world. He became a "catapulteer." Less vaingloriously, John Wayne is a flinger.

His is a world of people who throw things, and not just dishes when they get upset, or even knives when they grow particularly angry. It is a world of war weapons, of siege machines, of catapults of all sorts, the most popular being a seesaw kind called the trebuchet. John Wayne and his peers use them to fling bowling balls, commodes, pianos, even small cars. "I get choked up," he says, "thinking about it."

It is a world where the deadly and the daffy dance. Early flingers hurled horses into enemy castles, especially dead ones infected with plague. They hurled baskets of snakes and scorpions and casks of Greek fire, a kind of napalm made of oil and sulfur. They also hurled corpses, the heads of prisoners, even negotiators, whole and alive, with their rejected terms hanging around their necks — an early form of shuttle diplomacy.

It is a world crowded with inspiring people. One is Allen Gross, an Oakland inventor who baited a catapult to fling rodents into a cage so he could release them in the wild. He called the device a Ratapult and offered it for sale for $350. Another is Maj. Stephen Ressler, a West Point engineer who assigned his students to build trebuchets. Then he turned modern and analyzed their work with a computer.

Another is John Quincy, a Texas dentist whose fond hope is to build the biggest trebuchet in history. Still another is Hew Kennedy, a British landowner who uses a trebuchet to hurl dead pigs because they are "nice and aerodynamic." And still another is Ron Toms, a New York computer engineer who constructed a trebuchet with a chair on it. He flung himself into a river three times.

"Every once in a while," says Quincy, "you really want to do something that is really out of the norm, something really stupid — and, by damn, we have found it."

John Wayne Cyra, 49, comes to flinging naturally. "My whole life," he says, "has been like a Woody Allen movie."

Nuns banished him from class for chewing gum, for writing X-rated limericks and for putting thumbtacks on their chairs. He finally got thrown out of school altogether.

He joined the Air Force, trained as a paramedic, went to Navy diving school and volunteered for a top-secret 16-man spy satellite recovery team in the northern Pacific. He was a dead-on mimic, and he could imitate Walter Cronkite. After his Navy hitch, he got a job reading the news on a Honolulu radio station. He specialized in wacky stories.

Finally he came home to Washington state. He drove trucks and bulldozers and built log houses, including one for himself; his dog; his cat; his 200 handcrafted knives, stabbed into a pole in his living room; and his shelf of whaling ships, carved from walrus ivory by an Eskimo known as Three Fingered Arnold, once known as Nine Fingered Arnold.

One day four years ago, he heard gunshots. It was Skip, his neighbor, who had a bigger log house with a hand-carved spiral staircase, $1 million worth of antiques and, unlike John Wayne, a telephone. That was where John Wayne got his calls. Whenever the phone rang for him, Skip would fire a few rounds into the air, and John Wayne would hike over.

This time, however, it was a visitor. He was a location scout for a television show about Alaska called "Northern Exposure," and he wanted to shoot some scenes at Skip's place. On John Wayne's advice, Skip agreed — for a hefty sum — and John Wayne got to know the TV people well. What cinched their appreciation for him were toilet bowls.

"I walked into the production office one day," John Wayne says, "and this guy is on the phone, and he's going, 'Yeah, yeah. Yeah, we need prison toilet bowls. Yeah. Stainless steel. Yeah, OK. $1,200 apiece? OK. We'll take three of 'em. Put 'em on a Learjet.'

"And I'm going, 'Wait! Wait! Wait! Wait!'

"It just so happened that a buddy of mine was doing reconstruction work over at the state prison in Monroe, and I knew where there was a pile of old stainless steel toilet bowls. They were putting in new ones.

"So I said, 'Listen, I can get you toilet bowls from the prison for a lot less than $1,200 apiece.'

"He said, 'Don't mess with me. We need 'em this afternoon!'

"I said, 'Well, my minimum charge for breaking a toilet out of prison is $200 a bowl.'

" 'Get 'em! Get 'em!' "

The writers of "Northern Exposure" had created a quirky show. One character was a disc jockey who was partial to rock 'n' roll, Walt Whitman and performance art. After reading about Hew Kennedy and his pig-flinging trebuchet in Britain, the writers decided that their disc jockey ought to hurl a piano.

This time the production office told John Wayne it needed a catapult. It wanted one that would fling an upright piano 150 yards, and it wanted the catapult up and operating in 10 days. That sounded about as possible as tattooing a bubble, but John Wayne was game. He agreed to build it, and he said he would finish it in time. "Guaranballbearingteed."

The producers hired Kennedy and flew him in. Based on what he described, a studio draftsman drew a trebuchet at quarter-inch scale. John Wayne threw out some of the blueprint, but he kept parts of it. An important element was the weight ratio: With 10,000 pounds of counterweight, he decided on a foot of flinging arm for every 10 pounds of piano.

It was early January and colder than a cheap funeral. Equipment fell through ice and disappeared in mud. Hands and feet froze. John Wayne burned up three hair dryers thawing out oil lines. For the trebuchet frame, his men cut 12 logs. They tied them together with steel straps. For the flinging arm, they built a 45-foot beam. On top of the frame, they installed a chromium steel axle, and they lay the arm across it.

On the short end of the arm, they filled a metal box with 10,000 pounds of lead ingots. On the long end, they tied a sling. With a cable and a bulldozer, they pulled down the long end of the arm. Like a teeter-totter, the short end, weighted with the ingots, went up. With time to spare, the flinger was cocked and ready.

The director wanted to film the first fling, but John Wayne reserved it for himself and his crew. Besides, if his trebuchet flew apart, he did not want a lot of people to be hurt.

He selected a 450-pound log. He topped off a jug with gasoline, and he strapped the jug to the log with duct tape.

He soaked a rag and jammed it into the mouth of the jug. One of his men lit the rag.

"And we shot that baby.

"I saw 10,000 pounds of lead come down, and that log took off like the space shuttle. It pulled so many Gs that the force ripped the jug off the log. A gallon of gas went straight up. It was like the Fourth of July, man. It was great!"

The log?

"It went high," John Wayne says, with a hush in his voice. "I don't know really how to describe it. It was awesome."

Finally, with actors in place and cameras rolling, John Wayne flung a piano. "To see that piano go whoosh, like a little pebble! It gets smaller in the distance, and the keys are flying off, dark keys and white keys…. The way they sprinkled through the air: Oh, it was beautiful!

"Then there was a humming, like a harmonica sound. Air was blowing through the piano…. But the best sound of all was when it hit: a piano just smashing to pieces all over the frozen ground…. It's not a crash. It's a tinkly, air chime kind of — ta-king! — sound. And then there's a little after-tinkle … a metallic clink-clink.

"Then just dead silence."

John Wayne flung nine pianos in all; it took that many to satisfy the director's enthusiasm. All were uprights. Each weighed 450 pounds and sailed about 120 yards. From the nine flings, the director edited together a single flight. To Johann Strauss' "The Blue Danube," it aired in an episode that ran February 3, 1992.

Next the writers decided that a good friend of their disc jockey would die and that his body would be sent to Alaska to be enshrined in a Volkswagen Beetle and flung into a glacial lake.

So it was that the location scouts chose Rattlesnake Lake; it was pristine, the essence of Alaska. But it supplied Seattle with drinking water, and the city ruled out the greasy car. The writers had to settle for a coffin.

John Wayne flung five coffins in all, until the director had plenty of film. The drama was aired on October 19, 1992, to "A Whiter Shade of Pale," by Procol Harum.

Two of the five coffins were made of wood. They shattered when they hit the water.

The show, John Wayne says, "had to hire 20 people with those little mesh nets for cleaning out the fish poo-poo in your aquarium, and they had these bags, and they walked all around the lake cleaning up toothpicks."

Three of the coffins were metal. John Wayne could see them, torn open by the impact and stacked on the bottom of the lake like tuna cans.

He dove for them.

On a jagged edge, he cut one of his hands. He was taken to a hospital, where an attendant filled out a form.

" 'Was this an industrial accident?' she asked.

" 'Yes, yes.'

" 'Was this a piece of machinery?'
" 'It was a coffin.'
" 'A coffin?' "

. . .

If John Wayne Cyra comes to flinging naturally, then John Quincy comes to it as a Texan: He wants the biggest flinger in the world.

Quincy, 47, is a graduate of the Air Force Academy, where he majored in physics. He flew for a while and chased electrons around circuit diagrams until it bored him. He left the Air Force and went to dental school. At the same time, he got a master's degree in literature. Today he has a dental practice. He lives in the country, near the town of Aledo, 12 miles west of Fort Worth.

One day Quincy and a friend, Richard Clifford, an engineer and artist, watched a film, "Monty Python and the Holy Grail." What impressed them was a scene in which a catapult flings a Holstein over a castle wall. Not long afterward, they too read about Kennedy and his trebuchet in Britain. On an impulse, they flew over to visit. Kennedy flung a piano for them.

Quincy and Clifford came home hooked. They founded Projectile Throwing Engines, Texas Division, whose motto was: "Hurling Into the 21st Century." They built a trebuchet with a 24-foot throwing arm. It was powered by 2,000 pounds of scrap iron, and it flung things 100 yards, sometimes farther. They cocked it with a hand winch, but to fire it, they did something special.

They set in motion a mechanical man that kicked a support that disengaged a blade that cut a rope that fired a battering ram that hit a lever that dumped some kitty litter that turned a wheel that wound another rope that tugged a lever that triggered a crossbow that shot a pipe that set off a tiny catapult that threw a ball — usually a knuckle ball, but sometimes a slider or a curveball — at a garbage can lid that tripped a guillotine that sliced another rope that dropped a weight.

Sometimes the weight fired the trebuchet. Other times it rang a bell, "alerting," Quincy says, "another idiot" to fire it.

They called it Baby Thor.

Like kids with a new puppy, Quincy and Clifford started the International Hurling Society. They published a journal, called HEAVE. It offered acknowledgments. "We would like to thank Mr. Pearson of Weatherford, Texas, for the donation of five toilets for hurling, Mr. Armstrong of Tulsa, Oklahoma, for his donation of a typewriter (hurled 89 yards), Brian Lewis for the cash register (awaiting hurling), and the Burgett family, who donated two toilets and currently holds the toilet-hurling record of 123 yards."

Quincy also hurled computers, outboard motors, kitchen sinks and bowling balls. He longed to hurl a case of Spam, but his wife, a vegetarian, said this would be littering.

What he wanted most, however, was to have the biggest trebuchet in existence. So he and Clifford set about engineering it. This trebuchet is still on the drawing board. Their basic plan calls for a 110-foot throwing arm on an axle 40 feet above the ground. The arm will be powered by a weight box of no less than 15 tons. The frame will be steel, covered with wood and vines to make it look medieval.

They call it Thor.

The cost is projected at $50,000, and money is scarce. Indeed, HEAVE recently announced that Clifford has decided to "pull back to a consultant position due to work demands."

"I was sorry," Quincy says sadly, "to see him get rational on us."

Undaunted, he looks forward to seeing Thor throw "something the size of a cow about a quarter of a mile." Such talk has gotten him reported to animal-rights advocates. It has not helped that he plans a scientific experiment: He wants to smear a cow with peanut butter and jelly, fling it 10 times and record how often it lands jelly-side down.

Nor has it helped that he has published:

1. A photo of a flying pig, courtesy of Kennedy.

2. An article about trapshooting armadillos.

3. A recipe noting that "the meat of the armadillo is quite tasty and is often compared with spotted owl."

If he cannot hurl a cow, Quincy wants to throw a 1962 Buick. Not a Ford or a Chevy or anything as humble as a Honda: A 1962 Buick, he says, "seems bigger and sturdier, and some friends I know have had some problems with Buicks." It might be harder to fling than a cow, he says. "We won't get quite the distance out of it, unless we roll up the windows."

He has bought 80 acres next to his property so the Buick will have someplace to land. The site is away from his house, "thereby reducing the strain of hundreds of curious people on a heretofore tranquil marriage," he says, and back from the road, because "my neighbors certainly have been tolerant of commodes sailing past their homes, but…."

Failing a 1962 Buick, Quincy would like to fling a human being. "We have looked into that," he says, especially the possibility of throwing a mime. "Silent, night hurling," he says, "in appreciation and respect for the neighbors.

"If the mime were tied up," he muses quietly, "… or if his arms were akimbo — would it affect the distance?"

. . .

In Britain, at Acton Round, 150 miles north of London, lives Hew Kennedy, the proud godfather of all this.

He is in his late 50s. He is a landowner and holds a considerable estate, nearly 700 acres, most of it in woods and rolling hills. At the heart of it is a three-story, Queen Anne-style, brown brick manor house.

From the dining room chandelier swings a stuffed baboon. He shot it in Africa. Scattered about are coats of mail and horse armor. He restores them. At one point he had a coat of elephant armor, fitted over an iron frame in the shape of an elephant. It came from India in the days of the Raj.

Kennedy went to Sandhurst, the West Point of Britain, where he learned that Napoleon III had built a trebuchet and that it had not worked very well. "The French had done something wrong." He adds: "Of course." In time, he returned to his estate and talked a neighbor, Richard Barr, into building a trebuchet that would be the envy of the French and everyone else.

After some false starts, they built a trebuchet 60 feet high, on two A-frames fashioned out of the logs from 24 trees. Between the A-frames was an axle. On the axle pivoted a 3-ton beam powered by a 6-ton counterweight. At one point, one of the logs knocked Barr off a ladder. He landed face down in several inches of mud. The log fell on top of him.

"It forced me right into the mud," he says, "and Hew Kennedy, being so calm, cool and collected, having been trained at Sandhurst as an army officer, leaped out of a tractor, forgetting to put the hand brake on. In total panic, he leaped out of this huge farm machine, which had four large wheels on it, and it rolled forward on top of the log. I was sort of conducting him from underneath all this, telling him not to panic.

"There was another chap helping, and they sort of managed to lever it off of me, enough to sort of drag me out from underneath it, and I was put into Hew Kennedy's wife's car, because she was just sort of sitting up there watching with a picnic ready for us, and they took me off to hospital. I ought to have died."

The picnic, needless to say, was ruined. "We wasted a chocolate cake." Finally the catapult stood tall and ready, like a praying mantis, sling attached and cocked to fire. It was in a field where Kennedy grazed sheep. He and Barr invited other neighbors, properly tweedy. Some arrived in Rolls-Royces, but most came by Land Rover. The sheep grew understandably nervous. "None have been killed," Kennedy says, "but we have had some near misses."

To date, Kennedy and Barr have flung:

— Sixty pianos, most of them uprights, but several grand pianos as well. "They accelerate up to about 90 mph in about 2 1/2 seconds," Barr says, "which is about 14 to 20 Gs." Each was tuned and concert-ready.

— Half a dozen cars: Morris Minors, Hillmans, Austin Minis, even an Italian Lancia. "We like to throw the whole car," Barr says. "It's got to have the engine in it and the wheels on it." If the car will not run, they will not throw it. "Otherwise, there doesn't seem to be any point."

— Several dead cows, a dead horse and a lot of dead pigs. "A pig makes a good missile," Kennedy says, "because it is nice and aerodynamic, you know." Barr adds: "It's very amusing seeing a pig in a parachute."

The parachute was part of an experiment conducted by the Royal Air Force in Kennedy's sheep pasture to see if it was possible to hurl a man. "Fascinating," Kennedy says. "They spent three days at it, but it wasn't any good.

"It did establish that the man would have been dead when he landed."

· · ·

Ron Toms, however, lived.

A computer engineer, Toms, 35, was, perhaps significantly, still a Texan when he decided to build a trebuchet in a friend's backyard in the town of Kyle, between Austin and San Marcos.

Instead of a sling, he and the friend, whose name is Chris, attached a chair to one end of the throwing arm. The chair rotated and had a stabilizer to keep it upright. To the other end, they tied three 55-gallon drums of water, weighing 1,600 pounds altogether. Then he, Chris and another friend hauled the trebuchet down to the Blanco River.

After flinging some boulders into the water, Toms climbed into the chair. Chris fired the trebuchet. Toms flew 30 feet into the air. He arced out over the river. All the while, he stayed in a sitting position. He spread his arms like wings. "A lot of people have jumped out of trees or off of cliffs," he says. "The thing about being thrown is that it takes you twice as long, because you have to go up and then come down.

"Once I left the catapult, I was decelerating. It sounds obvious, but at the top of the arc, when my acceleration went to zero, the experience was something I didn't expect. It lasted for an instant, but hanging there in midair, 30 feet up, looking down at everything, with nothing but air everywhere, was an ethereal experience.

"It's a mysterious feeling. You are hovering, weightless and motionless. You actually have a forward component to your motion, but you're not going either up or down."

It chilled him, like a quiet stranger. Oddly, it was comforting to start falling. That was a feeling he knew. So was splashing into the water.

He came up laughing.

Toms did it again, twice. He flung his friends two times each. Then he climbed into the chair a fourth time, but the trebuchet disintegrated.

In time, Ron Toms left Texas to work in New York City. Now he plans to move to Los Angeles.

He will fit right in.

Researchers Edith Stanley in Atlanta and Lianne Hart in Houston contributed to this story.

❖

Harpin' Days Are Dying Out for Boont

In an isolated valley in Northern California, a few remaining old-timers have fun with a colorful dialect that's become an academic curiosity.

By Jenifer Warren • January 19, 1996

BOONVILLE, California — To the old-timers who gather for afternoon coffee at the Redwood Drive-in, there are few pastimes sweeter than sharkin' a bright-lighter with a slib of Boont.

Take the yuppie in his BMW, up from San Francisco for some weekend wine tasting. He approaches the men with a smile, asking directions to a local bed and breakfast. The response is quick — and earnestly polite:

"Take your wee moshe, pike toward the Deep End and you'll deek on the Big Crick chiggrul and sluggin' region. And jape easy!"

The hapless tourist might not appreciate it, but he has just been given directions in one of the most unusual homemade languages in the world: Boontling, hatched by settlers in this remote Mendocino County valley more than a century ago.

29

At its peak, the colorful lingo was used by virtually all of the 500 people who once made their living raising sheep and apples here. But now, only eight or 10 old-timers can speak Boontling with ease, and they are gradually passing on, taking the language with them to the grave.

"God has thinned us out, and we're getting thinner all the time," said Bob Glover, 74, one of those who occasionally "shark" — or play games with — an unsuspecting city slicker (bright-lighter) passing through town.

"A few of the words — especially the dirty ones — will probably be around forever," said Donald Pardini, 65. "But I don't honestly see much of a future for Boont."

Pardini has reason to worry.

Boontling's decline has not exactly set off alarms. In Boonville, population 1,200, high school teacher Ken Jones planned a course in Boont this year but dropped the idea when students greeted it with a collective yawn. The valley's elders have passed on some words to their children, but members of the younger generation don't speak the language enough to keep their skills sharp.

One small effort to preserve the language was made by Pardini, who included a poem in Boont in a time capsule buried in the town some time ago. The poem, a nostalgic ode to Boontling, urges those who eventually dig up the capsule to bring the language back to life.

"It makes you sad, seeing it die out," Pardini said.

If the curious sounds of Boontling do indeed fade away, the Anderson Valley will have lost a piece of heritage few other places can claim. There are many blended languages — such as the merging of French and Cree Indian by trappers in 17th century Canada — and numerous forms of jargon, like that found among thieves and carnival workers. Twins sometimes invent secret codes, and island populations often have their own dialects.

But experts say Boontling's history, durability and extensive original vocabulary make it stand out: "I don't know of many examples like it — if any at all," said Leanne Hinton, a professor of linguistics at UC Berkeley.

On top of its anthropological value, Boontling is fun. Its words and phrases — an estimated 2,000 in all — are colorful and tend to have amusing origins, often relating to local characters out of the past and their occupations or habits.

A prostitute is a "madge," after a madam in nearby Ukiah, while a "tombacon" is a handlebar mustache, in honor of a man who could twirl the ends of his whiskers around his ears. A "buckey walter" is a pay phone — a combination of "buckey," meaning nickel, and "walter," for Walter Levi, who owned the valley's first telephone.

A cup of coffee is a "horn of zeese," a tribute to a hunter with the initials Z.C.

whose coffee was so thick it could reputedly float an egg. And to be embarrassed is to be "charlied." A local Indian named Charlie Ball, an exceptionally bashful fellow, was said to inspire that term.

About 15% of Boontling is made up of dirty words, or "nonch harpin's," permitting its speakers to gossip about sex, bodily functions and other taboo matters without sounding vulgar or offending others. Wes Smoot, a retired state road supervisor who is fluent in Boont, explains how useful this can be:

"If I were in a mixed crowd I could say, 'That mink and kimmie were burlapin',' and it wouldn't sound bad. But you'd never catch me saying those same words in English."

(Translation: A "mink" is a woman, especially one of loose morals, and a "kimmie" is a man. As for "burlapin'," legend has it that a store patron once caught a clerk and his lady friend in a compromising position atop a pile of burlap bags in a storeroom. Thus did the witness exclaim, "They're burlapin' in there!")

Just how Boontling got started is a matter of lingering dispute. The leading explanation suggests that adults invented it around the 1880s so they could discuss delicate matters in front of children. Pardini and others subscribe to a more specific theory, involving women who were picking hops and wanted to gossip about a pregnant — and unmarried — girl in their midst.

Whatever the spark, Boontling quickly caught fire in the valley. During its heyday early this century, some locals became so comfortable with Boontling that they used it as their primary language. Indeed, during World War I, several GIs from Boonville reportedly had to relearn English when they left the valley to fight. At one time, members of a local baseball team used Boontling to yell signals, which sounded like crazy babble to visiting players.

As with island dialects, the lingo thrived largely because of the region's isolation, 120 miles north of San Francisco. When cars and telephones linked the Anderson Valley more closely to the outside world, Boontling began to fade. Hastening its decline was a minor community backlash: Some newcomers mocked the language as backwoodsy, while other residents feared that it might supplant standard English, putting local children at a disadvantage.

In 1971, Boontling got a lift when an English professor from Cal State Chico shined an academic light on the language. After winning the confidence of Boonters (proficient Boontling users) over a period of years, Charles C. Adams wrote a book called "Boontling: An American Lingo," which includes a comprehensive glossary.

Unlocking the mysteries of Boontling was a painstaking task. The most difficult part, Adams said in an interview, was persuading wary locals to share what they knew.

After all, a young anthropologist from UC Berkeley had already tried and failed. Boonters roll their eyes when they talk of him, describing a hippie whose looks and lifestyle bore no resemblance to their own.

But Adams — who has a quiet, unassuming manner and shares hunting and other hobbies with the Boonters — eventually broke through.

"One night I was at a meeting of the Boontling Club, and one of the leaders, sitting on his heels by the fire, said, 'Well, I think this guy is all for poison oak.' That was his way of saying they should help me, and so they did," said Adams, now retired.

After months of research, Adams concluded that Boontling is not, technically speaking, a language in itself. Its sounds, grammar and morphology — or word-building techniques — all fit the pattern of standard English. What distinguishes Boontling is its peculiar vocabulary, which makes it indecipherable to outsiders.

Some terms are borrowed from Pomo Indian, Spanish and the Scotch-Irish dialects spoken by some early immigrants to the valley. Sounds also were a common source for words. The digger squirrel was called a "squeakyteek" in imitation of its distinctive bark. A small-caliber rifle is a "spat," reflecting its short, cracking report.

Brevity is one of Boontling's most cherished features, leading to words formed from odd contractions and abbreviations. To wit: Whiskey is "skee," Grizzly bear is "leeber," and a schoolteacher is simply a "skoolch." Even Boontling, the name of the language, is a blend, of "Boont" (for Boonville) and "lingo."

Although the future looks dim, through the years Boontling enthusiasts have fought the odds to keep the language alive. For a time, a local teacher taught Boontling as part of her English classes, but that ended when she retired more than 20 years ago. Boont speakers occasionally make guest appearances in valley classrooms but lament that the kids "just don't seem interested anymore."

In the 1960s, a Boontling Club was formed. Among its missions was deciding whether to embrace new words — always a heated topic. Boontling purists believe that the language should be limited to terms coined by its original users; others insist that it should be a dynamic thing, open to new words so long as they fit its characteristics.

The purists, it seems, have mostly held sway, as few new terms have passed muster. One that was accepted is "posey tweed," or flower child, which proved a useful label for the hippies who invaded the valley in decades past.

It has been 10 years since the Boontling Club last met, and around the Anderson Valley — now home to a growing industry of highly respected winemakers — remnants of Boontling are increasingly difficult to find. The local microbrewery sells beers with Boontling names, and the pay phones still say "Buckey Walter" on the booth. At the local market, tourists can still buy a souvenir coffee cup marked with Boont words.

But if you want to hear Boontling spoken, it is nearly too late. Each year, a couple of the old-timers perform a brief skit in Boontling at the valley's spring festival, but they may boycott the event this year.

"Last year," Glover says with a scowl, "they wanted us to do it in rap. Can you believe that? I think this year we may have other plans."

For now, the only Boontling to be heard bubbles forth when the few fluent speakers who remain meet for gabfests at the Redwood Drive-in. Keeping with tradition, they all have nicknames. Glover is known as Chipmunk — after a grandfather who hoarded his money — and Pardini, caretaker of the valley's four cemeteries, is Ite, the Boontling word for an Italian. Smoot's alias — Deekin — takes some explaining.

"When I was a tweed [child], I was half-charlied [shy]," Smoot said. "So the other kids said I was always just 'deekin' — or just looking — and was too scared to say a thing."

Boontling's chronicler, Charles Adams, knows that the lingo's days are numbered. But he is philosophical about its fate.

"If Chaucer were to walk among us now, nobody would understand him," Adams said. "Language changes, cultures change and societies change. That's just the way it is."

Pardini is less resigned. He turns melancholy when musing about Boontling's grim prospects but holds out hope for a rebirth. Toward that end, he penned his poem, the one tucked in the time capsule buried by townspeople in 1983.

The verse, accompanied by a translation, closes with a poignant exhortation:

"We've all piked for dusties now, our harpin' days are gone. But we'll never be tebow, if Boont is pikin' on."

(We've all died off now, our speaking days are gone. But we'll never be deaf, if Boontling is carried on.)

"Maybe somebody someday will find a use for Boont," Pardini said. "It would sure be nice for it to survive, even in a small way."

A BOONTLING PRIMER

There are an estimated 2,000 words, names and phrases in the Boontling vocabulary. Here is a partial glossary:

apple-head: A girl, especially one's girlfriend. From a reference to a

Boonter's girlfriend whose head was noticeably small.

bahl: Good; of excellent quality. Possibly from Ball Band shoes, once the best brand available.

barney: To hug or kiss. After a Boonter named Barney known to greet women enthusiastically.

bill nunn: Pancake syrup. Boonter Bill Nunn ate syrup on nearly all food.

bluebird: To buck off a rider (said of a horse). Figurative allusion to flying through the air, like a bluebird.

doll: To foul something up. After a Boonter nicknamed "Doll" who was unkempt and confused.

fence-jumpy: Prone to adultery. Reference to straying from one's pasture.

haireem: Dog. Merging of hairy and mouth.

itch neemer: A person who no longer craves drink. Merging of itch no more.

keemwun keemle: A call to entertainment. From "come one, come all."

packem-out billies: Dirty socks. Origin unknown.

peerl: To rain. From the shape of a raindrop.

pusseek: A cat. Merging of pussy and cat.

set 'n ear: To scold. Reference to form of punishing sheep dogs by twisting their ear.

shoveltooth: A doctor. After a physician who had wide, protruding teeth.

skipe: A preacher. Merging of sky and pilot.

toobs: Twenty-five cents. From two bits.

trashmover: A heavy winter storm.

white oak: To work hard. After a tree that is difficult to process into firewood.

Source: "Boontling: An American Lingo," by Charles C. Adams

❖

Commodity Traders Take Their Lumps

With big money to be made in deals that last mere seconds, kicking and pushing are among the routine hazards of life in the pits.

BY LARRY GREEN · DECEMBER 8, 1977

CHICAGO — Last month, someone here paid $140,000 for the right to be yelled at, pushed, elbowed and occasionally sprayed with saliva.

For his money, he will also have his toes stepped on and is likely to be kicked or maybe even punched.

That big price tag was not the fee for joining an exclusive club for well-heeled masochists or even the fee for a fancy new kind of psychological therapy for executives. It was the cost of membership in the pits — the rough and tumble life at one of the nation's largest commodities exchanges.

The pits, literally depressions in the trading floors of commodities exchanges here, are probably the most physically taxing and least dignified arenas of high finance.

In the pits, high finance becomes almost a contact sport, and the lumps speculators and traders take may not just be in their bank accounts.

Jeffery S. Greenberg's nose was broken. Laurence M. Rosenberg has a black spot on his right palm where he was stabbed with a pencil. Daniel G. Kelly occasionally finishes a day's work bruised, sometimes even black and blue.

"I've seen blood," said Andrea Usher, a 25-year-old trader who has also worked as an exchange messenger.

"This is the National Football League of finance," said Joseph M. Kane, a bean trader at the Chicago Board of Trade.

"Once I creamed a guy's toe and he just turned and slugged me," recalled Ronald F. Young, who like many other traders protects his feet by buying shoes with hard toes and rubber heels. "And some days you walk out of the pits sweating and feeling like you just played a couple of games of squash in your street clothes."

"I get kicked and pushed, but I kick and push back," said Donald C. Lisle, a corn trader. Speaking of such close encounters of the unkind, he says, "It's not anything

35

you plan. But it is very physical in the pits."

Indeed it is. The Chicago Board of Trade, with 1,402 members, keeps a paramedic on duty during trading hours. He is there primarily to assist infrequent victims of heart attacks, but his usual tasks are treating sprains and aiding traders who faint from overexertion or are injured when they are bumped out of the pits, according to Robert G. Draper, the board's safety and security chief.

The rugged world of commodity trading is centered in Chicago, where roughly 80% of the annual transactions in the United States are completed. Situated here are the Chicago Board of Trade, the Chicago Mercantile Exchange and the MidAmerica Exchange. Respectively, they rank first, second and fourth in size among the 10 American commodity exchanges.

Contracts for the future delivery or sale of a wide variety of commodities — from soybeans, corn and livestock to lumber, foreign currencies and precious metals — are traded at the exchanges. The contracts specify the quantity, quality and date of delivery, usually sometime within the following 24 months.

For example, a speculator might buy a contract for delivery of 5,000 bushels of soybeans next March at $4 a bushel. Sometime later, maybe in a few minutes, maybe in a few weeks, the price of soybeans goes up to $4.02 a bushel. The speculator sells, making a profit of $100 on the contract.

Generally, trading is done in multiple contracts. In this case, if the speculator had purchased 50 contracts, his profit would have been $5,000.

Speculators are not the only traders in the commodities market. Producers, grain elevator operators and commodity dealers also buy and sell futures contracts so they can be assured a firm price for a commodity in the future, a process known as hedging.

A grain elevator operator might sell contracts for all the grain he is storing to protect himself against a drop in grain prices. A manufacturer of soybean products might sell contracts equal to the beans in his inventory. If the price falls, he can protect the value of his inventory by buying back the contracts at a lower price.

Speculators and hedgers need each other. The speculator provides the risk capital the hedger is looking for. The consumer, in theory at least, benefits because producers, processors and manufacturers know in advance approximately what commodities will cost at a future time and can therefore maintain reasonably stable prices for goods going into the marketplace.

Before the commodities markets existed, for example, the price of bread depended on the daily price of grain. If deliveries to the flour mill were delayed or suddenly stopped, the price of bread rose sharply, only to fall sharply a few days later when grain arrived in quantity.

The commodities markets differ from the stock market principally in that investors and speculators are not buying equity in a company. Another important difference is that a substantial number of speculators in commodities are actually on the floor of the exchange because price fluctuations of one-eighth or one-fourth of a cent occur for just split seconds sometimes, and the only way to realize the advantage is to be there. However, the public can and does deal in commodity futures through brokerage houses.

Both the mechanics of the market — the fact that a price change of a fraction of a cent can mean a substantial profit or loss to large traders — and the rules of trading account for the frenzied activity in the pits where the buying and selling of contracts takes place.

"You can make a trade involving $7 million in a second. That sounds mind-boggling to people in other fields of investment," said Young, who is a major soybean trader at the Board of Trade.

Rules of the exchanges require that all offers to sell and all offers to buy be made in "public outcry," and that the first trader to yell out an acceptance bid be awarded the deal.

The competition is often fierce as contracts are bought and sold back and forth in the octagon-shaped pits on the trading floor. The Board of Trade's largest pit, where soybeans are traded, is no more than 30 feet in diameter. Sometimes as many as 300 traders crowd onto its eight steps. When trading gets active, the scene looks and sounds like an angry mob behind home plate screaming for the umpire's scalp.

Picture this happening all at once:

A man in a red trading jacket suddenly yells, "Three for Deece, three for Deece," indicating in verbal shorthand that he has three contracts for 15,000 bushels of soybeans for December delivery for sale. "10 for Deece, I've got 10 for Deece," another trader in an orange jacket shouts. "Six for Acht," yells a man in a blue jacket with October beans for sale.

"Five for five, five for five," another trader screams in a raspy voice, looking over to the man who yelled "10 for Deece." That means the bidder is willing to pay five-eighths of a cent for five of the 10 contracts. If beans were selling for $4 a bushel, the new bid indicates the price has just gone up to $4.00625 a bushel because all trading is done in eighths of a cent.

Because one buyer one minute might be a seller the next, the traders are not separated in the pits, and offers to sell or bids can spring from anywhere in the pit at any time.

Hand signals, which are not required, supplement the audible bidding, which is. Shorter traders bob up and down trying to see or be seen. Traders push and shove to get closer to the action.

And there is noise. Shouts. Screams. Yells.

"The voice is the most important asset," says Leo Melamed, who has been trading at the Mercantile for the last 22 years.

Rosenberg, the Mercantile's chairman, had polyps removed from his vocal cords several years ago. "The doctor said it was from abuse."

Some female traders, particularly those with experience in yelling at children, think they have an advantage over male traders. "My voice is like a flute among bass drums," said Elaine Dann, who trades at the MidAmerica Exchange and is one of about 200 female traders in Chicago.

Flute or drum, most traders end a four-hour day in the pits hoarse. Some say it takes weeks to get their voices into shape after a vacation break.

The yelling poses another threat to traders. "A guy will suddenly want to get in on something, and if you're in the way, you get hit in the face with spit," said Myron Tiersky, a MidAmerica trader.

Size also is considered an asset by many traders.

"If you're a little taller it doesn't hurt," Melamed said, perhaps speaking from experience. He stands about 5 foot 7.

Six-foot-4 Charles Andrews, who resembles actor Dennis Weaver and spends his weekends roping and branding cattle on his Kansas ranch, agreed. "Once you reach over and grab somebody, you've got the trade made."

If Jeffery Greenberg had been bigger, he might have had only a bruised chest instead of a broken nose. Greenberg, who is 5 foot 5, was standing between two larger traders when the MidAmerica Exchange opened trading in gold futures for the first time on December 30, 1974. In the frenzied bargaining, at least one of the taller men, and possibly both of them, accidentally hit Greenberg's face.

"I didn't realize it until after the trading was over," he recalled. "People came up to me and asked, 'What's wrong with your nose?' I looked in the mirror and it was all over my face."

"You're talking about money, and people get emotional about money," a MidAmerica spokesman explained.

But there is more to trading than just yelling and pushing. Gamesmanship is important. Theatrics are frequently used.

"A good trader tries to intimidate people. I've tried to intimidate people. You have to represent your own interest and your customers' interests," Kelly explained.

"In the pit, anything it takes to turn a buck is done on a daily basis," said Lawrence Federman, a burly 6-foot-4, 240-pound MidAmerica trader. "You have to border on the obnoxious."

Daniel L. Bowman dominates the Mercantile pit where live cattle futures are traded. He has a voice that can be heard through the thick glass enclosing the visitors' gallery above. He dances around the pit, wiggles his hips and makes funny faces.

"People think I'm a clown, and they never know when I'm seriously trading a big deal," Bowman confided.

He has a reputation for being one of the shrewdest and most intense traders at the Mercantile. His theatrics are part of his skill.

Dann said she approaches a day in the pits much as she does a tennis match. "To be a success, I have to have a game plan and mental agility," she explained. "You look at your opponent. Each one has special characteristics. You learn to read them. And you can't be afraid to lose."

"You have to strip yourself of ego and not let your mistakes get so important that you can't admit them," added the Mercantile's Melamed, who has written about the psychology of commodity trading. "The pit is a total equalizer. It doesn't care who you are or what you are."

For those who trade in them, the pits became a way of life, sometimes the only way of life. Kelly calls commodity trading an addiction. Others agree.

"The pits take complete and total concentration. Trading becomes instinctive. It tends to get your juices flowing," Young said. "But it is extremely exhilarating. You can have a lot of fun and make money — once you've learned to cope with the risks."

James A. Donaldson, a Board of Trade grain trader, said that when he is right about a deal, "it's like a mental orgasm."

"There's no high like being involved in having things go right," Rosenberg added.

"Once you start, you really can't stop," Greenberg said. "On weekends I can't wait until Monday so I can come down and start trading again."

There are tensions, to be sure. A bad trade could send a pit man into bankruptcy court. Ulcers are common. Learning the art of not worrying about yesterday's trading is as important to survival as making good deals.

The lure is more than excitement. It is money. And there is the potential for making — or losing — money faster in the pits than at a Las Vegas roulette table.

"This is one of the few situations left in America where there's no ceiling on what a person can make," Young said.

"A good trader on a good day can make as much as a leading doctor can make in a good month," Greenberg believes.

Insiders on the two larger exchanges say that in a good year, a successful trader can earn hundreds of thousands of dollars. Losses can also run that high.

One measure of the profit potential is the price of a seat, or membership, on a commodities exchange. The last seat to change hands on the Mercantile Exchange sold for $140,000, and at the Board of Trade the last one went for $138,000. Recently some have traded for close to $170,000. At the MidAmerica, where trading is done in smaller contracts and the earning potential is smaller, seats go for about $12,000.

There are more than 3,100 members at Chicago's three exchanges, and few bow out each year. When they do, it is usually because of age or heavy losses.

There is a saying in the pits: "Commodity trading is a helluva hard way to make an easy living."

Dispatches from Abroad

❖❖

The Fatal Thaw of Russian Ice Fishing

Most of St. Petersburg's smelt anglers come back alive. But every year, scores do not. And hundreds, sometimes thousands, find themselves adrift on floes that shrink by the hour as they are carried away.

By Maura Reynolds • May 1, 2000

ST. PETERSBURG, Russia — Furry-hatted fishermen emerge like humpbacked trolls from stands of birch and pine at the shoreline. They carry stiff, square backpacks and strange, 5-foot-long corkscrews. They trudge out onto the ice, a white and gray expanse that glows faintly and stretches to the horizon.

For the most part, they walk alone and they walk for miles. They read the ice like oracles, seeking signs of life and tremblings of death.

Most come back alive. But every year dozens, perhaps hundreds, do not. And hundreds, sometimes thousands, find themselves adrift on thawing floes that shrink by the hour as they're carried away.

"I once spent a night on a floe. Actually, two floes. It broke in half," says a cranky fisherman in a black sheepskin hat who gives his name as Yevgeny Semyonovich. "Why do I risk it? Why not?"

Spring arrives in St. Petersburg with a lengthening of daylight, a quickening of wind and the sparkle of a humble little fish called koryushka.

The fish are just a few inches and a few ounces each. They smell like cucumber and taste vaguely of salmon. In English, they are known by a decidedly less melodic name: smelt.

Smelt may not be much to look at, but the annual migration stirs an instinct in fishermen as powerful and lethal as that which drives lemmings to the sea. Indeed, ice fishing is ruled by a cruel paradox: The more dangerous the ice, the better the fishing. When the ice begins to melt, bubbles dissolve and release oxygen into the water, which stirs the fish, sluggish after a long winter in the cold. When the wind kicks up waves and cracks appear, the oxygen level climbs higher.

Why risk their lives for a satchel of smelt?

Semyonovich says he can't feed his family on his pension alone. "I only caught

2 kilos [about 4 1/2 pounds] today," he spits in contempt. "My wife will scold me when I get home."

Boris Vilyo, a 64-year-old construction engineer with flyaway blond hair, says he likes the solitude, the fresh air and something useful to do on his day off. He says he once fell through the ice and spent three hours swimming and wading through slush before making it to shore. But year after year he returns.

"Of course, it's scary sometimes," he says, warming his hands in a homemade oilskin muff. "I don't understand people who don't pay attention to the dangers. But everyone understands danger in different ways, don't they?"

And that may be the crux of the matter. As well as the fact that nowhere else on Earth are so many people — about 6 million — concentrated around so much ice.

The city of St. Petersburg straddles a bridge of land just 25 miles wide. To the west is the Gulf of Finland, a tongue of ocean that pushes past Estonia and Finland to lick the city's shore. To the east is Europe's biggest lake, Ladoga: about 130 miles long and an average of 50 miles wide, and home to four dozen species of fish. When winter arrives, a layer of ice creeps across both bodies of water.

The ice is seductive. Underfoot, it seems almost alive. It breathes, shifts, sings in the wind. It seems to have moods, changing from white to gray to black. The black ice is stronger but thinner, without bubbles. The white looks more solid but is often porous or slathered with icy slush, which Russians call "porridge."

For the most part, the ice and the waters underneath bring life to this region, supporting shipping, fishing and tourism. When St. Petersburg, then known as Leningrad, was besieged for three years during World War II, the ice became a road of life. Trucks evaded the Nazi blockade by driving across Lake Ladoga, ferrying people out and food and ammunition in.

On this soft spring day, more than a mile out on the ice along the gulf's northern coast near the village of Smylyachkovo, Vilyo seems to be having the best luck among a cluster of a dozen anglers. They have set their holes a wary distance apart — just close enough to spy on one another.

Vilyo stabs the point of his oversized corkscrew into the ice and turns the crank. The bit bites with a growling noise, which grows deeper as it burrows. He pulls it out with a rush of water and slush, leaving a dark hole about 5 inches across.

Koryushka rods are only about a foot long, with tiny red bobbers on the tips. They look fragile, like toys, but the fish tug gently. He sets his rods.

Vilyo travels by train and bus for three hours to get here, and he makes the trip at least twice a week. "What else am I going to do, sit at home?" He jumps up, pushes back a green knitted cap and rapidly hauls in one of the lines hand over hand. On the end is a little silver fish. "What a cutie," he says.

Nikolai Stepanov, a 33-year-old security guard, watches from his spot about 30 feet away and cracks a morbid joke: "The fish are biting in this spot for some reason. Somebody must have drowned."

Looking back, Maxim Balachevtsev realizes he ignored the omens.

First there was the vehicle that broke through the ice. It was midmorning on Sunday, February 27, and he was driving onto Lake Ladoga with 10 friends in four cars. They were experienced fishermen. In fact, Balachevtsev, 27, is the editor of St. Petersburg's Sport Fishing magazine.

They had driven about 1 1/2 miles out onto the ice when they saw the minivan sinking. They ran to the edge and a man struggled to the surface. As they hauled him out, he asked for his friend and Balachevtsev realized there had been another man in the van. The second man didn't surface.

"He was the first victim of the day," he says.

Balachevtsev and his friends were undeterred. They left the cars behind and continued more than an hour on foot. They reached the end of the older, whitish ice and walked onto the newer blackish ice. They stepped over a crack.

"Usually I don't step over cracks like that, but because of the shock of the death, I guess I wasn't paying enough attention," Balachevtsev says.

The fishing, of course, was good. Balachevtsev caught more than 30 pounds of perch in less than two hours. And then he felt a new tug on his fishing line — not the jerk of a hungry fish, but the slow pull of quickening current.

The ice had broken free.

"You know right away when the ice starts to drift. We all jumped up and started shouting. Everyone started running."

He didn't know it yet, but the floe was huge: more than 10 square miles. There were more than 1,000 people on it.

One was Nikolai Tropnikov, a 57-year-old short-story writer. He was walking toward a cluster of about 200 anglers, scouting for a new fishing spot, when "all of them jumped up simultaneously, like a flock of blackbirds."

"I turned to face the wind and started running against it," Tropnikov recalls. "The others ran the same way. I was sweating like a pig when I stopped in my tracks at the edge, paralyzed. There was a big stretch of black water, and it was widening rapidly."

Often, when a floe breaks off, one corner clings to the rest of the ice, at least for a few minutes, and the quick-footed can get across before the floe heads for open water. But this time, the wind came up perpendicular to the shore and the break was clean.

Tropnikov watched a boy jump into the frigid water at the narrowest point, swimming about 80 feet to safety. A man followed but couldn't make it. He drowned. Tropnikov learned later that the man was the boy's father.

Soon local residents began to arrive with small boats. Some of the drifting fishermen panicked. Balachevtsev watched as several fishermen jumped into a vessel meant to hold four. The boat soon sank, and all eight men aboard drowned. Others stood on small floes and tried to paddle them like rafts to shore using their ice drills as oars. The wind pushed them back.

Some of the fishermen had mobile phones and alerted the rescue squad. The first helicopters began buzzing overhead in the early evening. Already that day, rescuers had plucked 30 people from the ice on the southern shore of the Gulf of Finland, and 17 more near the gulf island of Kronshtadt. It took them awhile to reach Ladoga, and they managed to pick up only a few dozen people before night fell. The remaining fishermen — about 800 — prepared to spend the night on the ice.

They had to keep moving. The wind stayed strong, and the waves chewed at the floe. As it shrank, the fishermen retreated toward the center.

"We could hear the edge of the ice crunching and breaking behind us," Tropnikov recalls. "We'd sit for half an hour and then walk for half an hour. At first, people carried their things with them, but we began to lose strength and started discarding stuff. I threw away my fish, then my drill. I tried not to think about anything, even about my wife or my children."

By morning, the floe had shrunk to one-fifth its original size. While waiting for the helicopters, Balachevtsev squeezed in some more fishing.

"We had time to kill," he says, only slightly sheepishly. "Why not?"

Four helicopters spent the better part of the day picking up the fishermen. By afternoon, the floe had broken into several pieces, some just a few yards across, and had drifted more than 10 miles out into the lake. As the choppers arrived, some fishermen were lying spread-eagle on partially submerged floes, stabbing penknives into the ice to keep from being blown off.

"When the helicopter came, I was at the end of my reserves," Tropnikov says. "I couldn't feel the toes on my right foot…. I tried to climb aboard, but my strength failed me. I clung to the [rescue ladder's] rungs lifelessly until one of the rescuers lifted me like a sack and threw me inside."

Officially, 1,012 people were rescued and eight died — the men in the overloaded boat. But many people, including Balachevtsev, say dozens of deaths weren't counted, including the man in the van, the drowned father and anglers who may have drifted off alone in the dark.

But both Balachevtsev and Tropnikov will fish again.

"When you have a car accident, you are in shock at first," Tropnikov explains. "But then you get the car fixed and you get back behind the wheel, don't you?"

"I don't have a death wish," Balachevtsev insists. "All I want to do is catch fish. I wish it was safer. Too bad it's not."

. . .

Alexander Shilin struggles into an orange dry suit. He is a trim man, 43, a veteran rock climber who is deputy chief rescuer for the St. Petersburg region. It's a warm day in mid-April, and he's having a busy weekend. "It's a mess up there on the northern shore today," he says.

It seems the ice off Smylyachkovo broke free late in the morning and dozens of fishermen are adrift. Boaters and a Hovercraft are picking up some. The chopper is heading out to look for stragglers.

"We have our own fishing season," Shilin jokes. "It starts in November. What we catch are fishermen."

St. Petersburg has just 45 professional rescue workers, employees of the national Emergencies Ministry, and they retrieve everything from cats in trees to fishermen on ice. Thanks to ice fishing, for most of March and April they barely get an hour off.

"Sure, sometimes I'd like to fine them, to punish them somehow," Shilin says. "But when you pull them out of the water like drowned kittens, how can you get mad at them? They're so grateful."

The helicopter passes over the new edge of the ice, which breaks off just 200 yards from the beach. The day before it stretched for miles.

Shilin points to a scattering of small dark dots along the edge — fishermen who ventured out as far as they could go. "Look how many there are," he says over the roar of the engine. "They look like little ants. You can even see their tracks."

The tracks weave over what remains of the ice, ending abruptly at the edge. They seem like the trailings of ghosts, and maybe some of them are.

Officially, the Emergencies Ministry rescues anywhere from several hundred to several thousand fishermen a year. Private citizens who have sharp eyes and quick boats rescue at least that many.

But fishermen are a solitary breed. Emergencies officials say there is no way to tell how many may go off on their own, get in trouble and die without anyone knowing. "Are they crazy?" Shilin asks. "No, they're Russian."

Shilin has traveled to disaster sites around the world and has conferred with rescue workers from many countries. He's convinced that Russians have a different sense of danger.

"In the West, you say that life is cheaper in Russia. Maybe that's so. Maybe we don't value even our own lives as much," he says. "But any way you look at it, our understanding of risk is different. And it's built into us. It's part of us."

His boss, Andrei Rubul, deputy director of the northwestern region for the Emergencies Ministry, notes that even though the Finnish capital, Helsinki, is also on the Gulf of Finland, it has no comparable problem with floating fishermen.

"A Russian knows that he shouldn't do this and he goes out on the ice all the same," Rubul says. "A Finn knows he shouldn't do something and he doesn't. He stays home."

After passing over open water, the helicopter finds the new floe. It takes half an hour to fly the length of it and circle back. The only signs of fishermen are their holes in the ice.

When Shilin returns to headquarters, another crisis is brewing. Two fishermen have been spotted 300 yards off Kronshtadt. Night is falling, the wind is strong, and they seem to be having trouble getting back to shore.

He's reluctant to send a crew. "Of course we'll go," Shilin tells his boss after conferring by phone. "But you understand how big a risk it is."

The team he sends has been out all day on Lake Ladoga and has already hauled in four wayward anglers. Wearily, the rescuers load a boat and outboard motor onto a truck and drive into the darkness.

Vadim Nenonen, 32, is the captain. He and two teammates, looking like cosmonauts in bulky hypothermia suits, haul the boat out onto the ice. Their headlamps contract to pinpoints, then disappear in the darkness. The bitter wind freezes all conversation among police and residents on shore.

The rescuers search for three hours before the headlamps bob slowly back. The ice has turned to porridge, Nenonen says.

"That's it for them," he adds. "No one can survive out there that long." He calls off the search.

Does he resent having to risk his life for foolhardy fishermen?

"Fishermen are all crazy, of course. It's probably some kind of psychosis," he says. Then he grins mischievously. "But I guess I have it too. I don't mind a little fishing myself now and then."

His attitude is common in these parts — half exasperation, half amusement. But if there's one person in St. Petersburg who can no longer shrug off the phenomenon, it's Anna Artamonova.

Artamonova's 45-year-old husband, Valery, was one of the men Nenonen was searching for on the dark ice off Kronshtadt. His body turned up the next day. He died of hypothermia around dawn.

"He was like any other fisherman in Russia — he always thought that if something bad was going to happen, it was going to happen to someone else," Artamonova says. "How desperate or reckless does a person have to be to risk his life for half a dozen fish no bigger than your palm?"

Sergei L. Loiko and Alexei V. Kuznetsov of The Times' Moscow bureau contributed to this report.

❖

Children Left by the Wayside

Each day, a U.N. truck makes its rounds, picking up youngsters Rwanda's war has abandoned. With no family, no food, perhaps not even a name to remember, their last hope is the 'orphan express.'

BY JOHN BALZAR · AUGUST 10, 1994

MUNIGI, Zaire — Death we have seen, and by the numbing long ton. But imagine this other ordeal: being left alone in the world with nothing.

Sick, naked, wet in a pool of your own uncontrollable excrement, too weak to do anything except tremble. Not a possession, no family or friends, no country, perhaps not even a name you can remember.

"And these are the lucky ones. There are thousands out here we haven't got to yet," says Christian Clark, a 33-year-old UNICEF worker who rolls another Rwandan child from the plastic sheeting of the Munigi camp cholera aid station onto a prickly blanket. He carries her to a rescue truck.

It is 9 a.m. and this is stop No. 1 in the daily round of the orphan express, the white U.N. Children's Emergency Fund truck that rumbles over the sad, teeming landscape of eastern Zaire, scooping up the children that Rwanda's war has abandoned.

The frail girl, who might be 8 years old, is placed on the dirty steel floor of the truck. Medical attendants load three more babies in a single blanket. Perhaps 3 to 6 months old, they too are naked. But one has a thin gold chain around her waist — the only thing she has to carry from this life into the great uncertainty of the next. That is, if someone doesn't steal it from her, which is likely in this cruel land.

There are only four orphans today at this stop, fewer than usual.

Suddenly, a man emerges from the mass of refugees — everywhere here people are compressed into epic throngs. He hands up a 25-pound girl in a soiled and shapeless blue smock. The last of her known family died and she has been sitting alone for two days, the man explains.

She comes into the truck without protest, standing perfectly still on her hard-bottom feet, eyes as wide with wonder as a child at the gate of Disneyland. She has been watching trucks rumble by on this road; finally she will see where one goes.

Clark hands her a biscuit, which she takes with her good hand. She holds the other as if it's hurt. Or maybe it's just rigid with tension.

The girl stares at you with questions you can never know. She is trembling. She is covered with lice and crusty with filth. A reporter puts an arm around her. "That's it," Clark says. "She'll warm up, you'll see. These kids are starved for affection."

Good God, you think, it's only 9 a.m. and the rounds are just starting. Wouldn't you be pathetic if you couldn't hold back these burning tears in front of this girl?

Next, the airport and the French army post.

Word has already spread among the refugees. Each day, lost and orphaned children who no longer can endure the camps on their own learn of the truck stops. Some parents also hear of the UNICEF rescue. They drop off a child to lighten their own load. Perhaps they say to themselves: Nothing could be worse than keeping children in the camps, even if that means sending them down the road alone.

So far 7,400 unaccompanied children have been collected here by relief workers. UNICEF estimates an additional 10,000 to 70,000 roam alone. Each day, the orphanages exceed their capacity and are expanded farther onto the lava rocks.

"We've never, never seen anything like this before. Maybe it's happened [before], but we haven't seen it," Clark says.

At these stops, the truck collects some older children. One, two and then another. They seem to appear from nowhere. You turn your back, and two have climbed up and taken a seat on the little school benches that ride unfettered under the canvas top of the truck. The children are quiet as they accept biscuits and water. Suddenly, two more have moved in.

We drive on, and Clark scrambles back and forth in the bouncing truck bed, smiling widely and trying to joke with the older children. There are no smiles back just yet, but a faint spark can be seen in their eyes — perhaps gratitude. A truck ride, a cookie and a hug are more than these children have had in a long time.

Wearing a dirty jacket and shorts, Joseph Bavurnda says he is 13, although he is only half the size of a Western teenager, with bony feet and big, curious eyes.

"My father died before in Kigali. My mother died with cholera after a one-week walk. I have two little brothers, but I don't know where they are. We became apart at the border."

On the roads, children, some of them very tiny, sit unattended in the dirt. In the teeming centers of the camps, who can know which of the thousands are attended to and which are not? Difficult as it is, the truck passes them all by. Surviving refugees are asked to help identify the lost, orphaned and abandoned, and bring them to designated pickup sites. No one wants to accidentally take a child whose mother is off looking for food or water.

The next stop is the public hospital in Goma, Zaire, which is considered adequate by African standards. There are two and three patients in each bed, with others lying in tents and on the ground. Flies and the sharp smells of urine and infection fill the wards. But there seems to be a large medical staff.

A girl who is perhaps 3 has lost her mother to dysentery and adopted another female patient as a surrogate. But the woman explains that she has two children of her own and cannot support this child. The girl screams and will not let go. The surrogate mother's agony shows on her face. A crowd gathers, noisily. Someone yanks the wailing child away.

Just this morning, reporters here learned via shortwave broadcast that some Western pundits were criticizing coverage of the refugees as exploitative. The critics should have seen this: the wailing, half-naked child clawing the air furiously for something to hold.

And there was the shoulder of Gloria Galloway, a reporter for the Canadian Press news service, herself a mother of three.

Her notebook in her pocket, Galloway carried the child back to the orphan express. Two other reporters lifted other children into the now-crowded vehicle and began the feeding chores. Somehow, counting the morning's total of orphans was forgotten. Was it 20 or 30?

"The last time people fled like this was when Moses parted the Red Sea," says Clark, a former scriptwriter for "Sesame Street."

Today's children are first taken to UNICEF headquarters in Goma, the town where relief efforts are coordinated. The children who are old enough to talk are registered here. Workers hope that if the outlying camps can be stabilized with food and medicine, at least some parents will come searching for missing children.

Then the truck drives to the final stop, the Carea Orphanage outside Goma. This is a tent city of tiny people, where the sick are separated by disease: cholera here, dysentery there, unknown over yonder.

The healthy move on to canvas tents with floors of plastic sheeting. Here, children care for other children.

And someone has done a good job of it already. A group of 6- or 7-year-old boys charges out of a tent to greet a visitor. With their arms folded, they bow in unison, smile and recite:

"*Bonjour*, papa!"

"*Bonjour,* boys."

None of them looks when a tiny body is carried through the orphanage in a blanket. It is placed along the shoulder of the road for a different collection truck.

Three days ago at this orphanage, a 5-year-old girl showed up at the gate with an infant she found along the roadside in the arms of a dead mother. Today, the 5-year-old returned and inquired about the health of "her baby." The infant died, but an orphanage worker lied and said everything was fine.

There are happier stories too, like the listless infant who would not eat or stop crying. A nurse held the dying toddler and happened to feel a bump. A surgeon extracted a bullet that had killed the mother and lodged in the child. The youngster grew plump in three days.

But what of these children a month from now when the rainy season turns the ground to mud? And a year from now when the eyes and hearts of the world have moved elsewhere? And 20 years after that, when they reach adulthood on this crowded and turbulent continent?

"I don't know how these kids will survive emotionally," says Pat Sheppard, a New Jersey nurse with the relief group AmeriCares. "I can hardly think about that yet. I only know it's not going to get better for a long while."

❖

An Island Transformed by a Small Screen

American Samoa didn't have TV entertainment until 1966. Today, village customs are fitted around favorite programs, and boys and girls alike want to grow up to be policewomen, after the island's most popular show.

By Barry Siegel · June 14, 1979

PAGO PAGO, American Samoa — Every evening in a small village not far from Apia, the capital of Western Samoa, a conch shell blows, announcing a communal gathering where villagers pray, read the Bible and share the day's experiences.

This gathering, called a *lotu*, is an ancient and much-valued part of *fa'a Samoa*, the Samoan way, one fiercely and diligently maintained by the village elders against the inroads of modern life.

But in recent years, the elders themselves — tribal chiefs marked with elaborate tattoos from waist to knee — have altered the custom in this village. They have changed the time for the Sunday *lotu* — so they can watch their favorite television program, "All Star Wrestling."

This is just one sign of television's arrival in the isolated South Pacific, one of the few regions in the world where entire countries exist without TV.

In the village of Alao in American Samoa, in a coastline compound of *fales* (huts) with no walls and thatched roofs woven from sugar cane leaves, 10 men sit cross-legged on the floor, eating a meal of boiled curried bananas and a steamed local fish called *pone*.

The food is prepared and served by the women of the village, who eat later, in the rear of the *fale*. Roosters and small brown pigs stroll through the surrounding banana trees and thick bushes of scarlet hibiscus. A central guest hut is open to whoever passes by.

The scene could be unfolding 100 years ago — except that as the villagers pick food off banana-leaf mats, a television set in the corner of the hut shows the NBC Game of the Week between the Pittsburgh Pirates and the St. Louis Cardinals.

The Pirates score two runs in the first inning. The scene cuts to commercials, taped off KRON-TV in San Francisco, for Pentax cameras, Delco shock absorbers,

Ortho lawn fertilizer, State Farm insurance and Gillette Foamy shaving lather.

In the nearby village of Lauli, Imo Tiapula, 8, rises early on Saturday morning to make his father's coffee and finish his other chores — so he can watch the Saturday-morning Godzilla cartoons.

On historic, remote Savai'i, considered by anthropologists to be the cradle of Polynesian culture, Mapuilesua Pelenato plugged in the island's first television set last February, four months after the first electric power poles appeared along the island's eastern edge.

The children and some adults in his village, who used to gather on the road most evenings to talk, now come to Pelenato's *fale* every night at 6, turn on the TV and keep it on until the broadcast day ends at 11.

The villagers watch whatever is on the screen, although they particularly like westerns, police stories and "The Midnight Special" when it features disco music. Late at night, Pelenato gently awakens youngsters who have fallen asleep before the TV. He does not mind: "It gives people here something to do and it helps them learn better English."

American Samoa is a place worth examining because TV researchers call it a classic example of what usually happens when TV is introduced anywhere.

President Kennedy dispatched H. Rex Lee to this island territory as governor in 1962 with orders to upgrade the place. So during his tenure, Lee built roads, installed utilities, improved medical care — and introduced television.

The initial purpose was educational. The government wanted Samoans to be competent in English, but lacked enough English-speaking teachers. So in 1964, the territorial Department of Education pulled together what English-speaking teachers they could find, put them before TV cameras, installed television sets in every class-room and began broadcasting to all Samoan schools.

At its peak, the Department of Education was producing 180 live programs a week over six channels and drawing a good deal of attention for what was considered a novel experiment. In one such program, a teacher appears on the screen, holding a bottle of paint: "This is a bottle of paint. Listen again…. Shhh…. This is a bottle of paint. Now you tell me…. (Pause.) … Tell me again…. (Pause.) … Now … shhh … listen. This is a brush. Now you tell me…."

Then Samoan TV made a fateful move — it added a handful of entertainment programs to the schedule in 1966, including "Cheyenne," "The Mickey Mouse Club," "Top Star Bowling," "Hawaiian Eye," "The Andy Williams Show" and "Bonanza."

Although these programs were being warmly embraced by Samoan viewers, edu-cational TV was faltering. The television had become the primary tool in the classroom, rather than a supplement. Students' language skills improved, but they missed the human contact.

All classes had to proceed at the pace set by the television, teachers in the classroom grew restless in their limited role of monitor, the first students graduating from the program floundered when they entered college, and some observers took to calling the whole program a "white elephant."

Two years ago, the Samoan TV budget was cut almost in half (from $1.3 million to $711,000), most of the staff was dismissed and the channels were cut from six to three. The TV station was removed from the control of the Department of Education, and virtually no new instructional programs have been produced since then.

More and more American entertainment programs were brought in to fill the evening hours, partly in response to pressure created by a community survey and phone calls to the TV station that indicated entertainment was what Samoans wanted. "There is good and bad in TV," explains a Samoan villager, echoing the comments of others, "but I don't mind it. The shows are entertaining, TV is a good baby-sitter for my kids, and it expands their vision of things, puts them in contact with the outside world."

After working all day on an island plantation, this villager lies on the floor of his *fale* in front of his TV set, watching "Cliffhangers," "Laverne & Shirley" and "Three's Company."

By 1970, there were two evening channels; by 1973, three. This gave American Samoa, with a population of 35,000, more television programming than nearby New Zealand, with a population of 3 million.

Critics of television in other countries may note with interest that this swing to mass entertainment programming in Samoa did not come about because of commercial, advertiser pressure. Samoan TV has always been government-financed, non-profit and noncommercial.

(Last year's TV budget was $528,000, provided by the United States government; this year, the $593,000 budget is being paid for by the territorial government from local tax revenues.)

Although Samoan TV does not sell its own advertising, the week-old tapes from the ABC and NBC affiliates in San Francisco are broadcast with all the commercials included, unedited. A Samoan TV official says this is required by their contract with Overseas Taping Service. But Mere Betham, the territory's director of education, believes the station is simply saving the time and expense of editing tape.

Whatever the reason, Samoans now watch commercials for items they had never heard of or seen before, such as carpet cleaners, room deodorizers, antiperspirants, sugarless bubble gum and San Francisco car dealerships. A Taco Bell commercial one night posed a puzzle for one Samoan: "What's a taco?" he asked.

"We have ended up with publicly funded, nonprofit TV showing 'Baretta' and Burger King," Betham says. "Our merchants benefit, and taxpayers are paying for it."

"When the budget was cut," explains Kirk Walker, chief engineer for the TV station, "there was talk of lessening TV altogether, not just the instructional stuff. We tried, but there was all hell to pay. They wanted those programs."

A 1976 study by Survey/Hawaii concluded that "the Samoan audience is deeply fascinated with television viewing." About 96 percent of the population has access to a television set, the report said; there were almost 4,000 sets on American Samoa, with an average of just under eight viewers per set.

It is an odd sight to walk along the American Samoan coastline on a warm evening and pass village after village where TV screens are burning brightly in the majority of the thatched-roof fales.

Programming begins at 4 p.m. and includes everything from "Days of Our Lives" and "Wheel of Fortune" to "Charlie's Angels," "Mork & Mindy" and "Rockford Files." One channel broadcasts PBS programs such as "Sesame Street" and "Wall Street Week." Samoans also watch a local news show, the "NBC Nightly News" and the "ABC Captioned News."

According to the Survey/Hawaii report, "Police Woman" was the most popular show in 1976, drawing 83 percent of the audience, followed by "Sunday Night Mystery Movie" (77 percent) and "Police Story" (75 percent). The lowest rated shows were PBS programs — "Great Performances," "Visions," "Nova," "Bookbeat" and "Masterpiece Theatre" — which drew only 2 percent to 6 percent of the audience.

It is not unusual today to hear Samoan young people's conversations punctuated with suggestions to "flic your Bic." Nor is it unusual to see 14-year-old boys, after a game of cricket, celebrate victory with the clenched fist salutes and hand slaps common among athletes on U.S. television.

Apparent effects of TV can be seen everywhere in American Samoa. But it is difficult to separate TV's influence from the general impact of the American presence and the American dollar.

The economy here used to involve subsistence farming and fishing, and little cash. No more. Almost half the work force is employed by the territorial government, which currently operates with a $50-million budget, about 75 percent provided by the United States.

Many Samoans have moved to Hawaii or the mainland, and those who stay here have a declining interest in hard labor on the plantations or at the two private canneries.

American Samoa today imports bananas, although they grow wild all over the island. One morning, the local hotel dining room could offer only canned peaches and pears. The waitress said they had no papayas, pineapples, bananas or coconuts, although a coconut tree swayed gracefully outside the dining room window.

With money to buy food, Samoans have shifted more and more to canned goods. The shelves of the small store in Alao are heavily stocked with canned corned beef, Spam, salmon, vegetables, fruit cocktail, sausage, beef stew and fricassee of chicken wings.

This shift to canned goods even affected a traditional welcoming ceremony in a Samoan village one evening. Such a ceremony normally involves a chicken, killed and wrapped in a banana leaf. This evening, the villagers substituted fricassee of chicken wings — from a can.

But if it is an affluent wage economy and extensive travel that have most affected American Samoa, people here generally agree that the travel and migration were in turn mostly prompted by what people saw on television.

"TV makes people here think that in America everyone is rich, with two cars," says Sandy Tiapola, an American from Denver who married a Samoan and now lives in a village east of Pago Pago. "They look and say, 'Wow,' then decide to journey to the mainland. They want things. I know women who didn't eat for two weeks in order to buy a sewing machine they saw advertised."

Spontaneous social gatherings have diminished since TV arrived, others say.

"When I first came here 13 years ago," says Jake King, editor of the Samoan News, "it was very usual to have village sings and socials. You could go to the villages and be entertained. Now it has almost entirely disappeared. When it happens, it's planned. Today, when you go to a village, they're more likely to be sitting around watching shootouts."

David Irvine, art director at the TV station, points to a yellowed, aging poster on his office bulletin board advertising the Island Community Theater. "That was very active before; now it's hanging on by its teeth."

When a recent survey asked schoolchildren what they wanted to be when they grew up, the greatest single response by far from boys and girls alike was "a policewoman" — and the explanation could only have been that "Police Woman" topped the list of popular TV shows.

In stores, products that have been sitting on the shelves — or had never been there at all — now sell out: Johnson & Johnson shampoo, all kinds of cereals, Clorox, frozen potatoes. Betham, the director of education, shakes her head when talking about this and says, "Samoans before TV never used hair shampoo or ate cereals."

Even in Apia, merchants now purposefully stock what they see advertised on television. S.V. Mackenzie & Co., the Apia general store that for 57 years has served as agent for many American products, reports sharply increased sales for such items as Tang, Scope mouthwash, Pringles and Shout.

"Pepto-Bismol never sold here before at all," Vernon Mackenzie says. "Now it sells like hotcakes. Also things like Bufferin, Nytol and Sominex. And the great thing is, we don't have to pay for the advertising." Business has been so good that Mackenzie is tearing down his current store and building a modern five-story supermarket with a parking lot.

Not only the merchants see good in TV's influence. "TV ended our isolation," says Pat Galeai, executive director of the vocational education advisory council, echoing comments by many others. "We can keep up with the outside world. Samoans are more outgoing, more able to express themselves now." When Samoans saw on TV the disastrous Agoura-Malibu fire in Los Angeles last fall, they prayed during Sunday church services for the homeless victims.

But others wonder how much exposure might eventually affect the Samoans.

Samoans, like most Polynesians, generally are not a competitive or commercially enterprising people, anthropologists say. The hotel at Pago Pago rarely serves fresh fish because the food manager cannot get the locals to supply any on a regular basis; they fish only for their own dinner. The scientists also say Polynesians tend to submit willingly to the strict authority of the chiefs.

So when Dr. Wilbur Schramm of the East West Center in Honolulu surveyed a carefully selected cross-section of Samoan TV watchers and non-watchers, he was interested to see that the TV watchers' answers to his questions demonstrated a much greater tendency toward materialism and competitiveness, less valuing of the family, tradition and authority, and an inclination to be more independent and individual.

Outside a restaurant that serves a traditional Samoan feast, three local Samoan teenage girls dressed in blue jeans leaned against a wall and explained why they did not go in: "That's too old-fashioned."

But the questionnaire's results also suggested that this pattern may not hold permanently. The longer Samoans watch TV, the more, it seems, they return to traditional values. At least this is one interpretation of Schramm's data, one he thinks has some validity.

University of Winnipeg anthropologists say they found the same trend among Cree Indians in Canada. Perhaps the exposure to modern values, the researchers theorize, eventually leads natives to appreciate more their own values.

The Canadian scientists also found that TV had much less impact on those Crees who came from a traditional family, as opposed to those from more culturally assimilated families.

One of the central conclusions: Although TV has an impact, it does not alter a fundamental culture but rather is absorbed into that culture. They say signs of Western acculturation, such as blue jeans and transistor radios, are misleading, because private values and concepts prevail below the surface.

The 70-year-old father of Samoan novelist Albert Wendt is one of those who has changed the time of his village's *lotu* in order to watch wrestling on TV. Albert Wendt tells this story to illustrate TV's impact — but also to point out the limits of its influence. After all, he observes, the communal gathering still takes place. "Culture adopts and adjusts," he says, "but is not overwhelmed by TV."

Perhaps Wendt is right. Much of the evidence points toward his conclusion. But the fact is, no one really knows for sure. Contrary evidence can be cited, and most scientists admit their methodology may be limiting what they know. There are those who believe that television causes certain profound changes that just cannot be observed or quantified.

"We know all the statistics," says Schramm, one of the most highly regarded TV researchers. "But what we don't know are the deeper things, such as how TV affects a person's sense of time and space. We must rely on the intuitive and the anecdotal."

❖

A Reverence for 'Noses'

In France, the inventors of perfumes are regarded as composers and their creations are considered works of art

By Stanley Meisler · March 22, 1988

PARIS — Perfume is a $3-billion industry in France, but it is also, for the French, a mystique, a cultural heritage, a work of art, a hallmark of national elegance and taste, an expression of sexual fashion, a reminder of past power, and an echo of great romantic literature of the 19th century.

Nowhere else in the world is perfume taken so seriously and treated with so much reverence. Inventors of perfumes — known in France as "noses" — are regarded in the same light as composers of music. To make the association clear, Chanel, the couturier and perfume house, even hands out publicity pictures that show Jacques Polge, the creator of its Coco perfume, standing in front of a music stand.

In his standard encyclopedic work on perfume in France, Edmond Roudnitska, creator of the Rochas perfume Femme, invokes the thinking of French philosopher Henri Bergson and the methods of French composer Pierre Boulez to explain the art of making a perfume.

"A perfume," Roudnitska writes, "can be a work of art like a symphony or a master's painting and therefore deserves the same respect."

The French study perfume from every side. Historian Alain Corbin produced an unusual study a few years ago of French attitudes toward odor, both foul and fragrant, for the last two centuries. The National Museum of Natural History in Paris is now presenting a major exhibition on the use of flowers in perfume throughout history and throughout the world. The museum pumps perfume into the air of each exhibition room.

The Paris Metro recently decided to perfume its stations. Subway riders, asked to sample several fragrances, selected two, Legende and Horizon, as the perfumes they would most like to smell underground. Workers then infused them into the soaps used for cleaning the stations. Unfortunately, according to a Metro spokesman, "you can only really smell them just after a station has been cleaned."

In 1985, Patrick Suskind, a German writer who had studied at the same university as Polge in southern France, wrote the novel "Perfume" about an 18th-century "nose" who murders beautiful young women in the town of Grasse to capture their scents for the creation of a magnificent new perfume. The book was dismissed by the New York Review of Books as "verbose claptrap," but the historical accuracy of Suskind's descriptions of perfume making in the 18th century astounded everyone in the French perfume industry, and the French translation was a bestseller in France.

The French still celebrate Grasse, just north of Cannes on the French Riviera, as the perfume capital of the world. Students in Grasse try to learn to distinguish at least 3,000 scents so that they can become "noses" someday. Workers in Grasse pick jasmine by hand, separating the flowers petal by petal for processing and then shipment to perfume houses in Paris.

Admirers of French literature still quote the great 19th-century poet Charles Baudelaire, who dwelt on the sense of smell in his "Les Fleurs du Mal" — "The Flowers of Evil." The book brims with lines such as: "There rises from her tensile, heavy hair, a living sachet, censer of the bed, a perfume savage, turbulent and rude."

All the mystery and mystique are sometimes obscured these days by marketing. Far more is spent on promoting a perfume in modern France than on creating one. It cost Christian Dior $11 million in 1985 just to launch the perfume Poison on the European market.

This kind of hoopla is deplored by some of the French industry's traditional leaders, such as 82-year-old Robert Ricci, president of Nina Ricci perfumes. "Perfume," he lamented at a recent industry conference, "is changing from a universe of charm into a universe of shock."

Yet even with aggressive marketing and advertising hype, a good deal of antique romance still hangs on in the perfume industry here. This is reflected clearly in all the homage paid to the artistry of "noses" in the industry.

To understand a "nose," an outsider must have a clear idea of what a perfume really is. A perfume is an alcoholic compound that generates a scent pleasing to the human sense of smell. The compound is made up of any or all of three primary materials: fragrant vegetable materials such as the petals of jasmine; animal scents such as musk from the male musk deer of the Himalayas; and chemical synthetics that reproduce fragrances such as violet and vanilla which are hard to capture naturally.

A "nose," who often carries an official title such as director of laboratories, is the creator and monitor of a perfume. A "nose" seeks new combinations that will seduce the market, and tests the quality of primary materials to make sure that the fragrances of old, popular perfumes are maintained.

A visitor finds on the desk of every "nose" a metal, fan-like contraption that holds several fingers of paper. Droplets of scents are put on each paper. A "nose" sniffs one and then another in his continual quest for new and old fragrance. A "nose" must learn to sniff with the times, trying to assess, for example, whether a more sexually overt era allows more powerful animal scents in a perfume or whether it demands, for contrast, more diffident and subtle smells.

There are supposed to be 15 great "noses" in the world, with another 100 of near-star quality. Almost all are French, and most come from Grasse, where, in a bygone age, "noses" claimed that they could distinguish the scent of one type of jasmine from another at a distance of several miles.

One of the best-known modern creators, Polge, the 44-year-old "nose" of Chanel, grew up in Grasse and returned home to train in the art of distinguishing scents after studying English literature at university.

In an age of computers and dazzling advances in chemistry, an outsider may wonder if all the veneration of a "nose" is no more than hocus-pocus dreamed up by publicity agents trying to infuse the business with even more mystique than it already has. Couldn't a chemist with a computer do the job as well as a "nose" sniffing from fingers of paper?

"I have no training as a chemist," Polge replied in a recent interview in Paris. "A formula for a perfume is not a chemical formula. A formula is worthless unless you know your primary materials. The formula lists the primary materials and the proportions used of each. But there may be at least 20 varieties of each material. You must know them.

"We keep the formula for Chanel No. 5 in a safe under lock and key. But, if you stole it, you would not know what to do with it."

The cost of launching perfumes is so high that a "nose," no matter how celebrated, cannot hope to be credited with a great many creations in a lifetime. Polge, for example, has established his reputation on five: Coco, Antaeus for men, Diva, Senso and Eau de Parfum No. 5, a less concentrated form of Chanel No. 5.

"I get 60 to 100 ideas a year," said Polge. "Very few, of course, ever become a perfume that is marketed. Those are the limits of all composers of perfumes. But that does not hold me back."

Perfumes are an ancient creation, dating at least to biblical times. The Old Testament tells how Queen Esther, for example, bathed "six months with oil of myrrh and six months with sweet odors and with other things for the purifying of the women" before her marriage to King Ahasuerus of Persia. Describing the elite of France just before the French Revolution, novelist Alexandre Dumas wrote, "Aside from philosophers . . . everyone smelled nice."

Over the centuries, the use and kinds of perfume have varied. In some eras, people perfumed themselves to mask body odors; in other eras, to excite or attract a partner; in still others, to drive away infections in the air. New ideas about hygiene, for example, lessened some of the need for strong animal scents in the 19th century. People no longer had to have something strong to overpower their own body odor.

The modern concept of perfume, however, dates mainly to the 19th century and France. The House of Guerlain, for example, was founded in Paris in 1828 and did not become established and powerful until much later in the century.

Historians attribute the development of the modern industry to three factors. The first was subtle. According to historian Corbin, a new modesty in women's dress in high society, with less exposure of the body, fostered the need to seduce men in other, seemingly innocent ways. Perfume filled that need handily.

Second, 19th-century French writers such as Baudelaire extolled smell as one of the great human senses. Before Baudelaire, a sensitive soul would look upon a field of flowers and see the beauty of its myriad colors; after Baudelaire, a sensitive soul would be expected to breathe in the beauty of its fragrance as well.

In his turn-of-the-century novel, "Against the Grain," Joris-Karl Huysmans devoted an entire chapter to his hero's obsession with mixing perfume in a quest to experience every possible human sensation. The novel was looked on as the master-work of the then-fashionable movement of decadence in French literature. It helped make the sense of scent and the art of fragrance exciting.

Finally, and perhaps most important, new discoveries in chemistry made it possible to create a large number of floral scents that were impossible or nearly impossible to fashion from the flowers themselves. This opened an enormous variety of combinations to the perfume maker. It made the art of perfume composition possible.

A perfume like Chanel No. 5, composed by Ernest Beaux in 1921, could not have been made without synthetics. This is true of almost all modern perfumes.

France, in this era of first great perfumes, was regarded as one of the most powerful nations on Earth, a great military and colonial power and a civilization that set a pattern of taste for everyone else. It was natural for the art and use of perfume to take the form, in the eyes of the rest of the world, of a French cultural phenomenon. Perfume became as French as fashion and cuisine.

The costs of producing a perfume are high. Elizabeth Sirot of Guerlain recently pointed to a small canister of jasmine concentrate at the company's plant outside Paris and said, "It takes 300,000 petals of jasmine to produce one kilogram of concentrate. That kilo costs us 450,000 francs" or $80,000. The company needs jasmine to produce Shalimar, the famous perfume created by Jacques Guerlain in 1925. Civet, another significant ingredient in Shalimar, comes from the secretions of a wild cat in Ethiopia, and Guerlain must pay heavily to get it.

Yet, whatever the costs, the luxury perfume industry, still dominated by France, remains an extremely profitable business. Chanel reportedly sells more than $50 million worth of No. 5 every year. It is regarded as the bestselling perfume of all time.

There is some concern in the industry that the decline in the value of the dollar has prompted Americans to buy less French perfume. The fall in the price of oil has also diminished some lavish buying of perfume by Arabs.

"A few years ago," said Guerlain's Sirot, "a eunuch came into our store on the Champs Elysees to buy perfumes for the 40 women in a harem. And there was a sheik who bought Shalimar to fill his pool. But those days are gone." But even while selling less, manufacturers have managed to increase their profits, at least in dollars, by raising prices.

Competition is intense. Manufacturers introduced 485 new women's perfumes between 1975 and 1986. The pressure from this competition shows itself in different ways.

Three "noses" were arrested and charged with industrial espionage in Grasse recently for trying to take the secret formulas from the Mero perfume company and use it in a new company of their own. The pressure is far more commonly met, of course, by enormous expenditures on advertising. Perfume ads are the staples of luxury and beauty magazines throughout the world.

Some specialists see a danger in this. Roudnitska, the "nose" who invented Femme, says that French perfumery — "this beautiful perfumery founded on an aesthetic conception and on the creative sprit of beauty" — could slide downward into a mass industry based on marketing.

Ricci, who runs Nina Ricci, argues that much of the money spent on marketing may be wasted anyway.

"Ninety percent of women choose a perfume for its fragrance," he said, "only 10% for its concept and marketing. I'm not against marketing, but the primordial thing is creating the fragrance."

But even as celebrated a "nose" as Polge does not agree. He insists that the success or failure of a perfume depends on several factors: the perfume itself, its flask, its publicity image and the way it seems to fit in with the culture of the times.

"Which is the most important?" he asked. "I know what you think I am going to say. As the creator, I should say that the perfume is the most important. But I prefer to put it this way: You must succeed in all these factors to have a success. If one fails, you will not have a successful perfume."

Paris bureau editorial assistant Sarah White contributed to this article.

❖

Japan Is Flush With Obsession

The country has an enduring fascination with the toilet — replete with cutting-edge technology, Web sites, symposiums and museums. The enthusiasm is largely lost on foreigners.

BY MARK MAGNIER · DECEMBER 13, 1999

KOKURA, Japan — It's got wings, it's sensitive, it's smart. It cares, it knows when you're around, it bleats when you arrive. Ignore it and you could be sorry. Treat it well and it will comfort you in your old age.

A new kind of house pet? No, it's the Japanese toilet in all its glory. And if you believe its makers, it's only getting better.

Japan has an enduring fascination with the toilet, replete with cutting-edge intelligent-toilet research, toilet Web sites, symposiums, antique toilet museums, solid 24-karat-gold johns and official Toilet Days. Nowhere else on Earth do so many people spend so much money on such expensive thrones.

Japan's enthusiasm is largely lost on foreigners. In sharp contrast to their receptiveness to the Japanese cameras, autos and Walkmans that have taken the world by storm, few Americans or Europeans seem to covet Japan's super bowls — some of which can cost $4,000.

Major Japanese manufacturers hope to change that by creating something with more universal appeal. Their latest project: a toilet that doubles as a doctor's office.

At Matsushita's research center in Tokyo, scientists explain how they are working on embedding technology in the porcelain that will catch a urine sample, shoot it full of lasers, and in short order test it for glucose, kidney disease and eventually even cancer.

One of the researchers, Tatsuro Kawamura, says future smart toilets will compile and compare test results day by day, allowing doctors to spot important changes.

Japan's undisputed king of toilets is Toto Ltd., which has noticed the enormous profits ahead in serving Japan's rapidly aging population, although it's moving slower on the medical front.

Toto set the industry standard in the 1980s with its high-tech Washlet, which got worldwide publicity at the time. With the slogan "Even your bottom wants to stay clean," it built mass appeal in Japan for the $1,000-and-up toilets previously confined to sanitariums and hospitals.

Nearly 20 years later, these once-luxury items can be found in about 30 percent of Japanese homes. The fully configured Washlet, the Lexus of toiletry, has enough lights, hoses, buttons, remote controls and temperature and water-pressure adjustments to bowl over even the most avid gadget freak.

Master the Washlet's controls — many foreigners don't and emerge soaking and embarrassed — and your bum will be warmed even as your undercarriage is squirted with warm water and blow-dried, obviating the need for toilet paper.

"Once you use it, you wonder how you could ever do without it," says Mariko Fujiwara, a researcher with the Hakuhodo Institute of Life and Living.

What's behind Japan's keen interest in toiletry?

Takahiko Furata, director of Aomori University's Modern Social Studies Institute, cites the Shinto religion's traditional emphasis on physical and spiritual cleanliness.

"Japanese hate impurities and think it's important to have a place to remove them. That place is the toilet," he says. "Japanese toilet culture is based on this idea."

Others such as Eiko Mizuno, a researcher at the Life Design Institute, note that the toilet may be one of the few places people in crowded Japan can go for a few minutes of quiet — akin to the automobile for some Americans.

And Dr. Hiroshi Ojima, a proctologist at Japan's Social Insurance Central Hospital, traces the popularity of Washlets to Japan's high constipation rate and low fiber intake relative to many other countries.

Whatever the reason, it all spells big bucks. Toto's most complicated model for the elderly is the EWCS120K, which includes armrests and something resembling an ejection seat for people unable to stand without help. A quick glance at its most elaborate configuration leaves the impression that there's a small aircraft in your bathroom.

Japan's toilet culture isn't limited to the plumbing, however.

One of several Japanese toilet Web sites asks volunteers to visit and rate Tokyo's public restrooms, a sort of twisted Zagat Survey. It invites photos of the most disgusting cases and posts them in the Harsh Site of the Day section.

Another site, called Toilet Television, offers global comparisons and a quiz. Sample question: What percentage of the world uses toilet paper? Answer: 30 percent — alternatives include hands, water, sand, small rocks, mud, leaves and rope. In the old days, Japanese used seaweed, while Americans used cornhusks, it adds helpfully.

For those in search of more theory, the southern island of Kyushu held in mid-November the 15th Japanese National Toilet Symposium, where 500 toilet experts from 15 countries and global groups schmoozed, feasted and voted for their 10 favorite toilets. In past years, the group has also celebrated the toilet's importance with an official day devoted to it.

People intrigued by toilet paper can chase down Hideo Nishioka, chairman of the Japan Toilet Association. His personal toilet paper collection features 400 samples from more than 50 nations. One of his favorites: an Italian roll with a rendering of Botticelli's famous painting "The Birth of Venus."

Out in the marketplace, meanwhile, the Japanese are spending more than $100 million annually on over-the-counter pills designed to prevent any odors they might generate while luxuriating on all these fancy Washlets.

They're also shelling out to fight noise pollution and save water. It seems that many Japanese women flush repeatedly to hide embarrassing sounds. Now some bathrooms include the Sound Princess, a device that mimics the sound of flushing water in place of the real thing.

There are toilet exhibits and museums. In Tokoname, near Nagoya, the Kiln Plaza museum displays porcelain toilets dating back 150 years. Rioh Semba, the collector who owns most of the antiques, says his interest in tea-ceremony porcelain sparked this rather unusual collection. He now owns 500 commodes.

A toilet museum with more popular appeal, meanwhile, is the World Toilet Exhibit in Nakatado-gun on the island of Shikoku. Unicharm, a sanitary-napkin company, contributed $535,000 in 1994 to craft a solid-gold toilet and gold bathroom slippers (the ultra-clean Japanese use different footwear for the john), an exhibit that has wowed the crowds from the start.

The willingness of the Japanese to spend big reached full flower in the 1980s, as disposable income grew, says Miho Mizuhaki, a planning official with Inax, Japan's No. 2 toilet maker. "That's when toilet culture really started to take off," she adds.

Not everyone hails this, however. In fact, some, like the toilet association's Nishioka, think Japan has gone a bit too far.

"The Japanese have become too obsessed with cleanliness," he says, citing recent news reports about students who refuse to use school bathrooms that don't have Washlets.

Japan wasn't always this way. A century ago, it used some pretty basic technology, if you can call it that. Until the early 1900s, human waste generated in the cities was hauled to the country and sold to farmers as fertilizer. The Hakuhodo Institute's Fujiwara says dealers paid more for rich people's waste because their diet was better.

In fact, when it comes to johns, Japan is a Johnny-come-lately. For most of its history, Japan used a variation on the hole in the ground. Plumbing didn't make much of an appearance until the 1923 Yokohama earthquake underscored the danger of disease.

After World War II, as the Western toilet became more popular, Japan relied on a tried-and-true tactic to catch up: It borrowed toilet technology from France, Switzerland and the United States, reverse-engineered it, improved it and voila: the Washlet.

"Japanese are keen about taking foreign ideas and fully developing them," says Aomori University's Furata. "It's a basic Japanese trait."

One of the dead ends on the road to high-tech toiletry can be found in the bowels of Japan's National Stadium, the showcase of the 1964 Tokyo Olympics. Directly under the field along a low, dusty hallway lined with electric wires sits one of Japan's few remaining female urinals, several hundred of which were made by Toto between 1951 and 1968.

The female urinal, which rises out of the floor like a modified cone, is a Japanese invention meant to save time. It never caught on.

"Women just didn't like to use them," says Miyuki Matsumoto, a Toto planning official.

After almost 20 years of Washlet revenue, Toto is searching for its next mega-hit as the old machines start to break down. The firm is weathering the bad publicity that followed when four old Washlets caught fire, prompting headlines such as "Check behind you."

Meanwhile, as Japan contemplates how far it has come with its advanced digital toilet technology, some wonder if there's a danger Japanese toilets will run amok January 1. Are they Y2K compliant?

"They all include computers," said Inax's Mizuhaki. "But we don't expect anything bad to happen. We don't see any danger that the water will shoot out or keep on flushing."

Etsuko Kawase of The Times' Tokyo bureau contributed to this report.

❖

Withering Brit Wit

Coping with hecklers isn't just a fact of life for England's politicians, it's also a skill they cultivate.

BY ROBERT C. TOTH · OCTOBER 12, 1968

LONDON — "Liar!" shouted the heckler. "Liar! Liar!"

"If the gentleman will tell us his name as well as his calling," replied the unperturbed English politician, "we shall be pleased to hear from him."

The British art of putting down hecklers with witty ripostes appropriately seasoned with invective must be envied these days by United States presidential candidates. To turn a rude interruption back with humor and grace is perhaps the best way to win over an audience.

"I'd rather vote for the devil than for you, John Wilkes," yelled a heckler two centuries ago. The reply from Wilkes has become a classic:

"And if your friend is not standing [running] …?"

This kind of heckler handling has earned British politicians a worldwide reputation, and deservedly so.

"Hey, missus, how many toes on a pig's foot?" called out a rowdy who obviously had a barbed answer prepared.

"Take off your boots, man, and count them," shot back the lady politician.

"Traitor! Traitor!" shouted a heckler, but the politician only cupped a hand to his ear and listened intently until silence was restored.

"Just waiting for the cock to crow," he explained mildly.

Americans may remember former Prime Minister Harold Macmillan's elegant put-down of former Soviet Premier Nikita S. Khrushchev at the United Nations in 1960. The Russian had finally stopped banging his shoe on the table to interrupt Macmillan's address when the unflappable Macmillan remarked dryly:

"I'd like that translated, if I may."

British politicians are far better at repartee than their American colleagues. Usually they are more articulate and better educated, particularly in the classics that provide source material for many replies. And most have graduated either from university debating societies or street-corner speaking schools where they have been taught to reply rather than rise to the taunt. Usually they wait for a favorable opening.

"Groundnuts," a young Tory yelled at Prime Minister Harold Wilson during a 1964 campaign address on nuclear missiles. "Groundnuts," he repeated periodically until Wilson either decided on a response or just had had enough of it.

"Now there's an aging young Conservative for you," he said. "His only contribution to the Blue Streak argument is to shout groundnuts [a kind of peanut]. Where have you been, Rip Van Winkle?"

Techniques vary, of course, but another favorite ploy by politicians is to seek out the heckler in advance and neutralize him. One used to follow David Lloyd George around, but when he kept unusually silent during one speech, the prime minister wondered aloud at his absence.

"Here, I'm here," the heckler called out.

"Yes, my man, but are you all there?" Lloyd George asked.

But the best heckling schooling for politicians here comes after rather than before they get elected, for the "clever interjection" in Parliament is a tradition as old as this oldest democracy.

"Wit and invective [in Parliament] do not so much affect legislation directly as they affect the standing of ministers," Lord Attlee, a former Labor prime minister, said in the book "The Fine Art of Political Wit."

"A pompous minister can be brought down by an excellent interruption. It also adds to the brightness of debate and an important point may often best be registered by a flash of wit…. Our politicians seem to have much greater training in ad lib controversy and impromptu debate" than in the United States, he added.

All ministers, including the prime minister, are regularly subjected to freewheeling questions in the House of Commons. Exchanges are fierce between opposing members who — standing behind red lines before each front bench — are literally separated by the length of crossed swords.

Interruptions are frequent but they must be brief, and this promotes the incisiveness of the rapier thrust rather than the ponderous assault of the broadsword. Not surprisingly, the most memorable heckling comes from the professionals in Parliament rather than amateurs on the hustings.

A minister making an interminable speech on economics lost whatever audience was still with him when he paused for a drink of water. "On a point of order, Mr. Speaker," interjected a member, "is it proper for a windmill to go on water?"

One of the most effective pieces of heckling was done by Sir Winston Churchill in the middle of a dull speech by the late Labor leader Hugh Gaitskill. Churchill abruptly sat bolt upright in his place, searched his pockets intensely, then began looking about on the floor. The rattled Gaitskill lost his theme as well as members' attention, and in the silence Churchill was heard to mumble:

"I was only looking for my jujube" or cough drop.

Churchill's ripostes are legendary. They were particularly biting to any remarks about his vices.

"You, sir, are drunk," said a furious woman MP.

"And you, madam, are ugly," he replied. "But tomorrow I shall be sober."

Female politicians are fair game when it comes to heckling. To a woman who was Tory minister of education and who irritated the Socialist firebrand Aneurin Bevan with a condescending grin during one of his speeches, Bevan said:

"I don't know what the honorable lady is grinning at. That is a face which has sunk a thousand scholarships."

Some of the witticisms "reek of the midnight oil," as a Tory once said of Harold Wilson's quips. But American politicians might do better against their hecklers if they burned some of that fuel in advance.

On the other hand, there is a qualitatively different kind of heckling here and in America these days.

The interruptions at American political meetings are aimed less at embarrassing the speaker into an admission of guilt or inconsistency than at deliberately creating chaos to prevent him from being heard altogether.

72

Tolerance of opposing views and a sense of humor about the most serious topic still rank high in British politics. Both seem to be absent from the American scene this year.

❖

Up and Down a River Lifeline

The riverboats that ply the Congo aren't merely a means of transportation. They bustle with traders and their goods — fish, monkeys, antelopes, even crocodiles.

BY CHARLES T. POWERS • NOVEMBER 24, 1983

KISANGANI, Zaire — The searchlight on the riverboat sweeps the shoreline, and the trees stand out brilliant green, dripping with the rain that roils the surface of the water.

The canoes approach like shadows, sliding out of the night, black forms on black water. Behind them, points of firelight flicker from huts scattered along the bank. Now and then someone on the bank whistles — children who have stayed up past midnight to see the boat go by.

Suddenly, the canoes surge forward, men standing in prow and stern and digging their paddles deep into the water, watching intently for a handhold on the big boat. A man in the prow of one canoe leaps for the rail and misses. Another leaps and misses. A third manages to grasp the rail and hold on, the muscles of his glistening arms standing out like rope.

Others follow — five, 10, 20, 40 canoes, seemingly out of nowhere, loaded with fish and dead monkeys trussed by their tails. In the morning, the riverboat's decks will be covered with monkeys and fish, and the buying and selling will go on while still more cargo is hauled on board. More canoes will slide away from the banks through the gray light that rises with the dawn mist over the Congo River.

The sea is still 1,000 miles away.

The mouth of the Congo River, now officially called the Zaire in this Central African nation, was discovered by Diego Cao, the Portuguese explorer, in 1482, a decade before Columbus sailed to the New World. Nearly four centuries would pass before the river's first explorer — Henry M. Stanley in 1877 — traveled its length and mapped it.

Now it takes two weeks to go up the river and one week to come down. Government riverboats, pushing barges packed with people and freight, ply the route between Kinshasa, Zaire's capital, and Kisangani, formerly Stanleyville, the town 1,200 miles inland on the great bend in the river.

The river is a stunning thing, as powerful today as it was to the first explorers, as it has been throughout the years to travelers whose awe from afar has not been diminished by the actual sight of it.

Perhaps no description can improve on that of Joseph Conrad, who saw it, on the map, as resembling "an immense snake uncoiled, with its head in the sea, its body at rest curving afar over a vast country, its tail lost in the depths of the land."

And at firsthand, as he wrote in his novel "Heart of Darkness": "Going to that river was like traveling back to the earliest beginnings of the world, when vegetation rioted on the Earth and the big trees were kings. An empty stream, a great silence, an impenetrable forest."

The river is 3,000 miles long, the fifth longest in the world (after the Nile, the Mississippi/Missouri, the Amazon and the Yangtze). It drains a huge basin of 1.5 million square miles, equal to a tenth of the African landmass. In its vast drainage area, crossed by the Equator and ranging into seven other countries, it is almost always raining somewhere, so that the river maintains a consistently high level and pours 1.5 million cubic feet of water per second into the Atlantic Ocean, a volume exceeded only by the Amazon.

It is a major lifeline for Zaire. Together with its tributaries, it provides 8,000 miles of navigable waterway, over which the produce of the interior and the manufactured goods of the outside world are exchanged, though not in equal measure.

Not much changes for the people who live along the river and whose lives are dominated by it. Physically, it all looks pretty much as Stanley and Conrad must have seen it. In the interior of the country, life along the river — certainly in the perception of a white man passing through — is difficult beyond knowing. The villages are low shacks of mud and dried palm leaf, crowded to the riverbank as if pressed there by the unending explosion of vegetation at their backs. If there is food for the people here — fish from the river, antelope, wild pig and monkey from the forest — there is precious little else.

On the trip from Kisangani to Kinshasa, the boat never follows a fixed schedule. A general rule is to add two days to whatever day the ticket-seller at ONATRA, the shipping company, says the boat will leave. The boat I took, the Colonel Ebeya, was scheduled to leave on Saturday but did not leave until Monday.

It arrived at Kisangani with three barges attached. Two were double-deck passenger barges lashed side by side at the blunt prow of the steamship, to be pushed along; in front of these was a flat, single-deck barge loaded with a dozen cargo containers.

The boat itself had four decks and housed most of the crew. There were several first-class and deluxe cabins for passengers. For the equivalent of about $80, which would include meals for seven days, I took a deluxe cabin. It had two beds, a couple of chairs and a private bathroom (river water for the tub) with a toilet that flushed ceaselessly. It also had cockroaches the size of mice. The second- and third-class accommodations, on the barges, were floating slums.

The boat was packed by the time it drew away from the pier at Kisangani. A day or two later, it would add two more barges. The total population of the combined vessels ranged from 1,000 to 1,200 people, not to mention the livestock — chickens, geese, pigs, goats, monkeys and at least two live crocodiles, both juveniles. We were more populous by far than most of the villages we passed along the river.

And a lot nosier. Two bars immediately set up competing loudspeakers, blasting Zairian music from dawn until midnight. A dozen restaurants sprang to life. Buying and selling went on constantly, in all corners of the boat and on the barges.

It was difficult to tell what impact our racket made on the enveloping stillness of the river, the quality that had made such an impression on Conrad. Crew members and veteran travelers insisted that word of our coming was passed from village to village by drum. But no drum could be heard on the boat. It seemed that we could be heard miles away, and after a few days it was probably possible to smell us at an equal distance.

In any event, we were too important to be missed. As if to make sure, the pilot would sound the boat's whistle as we approached a sizable town, but by then the first canoes would already be approaching, to get a head start on the trading.

Trading is what the riverboats are all about. Only a small percentage of the people who take the boat have just transportation in mind. Most of the people are here to buy along the river and sell in Kinshasa. They also sell along the river, but that is the smaller part of their business.

Kasimi Musuluka is 32 years old and has been traveling on the riverboats, buying and selling, since he was 9. This is how he makes his living. Sometimes he takes his wife along, and sometimes other members of his family — brothers, cousins, in-laws. Each has a small piece of the action.

Musuluka, who set up shop (a tray on three legs) just inboard from the first of the third-class barges, remembered his first trip and how much he paid for his goods, virtually to the penny, and what he got for them.

He said he left Kinshasa, his home, with six shirts to sell and a dollar in his pocket along with a ticket for Kisangani. He sold the shirts on the way and bought fish, then sold the fish in Kisangani. On the way back, he sold flashlight batteries, bought more fish and sold them in Kinshasa.

Currency values have changed a dozen times since then, but Musuluka must have made a profit of about $7 on a journey that lasted a month.

He operated today in the same fashion but on a larger scale. So do most of the other businessmen — *commercants*, they are called in French — who have become professional riverboat travelers. People along the river still buy flashlight batteries and shirts from Kinshasa, and the *commercants* still buy fish on the river and sell them in the cities.

The people want other things too, of course, and some of them are available on the boat. Musuluka's major item for sale along the river is medicine. On his tray, behind which he sits with great patience listening to the wailing music and smelling the dried fish, are cellophane-wrapped capsules of drugs and vitamins and minerals. He needs no prescriptions, either to buy or sell.

Among his other wares are shotgun shells used for hunting, mainly monkeys. Monkey is regarded as a delicacy by many Zairians. An undressed monkey carcass (its tail split at the end and looped around its neck) that costs 300 zaires on the river, about $10, will fetch two to three times that amount in Kinshasa. A live baby chimpanzee can be bought for the equivalent of $20 on the river and sold as a pet (chimpanzees are seldom eaten) to a foreigner in Kinshasa for up to $150.

Musuluka's principal moneymaker, though, is food. Upriver, he buys haricot beans, manioc flour, bananas, sugar cane and peanuts. A sack of beans that costs 700 zaires in Kisangani will bring a profit of $75 to $100. Throughout the trip, I could see Musuluka making lists and calculations in a notebook.

Similar notebooks were used by other businessmen and women, each noting carefully how much was paid for every fish, so he or she would remember what to ask for in Kinshasa.

As the floating city moved along, I marked off its progress on a map — Liteko, Basoko, Bolama, Bumba, Dobo, Lisala — but afterward it was difficult to recall, even from detailed notes, where the towns were and how they had fit into the stream of events on board.

For an hour or two at a time, I could stand outside my cabin above the main deck and watch the boiling activity below. Or I could walk forward and cross to the barges, smelling the smells and watching the people as they cooked and drank and slept and talked. Some dozed on benches along the passageways; some were jammed into little cage-like compartments. Women were washing clothes, plaiting hair, throwing buckets of slop overboard, dropping cans into the river on long ropes and hauling up water for drinking or bathing or scrubbing cookware.

Everywhere were piles of monkeys, freshly slaughtered or smoked. There were river eels that looked like sea serpents, and baskets of black soil wriggling with grubs (remove legs, toast lightly). There were terrapins and river turtles, tethered by vines threaded through holes in their shells.

Of all the livestock, perhaps my favorite was a young crocodile. He was about 4 feet long. A piece of wood was jammed between his bound jaws, and his legs were trussed behind. He was motionless, apparently not breathing, but he blinked if anyone tried to touch a malevolent yellow eye. He was still alive at journey's end, but someday he would be someone's dinner.

On the riverbanks, the land passed by, disclosing little. At places where the channel lies close to the bank, the bush looks impenetrable, netted with vine and creeper and the fresh green and dead fronds of 50 varieties of palm. It does not rise to a great height, and here and there the white trunk of some giant hardwood towers over all, a perch for fish eagles.

The river, at the northern apex of its bend back toward the south, is 2 miles wide at some points, although its true breadth is usually obscured by forested islands that give the false impression that other large rivers are joining the Zaire. At times, the river spreads out over vast marshes, utterly uninhabited. The people along the river prefer solid ground. They hack the bush away from the river's edge, then sweep the earth bare as a protection against snakes.

Evening comes with epic sunsets and towering storm clouds, steam-white against blue and orange and gray. Thunderheads catch the last rays of the sun, turn pink and quiver with lightning. The forest takes on a jagged, black quality, the dead trees rising above the line of the jungle like broken towers. Gray curtains of rain roar over the forest and across the river, and night comes. The rain might last a few minutes or as long as an hour.

Whether alerted by drums or by searchlights sweeping the banks in search of channel markers, the people along the river were always ready, their canoes loaded. At 4 a.m. on the third night out, we must have passed a sizable village. In the drenching rain, it was impossible to see, except for an occasional fire, but the canoes came in waves.

The boat kept its steady pace, about 14 miles an hour, as it moved along with the current. Bringing a loaded canoe alongside — these are graceful but heavy craft fashioned from a single hollowed log — requires daring, skill and timing.

Most of the canoes were loaded with fish, *capitaines* 2 feet long and catfish the size of a tall man's leg, but some also carried goats and pigs, sacks of manioc and chickens in bamboo cages, not to mention the human passengers who came to buy and sell.

The arguments were furious. Canoes coming up to the boat smashed into others already tied alongside. The oarsmen clutched desperately for handholds, jumping from their canoes with a vine rope in hand and then sliding the length of another canoe as they tried to bring their own to a stop, knocking over people and crates of chickens. People fell in the river and grabbed madly for other canoes as they passed. On the decks, the *commercants* shouted out prices and fought with one another over prize catches. In almost every canoe was a woman, the chief negotiator and handler of money, often with a baby strapped to her back with a length of colored cloth. The women seemed tough and shouted orders at the men.

It was cold and wet and miserable. Alongside, the tied-up canoes would be swamped as the wake from one would submerge another up to its prow. Brief fist-fights broke out among the oarsmen. The women scolded and bargained, handling money with one hand, a baby with the other.

But the business was vital. This was evident in the expressions of those whose handholds failed and were left bobbing, their canoes filled with unsold goods and a woman standing upright, palms upturned in exasperation, as the rain and darkness closed around them. At least they would have a short trip home; the others would be carried miles downstream and would be paddling back as dawn broke over the river.

Among the passengers were 13 whites — nine young Spanish students who carried backpacks and spread bedrolls on the deck outside the first-class cabins at night; three 23-year-old English schoolteachers — two women and a man, headed home after a year's work in Zambia; and I.

All of us, it seemed to me, were treated with great consideration, as if we were special cargo in need of special handling. Now and then my steward complained of backache, until I caught on and cured him with a small tip. The young English adventurers, quartered on the second-class barge, had no such largesse to distribute but were treated just as well.

We could go wherever we liked, even to the bridge. It was always peaceful there, high above the rattle and clamor and reek of the decks below, and it was especially pleasant at night.

We came late one night to Lisala, a brewery town, one of the four or five where the boat usually stops. It was dark and perfectly quiet in the pilothouse, with only the captain, the first mate and the pilot there. The boat had turned, nosing into the current — a slow process when there is 100 yards of barge in front of you. After 40 minutes, during which Capt. Mathew Mumbila (23 years a riverboat captain) issued perhaps a dozen murmured commands, the boat nudged the pier.

Most of Lisala seemed to have turned out for the arrival, but by the time we left, two hours later, the town's generators had been turned off, and lanterns and flashlights winked in the dark as the pilot ordered a slow turn and we headed back into the river.

The next night, the three English travelers were getting off the boat, at a dark little town just beyond the confluence with the Ubangi River, which they hoped to travel upstream to Bangui in the Central African Republic. Normally, the boat would not stop here, but Capt. Mumbila ordered it. He came down to the main deck, signaled for a canoe and saw the English safely aboard with their awkward bundles. He disappeared then, through the crowd on deck, before they could thank him.

As their canoe — at the hands of utter strangers — slipped away across the water, someone in the pilothouse swept the searchlight up and down over them in a sort of benediction, and they were gone.

The trip then moved into a quieter and seemingly slower phase. The river was wider here, 6 to 9 miles at its widest, and the boat kept to the middle, giving the impression of sailing a great elongated lake. There was less contact with the people along the banks, and the trading and hubbub subsided.

People played cards and talked, and the women spent hours plaiting one another's hair. On the roofs of the barges, young men spread fish to bake in the sun. In the luxury of my cabin, I could read or sleep and wish for the trip to end. There were two days to go.

The real world intruded. A dockworkers' strike had slowed work at the port at Kinshasa, so that, to delay our arrival, we spent two nights secured to the riverbank. On the last night, we tied up no more than two hours out of Kinshasa. Its lights glowed, as inaccessible as Paris.

The last great battle of the trip was getting off the boat when it docked in Kinshasa, where hundreds of people came not to greet but to buy. Out of the holds came the monkeys and fish, slaughtered antelope, the hideous eels. The boat was inundated by ragged porters who held loads on their heads with one hand and with the other fought for a grip on the single gangway railing. There were accidents; falling loads toppled half a dozen men and women at a time. People were too hurried to fight.

I waited two hours before I hauled my bag ashore. In the meantime, I went to say goodbye to friends made on the trip. But the captain and the pilothouse crew had disappeared. Musuluka, the trader, was busy arguing with porters and keeping track of his sacks and bundles of fish. He had reached the most crucial stage of his work.

Finding no one, I realized that I, too, was anxious to find a fresher environment. On the way to retrieve my bag, I passed my crocodile, still lashed to a passageway drainpipe, his owner unloading more valuable cargo. He was perfectly motionless, and I thought he had died.

But when I gave him a nudge with my toe, he bucked as if shocked. I felt sorry for him. It was a hard life along the river. One either ate crocodiles or was eaten by them. No doubt this one's forebears had fed on the forebears of his present tormentors, and vice versa.

Suddenly, his yellow eye snapped open and regarded me balefully, and I imagined him dreaming of what he would do if he ever caught me in the river without a boat. I said goodbye.

❖

The Long Shadow of 'The Crow'

**For years, the Villemin family was terrorized by an anonymous
letter writer who claimed responsibility for their little boy's death.
Now a French court struggles to resolve this tale of murder and revenge.**

By Scott Kraft · December 9, 1993

LEPANGES, France — The Crow knew the Villemin family intimately. He knew when they were home and where they dined. And he also knew their secrets.

He knew how they shunned a relative born out of wedlock. He knew about the grandfather who hanged himself and the son who had begun putting on airs since his promotion to factory foreman.

The Crow hated them all, especially the ambitious son, whom he called "the little boss."

For four years, in hundreds of anonymous letters and phone calls boiling with anger and jealousy, The Crow terrorized the Villemins. And he often threatened murder.

"He was near us, that is certain," said Albert Villemin, patriarch of the clan, an extended family of factory workers scattered among the deceptively quiet villages of the Vosges Mountains. "Every single word we said at home, he knew."

Then, one autumn evening, The Crow slipped his last letter into a box at the

Lepanges post office. Four hours later, the authorities found 4-year-old Gregory Villemin, the only son of "the little boss," in the chilly waters of the Vologne River. The boy's hands and feet were bound with rope, and a woolen cap was pulled down over his face.

Gregory's father, Jean-Marie Villemin, received the letter the next day. It read: "I hope that you will die from sorrow, boss. Even your money cannot give you back your son. This is my vengeance...."

Nine years have passed since little Gregory was buried with Kiki, his stuffed toy monkey, in the church cemetery here, high on a hill above the river.

Now, for the first time, a judge and jury, sitting in the 16th-century Palais de Justice in Dijon, are hearing all the grisly details, all the fragments of evidence and all the accusations that have fascinated this nation for nearly a decade.

At first, back in 1984, authorities accused Bernard Laroche, one of Jean-Marie's cousins. The charge was dropped, but Gregory's distraught father wasn't going to let him get away. He calmly waited at Laroche's house and fatally shot him.

Then, officials turned their attention to Christine Villemin, Gregory's mother. In 1985, she was charged with killing her son, but earlier this year that charge was dropped too.

Technically, all that is left for the judge and jury in Dijon to decide is the fate of Jean-Marie, who admits killing his cousin to avenge his son's murder.

But Judge Olivier Ruyssen, in a rare departure for French justice, has turned this trial into a freewheeling public investigation into *l'affaire Gregory*.

Who is The Crow? Who killed Gregory? And did French justice fail the Villemin family?

Judge Ruyssen, son of a decorated admiral and one of the country's most respected jurists, has vowed to find the answers. "This abominable affair has been made of suspicions and gossip," Ruyssen said. "We must take advantage of this trial to wash it out. Only the truth can bring a bit of peace from all this sadness."

The case of a little boy's death, the anonymous and terrifying Crow, the quintessential French family feud and the gossipy small town of Lepanges have enthralled the nation.

Tour buses still visit Gregory's gravestone. And, from the cafes of Paris and Marseilles to the tiniest rural villages, the French still debate the case.

Many believe that Christine wrote the anonymous letters, then killed her son — perhaps to spite her husband. Others blame Laroche. And still others believe that the true culprit has yet to be unmasked.

Even today, copycat "Crows" plague some family members, other witnesses and even the judge.

Ruyssen has put the French justice system itself on trial.

Along with pathologists, relatives and handwriting experts, the court has heard from the prosecutor who bungled the original investigation, police who may have pressured witnesses, and reporters who traded information for access to the Villemin family.

"When prosecutors are called to testify," Le Monde, the respected French daily newspaper, observed recently, "it is not a sign of the good health of justice."

Outside the courthouse, built by one of the last dukes of Burgundy, dozens of spectators wait in subfreezing temperatures for the chance to squeeze onto the hard benches of the gallery.

Ruyssen, his two assistants and nine jurors sit on risers facing the courtroom. Each of those 12 people will have a vote when the trial concludes this month.

On one side of the courtroom are the five black-robed lawyers representing Jean-Marie.

The 35-year-old defendant, who wears wire-rimmed glasses, conservative suits and a stoic expression, sits behind them in a bulletproof glass box. He has already spent 2 1/2 years in jail.

Jean-Marie's attorneys hope to prove that their client had good reason to take the law into his own hands because Laroche was, in fact, Gregory's killer.

Across from them are Laroche's widow, Marie-Ange, and her four lawyers. She doesn't blame her husband's killer.

Instead, she blames an incompetent investigation and the media for whipping Villemin into a deadly frenzy, for which he could be sentenced to life in prison.

"One must be human in this affair," Marie-Ange said during a break in the proceedings. She agrees with Jean-Marie's lawyer that the defendant "is not a killer. He's a victim."

But her goal is to clear her husband's name.

The case's roots are several hundred miles away, in Lepanges, population 1,017, one of dozens of villages among the low mountains, evergreen forests and winding rivers near the German border.

It was here that the trouble began within Gregory's extended family of more than 100 cousins, aunts, uncles, grandfathers and grandmothers.

The Villemins and their kin are part of what the French fondly call la *France profonde* — average people, the silent majority, punching clocks in the area's iron, steel and textile factories.

Gregory's grandfather, Albert Villemin, was the first to receive the anonymous letters and phone calls in 1979, but other relatives, especially Gregory' s father, were harassed.

The calls to Albert stopped abruptly after the police tapped his phone. But the letters continued to arrive, rambling missives written in longhand in low-class slang.

They urged Albert to disown his son, Jean-Marie. They chided him and the rest of the family for mistreating a son born to the elder Villemin's wife before they were married.

Although the letters were never signed, the family began referring to the writer simply as *le corbeau,* or "the crow." The name came from "Le Corbeau," a 1943 film in which a small French village is terrorized by an anonymous letter writer who signs himself "The Crow." The movie, made in Occupied France during World War II, has been shown on French television a dozen times over the years, inspiring successive generations of crows.

Everyone in the Villemin family knew about the letters and calls, and each had his own suspect.

But one thing was certain: The Crow hated Jean-Marie.

Jean-Marie, slightly built, was 26 at the time. He had recently become foreman, a $15,000-a-year job, in a car upholstery factory.

Ambitious and intelligent, he made no secret of his success.

He and Christine, who worked in a textile mill, had a new $50,000 house, and he liked to point out that his dining room furniture was oak and his couches were leather.

The couple had one son. Gregory, a bright, delightful youngster with long, curly brown hair, was the apple of his father's eye.

Bernard Laroche, Jean-Marie's cousin, was also a factory foreman. In fact, Bernard and Jean-Marie played together as children. But they had grown apart over the years.

Laroche was an unkempt, often profane man with a mustache. He and his wife had a 4-year-old child who was slightly retarded.

They didn't socialize with Jean-Marie and Christine, but one of Jean-Marie's brothers was a good friend of Laroche. And Laroche chafed at the way he was treated by the other Villemins.

"They've got what they deserved," he shouted at Jean Ker, a writer for the weekly magazine Paris-Match, soon after Gregory's murder. "They've paid for what they've done. I'm the poor stupid fool, because each time they [the Villemins] need me, I come. And they never invite me to their house on Sundays."

Gregory was playing outside the house that October day in 1984, around sunset, when he was abducted. His mother said she was inside, ironing and listening to the radio.

The body was found at 9 p.m. in the Vologne River, about four miles downstream from Lepanges.

There were no bruises on the body, and pathologists attributed death to drowning and contact with the cold water. But experts disagreed about whether Gregory had drowned in the river or in tap water; the water in his lungs contained none of the microscopic organisms one would expect to find in river water.

The local gendarmes, the soldiers who work as police in small French towns, were called to investigate. Although they assigned 50 officers to the case, they were swiftly outnumbered by reporters. And the young prosecutor reveled in the attention, often leaking confidential documents.

A few days later, the gendarmes found a hypodermic syringe and empty vial of insulin in a box near the riverbank. An injection of insulin could have rendered the child unconscious, the pathologists said, but it would not be detectable during the autopsy. None of the pathologists had thought to look for needle marks on the body.

Laroche emerged as a suspect after his sister-in-law, Murielle Bolle, then 15, admitted that he had picked her up after school that day and that they had picked Gregory up from his front yard and driven to the river. Laroche and Gregory took a walk, and Laroche returned alone, she said. Laroche had no alibi.

But after a few days at home with her parents, her sister and Laroche, Bolle recanted. She said the gendarmes had forced her to implicate Laroche.

He was released for lack of evidence. The prosecutor took the investigation out of the hands of the gendarmes and gave it over to their rivals, the national police, who immediately focused their attention on Christine.

The case against her was weak. Police found strands of rope, similar to that used on Gregory, in the Villemin attic, though many believe that the police planted them in their determination to find a culprit in the highly publicized case. Four of Christine's co-workers said they saw her mailing a letter at the local post office about the time Gregory disappeared. Christine couldn't remember what was said on the radio program she claimed to have been listening to when her son was kidnapped.

To the police, and to many in France, that was evidence she was The Crow.

She was portrayed by newspapers and magazines, with the help of the prosecutor, as an evil witch who harbored a deep-seated anger toward her husband. Even Marguerite Duras, the well-known author of "The Lover," traveled to the Villemin home and, without talking to Christine, wrote an article pronouncing her guilty.

As suspicions about Christine grew, Jean-Marie became obsessed with killing Laroche.

Mired in sorrow over the death of his child and fed daily by rumors delivered by reporters, Jean-Marie decided that Laroche's lawyers, the police and the prosecutor were conspiring to cover up Laroche's guilt.

Jean-Marie bought a shotgun and plotted several times to kill his cousin.

"The Crow said I would die of grief," Jean-Marie testified. "Maybe. But I wanted to have him first. It's true. I wanted to have him."

Laroche, 29, was fatally shot in front of his wife and father-in-law on his front lawn in March 1985, five months after Gregory's death. On his gravestone, his family wrote: "Here rests Bernard Laroche, innocent victim of a blind hatred."

Four months later, Christine was charged with murdering her son. Pregnant with her second child, she was jailed for a few days, then released.

By the time charges against Christine were dropped, last February, the Villemins had moved to a town near Paris and had two children.

Christine wrote a book, "Let Me Tell You," declaring her innocence, although a court later ordered her to give the proceeds to Laroche's children.

Jean-Michel Lambert, the first prosecutor, known as a *juge d'instruction* in French law, was replaced after Christine was charged. But in his autobiography, "The Little Judge," he said he remains convinced of her guilt.

In court in Dijon recently, Lambert, now a magistrate, defended his early investigation. But other witnesses contended that the inexperienced prosecutor, then 32, had made many errors. Among other things, Lambert had stopped pathologists from collecting enough samples at the autopsy. Referring to Lambert's book, Judge Ruyssen observed: "The case can do without this literary monument."

The only thing both sets of attorneys — and the French newspapers, magazines and television stations — agree on is that justice has failed the Villemin family.

"It's stupidity," said Paul Prompt, the Laroche family attorney. "All the mistakes in an investigation that could have been made have been made here."

Henri-Rene Garaud, Villemin's lawyer and one of France's most respected litigators, added: "The institutions only function if the people in them function. In this case, the people didn't function."

Meanwhile, the trial in Dijon has been filled with contradictory testimony.

Under Ruyssen's rules, no topic is off-limits. Witnesses with conflicting testimony have been called together to provoke debates, and the judge, jurors and even the defendant join lawyers in chiming in with questions.

But few believe that the crucial riddles — who killed Gregory and who was The Crow — will be answered.

"The judge is like everyone else who has come to this case," said Pierre Bois, a court reporter for Le Figaro, a Paris daily newspaper. "He wants to know the truth. But it will never happen."

Murielle Bolle holds fast to her latest story, saying she took the bus home from school the day of Gregory's murder and was never with Laroche.

But the bus driver said she wasn't on the bus, and a neighbor testified that he saw a mustached man and a red-haired girl, fitting the descriptions of Bolle and Laroche, park outside the Villemins' house that day.

A nurse who treated Bolle's diabetic mother in the early 1980s testified that she had showed Bolle how to administer insulin. But she no longer remembered if it was before Gregory's death, as she told Paris-Match, or after. (The personal lives of few have been unaffected. The nurse also admitted to having an affair with the brother of a Paris-Match photographer and, later, one of the investigating gendarmes.)

Christine angrily denounced accusations from four handwriting experts that she wrote the last letter from The Crow to her husband. A fifth handwriting expert isn't sure. And she contends her co-workers are confused about the day she was at the post office.

But the most emotional moment has been reserved for Jean-Marie. The ordinarily strait-laced defendant delivered a tearful monologue of grief and anger, saying he decided to kill Laroche after visiting Gregory's grave.

"I thought he spoke to me and told me, 'Go ahead, Papa,' " he said.

He blamed the prosecutor, the police and the media for egging him on and leaving him no alternative but to kill the man he still believes is guilty.

"Gregory was lively, tender," Jean-Marie said, pausing periodically to sob before collecting himself. "He grew up in happiness. You always had to eat lollipops with him. He danced to Michael Jackson music. I can show you the tape. He was a marvelous child."

Close to Home

❖❖

Care Amid the Chaos at County-USC

The center that sees nearly 100,000 patients a year is at once a marvel of medicine and an overcrowded 'hospital of last resort.'

BY PETER H. KING · JANUARY 27, 1985

There are many ways to wind up at Los Angeles County-USC Medical Center. Membership in what emergency room doctors call the Knife and Gun Club is one popular route. Drinking your liver into jelly is another.

A common path is via the womb. On average, 46 babies are born there each day, more than a few in the parking lot. "You are not initiated," one house doctor said, "until your first delivery in the back seat of a car."

Car wrecks and drug overdoses contribute heavily to the daily census of 1,400 patients. Cancer, cardiac trouble, kidney failure, pneumonia — all the major diseases are in evidence. Going crazy can get you there too, limbs lashed to a bed with leather bracelets.

Nearly 100,000 patients are admitted each year, and another 480,000 patient visits are recorded in emergency rooms and outpatient clinics. Seventeen thousand babies are born there — one out of every 200 in the United States — and 1,300 hospital stays end when patient becomes corpse, is bagged and tagged and stacked in vaults in a basement mortuary.

The medical center is the nation's largest acute-care hospital, a teaching hospital where doctors come from all over the land to feast on a diagnostic horn of plenty and make new medicine — despite conditions that can be little better than crude.

It is also the county's hospital for the sick poor, "the hospital of last resort in a system of last resort," Executive Director Paul Drozd said. Often, it is the only place where transients and illegal immigrants and other soldiers in the army of the down and out can find care and sometimes even comfort.

There was a hobo on one of the wards, and it was his birthday. The nurses surprised him with a bedside party, giving him one of the neatly wrapped packages that a volunteer group supplies for such occasions. The man began to cry.

"He was so moved," nurse Marcia Behmer recalled. "He said he had to come to

91

the hospital to find friends, and that no one had given him a birthday present for as long as he could remember.

"And then he opened the gift up, and it was shampoo and conditioner." That he was bald seemed not to matter.

Panhandlers troll the medical center corridors, and some of them are patients.

"On a good day," said Lloyd, a 31-year-old with a stringy red beard and a pallor approaching translucence, "I can make 6 bucks."

Lloyd came to the medical center a year ago. Chased by private demons, he said he had leaped off a freeway overpass in Norwalk and was left paralyzed. Now he is a hospital fixture. Clad in a white gown, legs folded up and fastened tightly to his wheelchair with a sheet, he scoots about the hallways cadging cigarettes from nurses, shepherding patients through the hospital bureaucracy, singing Jethro Tull ballads and, always, always, prowling for spare change.

"The best place is right over there by the front door," Lloyd said. "You say, 'Merry Christmas, *señ-or-i-ta,* do you have any change?'"

His prime hunting ground is the threshold of General Hospital, also known as Unit 1. A 20-story hulk of gleaming concrete, it sits atop Lincoln Heights in East Los Angeles like some great and terrible ark, its cargo all the kinds of injury and illness known to man.

Arrayed about Unit 1 are three smaller hospitals and 100 auxiliary structures. A network of subterranean tunnels connects the buildings.

It costs $1 million a day to run the medical center, and all but a scant fraction of the money comes from taxpayers. It is almost never enough.

Contradictions abound. A skillful diagnosis becomes moot because the patient can't afford to fill a prescription. A doctor speaks glowingly of the quality medicine practiced at the institution, and then admits that, no, he would not put a member of his own family in one of its cramped, chaotic wards, where patients sleep six to a room and where, in a heat wave, dimmed lights and opened windows must pass for air conditioning.

Drum-tight budgets force doctors, nurses and administrators to become Machiavellian strategists, competing among themselves — and other county hospitals — for money and material.

Likewise, patients become adept at working the medical center system for their own purposes. Some have been known to bounce around the grounds from hospital to hospital, persuading several doctors in a single day to prescribe them drugs.

Transients wishing relief from the cold will check in first at the emergency room to receive a plastic patient identification bracelet. This will discourage security guards from evicting them from the foyer of General Hospital, where they sleep, warm and peaceful, eyes closed to a magnificent ceiling mural of Hippocrates.

Nurses who notice a patient growing fidgety or grouchy know that it may signal an urge for street drugs. Quite often patients with this condition will concoct an excuse in order to check out for a day. They generally return on schedule, relaxed and cooperative, ready to resume their recovery.

Dr. Steven Horowitz of the Psychiatric Hospital tells of a patient who threatened the life of the president in order to secure a trip home to Pennsylvania. He had come to Los Angeles on business but only had enough money to arrange for a one-way trip.

"He called the Secret Service several times, making his threats, and then he walked in the door and said, 'I was the one who threatened the president.' They brought him here, and when I talked to him it became clear he only wanted to go back to Pennsylvania."

And?

"It worked."

Many medical center patients live in East Los Angeles and speak only Spanish. Doctors and nurses not fluent in the language often rely on pidgin communication. Each service develops survival phrases. For example, the key word for nurse mid-wives is *empuje*.

"It means push." Nancy Bolles, the head midwife, explained. "You go, *Empuje! Empuje! Empuje!*"

In the emergency room, the words are *donde*, where, and *duele*, pain, essential for determining where it hurts. Patients with stomach pains are called "*duele* bellies."

Women come from Mexico to have their babies at El Hospital, as the institution is known along the border from Nogales west. One reason is that babies born in this country automatically become citizens. Increasingly, pregnant women from El Salvador and other troubled Central America countries are showing up at the medical center. "You can always tell where the revolution is by our patient population," one old hand said.

Some patients seem to care little about their health. Doctors and nurses speak of the frustration of making someone just well enough to leave the hospital and return to the streets to do more damage to his or her body. "I mean, I discharge patients to a rescue mission," one doctor said.

"It has been suggested that the best thing we could do for some of these patients is give them a television set," a medical center pediatrician added. "That's because their priorities are food, shelter, entertainment and health care, in that order. So if we gave them a television, at least health care would move up a notch."

Other members of the clientele are just the opposite, impoverished mothers who manage to bring their children great distances to receive care, or outpatients who come each week for checkups. They spend much of their day standing in a line, waiting to see a financial counselor (always the first stop), waiting to see a doctor, waiting to schedule their next appointment.

It can be argued that medical center patients give more than they take, serving as teaching tools for more than 900 interns, residents and fellows each year. "All of us owe a great debt to these patients," said Dr. Alexandra M. Levine, a medical center cancer specialist. "The patients in this hospital, without knowing it, have taken on the responsibility for training a tremendous number of physicians in this country."

Handling heavy trauma is what the medical center does best. The General Hospital emergency room is its pride, a source of national acclaim, each day fielding a succession of frightfully wounded or gravely ill patients.

An apocryphal story told throughout the institution is that Los Angeles doctors carry cards or notes in their pockets instructing ambulance drivers, in the case of an acute injury or illness, to transport them directly to the medical center.

"Of course," added Medical Director Sol Bernstein, providing the equally popular punch line, "most of them also say that as soon as they are over that acute injury or illness, take them someplace else."

All this traffic in acute cases has a downside. The moderately hurt, sick or deranged often must wait ungodly measures of time to receive treatment while more critical cases play through.

"This is not the place to come for a nose job," is how one staff member put it.

Not all patients, of course, can be saved. Sometimes they appear to be headed for recovery and then, in the parlance of doctors, "go sour." Other times, they are terminal to begin with and essentially come to the hospital to die.

Mortality can be as tricky as a fun-house mirror. Intensive care nurses point out patients who "have been on the other side," only to be brought back with chillingly similar descriptions of lights and tunnels. In the emergency room, a doctor lamented, "bad guys always live and good guys die. It seems to be a rule."

And then there is this:

A woman drank ant poison after she fought with her husband. He rushed her to the medical center and house experts on toxins were summoned. She came around, it seemed, and husband and wife consoled one another, made amends, hugged and wept and vowed to do better.

Then a doctor took the husband outside. Even though his wife looked well and wanted to go home, the man was told, the truth was that the poison had begun a lethal chemical process and it could not be stopped.

"She probably won't make it through the day," the doctor said.

The husband was furious, disbelieving. The doctors were crazy, he said. Anyone could see his wife was fine. He demanded to take her away at once.

Four hours later she was dead.

The medical center can be a rough place. Employees who work nights speak of walking in fear to their cars. Security guards watch the ambulance entrance. Late last year, a patient was shot to death by a security guard in the emergency room after he allegedly reached up from his gurney, grabbed another guard's gun and opened fire.

It can, at rare times, be a boring place — drowsy doctors hunched over desks in the late afternoon, plowing through stacks of patient histories; medical students slumped in chairs as a lecturer drones on about the intricacies of a respirator.

And at all times, everywhere, around every corner, along every hallway, behind every door, there are people on crutches, people in wheelchairs, people in casts, grizzled hobos who look like Walt Whitman, skeletal transients who scream out that they are being "kidnapped, kidnapped I tell you, this is a kidnapping." And mothers with swollen bellies, and street brawlers with swollen faces, patients all.

On a November morning in General Hospital's orthopedic infection ward, many of the patients were young men flat on their backs, each with a single injured hand propped up on a pillow and covered with a green towel, faces sullen. They were there because they had punched someone in the mouth and neglected to clean the ensuing cut, allowing it to fester into a horribly infected wound.

"We always get a rush of these after a championship fight," one doctor said.

Not all the patients were fallen combatants. There was a woman who had cut her hand with a dirty kitchen knife, a young man who plunged into the Colorado River and received a gash on his leg that became infected, and a bulky weightlifter who infected his buttocks when he injected vitamin B-12 with a dirty needle. He kept at his bedside a mirror, a copy of Muscle & Fitness magazine, a Bible, and several snapshots of himself, with which he intended to illustrate a freelance story on the demise of his derriere.

There was a somewhat crazed-looking young man. A regular, he was in this time because he repeatedly punched his hand into the wall. "He comes here to get the TLC [tender loving care] he can't get on the street," a doctor said.

"Where do you live?" a skinny old man with a drawn, yellowish face was asked.

"I don't live anywhere," he said, his voice rising excitedly, as if he couldn't believe it himself.

On the next bed was a man whose feet had been ripped apart by swelling and become infected.

"I live in a mission and you have to sit up to sleep and my feet swole up," he explained.

"Don't they give you a bed to sleep in?"

"You only get a bed five nights out of 15."

Next to him was a dark, handsome man with a gallant mustache and a gold chain around his neck. He had been transferred from a private room at UCLA after his boss canceled his medical insurance, and now he was telling the doctors he wanted codeine at night to help him sleep. The snoring was keeping him awake.

To his right was a burly red-haired man with an injured knee. He was propped up against a wall. He took a long drag on his cigarette and exhaled slowly, satisfaction written across his face as clearly as the sign over his head that read, "No Smoking/*No Fumar.*"

Near his bed was the room's only television set. It was tuned to "The Flintstones," and the theme song was blaring loudly, promising everyone "a yabba-dabba-doo time."

The medical center employs 340 staff doctors. They train and supervise the 900 interns, residents and fellows. Interns are medical school graduates who must serve a year at the hospital before becoming doctors. Residents are doctors there to become specialists. Fellows are specialists developing sub-specialties. Together, they are called house doctors, and they handle the bulk of the day-to-day patient care. There are also 1,700 nurses, and 2,300 private doctors from the community who put in time as volunteers.

With all this brainpower, the conflict of ideas flourishes. Medicine is an imprecise science, and the hallways rattle with discussion about how best to handle difficult cases. The most profound ethical questions facing modern medicine today are everyday issues in the wards of the medical center.

Perhaps the toughest questions are asked in the several intensive care units scattered about the center.

"Here," said Robert Swinney, a 38-year-old staff doctor in one such unit, "we have an elderly lady who was bedridden at home and may have had another stroke and got pneumonia and, I think, represents one of the problems we have to deal with, those of us who work in a critical care environment."

He had stopped at the bedside of an 85-year-old woman. She lay motionless among a tangle of tubes and machines, mechanical devices performing essential bodily functions that her organs could no longer muster.

"For whom should we be utilizing these scarce resources?" Swinney asked. "It is a terrible problem. She is bedridden and unable to take care of herself at home.... But her family is very interested and very concerned and wants lots done for her. And we are doing it.

"Whether or not it's the best thing for her I don't know, because I think she doesn't have a really good chance of making it out of here alive.... The larger perspective is you have got 10 beds, and only one bed is available out of those 10, and there are two patients who need intensive care, and you have to choose between an 85-year-old with a terminal disease and an 18-year-old with a reversible disease."

A few days later, the woman was gone. "We had basically shot our wad," one of the doctors explained. She was now on a general ward, presumably awaiting death. In her place was a young man with a severe case of pneumonia. They were inserting a long tube down into a lung in an effort to assess the nature of the pneumonia. He had been transferred to the medical center from a private hospital, ostensibly because there were no slots open in its intensive care unit.

The medical center can be a place of dark humor. On the 13th-floor jail ward in General Hospital, a troubled soul tied to his bed told the doctors he had been carved up by unidentified enemies and eaten. The devil, he said, had taken him away. "That's right," one of the residents said, chuckling. "This is hell, all right."

It can be a sad place. Viveca Hazboun is a 35-year-old child psychiatrist. The children who come to her small ward tend to be severely disturbed.

Hazboun told of a 5-year-old patient, a girl. One day on the ward, she covered a shower drain with paper towels, turned on the water and put her face to the floor. She was discovered before suicide was accomplished.

Why would a 5-year-old want to kill herself?

"She said life just wasn't worth living," Hazboun recalled.

"I had another little kid," she said, "who was sleeping with her dead sister, who her parents had allegedly killed. They were force-feeding her and she died."

The parents refused to accept what they had done and left the dead girl in the bed. As the body began to decompose, the other little girl became convinced that her sister had the better deal and attempted to join her.

"These kind of things happen in the City of Angels," Hazboun said.

The medical center can be a cruel place. It was midnight on the fifth floor of Women's Hospital, and a pregnant woman whose horrible screeching had dominated the ward for what seemed an hour finally had delivered. Now she was being wheeled to a recovery room, her baby nestled to her bosom.

"What's her name?" a staff member at the ward desk hollered, preparing to complete a chart.

"Screamin' Mimi," one of the nurses called back. Everyone laughed. The new mother did not appear to understand, or at least was consumed by other thoughts.

Finally, the medical center can be a place of beauty:

At 5:15 a.m. one fall day, from the window of Room 8L36 in Women's Hospital, it was possible to look west across a sprawl of wrecking yards and railroad tracks that separate the hospital from downtown, and watch a city wake up.

Lights winked on in tall buildings. Freeways started to fill. The sky lightened. A fascinating process, it seemed to unfold in a succession of jerky moments, like those old time-lapse photography film shorts depicting the entire life cycle of, say, a tulip.

On the other side of the window, however, a distraction was developing to a rhythm of its own. A spotlight bathed a woman's belly with eerie whiteness. Her name was Sandra Lopez. She was 19 years old and had come to give birth to a child, her first.

"*Sople ... sople ... sople ... sople....*" The word is the Spanish command "blow out." Pat Alamos Donnelly, a 32-year-old nurse midwife standing at the foot of the birthing table, chanted it softly, like a prayer.

The expectant mother's large dark eyes appeared glazed, conveying both fear and weariness. She focused on a wall opposite the window. Her screams grew louder. "Push with your belly," Donnelly coached, "not with your mouth."

But the baby was not coming. The midwife took a pair of surgical scissors and with a few snips widened the passageway. A human scalp emerged. A few more moans, and then, an entire head popped out, delightfully. Soon the entire body was wiggled from the womb.

"*Nina, señora,*" Donnelly said. It's a girl.

A tickle induced the baby girl's first cry. The mother laid back her head and sighed. The baby was placed on her stomach, nature's incubator.

On the other side of the window, the day had grown lighter by several degrees.

In its 106 years, the medical center has endured doctor strikes and threatened doctor strikes, scandals, polio epidemics and Proposition 13 of 1978. It has been investigated by hospital commissions, supervisors, grand juries, district attorneys, television commentators and even a newspaper reporter named Alloysius Blatt, who in 1932 went to the newly opened General Hospital to snoop around on roller skates, a form of transportation intended to underscore his belief that at a cost of $13 million, the county had purchased a lot more hospital than it could ever possibly need.

There have been dire predictions aplenty about its impending demise. An authorized centennial history of the institution concluded with the somber appraisal that "beyond a few years, the future of the LAC-USC Medical Center is uncertain." That was six years ago.

Just last fall, medical center staff feared that passage of Proposition 41, a welfare-cutting measure, could cripple the institution; it failed.

Now there is discussion at USC about building a private hospital so that medical students can practice treating a wealthier clientele, and some staff members fret that this could siphon attention from the medical center and eventually undercut care.

It is a curiosity that the medical center enjoys a better reputation in medical circles than it does in its own community.

Dr. Larry Opas, director of inpatient services at the Pediatrics Pavilion, grew up in Los Angeles and did his residency at Childrens Hospital, providing him with a good perspective of the medical center from both sides of its creamy white walls.

"I think in general one is frightened of the county hospital," he said. "The story one hears on the outside is that it is a zoo. It's chaotic. Disorganized. No teaching. Mediocre patient care. That it's a step below every place else.

"Most of these comments are made by people who have never set foot inside this place. And it's not the Taj Mahal of medicine, I guarantee you that. But it is far different once you are inside, to the point where you can only take two attitudes toward County — you either love it and want to fight for it or you can't stand it. And those who can't stand it usually find a way to get out of it."

Indeed, those who stay at the medical center tend to be its strongest defenders. Medical center doctors boast about how they are summoned to national conferences to lecture on their latest work, or they let it be known how frequently they receive calls from other doctors at famous institutions seeking their counsel on difficult cases.

At the same time, these same doctors point out torn chairs that they requested be replaced months ago.

Or they nod disgustedly toward a long line of pregnant women waiting for hours to pay in advance for a clinic visit.

They say they need more lab technicians and social workers, and less paperwork. They complain of dirty toilets and the requirement that they fill out time cards.

"It's the personnel shortages that hurt the most," one doctor said. "For example, because there aren't enough X-ray technicians and transport people, you can't always get an X-ray when a patient's health depends on it, and that is very frustrating. Or patients won't receive proper wound treatment or care for bedsores because there aren't enough nurses.

"I don't mean to say that medical care is being compromised, because it isn't. It's just that these kinds of things make it harder, more frustrating to deliver it."

In Women's Hospital, its annual load of 17,000 babies exceeds by 7,000 the maximum number of deliveries that the 10-story facility was intended to accommodate. Things can move so fast and frantically on the maternity wards that nurses sometimes scribble vital patient information on gurney bedsheets, a concession to the likelihood that birth will begin long before the paperwork can catch up.

Only one operating room serves the entire 106-bed Pediatrics Pavilion.

In the General Hospital emergency room, patients with breathing problems until this month had to be assisted manually, with a nurse's aide pumping a bag to blow air into their lungs. A ventilator, a fairly common tool of the emergency room trade, was on order for a year before it finally arrived. "Inexcusable," one doctor said.

Ward 1234, the so-called "red blanket room," is where critical cases are moved after being stabilized in the emergency room. There, doctors determine on which ward the patients belong. But often there is no room in the wards, and so the patients stack up in the red blanket room and even adjoining hallways, waiting for hours on gurneys jammed closely together: medical gridlock.

Even those who wind up in the medical center mortuary sometimes face a final indignity brought on by overcrowding. The vaults are intended to hold four corpses in a bunk-like arrangement. Often, however, an overflow requires the dead to be stored eight to a vault, with two bodies sharing a single berth.

Lloyd, the panhandling patient, has been at County-USC for a year now, and he's seen a lot from the seat of his wheelchair.

"I've seen arrests. Guys all beat up. Girls screaming and yelling. All sorts of weird stuff," he said.

"But most of the people are pretty original."

Original?

"Just normal, everyday people," he said. "You know, married and have kids and all that. O-rig-in-al."

It eventually became clear that he was confused. What most people would call ordinary he defined as something original. Remember, he's been at the medical center quite awhile.

❖

A Proud Struggle
on the Field — and Off

Gangs and poverty and despair taint their lives. But come game time, the Garfield High Bulldogs get a chance to turn fear and rage and pain into glory.

BY BILL PLASCHKE · NOVEMBER 9, 1995

John Aguirre pushes a switch, and day becomes midnight in the gym at James A. Garfield High.

Dark, restless lumps line the floor. The only sound is the heavy breathing of teenagers nervously awaiting their weekly two hours of truth.

Feeling his way through the darkness, carefully stepping over these small men stuffed into big pads, is Aguirre, the head coach of the Garfield football team.

It is a Friday, 4:35 p.m. In less than three hours, the Bulldogs will step outside onto a patch of uneven grass in the middle of a temperamental neighborhood. In front of several hundred people, they will play a game against Bell.

"Gentlemen," Aguirre screams into midnight, "this game is not just for you. This game is bigger than you!"

This is one of nine Garfield games this season. This is one of about 30 games in the average Garfield player's career. That's 30 chances to throw out your chest, 30 chances to have the world scream for you until it is hoarse.

Thirty chances. And no more.

In the last 15 years, not one player from this East Los Angeles school has received a college football scholarship. Scouts rarely even venture inside Garfield's usually locked outer gates. The players are small. Their 40-yard dash times are slow.

All but one of the 48 on this year's team are Latino. The number of Latinos who've ever made it to the NFL is minuscule.

These 48 believe none of it.

They have spent the previous week practicing every day until dark. Juggling jobs and baby-sitting and housework. Dealing with muggings and gang colors.

All for a chance to step on the field and force somebody to notice.

"You are playing not just for yourselves, but for your entire neighborhood!"

101

Aguirre yells. "This is not just for Garfield, it is for all of East L.A.!"

On autumn evenings throughout America, to play high school football is to live a dream.

But for these children of immigrants, single-parent homes and dangerous streets — for these appropriately nicknamed Bulldogs — the dream is awkward, heavy.

The star linebacker sometimes leaves practice early to care for his mother, who is blind. One star running back works as an auto mechanic during the day.

Another starting running back — the team's only black player — missed several practices when Latino gangs tried to force him out of a nearby housing project.

Three of the team's players watched their estranged fathers die from drug- or alcohol-related problems this season.

Tonight, many parents will not be in the stands: Who will pay the bills? Who will watch the children?

Many friends are also absent, having lost a weekly battle to persuade a player to quit. More than 2,200 boys attend this school, these friends say. If only 48 play varsity football — on a team where nobody is cut — how good can it be?

None of this matters to the 48 who, at this moment, feel they have been granted a higher calling. They can sense outsiders looking at them on the street as if they were punks who would be lucky to live past their 18th birthdays. They watch on TV as Latinos are treated like thugs.

Tonight they will be something else. They will be heroes.

As Aguirre pauses to catch his breath, it is so quiet in the Garfield gym that you can hear the whispers of 48 prayers.

"Think about why you are here!" Aguirre shouts. "You just think about it! Just think!"

With the departure of the NFL's Rams and Raiders, critics nationwide have chortled about the fact that there is no football in Los Angeles.

Spend a week with the Bulldogs and you realize that, indeed, there is still football here. Football at its sweaty, soul-searching, heart-rending, triumphant best.

Monday

Willie Mercado is missing.

The team's first meeting of the week has begun. More than 40 shaved heads and pimply faces gather around a fuzzy TV in a classroom with barred windows.

They will watch films of Bell. They will study a mimeographed game plan. Both teams are 3-1. It is an important contest with playoff ramifications.

But their star defensive back is missing. Where is Willie?

Injury? Hooky?

"Nah," says Victor Ohm, equipment manager and trainer, with a shrug. "Guy got robbed again."

An hour later, as the team takes the field, Mercado shows up. He is wearing a grimace and stone-cold stare. He is 17. He dresses quickly in the cramped locker room. It smells like a subway. The yellow lockers are battered. The wooden benches are reed-thin and chipped. Most of the toilets are clogged up. One has a gang symbol carved into its seat.

Yes, Mercado says, his car windows had been smashed during school. His stereo and speakers were stolen. "And my damn books, they got my damn books," he says.

He will practice hard today, smothering smaller players with his long arms, leaping on them with a fury, sometimes kicking them before they get up.

"Kids like Willie, they keep coming here because this is where they are loved," Ohm says. "They don't need gangs, because this is their gang."

And Ohm, 35, is one of their leaders.

An imposing bald man with a stud in one year, Ohm has a constant scowl and a sharp mouth to match. He has been involved in Garfield football for 25 years, lives a few blocks down the road, walks to work every morning at 6.

Every high school team, it seems, has somebody like him.

And no team has anybody like him.

He is not just the equipment manager and trainer, but also the players' tormentor and their protector.

He sees their hunger, he buys them lunches. He sees them coming to school with holes in their pants, he buys them blue jeans.

Cleats are not supplied by the school. Many times, they are supplied by Ohm. He gives the sexually active players condoms.

Because of his intuition, most call him "Radar" after the character on "MASH." Some players, however, quietly call him "Dad." Ohm is most beloved for his medical knowledge. As in, he knows where to arrange for free X-rays and treatment.

This is important because the average Bulldog — about 5-foot-8, 180 pounds — is readily injured. Many players are uninsured beyond the school's limited coverage.

Sometimes Ohm relies on doctors who are former students, sometimes he hits up old friends. Other times he relies on his wits.

As practice ends, one of Ohm's children is attempting to hide a slight limp. It is linebacker Douglas Meza, who is recovering from a foot operation. It was performed last summer, after he played on a broken toe for two months during spring workouts because he couldn't afford the medical bills.

Ohm shuffled a few papers, held the boy's hand when doctors were allowed to make the correct diagnosis and arranged for the surgery.

Meza hopes to play in his first game, against Bell. "When I told my mom about the operation, she cried because we had no money," he says. "On Friday, I want her to see this."

Tuesday

Two hours before the first practice snap, and already there is a problem. A student walks up to Aguirre as he monitors the team during study hall.

"Coach, over there," the boy says. "I think somebody needs you." He is pointing to a player, sitting alone, head buried in his knapsack, softly crying.

Aguirre knows the problem from 10 steps away. It will involve the boy's family. Players have come to him when their father has beaten their mother, or beaten them. Then there are the times their mother has thrown them out of the house for fooling around with football and not getting a job.

Aguirre spends the final 30 minutes of study hall huddled over the player, a stocky defensive lineman with scared eyes. The boy will be sent home from practice. He will not be seen for two more days.

But he tells Coach he will be ready for Bell. Aguirre, a product of a nearby project and this high school, wants to believe him. "I grew up in the shadows; I was never anybody," says Aguirre, a small man with a big mustache and soft voice. "Adults would always ask me what I wanted to be, but the choice would always be janitor or machine operator.

"I listened to them, but in my heart, I always wanted to be a coach."

When Aguirre graduated from here 23 years ago, only his mother attended the ceremony. He never knew his father, his sisters were working, and his closest brother was in jail. Aguirre knows about being 17 and feeling alone.

Aguirre is also strict. Again, he says, he has no choice. His team is required to address every adult, in every situation, as "sir." They may miss a block, but they never blow that greeting.

During practice, players on the sidelines stand with their hands behind their backs and do not speak.

Gang members sometimes scream at them from the end zone. Neighborhood women flirt with them from the track.

They do not speak.

Midway through the session, though, bodies begin nervously shifting and eyes glance to the side.

It's Mario Hernandez. He is troubled again.

The star defensive end is pulled out of the scrimmage by two volunteer assistant coaches.

Unlike some schools in Southern California, Garfield has just two paid assistants. Aguirre must rely on seven volunteers, usually former players, who show up after work or between jobs.

Tommy Lopez, who will soon begin training as a prison guard, and medical supplies salesman Lawrence Galindo notice that Hernandez is not playing hard. They surround him.

"Don't b.s. us," Lopez says. "What is wrong with you?"

Hernandez stares down and says nothing. But the coaches know.

Hernandez's father died this season. His mother fears her son has joined a gang, and she wants to send him out of state. After Hernandez missed two recent school days and practices, Lopez and Ohm left the field during drills and drove to the projects to look for him.

They didn't know his address, so they walked through the streets shouting his name. They shouted and shouted until from behind one of the thin doors appeared a woman's face. Behind her was Mario.

Lopez explained to the woman that her son was one of the team's best players and that he was not in a gang. While the assistant coach talked, Hernandez gathered his gear.

He carried it past his mother and into the men's car before she could change her mind.

Today, Hernandez finally admits to his coaches, his mind is on his problems at home. Apparently he is not the only one.

It has been a warm day, the players are tired, but when you have just 30 chances, excuses are few. Aguirre calls the team together, glares and walks to his office.

The final speech of this day will be given, as it always is, by the team's leaders.

"Are you guys scared of something!" shouts receiver and defensive back John Cole, 5-foot-7 but with a 6-5 glare.

The team is kneeling, huddled before him and the other leaders in the end zone.

Linebacker Josh Villalobos is almost hysterical when he shouts, "Remember, every game is our last game. Every play is our last play!"

The day ends with several players walking backward on their hands across the darkened turf. They are being punished by their teammates for messing up, for not remembering.

Wednesday

A typical day in the life of a football team working without a net.

Jose Casagran, the paid defensive coordinator, begins practice by showing more videotape from Bell's last game. But one of the TV wires has corroded. Lopez must stand behind the set and hold it in place to maintain a picture.

They take the field in 90-degree heat and things get worse. Players begin complaining of dizziness. Ohm shakes his head knowingly. It happens about this time every week. Those are the ones who barely have enough to eat.

A couple of children — no more than 8 or 9 years old — gather in the end zone and taunt the offense. "I'm gonna rock you!" shouts one. "I'm gonna screw you up good."

In the other end zone, offensive and defensive linemen practice separately, alone.

Their volunteer leaders have not yet arrived from work and college.

Along the sidelines in this heat walks lineman Eddie Garcia, known as "Flounder," a genuine senior college prospect at 6-3, 245.

That is, if any recruiter could ever find these bleachers. There have been no obvious spectators at practice so far this week. Or for weeks before.

Today they couldn't watch Garcia play anyway. But they could understand a measure of his toughness. He is battling a fever that has reached 102. Yet he won't go home. He won't take off his pads. He won't even take off his helmet.

For the next two days he will circle the field in full uniform, not playing, not speaking, just circling.

"Sure, I could order him to go home," Aguirre says. "But would you do that to the kid? He would rather be here than anywhere in the world."

Somehow, in the late afternoon, from this madness a football team emerges. The hitting becomes louder, the tackling comes quicker, the players moan longer.

Villalobos has a sprained ankle but won't leave the field. Linebacker Tony Zamorano might have a broken hand but also won't go.

Ohm shrugs in frustration. Not that he could help. The average Garfield player has other ideas about healing. They are called *sabadoras*, elderly women who give massages and ointment rubs from homes and storefronts. The coaches liken it to visiting a witch doctor. The players believe it is magic.

Just the other day, a woman rubbed oils and a bit of shrubbery on Mercado's injured back. He hasn't missed a practice since.

"Doctors," Mercado snorted. "Those are for white people."

By the time practice ends, the players are in a good mood. They have seen the injuries, watched Garcia's struggle, felt the strength of their hits. They know they are becoming ready for Bell.

After congratulating themselves for a great practice, the players are screaming at each other about Friday night.

Reminding the players of the race of Bell's star running back, Villalobos yells, "Friday, we're all going to spill n——blood!"

There is silence. The teams looks uncomfortably at T.J. Sheppard. He is their star running back. He is the only black on the squad.

A long pause. Then from underneath his helmet, a smile. Relieved cheers.

Sheppard, a junior who leads the team with 350 rushing yards and two touchdowns, understands his teammates' hearts if not their words. He discovered this last season when gangs terrorized him and his mother.

All the windows of his mother's car were broken. The windows of their living room were adorned with "KKK."

His mother, Emma Birden, had seen enough. She made plans to move to another school district.

Then the Bulldogs showed up.

Zamorano and Cole, who both live in the projects, visited the gang members and asked them to back off. For the good of the team, they said. It was the only argument that would work. And it worked.

His mother is happy, and T.J. can't wait for Bell.

"I feel comfortable now," Sheppard says. "My sister and everybody used to say the Mexicans were racist. But not here."

It is dark. Puddles and tape clutter the locker room floor. The last player grabs his knapsack.

It is Zamorano. Senior captain. An SAT score of 1090. One of 20 players with grade-point averages better than 3.0.

These should be Zamorano's glory days. But these are also his days of drudgery. Back at home in the projects, he must clean his small apartment. He must make dinner. He must shoo away gangbangers.

It has been this way for several years, since his mother went blind after an illness. He has missed practice to drive her to the hospital. He has rushed home to be her eyes. But she will be here Friday.

That she can't see is the source of his inspiration.

"She sits up where she can hear the public address announcer. She listens for my name," he says. "That is why I make so many tackles. Because that is the only way she will know that I am there."

Thursday

The day begins with Ohm leaving the team to investigate reports of taggers on school property. Crime is as common around the Bulldogs as ankle sprains.

Paul Sarni, a junior linebacker, was wearing his blue-and-red jersey before last Friday's game when he visited a doughnut shop with teammates. He was the first to walk outside, where he was accosted by a gang member who demanded his jersey.

"I said, 'No way,'" Sarni recalls.

The gang member threatened to "shank" him.

"I said to myself, 'There is no way I can give him this jersey,'" Sarni said. "How could I go back and face my teammates?"

The punk then threatened to "blast" Sarni. That was enough. He was prepared to undress when his teammates rushed outside. The punk fled to his car.

That night, the team took out its frustrations with an 18-15 victory over South Gate.

Such endings have not always been happy.

Javier Perez, a junior wide receiver, was waiting for a city bus after practice recently when two men approached. One bumped him while the other reached under his knapsack and grabbed his helmet.

He chased the men but could not catch them.

"It was hard coming back to the locker room," Perez says. "I mean, that was my helmet."

Practice ends, as it does every Thursday, on a good, full note. In a small house on campus, Aguirre's wife, Maria, has arranged for a full meal for the team, paid for by Aguirre and donations.

"Tonight, you dream big!" exhorts Aguirre as the carne asada sizzles on the grill. "Then tomorrow, you come out and live it!"

Friday

A day that should be a celebration of life begins with death.

Kickoff for Garfield and Bell is 7 p.m. Just after lunch, three players can be found at Rose Hills Memorial Park in Whittier.

Zamorano, Villalobos and Mercado, decked in their jerseys, are planting flowers, weeping and wondering. They surround the marble gravestone of Carlos (Cooch) Alvarado, a fullback from two seasons ago who was gunned down on this day last year outside the school for no apparent reason.

Mercado sobs.

Six hours to game time.

"I used to think I could never leave East L.A.," Mercado says later. "Now that I look around, I don't see how I could stay."

Three hours to game time. One of the last to arrive at the locker room is Juan Marez, a starting running back. As other players are having their ankles taped, he sits talking with a girlfriend while hurriedly downing a Jumbo Jack.

But he can be excused for rushing. After all, he is a workingman.

Marez, who leads the team with five touchdowns, also is the leader in changed transmissions. He is a mechanic for Nungarey Tire Service. He works full time when he does not have a full class load.

"I support myself and help my family," he says. "Sometimes I am tired. But it is my choice."

At 4:30 p.m., the team files into the gym for its weekly hourlong quiet time. After Aguirre's speech, the players will spread out on the floor and sleep like babies.

At 6:30, they are preparing to take the field.

Unlike teams at many schools, during games they do not wear earrings or gloves or tape on their shoes. Some players in this league actually wear gang colors.

"My rules," Aguirre said. "We are not one person. We are one team."

The Game

The Bulldogs jog onto the grass amid virtual silence. The band has not started. The bleachers are not half-full.

But when the ball is kicked, the players behave like it's the NFL.

With Sheppard and Marez running through the bigger Bell defense, Garfield moves down to the 16-yard line. Marez runs 15 yards and prepares to score and … oops … he drops the ball.

Bell recovers.

The Garfield defense takes over. Garcia cannot be blocked. Zamorano has a hand on virtually every tackle. His name is announced so often, his mother cannot believe what she is not seeing.

Then, trouble.

Hernandez, who has forgotten his home problems and is playing with abandon, limps to the sideline. It's his ankle.

Ohm runs over. One problem. His tape-cutters are so poor, it takes him five minutes to unwrap Hernandez's ankle. The delay forces Garfield to call a timeout.

Things get worse. Late in the first half, the struggling offense has yet another chance to score. This time, it is Sheppard who fumbles. He stumbles to the sidelines and plops on the bench. Even beneath his helmet, you can see he is crying.

Teammates rush up to hug him. The sobs continue. On this team, the emotion is common.

Once, after a tough loss, Garcia lay down at midfield and refused to go home. Halftime. 0-0.

The players trudge to the locker room and sprawl in front of the showers. It is the only spot that will hold them all.

The outside doors are carefully closed, and for good reason. Several times each season, gang members wander in at halftime to try to inspire the players or scare them into losing. Each time, Aguirre shoos them away.

"We got 24 minutes, just 24 minutes!" shouts Aguirre tonight.

He says it as if they have but 24 minutes to live.

They begin the second half as if that is true. Moments after Cole recovers a fumble in Bell territory, quarterback Carlos Garcia scores on a 20-yard run.

The defense holds Bell after a long drive, then mounts another long drive. Sheppard runs one direction, Marez runs the other. Bell should stop them but can't.

Then just like that, Sheppard bounces outside with 8:45 left and runs 32 yards for a TD. It's 14-0.

Sheppard's tears are gone. His teammates engulf him.

The defense holds and it is over. Heroes again.

Eddie Garcia falls to the ground in excitement and exhaustion. Meza hops gleefully on his broken foot. Zamorano shuffles and waves his bad hand. Mercado slugs his teammates' shoulder pads, his last bit of anger diminishing for the week.

They run through a tunnel of cheerleaders to the locker room. While the boys dance and sing inside, Aguirre shakes hands and hugs well-wishers outside.

He has not seen any of these people this week. He knows he will not see them until next week. This task of nurturing flowers among the rocks must be handled alone, by him and his coaches.

Right now, it does not matter.

"Our players responded tonight, huh?" he says. "This is what makes it worth it."

He leaves for a steakhouse dinner with his staff. Most of his players are down the street at a loud hamburger stand.

The locker room clears except for one boy, Villalobos. A day that began in a graveyard is ending with a rebirth under a long, long shower. He remains under the water, laughing and singing, when he spots an adult bystander.

The smallest Garfield Bulldog steps out of the stall, covered in soap and a smile.

"Sir! Sir!" he says, as if this were the most wonderful, unbelievable thing in the world. "We beat Bell!"

❖❖

Cold Killers and Fearful Innocents

L.A.'s homeboys are players in a deadly drama.

BY BOB BAKER · JUNE 26, 1988

It's happened so many times. One of the homeboys would get back to the neighborhood all bleeding, saying, "Aw, such-and-such, they did such-and-such to me."

And just because I'm there I'd say: "I be back." Jump on my bicycle — whoooom — head back to the house, get my gun, come back out to the neighborhood, go to one of the homeboys' house, put WD-40 oil down the gun, put the bullets in — click, whiiiisssh — turn the revolver, make sure it's cool. Let's go. Get in the car, roll where we gotta go, talk about what we gon' do, park the car, walk about three, four blocks to where they at, shoot 'em — boom boom boom boom — run back to the car.

—David Stewart, a former Main Street Crip, describing a payback shooting.

Where do they come from, these audaciously violent young men? What rules do they play by? What kind of mentality is this?

The chief of police calls them cowards. The district attorney's gang specialist compares them to Al Capone. The minister who sees them one day in church and the next day in jail calls them "our children." The psychologist who counsels their parents calls them "Buicks," victims of deprivation mass-produced by a callous society the way a factory spits out cars. The probation officer who sees them on the street calls them angry harbingers of a new Watts riot.

Gang members are routinely described as cold killers and fearful, street-warped innocents. They are both. Their assaults are routinely described as the calculated byproducts of soured cocaine deals and drunken, spontaneous responses to the faintest insult. They are both. Their organizations are routinely described as large, disciplined rings and small, fragmented knots. They are both.

Gang members are too diverse to be captured by any generality. Their penchant for violence is too varied, their loyalty to their "sets" too unpredictable, their lives too riddled with contradictions and grand myths. Some are there for the thrill of hanging out with the toughest, coolest people on the block. Some are there for protection from the enemies they have made or plan to make. Many are there to sell drugs, something you cannot do without at least tacit approval of the gang that claims your neighborhood.

The madness percolates most deeply through the city's black neighborhoods. Here gang members immersed in an inside-out logic that makes killing reasonable collide randomly with one another and with innocents who live in the same milieu.

Start with Doc.

Doc is 16, tall, 6 foot 3, about 200 pounds, with a strong face and the rangy build of an athlete. But the streets — hanging out with Eight-Trey Hoover Crips, partying at the shabby Hoover Plaza apartment complex at 81st and Hoover streets, where his homeboys "kick it" — got to Doc before any coach had a chance. He has spent nearly three years in county juvenile camps for armed robbery and selling drugs. He figures he has lost 16 or 17 pals in gang violence since he started hanging around the Hoovers in the fifth grade. His older brother was a gang member. So were his five older sisters. He has developed a blase, fatalistic way of looking at the world.

Take the time his older brother got shot in a phone booth. It shook Doc. It made him think about trying to find excuses to spend less time around the Eight-Trey Hoovers, one of perhaps a dozen "sets" of Hoover Crips who claim territory along Hoover.

Yeah, he told himself, he'd start to cool it. But first there had to be revenge.

Most of the time you know which set to blame. This time Doc wasn't sure. His brother was wounded near the boundary line of two other Crips sets, Rolling 60s and Menlo Avenue. But Doc also thought a Bloods gang, the Brims, might have had something to do with it.

Doc got a gun, got in a car and rode into each neighborhood at night.

"Looking for anybody in they gang," he said matter-of-factly, "anybody in they territory who looked like a gangbanger."

Whenever he saw one, he'd stop and yell that he was looking for one of their homeboys. You spend enough time in the county camps, you learn at least one name from most of the other sets. All he wanted to do was to draw somebody close enough to his car.

"These other homeboys, they'd see me, come up, say, 'Who is that?' I like: Boom! Boom! Boom! 'That's who I am.' I didn't call out my gang's name or nothing." He just sped off. He still doesn't know whether he killed anybody during his spree. He figures he wounded some.

People outside the vortex talk about innocent victims. For most gang members, there is no such thing.

One of the powerful myths that gang members buy into is that they represent and protect their neighborhood. Gang members rarely talk about themselves as belonging to a gang. That is outsider language. Instead, they talk about being from a 'hood. This is more than semantics. It is one reason why no one in South Los Angeles ever feels completely safe. If your 'hood rides into my 'hood and fires on us, goes the unspoken threat between gangs, anybody in your 'hood could get hurt when we come back. We'll come looking for gangbangers, but if we don't see any, we might hit anybody — just to let you know we were here.

"My brother didn't know who done it to him, so I ain't gonna care who I done it to," Doc says, remembering his rage. "I'm just gonna get whoever around at a certain time — the wrong time — that's who I'm gonna get. If I can get somebody, it be off my back. I feel better about it."

For all the attention being paid to spectacular violence committed over soured drug deals and arguments over drug territory, the largest number of gang killings in South Los Angeles still occurs in this haphazard, chaotic way. These endless rounds of retaliation don't draw much notice because they're not spectacular, your basic stop-the-car-and-fire-the-revolver incident. There is nothing new about it. It's happened more than 2,400 times in Los Angeles County during the 1980s, five times every week.

For all the attention being paid to the war between Crips and Bloods, the two loose affiliations that all black gangs claim, a substantial number of gang attacks involve rival sets of Crips who have little loyalty to each other and often engage in festering rivalries.

Crazy? Hell, gang members spit back, life down here is crazy. It's not just the gang members who settle scores with guns. You see it every day. A grandmother shoots her grandson in the chest as they argue over $40 she wants to borrow. A mother shoots her ex-husband to death in a dispute over visitation rights. A woman shoots her sister's ex-boyfriend during an argument over a car.

What many gang members don't understand, since they have seen the world only through the most frenetic end of the prism, is that in their world the distance between increments of violence is very short. It takes frighteningly little time to drive from annoyance to rage to retaliation. The line between self-defense and a preemptive strike is badly blurred too. That's because you have to be ready. Anything could happen.

"It's all depending how your backbone is," says one gang member. "If you ain't strong enough to stop 'em from going in your house, they're going to go in your house. They ain't going in my house."

Inside a wood-frame home with a large porch near the Harbor Freeway, Doc sits on a couch in a darkened living room during an early evening and sifts the circumstances that ensnare him.

One of them is that the set of Crips he has spent his adolescence with is one of the most violent in the city.

In most of Los Angeles, gang members contend that for all the publicity about killings, the gangs themselves are pretty quiet.

"Ain't nobody banging no more," they insist.

What that means is that prolonged, organized assaults by one group of gang members on another are far less frequent than they were at the turn of the decade, when turf lines were less hardened and incursions tended to be more explosive. Gang members argue that less organized attacks, in which one or two members shoot somebody because they're trying to settle their own score, should not be called "gang killings." It's just a guy going off and doing his own thing, they say. This distinction is usually lost on outsiders, but it's an example of the peculiar logic of gang life.

The Eight-Trey Hoovers, by contrast, do bang.

You take a typical gang, Doc is saying, and it's probably once a month that a few of their members get their heads pumped up by any combination of adrenaline, alcohol and narcotics, and ride out to attack any rivals in sight.

Doc's homeboys "are straight crazy…. We be going through others' 'hoods every couple days, shooting them up. Don't care about nothing. All they [the Hoovers] care about is what's out there at the time. They don't have nothing to do. They get tired of sitting around drinking and smoking weed, so they just get up, 'Let's go roll on somebody. Let's go jack [rob] him. Let's go jack her.' "

The Hoover sets come from particularly dreary neighborhoods. A few weeks ago a local minister led a delegation of citizens to the corner of Hoover and 94th streets to decry gang violence. A newspaper photographer who pointed a camera at a house to take a picture found a Hoover Crip inside pointing a rifle back at him.

"A lot of the homeboys, the ones who still living in the 'hood, their mamas are drug addicts," says Doc, who has moved from his mother's house to the home of one of his sisters, about 30 blocks north. "They don't give 'em no money. Everybody want money; everybody want decent clothes. Lot of Hoovers don't go to school 'cause they don't have no decent clothes. So they just go out and sell dope and rob. That's the only thing to do. After they do some robbing, they get caught and go to jail. That's why they never go to school.

"Most of 'em are institutionalized. They been in jail since they was young; they figure they going back there anyway. One of my homeboys I known since I was banging, he got out after five years. Two, three weeks later he had killed a Mexican man in an alley. He doing nine years right now."

For all the impassiveness with which Doc discusses this, he's still trying to distance himself from the Hoovers without feeling as though he's betraying a way of life. He'd like to graduate from Manual Arts High next year and then study carpentry. As far as he knows, the only other members of his set who have graduated are his brother, who is no longer a gang member and is attending Trade Tech, and another friend doing time in Folsom.

Despite having moved out of the Eight-Trey Hoovers' 'hood, he periodically goes back to Hoover and 81st, and when he does, if there's a robbery or a drive-by going down, "I just want to get into it. I feel left out of something. You don't have to go. You can be smart and stay. But most of the time I just go."

He strides through Manual Arts High School with his pants sagging low on his waist, one of the most forthright fashion statements a gang member can make. Donald Bakeer, an English teacher who has befriended him, knows better than to push Doc too hard. The identification with being a gang member is deeper than most people understand. It was Doc's brother who used to sing: "Ain't just saggin', I'm blue-raggin' [blue is the Crips' color], don't you wanna look like me?"

"It's all they have," says Bakeer, who has written a self-published historical novel about the Crips and believes black gangs are a powerful family substitute for boys from poor, fatherless homes. "It's their daddy, and if you diss [disrespect] their daddy, they may go off and you may never get them back."

What makes the gangs of Los Angeles so unpredictable is that many of the young men who join or simply hang around the periphery do not see themselves as cut-and-dried murderers who wake up wanting to squeeze the trigger. Rather, like Doc, they tend to be so inured to violence that they think of themselves as nothing more than streetwise survivalists.

The trouble is, it takes very little — maybe a short evening of gulping 40-ounce bottles of "Eight Ball," Old English 800 malt liquor, a favorite gang pastime — to move from survivalist to aggressor.

Ask Kimberly and Tina, two 17-year-old cousins who were sitting around talking with five gang members in a motel room on Imperial Highway last January. Tina made the mistake of saying something negative about the gang that one of the men belonged to. He exploded.

"He said he should kill her, or he was going to, for disrespecting his 'hood," Kimberly testified in court recently. The gang members almost did. They gang-raped the girls and then shot them repeatedly with Uzis when the girls tried to flee, she said.

· · ·

This kind of hair-trigger life is not what Li'l Jake envisions for himself. But Li'l Jake, who lives in Watts, surrounded by even grimier poverty than the neighborhoods along Hoover, knows he could go either way.

He was scarcely into his teens when he asked to be initiated into Grape Street, probably the biggest Crips set in Watts and the acknowledged rulers of the huge, tattered Jordan Downs housing project. As a symbol of its independence, Grape Street disdains Crip blue for its own color, purple.

Li'l Jake, 16, grew up in a relatively quiet part of Watts, but as he was entering his teens, he moved and Cripdom surrounded him. Then a Blood killed his brother's 19-year-old uncle at Will Rogers Park in Watts, and Li'l Jake got mad. He told the older guys he wanted in. To prove himself, as an initiation, he fought five Grape Street members, one after the other.

Now he walks the tightrope. He still goes to school at Jordan High, but he hangs out with guys who don't. He watches the older guys who populate 103rd Street as it runs down the middle of Grape Street's territory, guys with no future except selling the rock, guys whose one-dimensional hardness is emphasized by gold chains shimmering against their rippling white T-shirts.

He wonders whether he'll wind up like that.

"Sometimes I think that'll probably be me," says the boy, a slender 10th-grader who wears his hair in a Jheri curl and has a pleasant, youthful face set off with hardened eyes. "I know I'm hanging out with the wrong people. Then again, if I stay on the right track, go to school, do my work, play football, then I got a chance."

A chance to be a pro football player. That's his goal, despite the fact that he's no taller than 5 foot 9. He played wide receiver on the B team last fall.

If he can't play ball? "I'll try to get a job or something."

His mother died four or five years ago after she went into a coma. He's not sure what caused it. He lives with his two aunts, their three children and his three brothers in a three-bedroom apartment in the Imperial Courts housing project. The aunts work. One of Li'l Jake's brothers comes home after school and looks after the smaller children. Li'l Jake keeps an eye on them after he gets home. "When my auntie comes, I leave."

Like most gang members, he's tried his hand at selling rock cocaine. He stood out on the street, conducted transactions, then went into a house, got the dope from "the head man" and brought it back to the buyer. He was not a big-timer. He grossed maybe $300 a day, kept half of it. But after a year he quit. He almost got arrested, and he was afraid of being shot.

"Friends getting killed," he says softly. "Buying it. Taking it. Buying up cars, shooting. They use kids 12, 13 years old. Little girls nowadays sell it. It's a trip."

Gang members listen to public service announcements about saying no to gangs and they sneer. People don't understand, they say. Theoretically it's a wonderful idea, but "even if you don't bang [attack rival gang members], you still go into another 'hood and they still gonna ask you where you from," Li'l Jake says. "Somebody might find you for some reason. They don't care. Nowadays, people is crazy. It hurts sometimes to see."

Crazy. Last summer he went over to his girlfriend's place with some friends when he found that some Hoovers, from a set around Hoover and 112th Street, were there. Hell, they should have known better. Hoovers just can't walk into Grape's 'hood.

"The Hoovers come out," Li'l Jake remembers, "so I told 'em, this is Grape. So they pulled out a .22 and fired. We dug who shot the gun, we left, I told my homeboy, he gave me a gun, I went back and I shot at them. I think I hit one."

He knows this is a ridiculous way to live.

"But you know," he adds with more resignation than bravado, echoing the words of so many gang members, "a person think he can shoot me, but if I don't die, I'm coming back for him."

. . .

George is the same age as Li'l Jake and dresses the same simple way: white T-shirt, dark corduroys, white sneakers. But sit across from him and you feel little of the pathetic world-weariness that washes off Li'l Jake's words.

Part of the reason is that George (not his real name) is sitting on a nest egg of $50,000, a settlement from a traffic accident, that he'll collect at 18. He talks about using the money to buy a Crenshaw Boulevard car wash, which is shorthand for the drug business. According to police, drug dealers often use car washes and auto body shops as bases of operation.

But there's more to George's outlook than that. George is from the West Side of South Los Angeles — in gang parlance, anything west of Broadway — and the difference between the two sides is night and day. The East Side of South L.A. is where you find the housing projects and the dented '79 Chevys. The West Side is where gang members who have the "snaps" — money — show off their "fresh" cars, the Benzes and the glittery sports trucks. Drug money and drug power are contemptuously on display. And even when they're not, the fact is that families on the West Side generally have more money than families on the East Side.

"My family, they got the money. They give me anything I want," boasts George, a student at Crenshaw High who lives with his mother. "My mama, she tells me I ain't got no friends, that my friends are in my pocket — whoever give me money is my friend."

For George, being a gang member — a Rolling 60s Crip — is a ticket to good times. To the younger guys at school, the ones who throw 60s hand signs and yell out the name but aren't really in the set — the claimers, the wannabes — George is a hero. A real gang member. Has been since sixth grade. He grew up in the 60s' neighborhood, at 60th Street and 8th Avenue, a collection of fading stucco homes, dried-out lawns and graffiti-strewn walls. He didn't need to be initiated. He'd grown up around the older guys.

On the East Side, they talk about being a Crip to survive. On the West Side, to George at least, what it's about is belonging, heading with the fellows to the skating rink, to the rap concert, or getting together in Hyde Park, which is impractical now that the police are conducting sweeps.

"It's about having fun, just being with 'em," says George. "The guys are cool. You gotta know 'em. If you don't know 'em, you think they crazy. For me, it's not about doing anything for money. If I was doing it for the money, I'd be out of town right now," joining older gang members selling drugs in other cities, he says. "I'd come back in two weeks with snaps."

Rolling 60s assured themselves of infamy four summers ago when three of their members, in what prosecutors said was a contract job, drove to a home on West 59th Street and killed the mother of former football star Kermit Alexander and three other family members. Only later did the gang members learn they had hit the wrong house.

Law enforcement officers estimate there are 500 to 700 members of the 60s. George figures he knows maybe 300, and that's another part of the lure: Everywhere you go, you see a homeboy.

George is one of his set's younger members. His nickname — again, he asked for an alias — is Baby Train. That means he's the third oldest member of the Rolling 60s to use that name. Above him is 19-year-old Li'l Train, and above him is Train, who's 25 and is considered an OG — Original Gangster — because he has held that nickname the longest.

"It ain't like they your brother," George says of Train and Li'l Train, "but it's like you're real close."

For all of his love of belonging, George willingly accepts the need to pay the price, to "be down" for his set. It means, simply put, that if he's around when a bunch of guys decides to avenge a real or imagined offense committed by another gang, he'll go along. In practice, there are ways of sliding out, but if you do so too often, you become known as a "buster."

As in war, fidelity to the set and hatred of all its enemies have become deeply ingrained. A cop who knows George threw a hypothetical question at him one day. He asked him what he'd do if he was at a skating rink and saw a girl he knew being hassled by a member of the Eight-Trey Gangsters. The two Crips gangs have killed off each other's members for years, ever since a fight over a girl who was dating members of each set.

"We woulda got him before he got that far," George said confidently.

"Let's say he got that far," the cop said.

"Aw, we gonna smoke him anyway, 'cause we don't get along with him."

But isn't that absurd, shooting someone you don't even know?

"He claiming that set. They don't care about us. So just get even. That's the way it's always going to be."

Doesn't George ever think of the senselessness of it?

"I think of it," he says calmly, but then, as if he has just caught himself sliding into a dangerous mind-set, his voice heats up. "But if I see one of 'em, I just think of the funeral I went to where I saw one of my homies, and I be like, I get mad. I just go off. I see my homie in his casket."

There are ways out of this, of course. One is to move to another neighborhood. That at least would decrease the odds of being shot by familiar rivals. But George, who proclaims, "I'll always be a 60 in my heart," is not about to do that. He thinks, like many gang members, that he can have it both ways. One foot in the future, one foot in his set. Besides, he says, "I'm not the kind of person to walk around letting everybody know who I am. I've got feelings for people. I'm not like those guys who don't got no feeling for people."

Wait a minute. What about the Eight-Trey Gangster you just hypothetically killed?

George's mood darkens.

"I don't care about him! They can do anything to him. They can torture him."

Would you? he is asked.

119

"I got feelings, but I'd still do it. I don't care. I remember my homeboy, my mind is going off."

OK, he is asked, let's say it's two years from now and the same Eight-Trey Gangster drives into your Crenshaw Boulevard car wash. Are you going to blast him?

George thinks for a second.

"Nah. I dunno. He got a fresh car, I'll have my homies jack him."

. . .

Listening, one is disarmed by the possibility that a lot of this talk about killing abstract enemies is just that, kid stuff, that it wears off with age. Sometimes it does. Too often it does not.

Ask Dwayne Jordan.

Dwayne was the same age as George, with the same kind of mind-set: He was cool, he was tough, he was a street warrior who hid his fears of being shot with stoic, time-tested sayings like, "Hey, man, whatever happens is gonna happen." He went to school only because it was a good place to find girls and other gang members. Privately, he was not planning on doing anything stupid enough to wind up in jail.

Dwayne's neighborhood was Eleven-Deuce Hoover.

"It was a second family in a sense. My mother was working a lot. I was always with 'em, basically spend more time with them than at home."

He began carrying a gun in the seventh grade after he was jumped by another gang. He kept it in an ankle holster. Such are the problems of being a Hoover. Enemies were everywhere. Raymond Avenue Crips on this side, N-Hoods, a Blood set, on another. You couldn't go anywhere without going in a group. His brother was an N-Hood, but that's just the way it is in some homes. Black gangs have little of the inviolate tradition of Los Angeles' much older Latino gangs.

Shootings abounded. "For the most part it was paybacks, but a lot of it was we'd just be bored at night, and one of the homeboys says, 'Man, let's go hoo-bang on the N-Hoods,' so we'd go over there and shoot up the N-Hoods, shoot up the Raymonds. You wouldn't always kill somebody. It would just be shooting to let 'em know Hoovers know where you hang out, can kill you anytime."

The thing was, you didn't feel like a potential murderer. Like another gang member puts it, you get so used to shooting at your enemies, it's like playing Laser Tag.

"At certain times people did get hit, but people didn't die every time. Some of the guys I'd be with, they'd feel like, 'I'm gonna kill one of 'em.' Some of us, it didn't really matter. We were just there for the ride, hanging out with the rest of the homeboys, followers, so to speak.

"It was usually shooting at people in a crowd. Everybody just be shooting. You couldn't tell if you was the one that shot that guy. There would always be that thought in your mind — did I kill that guy or did Li'l Bob kill that guy? — but you would never know. You'd be with five, six, 10 other guys, drive by, jump out the car, start shooting."

Dwayne never felt like killing anybody. Except for the time he did.

He was on his way to Washington High School when five guys from N-Hood jumped him. He knew it went with the territory. He'd been stupid enough to walk by himself across Normandie. They didn't beat him up badly. But they got him mad.

"I talked to a homeboy during school. After school I was home, lifting weights in the backyard, when a couple of homeboys came by to say they'd spotted some of those Bloods. They told me they had a gun and the whole deal. I was a little hesitant, but then it was like they were gonna call me scared. I went. I was the oldest one of that bunch in age, but streetwise I wasn't the oldest one.

"We went over there and me and my friend Eric, who had the gun, started arguing about who was going to do the shooting. I told them, 'Let me do the shooting.'

"We was on foot. They was in a big field. I lived on Mariposa. All I had to do was walk to the corner, go through an alley and I saw 'em in a big field, playing music, dancing around, 10, 15 of them."

He didn't know if any of these were the gang members who had actually jumped him. But he knew they lived in the apartments adjacent to the field, and that was enough. He raised Eric's .32-caliber revolver and fired one shot. Then he and Eric split.

"Later, one of the homegirls told me a guy had been shot in the head. I didn't think he would live. Three, four days afterward he died.

"That's when I decided to cool this gang stuff. Although I'd been shooting at people, I never knew I killed anyone if I did. This time I knew. It was my bullet that did it. It didn't seem impossible before. There was always that chance. But there was always that uncertainty."

It took a month or two for the police to catch up to him. One of his homeboys confessed. Dwayne spent the next five years in a California Youth Authority facility.

"For me, the main turnaround was being incarcerated. I had thrown away all of my teen years. Sitting up in that jail gave me a lot of time to think. Just like that was Dwayne Allison I killed, it could have been Dwayne Allison killing Dwayne Jordan. That wasn't what I wanted out of life. "

Today, 23-year-old Jordan works as a truck driver for $1,300 a month. Not much, but it's better than the $500-a-month job he started with when he came out of CYA.

He lives with his wife of nine months in a garage apartment, watches his friends sell cocaine and shakes his head.

"Some of them," he says, "they make my paycheck in a day, and I have more than they have. I don't know what they be doing with their money."

. . .

In a way, Jordan is lucky. He could have gone to state prison. He could have come out hardened and cynical, convinced that the deck was stacked and that crime was just a word. He could have wound up like Eugene Hooper.

Hooper (not his real name) is 27, a convicted thief who makes a living by doing auto detail work out of his car, dealing cocaine and hustling dice. He lives with his girlfriend and their 6-year-old son. He grew up as a member of the Harlem 30s Crips, near Exposition Park, had his share of wild, violent times during the turf wars of the late 1970s and then, as he hit his late teens, realized he had to come to terms with the real world. He started robbing jewelry stores.

"I was trying to beat the white man's system," he says, sitting in the bleachers of Denker Recreation Center on 35th Street, dressed in a white jogging suit and wearing a beeper on his hip. "I was trying to get the white man to lose some money — that's all they did, tried to make us lose. I was thinking, they leave all the jewelry out at night, why not get some? I made my money, and then again I did my time, too. But then again, when I get out I don't need to be labeled. They label you.

"If you mess up early, you never get back. I done tried. I was on parole two years ago. I tried to get a job for a whole year while I was on parole. I lied on my application sometimes. They call back and then deny me. Then when I put it down, they say your record show you were a professional burglar.

"And then I went to the point as far as trying to be a janitor, at my age," he says disgustedly. "I went to work, and for a whole two weeks they never took me off the toilets. They made me work toilets for two weeks, and I called up one morning and said find me some work where they ain't no toilets. When I went to work that night, they had me in some toilets. See, 'cause what they want me to be is what they want me to do. They don't want to see me go up, do nothing else. I couldn't accept that, and they weren't paying me more than $4 an hour. When I could come out on the streets and sell a rock $10 every 10 minutes? What would you prefer?

"Everybody's trying to survive in this world. The white folks is bringing us the dope…. Hell, the white man is making all the money. We getting the crumbs, the bottom barrel. They just issuing us our little crap. They made all their millions at the top.

"We just innocent bystanders stuck up in a mad-ass world. That's all it is. We just trapped in a world that we gotta survive until we die."

This is the adult voice that some of the children of South Los Angeles hear. The black middle class — the lawyers and the doctors and the civil servants and the entrepreneurs, the role models of opportunity and working within the system who lived there when segregation forced them to stay — have largely moved to nicer neighborhoods. "And if they come back to see the cousins or the aunts," grumbles one disgruntled youth worker, "they in and out in 15 minutes."

Hooper fills this void. It's not that he's recruiting anyone to his philosophy. It's that he's devoid of hope. It's not that he's exhorting anyone to gangbang — he's long been out of that. It's that he's an active voice for the hopelessness that makes the gang seem like a redemptive presence.

His bitterness is typical of older gang members.

"If a guy from the moon asked me about Cripping," said Chic, a slender, muscular, unemployed man of 22 with chiseled facial features who hangs out in an apartment courtyard on 69th and Main streets with other members of the 69th Street East Coast Crips, "I'd tell him it's a confused, disorganized, depressed kind of thing."

. . .

The young ones never think about this. It's too distant. The social pull is so strong. To belong. To be known. To be somebody.

"I wasn't a problem child. I still did the things my mother told me. I just got to the point where I wanted to be with everybody," remembers David Stewart, 20, who was a Main Street Crip from the age of 11 until he began to ease himself out of it two years ago.

"I used to be into drawing, sports, used to join the teams. It just wasn't fast enough for me. I needed something more. Just going to school and playing basketball, I needed something more exerting.

"I didn't want to sit in the house by myself and be neglected, not one of the fellas. So I just got out and wanted to dress down [flaunting gang colors] and be down with everybody, stand out and get drunk and have it all, 'cause when you a gang member you just have everything you want. When you a gang member, you have all the ladies. Ladies come around, be like: [he imitates a girl's voice] 'Where you from?' 'Main Street.' 'Oh, you from Main Street?'

"All gang members come out for is: They want ladies, they get easy money any kind of way. Guns, power, the excitement of the whole thing. Respect. You can walk up the street and people pass by in the car and say, 'Hey man, what's up? That's my homeboy.'

"Just having that respect. Having certain people scared of you. They see you coming, and [he gasps in mock horror] you 20 pounds lighter than him, he's a big guy and he's scared: 'Oh, that's such and such. He's bad. You don't want to touch him.' You have whole school grounds scattering because you from the same set.

"It was like that movie 'Scarface.' Everybody say, 'I'm gonna be like him, make all this money, be 17 in a Mercedes.' All you imagine is all this money, you doing this, you got all this. It blows your head up. That's all you think about.

"Most of the time your mama knows what's going on, but Mama's not going to be the one to tell the kid to stop it," said Stewart, who had his own apartment when he was selling cocaine but today, after serving nine months in jail, has moved back with his mother.

"Moms are too gentle. When I started gangbanging, my mother tried to get me to stop. I wouldn't; she saw that's what I wanted. If I did something I shouldn't, she was there to help me. She wouldn't, if I killed somebody, get rid of the gun. She wasn't that deep into it. But if I do something like: 'Hey, Mama, we just do such and such,' she sit me down, talk to me.

"I would tell my mother everything I did. That's the kind of relationship I had with her: 'Oh, Mama, we just broke into this house, and if the police come here, just tell 'em you haven't seen me since you don't know when.' I'd get out of the house. She would say, 'Hey, well if that's what you want to do with your life, hey, you do that with your life, but I see a better way. If you don't see it, you will in the future.'

"That's what happened. If she'd told me, 'You got to stay in the house,' that's gonna make me start arguing with her. And then she'd have been telling me, 'You can't do this and that in my house,' and I'll be: 'Forget it, I'll stay with one of my homeboys.' But she didn't want that."

The mothers are largely alone in carrying this load. In many sections of South Los Angeles, the majority of homes with children have no father, the majority of births are out of wedlock and up to 90% of the mothers with children are on welfare.

· · ·

Charles Baylor, a sweet-faced, 14-year-old boy, has both parents at home. He's lucky enough to have lived outside Los Angeles long enough to know what life beyond the vortex is like. His father moved the family to Alaska two years ago to take a job as a court administrator. Last year he moved back to a modest apartment in Inglewood, where Charles rediscovered gangs.

Charles is not a gang member. Most young black men are not. According to law enforcement agencies, there are about 25,000 Crips and Blood gang members or "associates" in Los Angeles County — an estimate based on arrests and field interrogations of people stopped but not arrested. That represents about 25% of the county's estimated 100,000 black men between the ages of 15 and 24.

Still, Charles must play the game, despite his innocence.

The Baylor family lives a few blocks southwest of Crenshaw, where the Los Angeles municipal boundary turns into Inglewood and the Los Angeles street gangs' boundaries turn from Rolling 60s to Six-Four Brims, a Bloods gang.

Charles, a good son and a dutiful student, is frightened of pressures around him. But he doesn't want to be messed with. So he feigns a certain toughness. He pulls his pants down so they sag at the waist. And he initiates fights between classes at Paul Revere Junior High in Pacific Palisades, where he is bused to school. His friends do the same.

He wrote an essay about it for his English class:

> On the outside of me, I want to be like everybody else. I try to be a gang-banger and act hard, as we say. I have a certain name people call me and I just try to mix in with the crowd and sag, talk slang talk and fight a lot because I mess with people. It's just like a sickness. You get ready to go through the same thing every day. It's just a trip.
>
> On the inside, I am the sweetest kid you could know. I know you probably don't believe it, but when school is over, I am very scared of the same thing I be doing. I pull up my pants, turn my hat [baseball cap] to the front and go on about my business. When I get in the house, I am a whole different person. I help my mother out when she needs me. I help my brother out from time to time and when I get to school it gets crazy. My mother keeps telling me you're going to need an education to make it. And I try to keep it in my head, but it slips right out. That's why someday I can do good and other days I act like a you-know-what.

Charles has nightmares about his family's modest apartment being shot up because gang members are pursuing him.

David Stewart, an intense, quick-witted young man who has gone back to school to complete his high school education, has lived that nightmare and awakened with an uncommon resolve.

Two things changed him. The first occurred two years ago when he was pushing his newborn daughter in a stroller to buy some diapers. He was walking through Rolling 60s territory when he was confronted by a 60 who put a gun to his head and complained about the color of the stroller. It was burgundy. Too close to red, the Bloods' color.

Later, Stewart went to jail for selling cocaine to an undercover officer. It made him do some more thinking.

"The only thing you think is, I could have done better than this. I got out seeing that gangbanging wasn't benefiting nobody. Long as I was gangbanging, I was Homeboy This, Homeboy That, but when I didn't graduate high school, none of them was out there to help me. Now I don't have my diploma, or this and that, I can't look at them and say, 'Can you help me do this? Can you help me take care of my family?'

"When you're really into it, and one of the guys goes down, the homeboys are usually there at the funeral. But in this day and age, with dope like this, they figure you die, I can't come to your funeral 'cause I got a big deal to take care of. It's like you don't really matter. I figure I don't need it. I went to jail for selling dope, but the man I was selling dope for didn't take care of my mother, didn't take care of my child."

Stewart did what most gang members never do. He cut off all his associations. He does not go back to Main and 94th streets, his old 'hood.

"You can stop doing anything you want," he says.

"In my mind it's nonsense. It's nonsense, black people killing off each other like that. It's not what's happening. I think it [should] make some people feel kind of funny to just kill another brother."

That was what one of Donald Bakeer's creative writing students at Manual Arts High, Miles Allen, was getting at a couple of months ago when he turned in a poem. It went like this:

> *Cooling out with the boys in the 'hood.*
> *Everything is OK and going good.*
> *But nobody no how up to no good.*
> *Big weed-smoking and 8-Ball drinking. Everybody was high as a kite.*
> *Budd smoked up, beer all gone, fall to the ground, nobody is paying*
> *attention, nobody looking around.*
> *Duck! Duck!*
> *Boom! Boom!*
> *'Aw, Cuz, aw, Cuz, they are blasting.'*
> *Silence went through the 'hood. That is all it was.*

Bakeer liked it. Miles (not his real name) was talking about trying to distance himself from the gang members he hung around with. About a week later, he was walking to a liquor store with a Crip friend when a Blood drove past and threw his gang's sign. In defiance, the Crip threw his gang's sign. The Crip went into the liquor store. Miles waited outside. The Blood made another pass in his car and stopped. He stepped out, walked up to Miles and shot him half a dozen times, killing him.

Silence went through the 'hood.

❖

50 Years of Moving History

The Pasadena Freeway, a first in the West, approaches its golden anniversary as a marvel of its age — and with a better safety record than many of its modern counterparts.

By Patt Morrison · December 21, 1990

Drive it the way you would dance. Curve, glide, turn; clutch, shift, accelerate. In the morning, it moves through alternate flickerings of shadow and light, cast by the lift and dip of the hills alongside. In the evening, it hurries through the black shade of green trees.

Whatever other symbols have come to represent Los Angeles, the freeway is its most fitting. The movies are older, the climate is none of our doing, but the freeways are our gift and our endless joke. They make the place run or not run. The first of them, the mother and father of Western freeways, will turn 50 on December 30 — the golden anniversary of the Pasadena Freeway.

In an age of technical marvels, it was a marvel of the age, a sunken six-lane parkway that snaked and bent along the riverbed of the green and pleasant Arroyo Seco, from the august *banlieues* of Pasadena to the nubby buildings of downtown. Over the miles their grandsires had needed a day to conquer on foot and horse, 1940 drivers could transit in the time it took to smoke a cigarette. Some committee, in a flush of civic lyricism, named it the Arroyo Seco Parkway. Locals called it "that ditch."

This first of the freeways, like the rest that would come, put form to fantasy. To drive a freeway became "a special way of being alive," wrote urban critic Reyner Banham, "a state of heightened awareness that some locals find mystical." To drive a freeway was to move "as a riverman runs a river," wrote Joan Didion, "every day more attuned to its currents, its deceptions."

Rivers they are, great concrete rivers that in 50 years have carried our commerce and concerns farther afield than had been envisioned, farther indeed than many now wish they had. Freeways now divide our days as they divide the city.

To the grim-eyed, hurried 1990s, the Pasadena Freeway has the look of a museum piece, dated as a zoot suit, narrow, awkward, pokey, perilous to the driver who does not know its quiddities and tricks. Along its 8.2 miles, from lower Pasadena past the Art Deco tunnels that once arched over Figueroa Street, it has no shoulders, almost no turnout bays and permits no big trucks. Its curves are thrill-ride sharp, its lanes a foot narrower than the current standard. People pull into their driveways faster than some of the Pasadena's exit ramps can accommodate.

"There's a level of discomfort on the part of the motorist," says Keith Gilbert, the Automobile Club's manager of highway engineering, "but basically it's such a beautiful historic road, and learning to cope with it has made it an important part of the Los Angeles infrastructure."

The Pasadena Freeway ranks as the 12th busiest among Caltrans' 26 regional freeways. At a point near the Golden State Freeway, where it first carried 27,000 cars a day, 127,000 now pass. On workday mornings, at each entrance ramp along its length, 10,000 cars join the inbound stream, to be siphoned off again each night. The stop signs and the hairpin ramps make it as self-metering as a modern freeway, without aid of red and green signals; its path through parklands is aesthetically and environmentally aware, if not altogether sensitive; a ban on trucks helps make it safer than some newer, more frantic lengths of urban freeway.

In sum, it still moves.

· · ·

"The problem is the on- and off-ramps.... Those of us who use the freeway during morning hours I think are experienced enough to know how to merge.... I tell my friends, 'Don't be in that outside lane, it's dangerous.' I have many friends who say they don't like it all — too many curves."

Sally Stanton Rubsamen was 17 in 1940, a high school senior plucked from a gym class to be later crowned Tournament of Roses queen.

She lives in Pasadena, drives every day to her paralegal job downtown, along the length of what her son and daughter still call "mama's freeway." If she speaks of the Pasadena Freeway with crisp and analytical propriety, she is entitled. She is the one who officially opened it, she and the governor of California, tugging opposite ends of a red silk ribbon on a December morning she remembers chiefly for the throngs of people and the "rough policeman" warning a man — her father — not to touch the queen.

. . .

"It works fairly well for being a small old freeway, but you probably have fewer strangers driving the Pasadena Freeway than you do most of the other freeways. If you've driven that thing a hundred times or a thousand times, you get used to all the quirks and curves and drive it a whole lot better than some guy who's never been on it before."

Nick Jones, Caltrans associate transportation engineer, is among those who believe that the Pasadena Freeway, for all its antique shortcomings, remains a pretty well-mannered piece of road, if sometimes balky.

When it was first proposed, the publicity of the day promised Pasadena to downtown in 10 minutes, a breeze of a journey past the fusty trolley lines that rattled alongside for a ways. The parkway designers intended drivers to enjoy the view at 45 mph. Today, the trolleys gone, rush-hour motorists can enjoy the view at even greater leisure, like dead stops.

. . .

"We didn't know much about freeways in those days. In fact, the Pasadena Freeway, what we now call a freeway, was conceived originally as being a leisurely scenic route. Speed and volume were not considered as being the main purposes of it. You were supposed to enjoy the park and view, and leisurely and safely go from L.A. to Pasadena."

Al Himelhoch worked on the Pasadena and virtually every freeway in Los Angeles, starting in 1936 as head chainman on a survey crew and retiring in 1974 as Caltrans deputy district engineer.

Himelhoch recalled that at the time, the Pasadena Freeway defined the cutting edge of transportation development — a "learning laboratory," said one engineer, for how to build more.

An arroyo road had been talked about since it was surveyed in 1895. One man tried to start a bicycle trail, but nothing came of it. It took legislation to allow the designing of such a highway, with no intersections, no right of access from adjacent property. They didn't even know what to call it: "stopless motorway" was one suggestion.

One or two parkways had already been built in the east; the beginnings of the autobahn were crossing Germany, broad enough to accommodate tanks, which they soon would. But an urban roadway — there was no state of the art; they had to invent it as they went along.

This, by the numbers, is what they built in 33 months:

Size

Lanes at least a foot narrower than those mandated since. Originally, the two outside lanes were paved with white cement, and the two inside ones with black, on the curious theory that different-colored pavement would keep people from lane hopping. Emergency turnout bays were added in the 1950s, but nothing ever came of the notion that all six lanes be converted to one-way for morning and evening rush hours, nor of the idea to install coin-operated gas pumps for stalled cars.

Ramps

Better suited to circus clown acts than modern cars. Unlike newer freeways, it has virtually no merging lanes on or off. The stop signs at the bottom of on-ramps were put there as a safety measure. Today, as traffic rushes by at shooting-gallery speed, you choose your moment and floor it.

Curves

That slight lift and tilt you feel instinctively when you take a curve, a sense that the road is banked to meet the centrifugal lean of the car — that's called "super elevation." The Pasadena Freeway was super elevated, but for 45 mph speeds, not 60. Hence the panicky feeling at taking those curves too fast. "We didn't understand freeways as high-speed, high-volume facilities, so the fact it had relatively tight curvature wasn't considered that important in those days," Himelhoch says. "It's a matter of comfort, at least that's the word we use." Because of those curves, says California Highway Patrol Sgt. Michael Moses, "every so often you get somebody not real familiar with the freeway, and they realize, 'Well, I'm too hot into this.' … It gets tighter as you get into it, and you've got to constantly reduce your speed or you wash out."

Median

About 4 feet wide, the median in 1940 was pleasingly landscaped with shrubs to screen out the glare of opposing headlights and "so nobody would have a head-on collision," the designers noted with naive assurance. Naturally, the early smashups were gory head-on affairs, cars leaping across that scant 4 feet. Most medians today are as much as 30 feet wide.

Trucks

Almost alone among freeways, no trucks more than 3 tons are allowed, although out-of-state truckers who see only a freeway line on the map sometimes get stuck on it. For a time in the early 1950s, the freeway was opened to trucks after a truck driver appealed his conviction. But the weight restriction was reinstituted, and has held up. So — mostly because of the truck ban — has the pavement.

Regulars

Because it begins on a Pasadena street and is not fully a part of the great tributary flow of freeways, it lacks much through traffic, says Jerry Baxter, district director for Caltrans. "You take the Santa Ana, Golden State, Ventura — there's a lot of interstate traffic on those. The Pasadena is mostly local people."

Safety

With local drivers perhaps intimidated by the road's limitations into behaving themselves, the Pasadena Freeway does a bit better than its old roadbed might suggest. Its accident rate, says Caltrans, is 1.84 — meaning 1.84 reportable accidents for every million vehicle miles traveled. That is higher than, say, the Long Beach Freeway, but lower than stretches of Interstate 5. In workaday terms, says Caltrans' Gary Bork, chief of the traffic operations branch, "I would say someone could travel the total length of that Pasadena Freeway every [workday] for 61 years and shouldn't expect to be in an accident" of reportable size. Compare that with an average of eight or 10 years of accident-free driving on city streets.

Speed

With all those Le Mans curves curling out in front of your hood ornament, there are times on the drive to work, says commuter Blanca Dalziel, that "I sort of pretend I'm a race car driver. Not going 100 miles an hour but...." We're conditioned to it — when the signs say "freeway," the pulse says 65. But the Pasadena tends to enforce itself. When "some guy doing 65, 70" careens by, says Moses, and an officer gives chase, "we don't have to wait for him to see us. He has to slow down because one of the locals is up there ahead slowing him down." In a World War II "Drive for Victory" gas-saving campaign, squads of volunteer enforcers patrolled the lanes, holding traffic to a patriotic 40.

Price

About $5 million for the upper six miles, opened in 1940. A total of $12 million by the time the final 2.2-mile link to the four-level interchange was done in 1953, before the name was changed to Pasadena Freeway, and the Ramona Freeway renamed the San Bernardino. Says Baxter: "We've gone from about a million dollars a mile to a hundred million" — the unfinished Century Freeway. The Pasadena will stay the bargain it always was; to straighten it out, to widen its lanes out into parkland on either side, would require difficult engineering, ill-advised politics and impossible expense.

"You always wonder 'what if?' "

Baxter has worked at Caltrans since the great master plan of the 1950s was drawn. Once, he went home to Missouri, but farm-to-market roads held no challenge for him after freeways, and back he came.

In his office is the vast map of freeways built and unbuilt, a vision of 1,200 miles crosshatching the area — the Industrial Freeway, the Beverly Hills Freeway and one or two whose names he has forgotten. About half were built, most in the great years of the 1950s and '60s, before gas shortages and inflation.

There, on the wall, is the stub of the Pasadena, the first, and the Century Freeway, maybe the last for a long time.

"If we had built more Pasadena Freeways to a lower [speed] standard and snaked them through the community and had less community impact in terms of land acquisition…. If you get hardheaded about freeways, which I suspect we probably did, and you say every freeway's got to be eight to 10 lanes and every freeway's got to be designed for 70 miles an hour, there's no room for compromise. And it seems to me there's room for compromise. And maybe in some areas you say, 'Why don't we design a four-lane? Why don't we design one that has 50 mph speeds?'

"Everything doesn't have to be the same."

❖

When Loving L.A. Turns to Heartache

Editors' note: In the early 1990s, a series of events raised searing questions of race and justice for Angelenos. Rodney King, an African American motorist who led police on a slow-speed chase, was beaten by officers in an assault captured on video and broadcast around the world. Two weeks later, a video camera was also on hand when Latasha Harlins, a South-Central teenager accused of shoplifting, was fatally shot by a Korean grocer. The grocer was convicted of voluntary manslaughter and sentenced to five years' probation, but served no jail time. A jury acquitted four white officers of most of the charges in the King case, touching off riots in the spring of 1992.

. . .

A woman who adopted this city as a student sees its myths unmasked. And she knows the rebuilding must be of the soul as well as the structures.

By Patt Morrison • May 5, 1992

I came here two decades ago to go to college. My mother and father ran out of fingers ticking off the reasons I shouldn't. Charles Manson. Smog. Bobby Kennedy. Bobby Seale. Earthquakes. Drugs. Watts. Freeways.

The smog was so bad that for the first month I didn't know the San Gabriels existed. Then it lifted for a brief, clear autumn moment before the Santa Anas whipped the smoke of burning shake roofs back to where the smog had been.

On the sidewalk outside the old Hall of Justice, I stepped uneasily past girls my own age, girls with shaved heads and "Xs" hacked into their foreheads, to sit in the courtroom where Charles Manson was sentenced to death, his mad eyes raking us like lasers.

I got my first bite of tear gas during the SLA vs. LAPD match. My first earthquake knocked down the shelf I had unwisely built over the head of my bed. If I hadn't already been awake, I could have been killed by my own books, just as I could have been killed by my own typewriter 10 years later, when my car got hit on the freeway. It rolled down the No. 4 lane like a big steel die, and my typewriter — which was in the back to go to the repair shop — was tossed around too.

It missed me. But what a great reporter's obit it would have made; I repeated it with bravado.

I never told my folks that stuff. But by God, I loved it. I loved knowing where to get bialys or burritos at 3 a.m., how the SigAlert got its name, and the best songs to ask the mariachis to play. I loved Occidental College's Tudor rose gardens blooming absurdly below Spanish-tile roofs.

And I loved my job. In this big urban midway, journalists went everywhere, fearlessly, with the blithe air of invincibility that reporters share with teenage boys who have new driver's licenses. The only color I was, I assumed ingenuously, was the color of my press tags.

The world had L.A. pegged as the epicenter of mellow, but we knew we were tough. We inhaled particulate matter and held off brush fires with garden hoses and clung to an Earth that tried to fling us off. We could handle anything.

All this time, it turns out, we've been preparing for the wrong Big One. The Earth didn't shake L.A. apart this week. We did that ourselves.

Multiculturalism was the civic mantra, L.A.'s special take on the myth that I chased — we all chased — out here to the edge of the continent: There is enough to go around. My gain does not mean your loss. We can all Make It.

And every sunlit morning, mainline L.A. looked in its mirror and admired its white, educated, prosperous self, its forward-looking, tolerant self — while the other L.A. sat in the closet like Dorian Gray's portrait, getting darker and poorer and angrier.

The fissures of race and class were there, if you bothered to connect the dots. There was no citywide outcry about murdered black hookers, but when the Hillside Strangler started offing "nice" women, there was hell to pay. All of us wrote endless inner-city gang stories, but L.A. didn't "discover" gang warfare until one night in Westwood, when the crossfire killed a young Asian American woman. That raised an outcry; that raised a reward.

Last Wednesday afternoon, we all gathered at the city desk to watch the verdicts read. My heart hadn't hammered in my chest like that since I took my SATs — so much was at stake here.

Not guilty? Of anything? After that tape? I must have made an odd noise, because a black friend glanced over at me. It was the look of tender pity reserved for the last kid to find out that there is no Santa. Poor Patt, it said, now you really get it.

This week, scared, white L.A. got it. So this is what it's like to be incidental in a city that uses you as window dressing for its rainbow PR. This is what it's like to sit in your locked home and wonder whether the sirens you hear are on TV or right out front.

At first I was angry at the white-flight crowd who got the hell out of L.A. to escape from what one of the four cops' defense lawyers called "the likes of Rodney King," and they aren't afraid to admit it. They watched the smoke on TV from the safety of their own R-1, 3 bdr 2 ba, and said, "I told you so." They may be bigots, but at least they're honest bigots.

But then I got angrier at the other white crowd, the right-minded, PC crowd that has piously peddled a sanitized, "We Are the World" boutique multiculturalism of Caribbean music and Native American sweat lodges and Malcolm X hats on $50 blond razor cuts. They preached it at the same time they sent their kids into the safety of private schools. They signed checks at fund-raisers for justice in Central America while the Central American housekeeper in their kitchens couldn't afford to buy the food she was preparing.

They're thrilled to discover a new Nigerian restaurant, but they've never been downtown, let alone to Florence and Normandie. If they have, it's for the Oscars or MOCA or "Phantom of the Opera."

"Phantom" was canceled this week. Another mask, a bigger one, was yanked away instead. What's underneath that one is pretty hideous, too.

I live far east of La Cienega — three blocks from Figueroa. We hear gunshots in our neighborhood, but they aren't next-door. I've bought meals for homeless women, rescued stray dogs, volunteered at my college, played pen pal to a barrio kid, picked up trash off the street.

I thought I was doing all right; to see it written down, now, it looks paltry. For the first time in a long time, I feel very white and very middle class. Somebody said of Mike Dukakis that he may speak Spanish but he doesn't speak our language; suddenly, my good Spanish isn't good enough. My glibness in English sounds mealy-mouthed and tongue-tied. I don't feel so much fearful as inadequate.

Thursday night, Friday night, I drove around with more caution than I'd exercised in years. There was a curfew on, but the police enforcing it drove right by me. If they bothered to look twice, they just shook their heads at the foolhardiness of a white lady driving around after dark.

I haven't cried over a story since the library burned. I didn't cry this time, until Saturday morning, when I saw the guardsmen along Wilshire Boulevard — dear, funky, passe old Wilshire Boulevard. Whatever we thought we saw in the mirror every morning, it wasn't a city fit for martial law.

We're rebuilding this week, as we would after any earthquake, but this is rebuilding soul as well as structures. I haven't heard the power brokers' standard line about multiculturalism; that record got broken last Wednesday. Instead, I see black people rescuing a white man and Asian Americans from a mob, and two days later, white folks in Saabs from San Fernando Valley dealerships bagging broken glass outside a gutted store on Normandie. I don't have any idea how long it can last: maybe only as long as summer camp friendships, maybe only until the TV cameras go away.

But I do know we shouldn't get back to normal. In L.A., normal doesn't work anymore. We don't live in the city we thought we did.

On my way to work, at the corner of two empty streets stood a scruffy young man holding a sign: "Please help — I'm homeless."

Hey, man, today, aren't we all?

· · ·

A third-generation Chinese American comes to a haunting realization about multiracial L.A. For the first time, she feels prejudice — and fear.

By Elaine Woo · May 5, 1992

On Saturday morning, I saw a woman wearing a T-shirt that said, "Love Knows No Color."

Fear, however, does know color. That, I'm afraid, was the rude lesson of last week for many Asian Americans like myself. It is a startling, deeply troubling realization.

I am a native of this city, born 37 years ago at White Memorial Hospital in East Los Angeles. I am also a third-generation Chinese American. In my nearly four decades — living first in the Crenshaw District, then in Monterey Park and now in a community near Pasadena — I never felt fear because of the color of my skin. Prejudice was a remote concern.

But after the not-guilty verdicts were returned Wednesday against the four white officers in the Rodney King case, the city — my city — blew up in a firestorm of racial suspicions. And the whole equation of living and working in multiracial L.A. changed.

Suddenly, I am scared to be Asian.

More specifically, I am afraid of being mistaken for Korean.

Having acknowledged those fears, I feel shame, guilt and an almost paralyzing puzzlement over where to go from here. Family members and Asian American friends made these same admissions to me during the past few days — some quite gingerly because the awareness leads to all kinds of politically incorrect thought.

Ever since last year's rash of shootings involving Korean merchants and black customers, Koreans have taken center stage in the public consciousness of who Asian Americans are. It is not a prominence Koreans asked for or want.

But I raise it because sorting out who Asians are has become a complicated proposition during the past decade, which brought waves of new immigrants to our city, and that sorting out is important if we are to explain the dilemma other Asian Americans feel in the wake of the violence that has rocked us to the core.

When I grew up in the 1960s and '70s, the mix wasn't terribly complex. You had your whites, your blacks, your Latinos — almost exclusively Mexican Americans. And Asians, for the most part, were of either Japanese or Chinese descent. But as a Japanese American colleague pointed out recently, Japanese and Chinese Americans no longer provide the dominant image of Asians.

Today, the Asian man from whom you bought cheap toys on downtown's 4th Street is probably from Vietnam. The pharmacist at your neighborhood drugstore could be second-generation Filipino American. The developer who built the shopping mall where you buy frozen yogurt and submarine sandwiches could be a recent arrival from Taiwan. The attorney who handled the real estate transactions for the mall could be an "ABC" — American-born Chinese. The dentist who fixes your kid's teeth could be an American-born Korean.

Knowing the difference is important to most Asians, who want as much as anyone to be seen as individuals. But we fear our unique cultural identities still aren't recognized by non-Asians — the old "Asians all look alike" trap. We know we're different from each other, but do they? Will it even matter if we're caught on a dark street with an angry person holding a weapon?

To many Asian Americans in L.A., that is a question that haunts.

Here we are, stuck somewhere between the images of the victim and the vigilante. There's the Vietnamese man — a boat person fleeing his country only two years ago — bloodied after being pulled from his car and beaten in a South L.A. intersection. And there are the Korean shooters, brandishing shotguns and automatic weapons to protect their businesses from looters. I suspect the more troubling image for many of us is of the vigilantes.

When I raised this with my ex-brother-in-law, Rich, he blurted out straight away the awful, new truth: "I'm afraid someone is going to take me for a Korean and kill me."

Another Chinese American friend, long involved in civil rights, expressed his anguish over the same unfounded fear.

"I feel vulnerable in the black community because of the fact they might mistake me for something else," he said. "It's that vulnerable feeling among people I respect and love that I find the most troubling. It brings out the racism in me."

A Japanese American colleague, when she found herself thinking along similar lines, mentally kicked herself. Politically incorrect for Asians, who have tried to build coalitions. "God, that's terrible," she said. "We should try to protect solidarity with Koreans.

"But it's different now. Everybody is polarized. I find it real unsettling. What you knew, and who you thought you were, is going through an upheaval."

For a Korean American colleague, there is hope and despair to be found in sorting through last week's eruptions.

Hyung is not embarrassed by the Korean vigilantes and does not believe other Asians should be, either. "I think we need to have that image instilled in mainstream culture," he said, "so they don't think we could be taken as wimpy Asians. What is America? It was won with guns. It was built by individuals who defended their dignity with guns. These Korean vigilantes may help balance the view of Asians. Some are gentle, some are tough enough to stand up for themselves."

A part of me winces every time the television news replays the footage of the Korean gunslingers. But another part of me is with Hyung. I want to shout: "All right!" Stereotypes of Asians as wimps and nerds go up in smoke.

Of course, many Korean Americans were appalled by the vigilantes, just as they — and so many others — could not condone the looting or other violence that impelled the merchants to take a stand. And the countervailing image of thousands of Korean Americans marching for peace Saturday conveyed another important and powerful message that I hope we all absorbed.

At the same time, Hyung said, he could identify with the more generalized fears other Asians express. A Times photographer, he was sent to South Los Angeles on Wednesday evening as the violence spiraled upward. Angry blacks chased him and hurled beer bottles and rocks at him. He fled the area when it became clear they would not let him do his job. The next day, on assignment in Koreatown, he was hassled by Latino youths, who cussed and threw gang signs at him and revved up their engines in a taunting way.

Hyung, who left Korea 15 years ago, grew up among blacks in Inglewood and lives — harmoniously, he thought — among Latinos in the neighborhoods along the Olympic corridor. But he was shattered by their hostility. "I think what has been happening the last few days is the ultimate expression of mistrust and distrust of each other in this city. Suddenly, I'm not welcome in the black community and I'm not welcome in the Korean community where many Latinos want to live. What is the meaning of this? Is this a sign we are supposed to get out of here? Whose land is this? Whose city is this?"

I think much of this soul-searching is peculiar to my peers in the assimilated generation, who can laugh at and feel the sting of recognition in these lines spoken by Chester in the David Hwang play "Family Devotions": "I live in Bel-Air. I drive a Mercedes. I go to a private prep school. I must be Chinese."

So when I explained to my mother how last week's events served as a wake-up call that soundly disabused me of melting-pot dreams, she said of me and my four siblings, "Oh, you people never did feel prejudice."

It's true, we kids rarely encountered the open bigotry that earlier generations did. She recounted how Grandpa Woo, who came to Los Angeles from China in the early 1900s, complained about laws that prevented Chinese from owning property. She recalled how, during her school days in Stockton, all the Chinese students were "stuck in a corner" of the classroom, not allowed to socialize with the whites. And how, in the late 1940s, when she and Dad went house shopping in the Crenshaw area, whites refused to sell to them.

Several years ago, when my brother decided to become a politician, Mom said she warned him: "You're going to run into a lot of racism." She says he scoffed at her, told her she was being racist to even think that.

She was right, though. In campaign literature, the opposition raised the specter of "Chinatown influence" and all that it connotes. When I knocked on doors for him in Hollywood, I remember an elderly white woman shooing me away with the inevitable "Go back to China."

On a second run for the office, he won a seat on the City Council, the first Asian elected to that body in the city's history. I think he's more hopeful about the city's future than I am.

On my way from the parking garage to the office the other morning, I saw a young black woman striding toward me on an otherwise desolate street. In the seconds before our paths crossed, I wondered: Should I smile? Say hello? Would I do so normally? Will she be pleasant in return? Or will she say something hateful because of the color of my skin?

The moment passed, and was lost. I did not look at her. That bothers me, and will for a long time.

. . .

A woman who came of age during the Watts Rebellion sees years of disrespect explode in anger and frustration.

BY JANET CLAYTON · MAY 4, 1992

In August, 1965, I was 10 years old, a then-Negro girl spending the week with her aunt, who lived near 116th and San Pedro. The Watts Rebellion — black people often deliberately call it that, not a riot — erupted nearby while I was there.

On the day after the trouble began, my aunt sent me to a store down the street to stock up on bread, meat and canned goods. "Soul Brother" signs were being nailed to stores along the way, and many of the stores were already shuttered. I didn't think much of it. I figured some people — I wasn't sure who — were just mad at each other and had gotten into a fight. I could see that everyone was nervous, though.

Soon, my parents came and picked us up. We headed home, to 75th Street near Crenshaw Boulevard, well away from the fighting and looting taking place to the south. We would be safe there; there would be no violence anywhere near our neat working-class neighborhood.

But there was a curfew in the riot area — and to my surprise, it was being imposed on us, too. Why? Why were they treating us as if we had done something wrong?

"Janet, you are so lame," my 17-year-old sister informed me. "Why is there a curfew on us? Look in the mirror."

In fact, the curfew was imposed virtually everywhere in the city where black people lived. That's when I began to hear in my head what my Uncle Ray B used to say during Friday-night political discussions in our dining room, when the adults always thought the kids were safely away, glued to the TV.

"What does the white man call a Negro with a Ph.D.?" My uncle would always pause for effect and then draw out the answer. "An ——. Maybe Dr. n ——."

Disrespect. A woman I talked to last week used that as a reason why she, a normally law-abiding citizen, walked into the rubble of a torched liquor store on Western Avenue and picked up a box of cigars. She said she couldn't stand the Korean American owner. I asked her why.

"Because the first time I walked into the store, he didn't say 'Hi' or 'Good morning.' He said 'Hey, Mama' — trying to talk as if he thought that's how black people talk. How dare he! He thought so little of me, thought so little of my community that he didn't even bother to find out the most basic things about us. He took his cue, I guess, from the white people who run this country and diss us daily. So he can take this cue: I didn't start anything at his store. But when I saw all those people in there, when I saw it was going on, I went in there and grabbed some cigars. I don't even smoke them, but somebody's gonna have a smoke on Mr. 'Hey, Mama.' "

Sounds like a petty reason to gloat over a man's lost business? In isolation, it is. Except nothing is in isolation. This woman is unemployed. She is, as she described it, "pissed off a lot." There is something about not having money, and not having any legitimate prospects for getting it, that makes you mad, irritable, resentful. There's nothing race-specific about that.

But there is something race-specific about other little hurts and indignities that can pile up on African Americans. Although many Americans really don't believe blacks still suffer prejudice, people who study these things say we do — and in consistently virulent ways. It plays out in most cities as cabbies zoom by us to pick up white passengers; as store clerks often assume we are thieves; as many whites cross the street or clutch their bags when they see a black man walking toward them.

I'm reminded of the time Condoleezza Rice, a top Soviet adviser to President Bush and a black woman, was shoved and shooed away by government agents who assumed she was a threat to visiting then-President Gorbachev. I can just hear it: "Oops! You mean you're with the prez? Sorry! Here's your dignity back!"

Here in Los Angeles, the land of image-is-all and air kisses, insults are also disguised as compliments: "Gee," say astonished first-time visitors to West Adams, Baldwin Hills, View Park, Leimert Park, Inglewood, Compton, "your house is actually quite nice!" Or, the personal favorite of my husband and me: "You two are so articulate! You speak so well!" Would any of this be surprising, or merit special comment, if two white, college-educated people lived in a nice house and spoke proper English?

Under normal circumstances, thoughtless remarks are ignored. Most people don't make a big deal of them. But last week, every slight, every rudeness, every wrong added up to be a very big deal indeed.

My niece, Angel, 23, had been watching TV coverage for hours and was fed up with it. She started shouting at the news anchor as if the two were in the same room.

"Encroach!" she said angrily. "This woman says the riots are 'encroaching on the Westside.' Give me a dictionary! Encroach means intrude. So it belongs in our part of town, not hers. Well, forget that, lady."

What's this got to do with last week's riots? It's not just the verdicts in the Rodney King or Latasha Harlins cases that make African Americans in Los Angeles, and elsewhere, feel so violated and disrespected. It's the everydayness of racism and the pretense that it is mainly a thing of the past, not of the present. Everybody loves Magic Johnson, a man most don't know personally — but few want to even drive in the lane next to a car full of young black men who, in many basic ways, are much like him.

Of course, a lot of African Americans in Los Angeles don't really care whether a white person wants to drive near them or live near them. As a matter of fact, many blacks prefer to live in areas where they can recycle black dollars to black business-es and where their children can see black authority figures — teachers, ministers, doctors, lawyers — who will set positive examples and push them to excel. That's why many blacks who can afford to live in other areas of Southern California don't move from South-Central and southwest Los Angeles.

The "Black-Owned" signs that went up on businesses last week expressed more than the current version of 1965's "Soul Brother" signs. Black-owned is an assertion of 1990s "black power," with the emphasis now on economic power.

Last week, after I passed by the rubble at Vermont and Vernon, I had to wonder: Why, in effect, burn down our own community and hurt ourselves just because the system — again — hurt us? Why turn the anger back on ourselves, destructively? Why commit economic suicide?

"Haven't you ever been so mad you hit your own hand and hurt it?" a friend replied. "Why is that so hard for people to understand? It's like a man who is belit-tled and put down by his boss constantly, and then comes home and takes it out on his wife and family. It's not right, but there's a lot of self-hate involved."

Of course, that man in the example doesn't gain power by coming home and abusing his family. He gets it by finding legitimate ways to better his situation. So I felt somewhat encouraged when I saw South-Central residents — and people from other parts of the city — working together to sweep up debris Saturday.

And there's serious talk of organizing to create legitimate moneymaking oppor-tunities, linking people and communities separated by the Santa Monica Freeway divide. Dare we all hope this isn't just another feel-good trendy thing to do in politi-cally correct and privately paranoid L.A.?

When I was 10 and the riots hit, I never dreamed that as an adult I would relive so much of what my parents thought they were escaping when they left Texas and Louisiana. I never dreamed that schools I attended in Los Angeles in the late 1960s and early 1970s would be better integrated than the L.A. schools that will be avail-able to my 3-year-old daughter. I never dreamed that Los Angeles would re-segregate as it has. And I never thought that I would again see my mother scrub as she's been scrubbing this past week.

I've seen her do it before; cleaning and gardening are her ways of keeping herself busy when she is upset or anxious. Gladioli sprouted in record numbers the spring after my father died. This week, her seeding is furious, and she can't seem to use enough ammonia on the kitchen floor.

. . .

A native son's affection for the city is lost amid the flames and the violence. For him, everything has now changed.

By George Ramos • May 4, 1992

Los Angeles, you broke my heart. And I'm not sure I'll love you again.

That's not an easy thing for me to say. I know, I know — reporters are supposed to be detached observers of the routine and the unusual. Notebooks in hand, we are historians on the run, asking the obvious, repeating the answers and wondering — after the story is done — if we really understood what it was all about.

But I'm also a native son, born 44 years ago in a little hospital near the corner of 4th and Soto streets in Boyle Heights. There's an air of pride whenever I tell a listener I wasn't transferred to L.A. like some pro sports franchise.

I know, for example, that real baseball was played at 42nd Place and Avalon Boulevard, where the old Pacific Coast League Angels taught me about balls and strikes long before the Dodgers got here. Ask me about the people of East L.A. and I'll recite a story about somebody I met inside the First Street Store. Ask me how to get from Downey to San Fernando, and I'll tell you how I was taught: Take Florence Avenue toward downtown; hang a right on Broadway and head north to San Fernando Road. Then, turn left and cruise. It'll take you awhile but you'll see more of L.A. than just freeway offramps and billboards.

Long before Randy Newman sang it, I loved L.A.

That, I'm afraid, changed last week when the not-guilty verdicts were returned in Simi Valley.

Everything changed.

At first, I didn't notice. I was too busy being a reporter. Right after the news broke, I interviewed dozens of folks, mostly Latinos, out on my Eastside. At the student union building at Cal State Los Angeles, a black student screamed at the TV set: "How can you look at that video and say those four white officers are innocent! Screw it! We oughta burn this city down!"

Back at the paper, I was taking dictation from reporters out in the field. They were describing frightening images — looting, arson fires, shootings — that reminded me of the violence in 1971 in East L.A. after Ruben Salazar, a Times columnist and news director of KMEX-TV, was killed during a Vietnam War protest march.

My note-taking was interrupted when demonstrators left Parker Center, the LAPD police headquarters, and began trashing downtown, starting with The Times. I rushed outside, to the corner of 1st and Spring streets, to report on the destruction of my newspaper's first-floor offices, when a black man in Raiders garb pointed a gun at me.

After a tour in Vietnam, I thought I'd seen everything. In the years since my return to the U.S., I have tried to discount the increasing violence in my city, most of it the street-gang variety. I guess I hoped that what I wrote about the tearful predicaments of its victims might help change things.

Now, with my own life in the balance, I told the gunman matter-of-factly: "I'm a reporter. I'm taking notes. I'm doing my job. I don't know what you're going to do, but I'm going to do my job."

He didn't shoot. He just picked up a rock, flung it at The Times and ran away.

There was no time to ponder what had happened. There were more notes to take and more hot spots to check out.

By Friday morning, I was hurt and depressed. I looked at the morning edition of The Times and thought: My city is getting trashed and I can't do anything about it. The next time I say "42nd and Avalon," people will forget beloved Wrigley Field and remember instead that it's in South-Central L.A. "Hey, I'm not going there," they'll probably say.

I tossed the paper aside and started "working the phones and hitting the streets" — something that all reporters turn to to get a real feel for what's happening outside the confines of the newsroom.

First, I called Middle America. I called Mom.

She was moved to tears by the TV pictures of the beating of Reginald Denny, the truck driver pulled from his rig in the early hours of the rioting. "How could they?" she cried. "How could they?"

A native herself of Los Angeles, she went on to lament whatever she heard, saw or read about the disturbances.

"These looters never heard of Rodney King," she said. "You see these people on TV? They're proud of what they are doing. Can you imagine? Here in Los Angeles? When you start seeing a breakdown in society, laws don't mean anything. Then you start getting scared."

Mom admitted she was scared.

Then, talking like a Middle American perhaps living in Simi Valley, she reminded me that she was surprised only up to a point by the King verdicts.

"I was very surprised at first, but then after that juror talked about watching that videotape for three months, I kind of understand how they felt. They were doing their duty as best they could."

I wanted to argue, but she's my mother.

I then telephoned the home of Cristal Anguiano, the brave 12-year-old girl who risked her life to save her 2-year-old brother after she was struck in the heart by an errant bullet fired in a gang fight. I wrote about her several times in the weeks following the shooting in February. The family lives near Manchester Avenue and San Pedro Street in South-Central and I wondered if they were OK.

They claimed to be fine, but I won't forget the tone in the father's voice. My heart sank when he said: "I want to stay in Los Angeles but we may have to go back to Mexico. The city is loco."

I had to agree.

Out at Lupe's modest hamburger and burrito stand on 3rd Street in East L.A., the business was brisk but the atmosphere was tense. Lupe Portillo, an aunt of one of the five La Verne Avenue soldiers I wrote about during the Persian Gulf War, said she banned any riot talk with unfamiliar customers because "I don't know who they are.

"They could start something, trash the place," she said.

Wolfing down a chorizo-and-bean burrito, I wondered aloud: "Who'd want to trash this place?"

"Anybody who was loco," was the reply.

Things are getting bad when you can't even have a burrito and a diet soda in peace.

I drove around looking for reassurance in familiar places. Old haunts on Whittier Boulevard, Soto Street, Brooklyn Avenue and Atlantic Boulevard were safe. The First Street Store was open, although the windows were boarded up as a precaution.

Frank Villalobos cornered me after a news conference of Latino politicians at the Hollenbeck Youth Center. He is a community activist who owns an urban planning firm on Beverly Boulevard, and he wanted to remind me that there were signs of optimism in the midst of despair and depression. The landmark Sears, Roebuck & Co. store at Soto and Olympic Boulevard had been looted, but when the young culprits came home with their booty — TV sets and the like — their parents ordered them to return the merchandise.

And they did so, Villalobos said proudly.

The ultimate dose of optimism came from Diane Gonzalez, a diminutive worker on Leticia Quezada's congressional campaign whose voice can match the roar of a jet engine. "Don't you dare call me a political insider," said Gonzalez, who is on leave from the staff of Democratic state Sen. Art Torres of L.A. "I'm a public servant!"

In between pushing her buttons for lively quotes, she told me not to give up hope.

"We need to return to basic values," she began. "God, government, faith in the system, family and respect. I believe in basic democracy."

She argued that those components, coupled with a new president, would make this country a more compassionate place. It would also save my town.

It's hard to argue with her, especially because she is so articulate, so persistent.

But I'm not sure she is right. And it pains me to say so.

People are afraid. They now talk about South-Central L.A. as if it were a territory in Libya. Before the riots, much of the city's population barely tolerated driving through those neighborhoods. Now, they will just avoid the area altogether.

I know how hurtful and divisive this can be. I come from a place that has been treated the same way at times.

"Is it safe to go to East L.A. for dinner or a movie?" I am asked. "Of course it is," I thunder in righteous indignation, "East L.A. is safe. I'm from there."

Now, I'm beginning to understand why the question is asked. That is why I grieve for my L.A.

Tales of the City

❖❖

Miami, So Lovely and Bizarre

Bodies wash ashore. The mayor packs a Beretta. For robbers, it helps to be bilingual. A reporter reflects on 15 years of living amid beauty and covering the macabre.

By Barry Bearak · February 21, 1991

MIAMI — The memories are mostly of beauty and weirdness, of sunbeams that made the bay waters sparkle like a carpet of gems and of news stories that seemed to warp toward the surreal in this city's subtropical heat.

At times, the beautiful and the bizarre layered over each other the way they would in a Salvador Dali painting. Always, the sky was the most luminous of blue; often, the world below the most haunting of dreamscapes.

There was the morning when dead Haitian boat people washed ashore onto the talcum-soft beaches behind the luxury high-rises, first five, then 10, then 20, until every shape in the mesmerizing surf seemed a corpse.

There were the evenings, woefully repeated, when racial combustion lit into ghastly towers of smoke. The police fanned out in riot gear, and the streets took on an unsteady pulse, the pinging of gunfire and the smashing of glass.

There was the night when a hurricane wind sent palm fronds rolling across the sand like tumbleweeds through a ghost town. Civil defense teams rushed to evacuate nursing homes near the oceanfront.

Without medication or caretakers, the confused residents were dispersed into the expedient shelter of a convention hall. I roamed among them with a spiral notebook. Four of them asked me the same question: "Are you my son?"

This has been my job, observer of other people's pleasures and pains, a newspaperman in Miami. Now, after 15 years, as I leave for another place, there is an inevitable incompleteness and an urge to write a few final things.

Did I say the city is beautiful and weird?

Miami is an enchantress who comes on to you with hot breath and moist lips. She likes tourists the best and used to coax them onto the dance floor for a fox trot and a hora, though it is now more often a samba and a merengue.

A metropolitan knockout, the city is confident of its good looks and sunny disposition, yet, at important moments, it somehow manages to appear hideous.

Honchos of the National Hockey League recently met here, choosing sites for new franchises. Miami wanted one. Instead of showing off its pretty face, the city broke out in untimely hives, suffering its fifth riot in a decade.

The previous street rebellion had come in January 1989, a week before Super Bowl XXIII, when 1,500 reporters were in town searching for a pre-game angle. They could watch the sporadic fires from their hotel windows.

That same year, the producers of TV's "Today" show decided to broadcast from balmy Miami, only to endure the worst cold snap since "The CBS Morning News" had tried to do the same thing three years before.

In 1987, Pope John Paul II led an outdoor Mass. He almost made it to Holy Communion before an electrical storm chased him indoors. Lightning cut off the TV transmissions that would have shared his prayers for Miami with the world.

There is a tendency to defend this city, to say it is soulful and fun and a lot safer than presumed. There is not as much shooting as you'd think, you tell people: Really, Miami is a great place. Really, no need to pack heat.

But the convincing is hard. Just reading the newspaper is like watching an Indiana Jones movie. The stunning and macabre are frequent and routine.

People are strangled with dead snakes or murdered in their autos for making a left turn too slowly. Body parts get fished from the bay. A decayed finger is discovered at the prison, wedged in a hollowed-out part of an inmate's Bible.

A buffalo herd is loosed on the turnpike. The school board excuses a first-grader so she can partake in the animal sacrifices of a Santeria priestess. Clusters of police officers always seem to be on trial for homicide.

Miami's elite is alert to such occurrences. When prominent civic leaders David and Dorothy Weaver were burglarized in 1989, an Uzi semiautomatic assault rifle was stolen from their bedroom. David had bought it on impulse.

"It's like when you go to a dress shop and [they] push a particular item," explained Dorothy, recent head of the Chamber of Commerce. "That day I guess the salesman was saying this was the best particular gun to buy."

Miami Beach Mayor Alex Daoud owns four semiautomatic handguns and a night sight. Acting U.S. Atty. Dexter Lehtinen has lost two AR-15 assault-type rifles to robbers.

Thieves stole Miami Mayor Xavier Suarez's car in 1987, making off with the .380-caliber Beretta in his briefcase. He got a new pistol. A few months ago, he flashed it at the intruders who held his wife at gunpoint in the family room.

Eccentricities have come to be a hallmark of Miami officialdom. "Animal House" has nothing on City Hall; nor does "The Price Is Right." In the Hot Suit Case, a Who's Who of spiffy Miami residents — among them a city commissioner, the statewide prosecutor and a police sergeant — were found to have shopped at a duplex with huge racks of clothes in every room. Designer garments carried expensive retail tags from department stores such as Bloomingdale's, but the new prices had been marked down by a very reasonable 90 percent. The formalities of sales tax were over-looked.

"I had no knowledge whatsoever the merchandise could have been stolen," said one of the best customers, Sergio Pereira, then the county manager. "I don't think any-one who went there could have imagined it."

Two years ago, shame even befell the usually heroic Miami Fire Department. Herman Skinner complained after he was handcuffed by several of his fellow fire-fighters; one of them had rubbed his genitals on the bound man's scalp.

At first, this was thought to be an isolated incident of harassment. But city inves-tigators later learned it was a fairly common way to pass time at the station house. The firefighters had a name for it: Scrotum on the Head.

One hot afternoon, a crowd of nearly 500 people, some sipping lemonade and others bouncing children on their shoulders, waited six hours in a shopping plaza for detectives to remove two bodies from the trunk of a gold Lincoln. The deceased had already begun to smell. Police attempted to wall off the gruesome scene with vans, but onlookers crawled under the vehicles or climbed atop their own cars after hurry-ing home for binoculars.

"Only in Miami," was the reaction of many to the event, not because of the dou-ble murder — common enough in other cities — but because of the casual manner of the onlookers. It was as if Miami residents felt entitled to such diversion.

There is a civic pride in the city's wildness, in living in a place of mysteries and intrigues and extremes. People wonder aloud: What is the weirdest thing to happen here? And the choice is most often "the head."

A naked man cut off his girlfriend's head and carried it by the hair through a quiet neighborhood. He finally stopped along one of the city's busiest streets. He hurled the memento at a passing cop.

"Arrest her ... she's the devil!" he shouted as the stunned policeman moved clos-er. The head landed on the ground and rolled a few feet. The man rushed to retrieve it. He threw it again.

Of course, bizarre things most often happen to other people, not to you. The rest of the city watches from a safe distance on the evening news. Only rarely do the inno-cent bear witness. One who did was Jorge Luis Gonzalez.

On a Saturday night, he was taken to police headquarters to tell what he saw of a barroom shooting. He was happy to help, and, after being questioned, he was offered a ride home by Detective Tony Rodriguez.

Just wait here, the detective said. But then there was a mix-up. Rodriguez went off duty, and the witness sat patiently in the unlocked fifth-floor interrogation room for the rest of the day.

He also waited Sunday, then Monday, then Tuesday too. There was nothing for him to eat or drink. He urinated in a plastic foam cup.

"What are you doing here?" curious police officers occasionally asked.

"I'm waiting for Detective Rodriguez," the dutiful witness replied.

Reporters earn adequate salaries, but nothing that would have permitted me to live in Los Angeles in the style I enjoyed in Miami.

My apartment's balcony hovered over the bay. The water view held a backdrop of the colorfully lit downtown skyline and the nation's busiest cruise ship port. Dolphins swam in the front yard, and pelicans sunned on the dock.

Management was obliging, and the upkeep of the pool, sauna and hot tub was superb. It startled me to find a photograph of the building in the newspaper. The government alleged it was part of a cocaine cartel's sizable holdings.

This city holds such occasional surprises: the suburban home that turns out to be a drug lab, the office space used as a base for counterrevolutionaries, the hotel that offers discounts for vacationing Contra "freedom fighters."

In 1988, county commissioners declared Leonel Martinez Day and renamed a street for the socially prominent, politically connected developer.

The honors barely preceded the indictments by a year. Martinez, it turns out, is a drug smuggler. He is also an alleged murderer.

About 40 percent of the people who live here are foreign-born. It is useful to speak Spanish as well as English, and those who have not schooled themselves in at least two cultures can be seriously disadvantaged.

Three masked men barged into the Tequendama Restaurant, one sticking a gun into a kitchen worker's chest. "Where's the money?" the robber demanded.

The man was stymied to answer. "I don't speak English," he apologized. So the gunman turned toward two waiters, who also failed to understand. All around, people were shrugging. Finally, the exasperated thieves left.

Moises Faroy, a recently freed political prisoner from Cuba, settled his family into a modest Miami home, and most of them were watching TV when detectives came to the front door.

The investigators merely wanted to ask a few questions about a kidnapping, but to the Faroys, the sight of armed men meant only one possibility: Castro's agents were there to kill them. Faroy's brother opened fire with a pistol.

In the ensuing gun battle, Moises hid his young son in a bedroom closet and then hurriedly made a phone call. Finally, he too joined in the fierce shootout until a high-powered slug ripped through his chest and killed him.

The number he had dialed was 911, pleading for the police to help.

The most important man in this city's history has not been here in 35 years. He resides in Havana. On weekends, dozens of Cuban exiles gather in the Everglades, wearing Army surplus fatigues and practicing to kill him.

Fidel Castro's Communist revolution inadvertently transformed Miami from a dowdy resort into the prosperous capital of Latin America. In 1960, only 5 percent of the city was Latino; now the percentage is nine times that.

The immigrants are primarily Cubans. They hate the bearded Red brute who uprooted them. It is as if Judas himself were alive, operating the business he began with his 30 pieces of silver.

In 1986, a rumor skipped lip to lip that Castro had died. Radio stations broadcast the hopeful news. There was dancing in the streets, and people broke open the good whiskey.

As things turned out, Fidel had only given up smoking cigars, a possible sign of ill health but nothing decidedly fatal. Still, it got officials to thinking. What will Miami do when the Cuban dictator falls?

Since then, there has been planning. The celebration will be tremendous. It is expected to take place in the Orange Bowl.

Miami is notorious for race riots; there is one about every two years. This owes to the horrid poverty and powerlessness of the city's blacks — and also to the periodic killing of unarmed black men by white police officers.

In 1980, four cops were acquitted after they were accused of beating to death insurance man Arthur McDuffie. The all-white jury agreed that something very wrong had happened, but the details were so hard to sort out it simply let everyone go.

Eighteen people — black and white — died in the cruel, spontaneous violence that followed. I recall running toward a crowd of people who were battering automobiles, overturning them and setting them ablaze. My aim was to gather quotes to explain their fury. The verdict had outraged me too, but in my ardor I overlooked the obvious, that I was easier to pound on than a car. Only the coincident arrival of 50 police officers rescued me.

Two years later, I again found myself in the midst of inflamed resentments and burning vehicles. Three black teenagers walked toward me. As a white man trying to calibrate the racial heat, I sensed danger. But I kept still.

This motionlessness was rooted — I hope — in humanism. Who knew for sure what these teens wanted? I thought it wrong to make a hasty judgment.

As they got closer, the one in the center became the spokesman. He pulled a brick from behind his back and said: "We want what's in your pockets."

I had once been a competitive sprinter, and my guess was that I could race away. This presumption turned out to be correct, though there was an obvious flaw to such a hastily devised escape. I did not outrun the brick.

Why did I stay in Miami so long? This is a fascinating place, a good news town, so beautiful and weird. But 15 years? Why?

Sometimes, I think I chose to stay because of that inexplicable wisdom known as intuition. Good things seemed about to happen. And indeed, in my last years here, I married. We have a child. The Earth spins reliably on its axis.

But other times I think the strong glue that held me was nothing more than inertia. I don't lead my life so much as follow it. Life does the leading.

So who knows? Maybe I was only waiting for the sheer sake of waiting — obediently waiting, as people do, for the return of Detective Rodriguez.

❖

Naples Puts On Its Best Face

Although the Italian port wallows in corruption, crime and decay, VIPs see a sanitized view of a city that is trying to clean up its act.

By William D. Montalbano · July 7, 1994

NAPLES, Italy — The question being tested here under the volcano is whether, beginning with one world-important and summer-scorched weekend in July, it is possible to hew order from the chaos called Naples.

Will President Clinton, who arrives Friday, find a historic and beautiful city that is belatedly recovering its health and pride? Or will he and leaders from the six other richest nations see hastily applied makeup caking an urban corpse as the setting for their Group of Seven meeting this weekend?

Reform Naples! O sole mio. What a giggle. Easier to stay the tide.

But don't laugh too hard. Overdue change is afoot in Italy's messiest metropolis. Reforms are being launched, and some serious people are taking them seriously: "I have begun to stop for red lights," said Tullio Pironti, the city's last remaining book publisher. "I used to feel stupid if I stopped, because nobody else did."

Whether this sudden modernization will outlast a limelit international gathering is the real question. Although the Italian government, the Secret Service and Neapolitans themselves will make sure Clinton sees no trace of it, there is an ever-lasting seamy side of Naples: When I exclaimed at a white-bearded body in blue jeans lying in the gutter, my cab driver scarcely braked, explaining, "No, he's not dead, that's Alfonso, who's quite comfortable there. He's a habitue. Alfonso drinks and drinks. I think he drinks to forget."

Oblivion and disorder, thy name is Napoli.

Little moves under the broiling sun except hands jammed on horns. Motorbikes weave on sidewalks around pedestrians, pickpockets, con men, preteen apprentice hoods called *scugnizzi*. Vendors hawk African gewgaws, Miami Dolphin hats, smuggled cigarettes and pirated copies of X-rated movies.

Naples' throbbing streets are home to a nasty branch of organized crime called the Camorra, and support some of Europe's highest official unemployment and worst civic services. Naples is a noisy, noxious, insufferable and dangerous city that often seems more of the Third World than the First.

And yet …

Neapolitans agree that their city is ungovernable and unlivable, but 78% tell pollsters they'd never leave. Naples is a madhouse in which nothing ever works, a stress-and-angst factory in which suicide is almost unknown.

It is a slums 'n' squalor, palaces 'n' princes southern port, with world-class architecture and museums. That kid on the corner may steal your watch while your park bench neighbor is reading Pliny the Elder in Latin. And how can anybody stay angry at a city in which one sips cappuccino while watching clouds play atop the Vesuvius volcano on the far side of a fairy-tale bay?

Naples may even seem quite magical from Bill Clinton's sanitized view of it in the (Enrico) Caruso Suite of the Hotel Vesuvio at the heart of a newly coiffed city core, where the G-7 participants will live and meet for three days beginning Friday. Christened the "red zone" and closed to traffic, it will perhaps be the most protected place on Earth until Sunday night. Even residents on foot need a special pass to get into the area.

The security and the fresh paint are symptomatic: What a difference a year can make! Last summer, Naples touched bottom, befouled and overwhelmed by corruption and decay. Uncollected garbage festered, few traffic lights worked, potholes swallowed roads, the water was brown, the city government wasn't paying its bills.

The crisis marked the local climax of a national scandal in which political parties, organized crime and big business were belatedly caught conspiring to get rich at public expense. Lire flowed into Naples by the billions: Special funds for a 1974 cholera epidemic, a 1980 earthquake and the 1990 World Cup came in a torrent. Many repairs and projects were started: a sports palace, schools, a new Justice Ministry building. Hardly anything was finished.

"It was like the pyramids. The question was not when a project would be finished, but how long it could be kept alive to eat money," newspaperman Vito Faenza said.

Change began August 6, when Prefect Umberto Improta, the Italian government's senior representative in Naples, dissolved the feuding, corrupt and inept city government to remedy what he deemed a lack of public order.

Improta, formerly police chief in Milan and Rome, does not take kindly to civic malfeasance. During the past two years, he has dissolved 16 local governments in the region around Naples for having links to the Camorra and 40 others for administrative paralysis. In Naples, Improta named administrators to run the bankrupt city until elections could be held in November.

Before that, though, then-Prime Minister Carlo Azeglio Ciampi, himself an interim technocrat, amazingly asked Improta if Naples could possibly host the annual meeting of the world's seven largest economic powers plus their newfound Russian ally.

"I said yes, if certain things were done first," Improta, 61, said in an interview. The central and regional governments dutifully anted up about $35 million for infrastructure preparations.

When the mayoral elections came, Naples, like most other large Italian cities, turned to the left in protest against corrupt establishment parties. Antonio Bassolino, 47, a longtime apparatchik of the former Italian Communist Party who now leads its Social Democratic successor, defeated right-winger Alessandra Mussolini, granddaughter of the former dictator.

Naples' new mayor cut his political teeth on fierce partisan politics. But Bassolino has proved an unabashed Naples booster, reaching across party lines in search of renewal.

"I've been critical of him, but as mayor, Bassolino has certainly overcome his combative past. He has appointed a good team of people, and he understands that restoration cannot be done by government alone," said Cesare De Seta, a Neapolitan author and history of architecture professor.

Together, Improta, the crusty ex-cop-turned-administrator, and Bassolino, the rookie reformer-mayor, are proving an effective odd couple.

They have begun stitching the southern metropolis of 1.2 million people back together: Public works contracts are now let on a fixed-price basis in a blind draw of competing companies — a revolution in the Italian context.

"Work is being finished in record time and at great savings — 55 percent to 60 percent cheaper than in the past," Bassolino said in an interview. "Everybody is interested in making the city look good. For G-7, Naples wants to prove itself to the world."

Repaving of the main bayside road, a civic priority for decades, is finished. The Piazza del Plebiscito and the Via San Carlo have been redone and antiqued to restore them to the way they looked in the early 19th century, when Naples, home of a ruling Spanish king, stood with Paris and London in the front rank of European capitals.

The 17th-century Royal Palace, where the G-7 leaders will meet in the tapestry-draped Hercules room, has had its face lifted along with a number of major thoroughfares and buildings including City Hall.

"The city is recovering. There's a new spirit of collaboration. We must show that the government keeps its promises. To combat decay, antipathy and indifference is the best way to fight crime," Improta said.

Cops are giving traffic tickets; trucks are towing illegally parked cars. Bassolino has reopened half a dozen parks. Improta has overseen the refurbishing of 280 schools. This month, Naples Police Chief Ciro Lomastro astonished and outraged 160 phantom city workers who collect pay for jobs they never go to — a hallowed Naples scam. He had them arrested.

Naples patriot Jean Noel Schifano, director of the French Institute that teaches French language and culture, sees marked improvement in the life of a city he loves and has written about extensively.

There is poverty aplenty, but some appearances are misleading: Swiss patients come for eye operations at one Naples clinic, Schifano says. Tens of thousands of the nominally unemployed in fact work hard in businesses and industries that do not officially exist — and therefore pay no taxes.

"Things are getting better. You can take a Sunday-morning walk by the sea and smell the sea. Ten years ago, people were afraid to go out at night. Now there is nightlife again. We are going in the right direction. This is how Naples used to be," Schifano said.

Wrong, says 78-year-old philosopher and social commentator Luigi Campagnone, a lifelong Naples resident: "I never go out anymore because I cannot bear to see Naples. It's unlivable.

"People go into raptures about the music, sky, sun, sea, sand. Lies, all lies. I define Naples as a collective infection. Two weeks after G-7 it will be exactly the same mess as before," Campagnone said over coffee at his home recently. "I was here during the Naples uprising in the war, when kids leaped bravely on German tanks and some got killed. Three days later, the Americans came, and these same kids were selling their sisters and mothers to new soldiers. It's a stupid, diabolical city."

In context, says Neapolitan sociologist Domenico De Masi, Naples is no stranger to big international gatherings — or the fact that little lasting good usually survives them. The Roman emperor Tiberius held ancient-world versions of G-7s on the island of Capri off the Naples coast, he says.

"Greeks, Romans, Renaissance princes, 16th- and 17th-century kings have always met here — it's an excuse for a party," De Masi said.

Others are less skeptical. Surveying clean streets blessedly free of cars one morning this week, Fulvio Milone, a longtime newspaper correspondent based in Naples, says nobody expects the G-7 overhaul to be the opening salvo in a social revolution. "Rather," he said, "it could be a trampoline toward renewal."

Bassolino and Improta recognize that they are sailing against the wind of both history and expectation, but they are not discouraged. "We will change the cultural and civic image of the city," Bassolino promises.

Improta, whose security forces have been nearly doubled to about 11,000 for G-7, says crime rates have fallen dramatically in the past two years, 50 percent in some cases.

One works project that is finished is the big, new Secondigliano prison in the northern reaches of the city. Its denizens include not only former political grandees snared by corruption investigations, but also Camorra bosses corralled by better police work and more vigorous judicial prosecution.

"We still have a long way to go, but I think we have turned the corner," Improta says.

From their different perspectives, Bassolino and Improta both point to what appears to be a changing perception about the role of government in Naples: Some grudging respect appears to be growing among a people that has historically mocked and undermined authority.

"I think Bassolino is trying to say that Neapolitans have their dignity and can take on formal commitments," sociologist De Masi said. "There are those magic moments in which a group of people becomes open to change.... Bassolino seems to offer some hope — a little brake in a fatal descent."

Neapolitan jewels long obscured by urban blight are beginning to reassert themselves. On Sunday now, cars are banned on some seaside roads, and Neapolitans gather along them to promenade. A private volunteer group arranged to open about 200 often-closed churches, museums, monuments and archeological sites one weekend this spring. They drew nearly 1 million people.

Recently, inspecting the city's often-shut archeological museum — one of the world's best — Italian Prime Minister Silvio Berlusconi noted that he had never been there before.

Naples will never be Florence. But it will always be Naples, a vibrant and gritty port whose people long ago learned that survival, tolerance and hospitality are three of life's great virtues.

Fingers crossed, the reforming mayor of a reawakening city quietly tells visitors that in recent months, Italian and foreign tourists have begun to return to Naples for the first time in many years.

Times Rome bureau researcher Janet Stobart contributed to this report.

❖

The Lowest Crime in New York

Lawyer, courier, porter, pauper — fare-beaters all. In the sweaty subway they jump turnstiles, enter via exits and worse, much worse. Deep down, this is what the city is like.

By Barry Bearak · June 4, 1991

NEW YORK — There they go, great gusts of people, some numb as sleepwalkers and others growling like curs, a sweaty herd of humanity entering the dank underground that is America's biggest subway.

Down the steps they descend into the morning rush, toward the deafening screech of the trains, toward the stomach-turning smell of the electric sewer, toward the annoying shuffle of the long, god-awful lines.

They stop. Commuters must first buy a token at a booth and then place it in one of the old mechanical turnstiles. The unwieldy $1.15 fare creates a puzzle of arithmetic with every multiple purchase. Things move slowly.

And there is larceny. In a city of startling extremes, the $1.15 is simply too much for the many too poor to pay, and the line is too long for the many too impatient to wait. On average, one in 13 riders sneaks in — in a ceaseless march of petty crime that costs New York an estimated $80 million a year.

The cheaters are known as fare-beaters. They enter through the exit gates. They shimmy through the turnstiles. They vault over, they limbo under. Imagine this: They stuff the coin slots with paper, then suck out the jammed tokens, their lips a pump atop cold metal that has been touched by a million fingers.

"Won't take long," says Capt. Francis M. O'Hare of the transit police, on a routine sweep for beaters, ready to arrest the first 10 who come by. He is in plainclothes, as are the six officers with him, blending in.

And he is right. It does not take long. The station at 86th Street and Lexington Avenue, on the Upper East Side, offers a mix from the cultural strata. The cops nab nine people who are currently males and one transsexual who used to be.

An 11th suspect is released. He is only 14, a skinny kid with sad, rheumy eyes. The papers in his pocket confirm that he is in a hurry to get to court on a robbery charge. "I don't think he should miss that," the captain says.

Other excuses get only polite nods: Tell it to the judge. One of the first with a breathless alibi is wearing a fine blue suit. He is Thomas McArdle, 28, an attorney for the city's Department of Social Services.

They cuff his hands behind his back and lead him into a hot, grimy women's bathroom taken over as a holding area. He is told to stand near one of the two toilet stalls. Anger turns his face the color of borscht.

"I was in line for 15 damn minutes," McArdle says, his voice all huff and fire, trying to clear himself some moral elbow room. "They got two lousy clerks and only one is working, the other doing whatever it is they do instead.

"So I give up and go to the automatic [token] machines. They got three, and two of the damn things are busted. I try to put my $10 in the one that's left. It won't take it.

"People behind me are telling me to get screwed, you know: 'Give it up, buddy!' Finally, I just did what anyone fed up with the system would do. Out of frustration I went through the gate."

One by one, he is joined in the tiny room by the others. It gets cramped fast. There is Richard Cendo, 26, a sharp dresser in a gray plaid suit. The police stand him next to the yellow-stained sink. He has $83.10 in his pants.

Cendo has shown the cops what he hopes is a clout-laden ID from the New York Times (the former newsroom clerk left the paper in 1989). It did him no good.

"Listen to this," the arresting officer says. "He told me he paid once, over the weekend, and the train didn't come, so he figured he was entitled to even up today."

The rest are lined up against the walls. There is Edgar Velez, an express courier. There is Tyrone Slade, 18, a high school student earning a few bucks delivering flowers. There is Joseph Hagar, 72, a retired porter on his way home from the bank with $239. "This is a bunch of raggedy crap," he says.

There are four paupers — ages 26, 35, 50 and 53 — their pockets empty of a single penny or identification or any other latchkey to the social order. There is the transsexual, Demetrice Haywood, a homeless panhandler.

"Constellations are against me, entire revelations to be classified," she mumbles to herself in a mad, disjointed rap. Her clothes are filthy, her hair matted, her skin leprous with mange. They let her go with a citation.

Capt. O'Hare explains: "She's a token-sucker, but not a bad one; she doesn't give the people in the fare booths much trouble. Besides, if we take her in, we've got to spray everything for lice."

Ah, New York. They say this is the city that never sleeps, but that's just because the garbage trucks and ambulances make noise all night long. This is urban America to the nth degree. It has a great and horrible subway.

At its best, the system is all rumble and blur, the trains speeding beneath the traffic-clogged streets 24 hours a day — every day — only a few minutes apart during rush hour. They stop near almost everything, a marvel of convenience.

Some 3.7 million people ride them on weekdays. The routes feed into each other like arteries on an anatomy chart. They cover 236 miles, second only to the London subway. New York spends $130 million a year just for the electricity.

At its worst, the system is an octogenarian geezer that goes out more often than a trick knee. Uncertainty prevails. A crackly voice on the station loudspeaker making some unintelligible announcement is the dreaded omen of 30 minutes shot to hell.

Societal rot is here in all its awful vaudeville. Hundreds of the homeless inhabit the tunnels. Pickpockets let their hands browse amid the crowds. Ads on the trains are a mosaic of personal misadventure: drug treatment, victim hot lines, laser therapy for anal warts.

The transit cops on subterranean patrol make up the sixth largest police force in the nation. The job is formidable. Besides muggers, drunks and gangs, there is the bloody debris of the pushed and fallen.

Two riders died on May 17 alone. One tripped while lurching for the Uptown No. 4. Another hit a concrete overhang as he hoisted himself for a thrilling look from atop the Downtown 6. A third rider lost a hand while hopping between cars on the Uptown 5. Service was disrupted for an hour as workers searched for a missing finger.

Then there are those fare-beaters. No other U.S. transit system reports even a fraction of the problem of New York. It is embedded in the municipal culture, as visible a part of subway life as derelicts taking a snooze.

Scams are abundant. Thieves get keys to out-of-use entrances, open up and collect fares from those who mistakenly follow. In 1987 and 1988, $4 million in tokens was stolen right out of the turnstiles until the collection bins were replaced with heavy steel vaults.

"Here at 116th Street hardly nobody pays," said Levi Bell, an occasional token-sucker indiscreetly working the B and C lines. He uses matchbooks to jam the coin slots. He sells the stolen fares on the street for 75 cents apiece.

"Yes, I know it's unsanitary," he says of his craft. He is a tall, older man with red lines in his eyes like the squiggles on a polygraph. "Hard times makes you do it. Anyways, I've kissed women that's worse."

The fare-beaters' best pals are the turnstiles themselves. Most are about 40 years old, mechanical sentries long obsolete against modern wile.

The transit authority has proposed buying a $670-million fare collection system from Cubic Corp. in San Diego. Cards would replace tokens. Passageways would be narrowed at the bottom to inhibit crawlers, inclined at the sides to stop leapers. A light would flash when the machines were stuffed with paper.

"Yes, I've heard something about that," the token-sucker says. "It will be a challenge, yes. But you wait. This is New York. People will find a way."

The transit police have converted buses into mobile booking centers. Right on the street, the accused are checked for priors, their fingerprints taken, their photographs shot, their addresses verified.

Forms are completed: desk appearance tickets, arraignment cards, court availability schedules, pre-arraignment notification sheets, supporting depositions, field investigation work-ups, online booking arrest reports.

Four hours of processing await the alleged fare-beaters. And there they go, out of the women's room and up the stairs onto the sidewalk, led in manacles two by two toward the bus. The crowds wonder just what kind of criminals the cops have got here: Hey, look — they've busted two guys in suits and ties!

Once inside the portable jail, most of the arrested men remain quiet. For them, this is just another hitch in a long run of woe. But the two in ties are different. They still can't believe it.

They protest. "Let's talk morals," says Richard Cendo, the sharp dresser with the outdated New York Times ID.

"OK, let's talk morals," says Capt. O'Hare.

"You're supposed to be providing a service. I can't count the times the trains have broken down on me. In the aggregate, the system owes me money."

"Listen, we handle an enormous volume of people. We handle 250,000 a day just coming through Grand Central Station."

"That means you have a larger economy of scale. You ought to be able to do better than other transit systems. But you don't. Look at Washington, D.C. There's never a line in Washington, D.C."

The captain considers this. He is likable and talkative, a heavyset man, 27 years on the force. "But the important thing about your situation is that you took something without paying," he says earnestly.

That is logic that appalls the attorney, Thomas McArdle: "Not pay. Not pay! Eighty percent of this system is federally and state subsidized. I pay taxes. I pay a lot of taxes!"

"Yes, but you didn't pay the fare today," Capt. O'Hare answers.

"The line was so long it was going up the stairs. You picked the busiest time of the day on one of the busiest days of the year to make your arrests. Some would consider that entrapment."

"It wasn't entrapment."

"It was enticement."

The captain shakes his head no. Can't they understand it? The case is open and shut, airtight as a coffee can. These guys know the law. They got caught.

Every year, some 28,000 fare-beaters get summonses; they are allowed to mail in the $60 fine. Others, about 1,600 a month, get caught in arrest sweeps. They are given a court date and usually end up paying a fine or performing community service, scraping the crud off the subway station floors.

"Why don't you just buy your tokens in ten packs?" O'Hare suggests amiably. "That way you've always got one."

But Cendo wants to talk morals again. "Is cheating the city out of $1.15 really worth all this?" he asked. His right hand is cuffed to the metal handgrip of the bus seat. "If I was speeding in a school zone, endangering children's lives, all I'd get is a traffic ticket. Is this justice?"

The captain rubs his chin. He wants to select just the proper response.

"Let me ask you," he says finally. "Will you ever do this again?"

"No."

"There you are. There you are."

❖

A PhD for Would-Be Cabbies

London may be unique as a place where standards in a major urban service industry refuse to be eroded — as exam-plagued aspiring 'black-taxi' drivers know too well.

BY CHARLES T. POWERS · OCTOBER 15, 1992

LONDON — The setting is grim, and the air stifling with tension. Six men sit on straight-backed chairs in a small waiting room, wearing dark business suits, white shirts and neckties knotted with noose-like firmness. No smile is visible here. Pulses pounding, they wait, as for the executioner's summons.

Eventually, it comes.

"Mr. Hollands, please."

Barclay Hollands, 24, stands up and, with as much confidence as he can muster, strides down the hallway.

"Good morning, Mr. Hollands. Be seated, please."

Another small room, another straight-backed chair placed directly in front of a high-fronted desk behind which a man sits, hidden except for his head and shoulders.

"All right, Mr. Hollands, the London Metropole Hotel to Wormwood Scrubs Prison."

No, this is not a sentencing, despite the inquisitional design of the setting. Hollands replies: "Harbet Road to Ducane Road. Leave by hotel forecourt. Right into Harbet Road. Left Praed Street. Left into Harrow Road. Forward the Westway…."

Ten minutes later it is over, and Hollands is released to the bracing air of the street, where his elation (fist punching the air, the folds of his stylishly baggy black suit flapping maniacally) might even infect passing motorists.

"I just flew," he says, "I just flew. Hit the elephant and went. Brilliant, boys, brilliant."

Among his mates on the street, Hollands' tap dance of joy is witnessed with a mix of envy and understanding, for, after 19 months of toil, he is now only a few weeks from his goal: a London cabby's license — the green-enameled, numbered medallion that hangs around every cabdriver's neck, the symbol of his struggle with, and his eventual mastery of, The Knowledge.

There are 20,000 or so licensed cabs in London — the famous "black taxis" —

and the driver of every one has gone through this ordeal, taking, in extreme cases, as long as five years to complete. It has been done in less than a year, but so rarely that examples of such dedication and brilliance tend to the legendary. The average struggle with The Knowledge is between two and three years.

The Knowledge is focused on an area within a six-mile radius of Charing Cross Station in the center of London, and involves some 15,000 miles of twisting streets and the names of some 25,000 streets, buildings, parks, monuments, apartment blocks, pubs, hotels, subway stops — a seemingly infinite number of places, called "points" by the examiners of the Public Carriage Office.

"You will know these 25,000 points," chief examiner-designate William Mayhew told a class of 17 appropriately daunted potential taxi drivers recently, "or you will not become taxi drivers. What you have to remember is that no one has ordered you to become cabdrivers. You will comply with our standards, and we will not lower our standards for anyone...

"You are about to undertake the hardest work you've ever done in your life," Mayhew told them. "Statistically speaking, about nine of you will not make it. One or two of you will be injured in the process, so seriously that you will have broken bones. Also, statistically, two of you will get divorced while learning The Knowledge."

Grim stuff. As far as anyone here knows, the system of licensing London taxi drivers is unique, and this city is perhaps the last place in the world where the standards in a major urban service industry refuse, stubbornly and sometimes under pressure, to be eroded.

In fact, the taxi industry now clings to The Knowledge as a prime reason to retain exclusivity in the London market. In the past 10 years, cheaper mini-cab services have eaten into the revenues of black-taxi operators, launching what some in the business refer to as "the taxi wars."

Although a few taxi fleets do exist, most London taxi drivers are independent owners and operators, and indeed cite the independence of the job as one of its leading attractions. Their cabs have no connection with the government, apart from the rigorous control exerted by the Public Carriage Office, the licensing authority whose bureaucratic forebears date to the time of Oliver Cromwell in the mid-17th century.

The mini-cab services — which use passenger cars, ranging from economical Ford sedans to luxury limousines — began operating more than 30 years ago, largely in suburban areas where taxi service was sparse, thereby filling an economic niche. Gradually, though, the mini-cab services moved into the central city, focusing on telephone orders for runs to the airports, then on getting sweetheart deals with nightclubs or hotels.

"Back when there was an economic boom, through the mid-1980s, it didn't matter much," said Stuart Pessok of the Licensed Taxi Drivers' Association. "But as times have gotten tougher, so has the competition, and that's when the mini-cabs tried hard to make inroads into the business, working hotels, air terminals, theaters, nightclubs. They started using two-way radios. Now, the basic problem is that there is no legislation covering them."

In the Thatcher era, when the watchword was to restrain government intervention in the marketplace, the licensed taxi industry had a hard time getting a sympathetic ear in the dispute. Now, under ex-Prime Minister Margaret Thatcher's successor, John Major, the Transport Ministry is studying legislation that could result in some form of licensing for mini-cab drivers.

The Public Carriage Office is largely manned by former Scotland Yard police officers, and every applicant for a taxi license undergoes a rigorous background check. The mini-cab drivers are given no such scrutiny, the black-taxi drivers point out, nor are their cars made to pass any inspections.

But the argument that may carry the day for London's licensed cabbies is The Knowledge, the trial-by-traffic and rigorous examination that drivers remember, with horror and pride, for decades after they have passed it.

"God, yes, I remember it," said Joseph Cane, 67. "I did it 40 years ago, and I still remember it. Took me 13 months. Didn't do anything else. Went out and made the runs on a motorbike, then sat with my mates calling over the runs. Did it 12, 14 hours a day. Had a map of London taped on the ceiling over my bed. Used to have to go to the Public Carriage Office for examinations at 6 a.m., sometimes sit there for hours. Men would get so nervous they would throw up. One man, I remember, sat there for hours, and when they called his name he stood up and fainted dead away."

Although the examinations now begin at the more reasonable hour of 8 a.m., Cane's memory remains an accurate reflection of being "on The Knowledge."

A good deal of the tension results from the demeanor of the Public Carriage Office examiners, who proudly quote a visitor's remark that their office operated "like the last outpost of the British Empire." The strict adherence to standards is, as much as anything, a matter of tradition, enforced by the office and accepted by the taxi industry. When a visitor remarked that the examiners were a bit like Supreme Court justices, one of them joked in reply: "A bit higher, actually."

The examiners all wear dark, judge-like suits to work and expect the same of the applicants showing up for an examination appearance. (Mayhew to entering applicants: "Those of you men who have various bits of jewelry hanging from your ears or other parts of your anatomy, I suggest you get rid of them before you show up here again. You are adults now, and we expect you to look like adults.")

Applicants are given a booklet with 468 "runs" (examples: Manor House Station to Gibson Square, Gray's Inn to Victoria Park), and before they finish, they must be able to "call over" to the examiner those 468 routes, street by street and turn by turn, following the nearest course to a straight line. The catch is that examiners seldom use the starting points or destinations listed in the book, but will name a building or street in the general area. If the applicant isn't able to remember where it is, he misses the question. No arguments are allowed. A simple "Sorry, sir," is the only acceptable reply. "We're testing their character," Mayhew says. "We don't want drivers who lose their tempers, who get rattled. We figure if they can take what we dish out, they can handle anything out there on the streets."

The only way to pass the series of examination appearances, which progress at intervals ranging from 56 days to two weeks, is to get out on the streets, usually on a moped or motorcycle, and do the runs. Not only do the runs, but search out buildings and alleys and mews along the way and surrounding each point.

"You don't have time for anything else when you're on The Knowledge," said Tim Overington, 35, a former milkman who worked 90 hours a week to learn The Knowledge and hold down his milk route job. He dropped the milk route six months ago and has lived on welfare for the last, intensive push to win his license. Now, after 3 1/2 years, he is facing his final exam. Except for the driving test (which has a 51 percent failure rate itself) and a much less rigorous test for knowledge of suburban routes, he is getting close to receiving his license.

"You find that you lose all your old friends," Overington said. "The only friends you see are your mates doing The Knowledge. You go out and do the runs, and then you sit down with the other guys and take turns calling over. That's all you have time for."

Overington has buddied up with John Howard, 26, and Sim Yiannikaris, 30, and they meet every day before noon at the Mann and Overton "knowledge school" (one of several such enterprises) near the Public Carriage Office, where they spend a few hours sitting over a tabletop map of London, practicing for their appearances before the fearsome examiners. Howard is now on 28-day intervals, Yiannikaris on 21 days.

"It's terrible before an appearance," Howard said. "You have trouble sleeping for a week before. You walk around muttering the names of streets to yourself. It's not only you that suffers, it's your family too."

"A lot of people underestimate it," Yiannikaris said. "They say learning the London Knowledge is like learning a Ph.D. You are supposed to know everything out there, everything that is of public interest. Sometimes you do these runs 15, 20 times.

It's hard to believe, but eventually it begins to stick."

None of these three have been seriously hurt riding their motorbikes around the London streets, but they've been run off the road and over curbs, soaked and splattered for hours in London's sopping weather, trying to cram every point possible into their memory.

Why do it? It's good money. Officials at the Public Carriage Office estimate that the average taxi driver can earn about 10 pounds ($17) an hour. Aspiring drivers hope that's conservative.

"My wife's uncle drives a taxi," said P.E. Evans, 30, who is also, he hopes, weeks away from his last Knowledge exam. "Last week he made 900 pounds, and that was with no weekends and no late nights."

"It gives you a lot of independence," Howard said. "Where else can you earn good money and set your own hours? You want to take the morning off and play golf, you can do it. You want to work, you can do it."

"The three of us here," said Overington, indicating his two study companions, "we're working-class guys. It's a good way up for us. You know, I should have studied this hard when I was in school."

Around his neck, Overington wears a gold chain tucked inside his sweatshirt. On it dangles a gold replica of, naturally, a taxicab.

"If I studied this hard when I was in school, I could have been a lawyer or something. But when you're in school, you don't care about anything. So now," he shrugged, "I'll be a taxi driver. That's pretty good, I think. When I'm finished, I'll be proud."

❖

A Newcomer to Beijing Learns How to Cope

For a foreign journalist and her family, adjusting means living with bureaucracy, co-workers who may inform on you, and doting strangers who are always called uncle.

By Linda Mathews · November 27, 1979

BEIJING — Strangers meeting for the first time in China are less likely to ask each other's name than to inquire politely, "What is your unit?"

That is because China is organized by units — factories, offices or communes — and they are all-important.

Every Chinese has one. His unit provides a citizen of China with the necessities of life — employment, ration cards and housing — educates his children and offers welfare subsidies in his old age. Even the decision to bear a child is usually made by the unit: The married women of the unit decide whose turn it is.

A newcomer to China without a unit feels absolutely lost, as I discovered when I arrived in August to open the Beijing bureau of The Times.

Without a unit, I could not reserve a hotel room, buy a train ticket or apply for ration coupons. "If you don't have a unit, you can't even communicate with other units," fretted my government-assigned interpreter.

The manager of the Peking Hotel, though spurning my request for a room, kindly suggested that as an American, I could get the U.S. Embassy here to be my unit. That was out of the question; as a journalist, I am supposed to maintain my distance from the government.

Another possibility was for the information department of the Chinese Foreign Ministry, the agency that accredits all foreign journalists, to become my unit. But if I didn't want to get too close to the U.S. government, how could I align myself with a unit of the Chinese government?

My interpreter, Hou Ying, supplied the solution. Realizing that the essence of a unit is a rubber chop, or stamp, that can be used to imprint the unit's official name on documents and correspondence, she had made for our office a chop that says "The Los Angeles Times of America" in English and Chinese. With our handsome new

171

chop, we have succeeded in buying plane tickets, renting hotel rooms and running up sizable bills. Our chop is accepted unquestioningly even by the best units.

And, somewhere in the process, Hou Ying, our part-time secretary who is the daughter of a diplomat, and I became a unit.

For a foreigner, the most bittersweet aspect of life here is the realization that the Chinese with whom you are most likely to make friends are those whose job it is to inform on you.

Hou Ying, a cheerful, bespectacled Cantonese woman of 33, has already proved herself a conscientious employee. Besides turning out reams of Chinese-English translations every day, she also spars with the Chinese bureaucracy on my behalf, pre-scribes Chinese herbs for my husband's colds and tolerates the occasional presence of my two sons in the hotel room we must use for an office.

What especially endears her to me is that she is just about as untainted by politi-cal cant as any Chinese I have met. She has a 4-year-old son and confided recently that she never intends to have any more children. "Oh," I said, "is that because of this new government policy that offers financial awards to couples who stop after one child?" She laughed, looked at me as if I were daft, and said, "No, because having a baby hurts too much. Childbirth was the most painful experience of my life."

We had some difficulty deciding what to call each other, but in the end opted for the Chinese custom, on the theory that when in China do as the Chinese do.

In this age-conscious society, Chinese co-workers address each other by their last names but soften it slightly by appending an adjective that indicates whether the other person is older or younger. So Miss Hou, five months my junior, is "Xiao Hou" ("Young Hou"), and seems happy with it. I'm not crazy, however, about being called "Lao Ma," or "Old Mathews."

Whenever I find that I am becoming fond of this woman who is glued to my side eight hours a day, I remind myself that she actually works for the Chinese govern-ment, not for me. That is where her first loyalties lie.

She is paid by the government (about $45 monthly, or one-eighth the sum the government collects from me for interpreter services), and once a week, she disap-pears for a mandatory political study group, where she and other interpreters discuss the latest People's Daily editorials, political campaigns and, I am told, their bosses. Seasoned diplomats here say I should assume that in her cheerful way, Xiao Hou is keeping tabs on me and reporting anything unusual.

Occasionally I sense that in this self-absorbed, xenophobic country, it will be a long time before foreigners are accepted as human beings, not regarded as potential enemies to be kept under surveillance. Sometimes, when Xiao Hou is chattering away in Chinese on the office phone, she refers to me not as Lao Ma or Linda, but as "the foreigner."

Along with gunpowder, spaghetti and printing, the Chinese invented bureaucracy, about two centuries before the birth of Christ. The first bureaucrats were scholars, certified by the Han emperors, who were dispatched to the far-flung parts of the realm to keep official records and administer imperial decrees.

In 30 years, the Chinese Communists have managed to eliminate many feudal traditions, but this country is still one of the most bureaucratic in the world. The average GS-14 in Washington may think he knows something about eliminating responsibility and postponing decisions, but compared with the legions of Chinese paper shufflers, he is a rank amateur.

Most Chinese are resigned to the fact that their government moves with glacial speed, if at all. It takes officials here up to two years to assign jobs to high school graduates. If you ask a young Beijing resident what he is up to, the answer is likely to be "dai fen pel," or "waiting for assignment."

Foreigners brushing up against this system for the first time are often enraged to discover that something as simple as a trip to Hong Kong, 1,200 miles away, requires the permission of four government agencies: the Foreign Ministry, the Public Security Bureau (the police), China International Travel Service and the government airline, the Civil Aviation Administration of China. If there is some mishap along the way — if the airline cannot supply a ticket for the day you told the Foreign Ministry you were leaving — you must start all over again. Naturally, all these stops must be made in person.

And woe unto him who because of illness or other business must cancel his reservations. Even if he calls in advance, he forfeits 20 percent of the plane fare and must pay double for his next train ticket.

The Cultural Revolution of the 1960s, the late Mao Zedong's unsuccessful campaign to rid China of entrenched bureaucrats, has been officially condemned as a catastrophe. But there are moments, usually when I am standing in some long line, when I feel a sympathetic twinge for Mao and wish that I, too, could purge a few bureaucracies.

At least once a month, the frustration of living here leaves me sputtering with rage. Our children, on the other hand, love it. Chinese adults are unfailingly solicitous, even indulgent, of small children, other people's as well as their own. So to 6-year-old Joe Mathews and his 2-year-old brother, Peter, China is a place where strange grownups bestow candy and peanuts, bounce you on their knees and offer to push your swing for hours.

To Peter, every Chinese is a *shu-shu.* That's Chinese for uncle, and children are encouraged to use it or the female equivalent, *aiyi* (auntie), to address all adults. "*Nihao, shu-shu?*" (How are you, uncle?) Peter says automatically to the room attendants, all of them male, on our floor.

The sheer number of *shu-shus* and *aiyis* means that it is impossible for a small, red-haired foreigner like Peter to get lost or hurt. There is always an adult around to keep an eye out.

The first time Peter sped down the hall on his tricycle and failed to reappear, I frantically searched for him, certain he had run afoul of elevators, open windows or other hotel hazards. But I found him in another room, lying flat on his stomach, showing off his Matchbox cars to an appreciative circle of *shu-shus,* all also on their stomachs.

When he goes off in search of amusement and exercise, we know he's likely to be down the hall playing with the *shu-shus* or helping them push the big carts of clean linen.

Eventually he always wanders back, his progress checked by the *shu-shus* along the way.

Joe, a rabid baseball fan, brought his beloved ball and bat and a tattered California Angels program to Beijing, and he has succeeded in transforming a corner of the Peking Hotel parking lot into a baseball diamond.

Batting practice, with my husband serving up pitches, sometimes attracts a crowd of several hundred Chinese. They congregate just behind the evergreens that mark the edge of the parking lot, eager for a glimpse of the American father chasing balls rapped out by his frenzied small son.

Order is preserved by a squad of People's Liberation Army soldiers, their weapons gleaming, who guard the parking lot. Over many weeks, they have become enthusiastic and knowledgeable fans. The drivers of the long Hong Qi limousines that line the hotel driveway have also been drawn into the game. They fetch foul balls and have agreed that whenever Joe's ball strikes their bumpers, it's a ground-rule double.

School for Joe, a first-grader, is a makeshift classroom in what used to be the garage of the U.S. Embassy. The Beijing American School, as it is known, has 13 students and, with three teachers, an enviable student-teacher ratio.

We could have sent Joe to a Chinese school, where foreigners are segregated all day into a separate classroom for intensive Chinese lessons, but decided he ought to become literate in English first. As it turns out, the pupils at the American school diligently study Chinese every Tuesday and Thursday with a local teacher, with good results. Joe can already manage such useful phrases as "hold the elevator, my mommy's coming," but he views the ancient and honorable language mostly as a vehicle for plays on words. It is a source of never-ending hilarity among the first-graders, for example, that in Chinese, the question "How old are you?" sounds almost exactly like the Chinese for "You are an orange soda pop."

The current U.S, view of the Soviet-Chinese-American power balance somehow seeps through at the American school. Joe came home the other day with his latest art project, a 6-foot-long scroll-like drawing of the Great Wall of China, on which he had labored for weeks. Some fierce and ugly figures near the wall were, he reported, "the Russians attacking on horseback." Fighter aircraft with Soviet and Chinese insignia clashed overhead. Atop the wall, repulsing the invaders with crossbows and cannons, were Chinese troops. "They're the good guys," Joe declared.

❖

Private New York Streets: A Walk in Yesterday

On these quaint blocks studded with charming period homes, a visitor can feel lost in another century — a quiet refuge amid the urban din.

By John J. Goldman · December 10, 1978

NEW YORK — With its cobblestones, old-fashioned lights and black wrought-iron gate guarded by statues of two antelopes, the street is a Dickensian delight right in the middle of Manhattan.

The block of small ivy-covered brownstones — only four houses long — stands just off Sutton Place overlooking the East River, but most New Yorkers do not know it exists.

In mood and tone, time has retreated along its sidewalks. Only the hum of traffic on a nearby bridge reminds visitors the scene is the 20th — and not the 19th — century.

"It is a little oasis," said Pamela Simpson, who lives with her family in one of Riverview Terrace's charming small houses. "It is one of the oldest places to live in New York.

"You get more of a feeling of being in a very special, private, removed kind of place. I really feel I am not in the city. You have the little gardens in front. You could be in Paris or Rome or the country. With the river going by, you could think you are on an island. It is really off the beaten track."

Riverview Terrace is not only a cranny from another century, but also a leading example of a subspecies of pavement — the privately owned streets of New York City. Often, on such streets, one can still live in privacy, elegance and style.

Private streets are found in all five boroughs of the city. They range from narrow trash-strewn alleys to enclaves of elegance. The homes on some private streets contain appointments missing in most of Manhattan: spiral staircases, ornate fireplaces (several to a floor), private gardens, terraces, exteriors with old-fashioned lights and cobblestones just outside the front door.

Several private streets are historical landmarks, favored by fashion photographers and movie companies for their picturesque settings. Landmarks include the quaint redbrick Queen Anne-style houses of Henderson Place, a cul-de-sac that poet Carl Sandburg visited, and Patchin Place in Greenwich Village, where E.E. Cummings once lived. On the West Side of Manhattan, tucked away from public view, is Pomander Walk, a page out of Tudor England. It is modeled after a street in suburban London. The London Mews served as the setting for a British play in the early 1900s, and when the show came to New York, the stage set became the model for the Manhattan street with its 16 Tudor houses.

Manhattan has about 30 private streets. The best known, perhaps, is Rockefeller Plaza. That almost-600-foot-long stretch of precious real estate is owned by Columbia University, which leases it to Rockefeller Center.

One day a year in July, to maintain its private character, the busy street is closed to all traffic. A sign is displayed announcing that it is private, and the university receives an affidavit signed by witnesses showing that the street was shut. To minimize inconvenience, it is generally closed on Sunday.

Rockefeller Plaza was part of the architectural plan for Rockefeller Center and was paved as a private street in 1937. It was designed to give adequate light and air to the skyscrapers and to provide spacious entrances and exits for tenants. Maintenance and the street's legal liability rest with Rockefeller Center's management.

Streets in New York City are classified as private when title to the land has not been acquired by the municipal government. Generally, private streets and alleys were developed by their owners or simply came to be accepted as private after years of private use. In most cases, because the streets do not conform in width, alignment or continuity to standards for public streets, the city isn't interested in adding them to public lists.

However, some private streets are owned by quasi-public agencies. Dyer Avenue, an approach to the Lincoln Tunnel, which links Manhattan with New Jersey, is owned by the Port of New York Authority. Cardinal Hayes Place is part of the Manhattan County Courthouse site and is under jurisdiction of the judges of the New York State Supreme Court.

But these are exceptions. The essential character of most private streets is residential.

Dr. Jerome Simpson and his family moved into their three-story home on Riverview Terrace about four years ago. They wanted a small private house with a bedroom suite on the second floor. Their house is only 16 feet wide and was built in the 1860s, but it has niceties not found in newer dwellings. At least two fireplaces grace each floor; a little garden decorates the back. A terrace allows the family to sit outside on warm days and watch the flow of shipping along the East River.

"It's like being on a boat," Simpson said. "When you have a home next to the water, it's like owning acres of land. It's a very pleasurable experience."

Outside the front door, the dead-end street is decorated with trees and bushes. They stand near a small private park overlooking the river. A visitor can quickly feel lost in another century.

Riverview Terrace is 30 feet wide. It first appeared on New York City's tax maps as a private street in 1880. Just outside the terrace's wrought-iron gate are the much larger townhouses of Sutton Place. One theory is that the smaller houses on Riverview Terrace belonged to the servants of the big houses; another holds that the smaller homes once were slaughterhouses.

Riverview Terrace was deliberately laid out to resemble an Old World street. When East River Drive was designed in 1938, the city decided to maintain the privacy of the neighborhood and approached each of Riverview Terrace's homeowners. In exchange for an easement under the private street, the city restored it to its original appearance after the drive was built. East River Drive runs below Riverview Terrace.

For residents of that and other private streets, life carries added responsibilities but also extra conveniences not found on public thoroughfares. Traffic isn't a problem. Parking is private, so spaces are generally available. Policemen don't give parking tickets. Unlike their neighbors just around the corner, residents of private streets don't have to get up before 8 a.m. several times a week to move their cars so the Sanitation Department street sweepers can come through.

That's not always an advantage. Residents complain that their private streets are sometimes dog-walkers' delights. The Sanitation Department doesn't clear away the snow either — a particular pain during last year's harsh winter. Residents of some private streets had to dig themselves out or pay to have their streets cleared. Their garbage is collected by private sanitation companies.

Homeowners on some private streets are on constant guard against parking pirates. These drivers glimpse an empty space on a private street, drive their cars in and leave them.

For a time this was a particular problem on Henderson Place just off 86th Street near Gracie Mansion, the official residence of New York mayors.

"The parking spaces belong to the owners of each house," said Gregory D'Alessio, an art instructor and resident of the street for 20 years. "We used to have a lot of stray cars come in. But we have signs out and leave all kinds of discouraging things in the space."

When some Henderson Place homeowners drive off, they leave a wooden sawhorse behind in their parking space. A phony fire hydrant serves the same purpose on at least one private street. Most private streets have a chain or gate as the chief safeguard.

The costs of repairs to Henderson Place and other private streets are shared by the homeowners, who often form a block association.

A common complaint among residents of some private streets is the cost of home upkeep. Simpson said his taxes were quite high, "in excess of $10,000 a year," and that Consolidated Edison, New York's utility company, had a field day charging him for steam to heat his house. The physician says that some months he is forced to pay for steam that isn't even used.

"You buy a house like this for the pleasure of it," he adds philosophically. "Economically, it's costly."

D'Alessio, who heats his Henderson Place house with a gas furnace, agrees that upkeep can be costlier than on public streets.

"The houses are quaint and so is the plumbing quaint," he complained. "And you call in a quaint old plumber and he gives you a not quaint old bill. The plumbers and the electricians think you are rich on this street and they really soak you."

But he shows no inclination to move from the home, built in 1881, with seven working fireplaces and some rooms connected by sliding doors.

"I don't want to sell. We like it here. It's a retirement from the city," D'Alessio said.

Many of New York's private streets are steeped in literary and artistic history.

Sniffen Court on East 36th Street in Manhattan is flanked by two black iron horse heads with a chain between them. This tiny street is paved with flagstones, and its buildings were constructed in early Romanesque revival style at the time of the Civil War. They were originally used as stables. The rear of the court is the exterior wall of the former studio of sculptress Malvina Hoffman and is decorated with a relief of horses.

Washington Mews, just off lower 5th Avenue, also contains converted stables. The mews stands at the heart of American literary history.

A few hundred feet away lived Willa Cather. Edith Wharton resided nearby. Henry James spent many childhood hours at his grandmother's house on Washington Square North, an experience he described in his novel "Washington Square":

"It was here that your grandmother lived, in venerable solitude, and dispensed a hospitality which commended itself alike to the infant imagination and the infant palate; it was here that you took your first walks abroad, following the nursery maid with unequal step.... It was here, finally, that your first school, kept by a broad-bosomed, broad-based old lady with a ferule, who was always having tea in a blue cup, with a saucer that didn't match, enlarged the circle of both your observations and your sensations."

One boardinghouse on Washington Square contained so many literary luminaries it was nicknamed the House of Genius. Distinguished boarders included Stephen Crane, John Dos Passos, Maxwell Bodenheim, Eugene O'Neill and Frank Norris, who wrote "The Pit" in his room there.

The Washington Square of James' description in 1835 already had "the look of having something of a social history." Handsome, wide-fronted houses, with drawing rooms and white marble steps, graced the north end of the square. These redbrick houses, James wrote, were supposed "to embody the last results of architectural science." Some of the houses still stand, substantial structures with solid front doors and proud, wide front steps.

The stables of Washington Mews served the great houses of Washington Square. So did stables in Macdougal Alley, another nearby private street. Over the years, Washington Mews drew prominent artists who set up studios. These included William Glackens, Rockwell Kent and Edward Hopper. Jackson Pollock lived in Macdougal Alley, as did James Earle Fraser, designer of the buffalo nickel.

The artists are all but gone, victims of high real-estate values. New York University now owns a good number of houses in Washington Mews. But like Riverview Terrace, Henderson Place and other private streets uptown, an air of James' time, an air of life well lived, remains.

You find you're in an unusual enclave in an unusually busy and noisy city," David Robinson, a foundation executive who lives in the mews, said, echoing the sentiment of private street homeowners to the north. "It has all the advantages of living in New York and none of the disadvantages. You can have a home and retreat from New York City."

Finders Seekers

❖❖

The Legend of a Jet-Age
Jesse James

Some 25 years after D.B. Cooper hijacked an airplane and disappeared with $200,000, he is celebrated by revelers and reviled by a pursuer.

By Richard E. Meyer · December 6, 1996

ARIEL, Washington — Music thumps. Boots stomp. Smoke swirls.

It rises like a dry mist from red-glowing cigarettes. It ebbs around an elk's skull, five-point antlers still attached, and a muzzleloader hanging on the wall.

A potbellied stove washes its warmth over strutting men, women and children. A skinned-out bobcat dangles from the ceiling. A two-man chain saw with a 12-horse-power engine roosts on a canopy over the bar. A sign says: "This Business Is Supported by Timber Dollars."

Tab tops pop. Bartenders slide Budweiser and Rainier and Miller and Coors across the varnished bar top, 3,120 cans and bottles in all. On a wall nearby, these people have tacked up $40. The money is waiting for D.B. Cooper. If he ever shows up, they would like to buy him a drink.

All of this is in his honor. For 11 hours, a guitar and a bass and a mandolin and a sax and a dobro and an accordion and some drums do not stop, and neither does the dancing nor the singing nor the drinking nor the joking. One husky man lifts his red-headed lady high in the air, puts her feet gently back on the floor and gives her a big kiss.

Maybe that is him. Or maybe that is her. The thought stops conversation cold. If D.B. Cooper were a woman, would she be a redhead? "Nah," shouts Bill Partee, over the pounding of the band. He is 64 and has lived here a dozen years. He has a full, white Old Testament beard, and he wears a cap that says: Ariel Store, Home of D.B. Cooper Days. "She had dark hair when she did this thing, but by now she's a blond."

What D.B. Cooper did was hijack a plane. It had just taken off from Portland, Oregon. At Seattle, he forced airline officials to bring him four parachutes and $200,000 in $20 bills. In the air again, somewhere around here, high over the cedars and the firs and the hemlocks that cover the Cascade Mountains, he strapped on two of the parachutes, and he jumped out. He disappeared. Vanished. No ripped rigging.

183

No bones. Nothing.

That was 25 years ago on Thanksgiving eve. People have found only two things in the wilderness to show that this hijacking ever happened: a placard that blew off the back door of the plane when he opened it, and money — a few bundles of $20 bills with serial numbers that match the loot. These prove that he died, some say. Others say no, he simply dropped some of the dough. Too bad, they add, not unkindly.

To many, D.B. Cooper is a folk hero. Nobody else in America has ever hijacked a commercial airliner for money and never been caught. He has become a legend, a new Jesse James, Butch Cassidy, Billy the Kid. Books have been written about him, a play staged, a movie filmed. He is the inspiration for ballads and bumper stickers and T-shirts and coffee mugs. Saloons across the country adopt his name and invite people to "drop in on us sometime."

Every year, on the weekend after Thanksgiving, his fans gather here at the Ariel Store and Tavern, in this mountain town of 50 people, 35 miles north of the Oregon state line. This year, they are 500 strong, and they come from as far away as Brooklyn, New York, and Birmingham, Alabama, and even Seward, Alaska. Their appraisals of D.B. Cooper and what he did offer a case study in how Americans create mythic figures and the ways in which they worship them.

Some stand and read the walls in the southeast corner of the bar, which are covered with newspaper accounts of D.B. Cooper's exploit. They scrawl their names on a white parachute canopy spread across the front porch. They eat D.B. Cooper stew and D.B. Cooper sausages. They shake their heads at a photograph of a headstone someone put up in a front yard across the Lewis River. "Here Lies D.B. Cooper," it says. "We spent your money wisely."

The headstone, regardless of its attempt at humor, runs contrary to an article of faith: that D.B. Cooper is very much alive and enjoying a modest and well-deserved decadence. To his fans, the headstone shows an impertinence that borders on the unseemly. They are relieved to learn that the stone and an oval of smaller rocks outlining a faux grave were judged in bad taste and that the attempted humorist finally removed them.

Mostly, though, they party. For much of Saturday and often into Sunday, they holler and dance and set off roaring fireworks. Each explosion sends clouds of white smoke billowing into a light rain and then up through the trees. They draw for prizes, mainly D.B. Cooper T-shirts, and they stage a D.B. Cooper look-alike contest. One year the winner was a basset hound in D.B. Cooper's trademark disguise: sunglasses.

This year the contest is hard-fought. Dona Elliott, 59, owns this combination country store and saloon, built in 1929 of clapboard and shingles, uphill from the river and hard by a narrow woodland road. She holds one hand over a young man, then an older man, both in sunglasses; then a man with a $20 bill pasted on his forehead; then a couple wearing torn clothes and parachute rigging with fir twigs snagged in the straps.

By hooting and yelling and applauding, the crowd decides. Jim Rainbow, 48, a Susanville, California, mortician, tangled in the rigging and the twigs, is here with his wife for their 10th anniversary. He runs second. The older man in sunglasses, Eldon Heller, 70, a retired contractor from Washougal, Washington, wins by a hair. He thinks for a minute about D.B. Cooper's current age and then smiles. "I'm just about right, huh?"

The crowd cheers again, and the band, called the Enlightened Rogues, swings through another verse about "good women who drink with the boys." Dona Elliott is short, soft-spoken and has wavy brown hair, but she has been known to throw unruly drunks out the front door bodily and by herself. She pronounces the event a good one.

She knows that celebrating D.B. Cooper angers pilots, the airlines and especially Ralph Himmelsbach, 71, a retired FBI agent who spent the last eight years of his career trying to find him. He has written the most authoritative book about the hijacking, called "NORJAK: The Investigation of D.B. Cooper."

Himmelsbach, who code-named the case NORJAK when he was still with the agency, spends D.B. Cooper Day at his home in Redmond, Oregon. To him, Cooper is "a bastard," nothing more than a "sleazy, rotten criminal who jeopardized the lives of more than 40 people for money."

"That's not heroic," he declares, and he means it. "It's selfish, dangerous and anti-social. I have no admiration for him at all. He's not at all admirable. He's just stupid and greedy."

Elliott understands. She knows why people on the hijacked plane, for instance, might not appreciate what goes on here. But she wishes that Himmelsbach would come up anyway.

Himmelsbach, for his part, says: "I know I wouldn't be welcome there."

"Oh, sure he would!" Elliott responds. She chuckles. "He's chicken."

As people here tell and retell the tale of D.B. Cooper and his feat, they praise Himmelsbach's book as the most thorough.

Folklore has entwined itself around the story like heavy brush. But from Himmelsbach's account and news reports at the time, this much can be said:

Shortly before 2 p.m. on November 24, 1971, a man stepped out of a blowing rain at the airport in Portland, and walked to the Northwest Orient Airlines ticket counter.

He asked for a seat on the next flight to Seattle.

The man was middle-aged, pleasant. He stood nearly 6 feet tall. He had olive skin, dark brown eyes and dark hair. It was cut short, neatly trimmed. He wore a lightweight black raincoat and loafers, a dark business suit, a crisp white shirt, a narrow black tie and a pearl stickpin.

He had no luggage to check. In his left hand, he carried an attache case.

Returning?

"No," the man replied.

His name?

"Dan Cooper."

The fare was $20. He placed a $20 bill on the counter.

Ticket in hand, he walked to Gate 52, unhindered at the time by X-ray machines or metal detectors. As he walked, he slipped on a pair of dark glasses.

Departure was scheduled for 2:50 p.m. He waited and smoked a cigarette, a filter-tip Raleigh. Finally a gate agent called Flight 305 for Seattle. Dan Cooper shuffled into line. He handed his ticket envelope to the agent, who took it and checked off his name on a boarding list, then handed back the envelope and his boarding pass.

Cooper stepped onto the plane. It was a jet, a Boeing 727. It had a pilot, a co-pilot and a flight engineer. It had three flight attendants, and it offered nearly 100 seats. But it was less than half full. Besides himself, there were only 36 passengers. He walked to an empty row in back and sat in seat 18C. But he did not take off his sunglasses or his raincoat.

The plane began to taxi. A flight attendant, Florence Schaffner, took a seat nearby. She asked him to put his attache case beneath the seat in front of him.

She settled in for the rollout and climb.

He handed her a note.

It was Thanksgiving, and he was away from home, and she was attractive. She thought that he was proposing something indiscreet. So she paid no attention and put the note aside.

"Miss," he said, "you'd better look at that note."

He paused. "I have a bomb."

To Jim Lissick, 69, of South St. Paul, Minnesota, who is here at the Ariel Store and Tavern to celebrate with a son and a daughter, such good manners are a sign that Cooper is a gentleman. "He was a caring person," Lissick says, then catches himself. "Still is."

Certainly, Lissick says, people such as D.B. Cooper can be tough and extremely demanding. But history, he says, is full of hard cases who were unfailingly polite to women and always kind to children. All of this, he adds, simply becomes part of the mythology that grows up around them.

Mike Holliday, 40, agrees. He has lived in this area since the days when loggers came to the Ariel Store and Tavern after work, hung up their wet clothes to dry and sat around the potbellied stove in their long johns drinking beer and telling stories.

To him, D.B. Cooper shows the unflappable cool of a modern Robin Hood. "But I doubt like hell that he is the kind of guy who gives money away."

Florence Schaffner glanced at the man's note. It was neat, clear. She looked at the man's face. He was not joking.

The note specified his demands. Take it up to the captain, he ordered, and then bring it back with his response. The man repeated: Return the note.

She hurried to the cockpit and gave the note to Capt. William Scott and First Officer Bill Rataczak. They radioed that Flight 305 was being hijacked: A man with a bomb wants $200,000 in negotiable bills, a money sack and a pair of backpack parachutes.

Schaffner returned to Dan Cooper with his note. He opened his attache case. She saw red cylinders, a battery and wires. She hurried back to the cockpit and described the contents to Scott and Rataczak. They radioed authorities on the ground: It looks like dynamite.

Cooperate, responded Northwest Airlines headquarters in Minneapolis, and try not to alarm the passengers. By now, Flight 305 was over Seattle, but Cooper refused to let it land until the money and the parachutes were ready. Scott told the passengers that the plane had a mechanical problem requiring it to circle and burn off fuel. The flight attendants served drinks. Cooper had a bourbon and water. He paid with a $20 bill.

Tina Mucklow, another of the flight attendants, sat down next to him. She was easygoing, pretty and wore her hair long and flowing. They developed a rapport. He smoked another Raleigh. She lit it for him so he could keep both hands on his briefcase. "He wasn't nervous," she recalled later. "He seemed rather nice. He was never cruel or nasty. He was thoughtful and calm."

Now Cooper wanted two more parachutes, for a total of four — two front packs and two backpacks. Four meant that he might jump with a hostage, and this signaled: Do not tamper with the gear. The Air Force offered two. But Cooper demanded civilian models. Civilian parachutes meant that he might free-fall away from the flight path before pulling the ripcord, and this signaled: A tail plane will be useless.

As Flight 305 circled over Seattle, airline officials, FBI agents and Seattle police scrambled to get the money that Dan Cooper was demanding. They rounded up $20

bills from several banks. Twenties would be easy to pass and would signal cooperation. It took time, but they found enough — 10,000 of them. The bills weighed 21
pounds and filled a white cotton sack. The FBI microfilmed every one.

Cooper grew impatient. He ordered another bourbon and water. Then he demanded that a truck meet the plane and refill it with fuel when it landed in Seattle. He said
he would release all passengers, but he wanted meals brought on board for the crew.

A skydiving school finally came up with four civilian parachutes. In a mistake
that the rigger would not discover until later, they included a dummy chute that would
not open.

At 5:39 p.m., a message went by radio up to Flight 305. "Everything is ready for
your arrival."

Capt. Scott eased the jet onto runway 16R. He taxied to a corner of the airfield.
"He says to get that stuff out here right now."

A fuel truck drove over.

Dan Cooper sent Tina Mucklow out to get the money and the parachutes.

Then he let the passengers go.

It is commonly held in Ariel that all of this demonstrates beyond the silly doubt
of any pinch-nosed naysayer exactly how brilliant D.B. Cooper really is.

"He pulls it all off pretty good," says Steve Forney, 40, of Kelso, Washington, a
biker who parks his 1979 Harley shovelhead in a special spot at the door that Dona
Elliott reserves for motorcycles.

A friend, Jim Smith, 49, of Castle Rock, Washington, who pulls up on a 1987
Harley blockhead, wipes the rain off his leather jacket. He declares with approval:

"D.B. Cooper is one smart outlaw."

Arguably, ground crews were less smart. The first fuel truck they sent out to the
plane had a vapor lock. The second ran dry. Finally, a third topped off the tanks.

Inside the plane, Cooper announced that he wanted to go to Mexico City, and he
wanted to fly in a certain way: with the landing gear down, the wing flaps down and
the aft air-stairs down.

Flaps?

"Fifteen degrees," Cooper said, with precision.

This meant that he knew the rear stairway on a 727 could be lowered in flight. It
also meant that he knew flying with the gear and the flaps down would slow the plane,
and he knew how far the flaps could be lowered to do it safely.

He gave another order: Stay below 10,000 feet.

This meant that he knew flying any higher with the aft door open would be risky.
At 10,000 feet, the outside air had enough oxygen in it to make it safe to breathe. But

any higher it did not.

First Officer Bill Rataczak figured that flying this way would burn a lot of fuel. By his calculation, the plane would have a range of only 1,000 miles. Mexico City was 2,200 miles away.

This called for refueling stops on the way. Cooper agreed that one would be Reno, Nevada.

He freed attendants Alice Hancock and Florence Schaffner but kept Tina Mucklow seated next to him. At 7:37 p.m., Flight 305 was back in the air.

Cooper told Mucklow to go up to the cockpit and pull the first-class curtain closed behind her. She glanced back once. He was cutting cord from one of the parachutes and tying the moneybag to his waist.

At 7:42 p.m. Capt. Scott saw a cockpit light indicating that the aft stairs were down.

The plane leveled off at 10,000 feet and cruised at 196 mph. Outside it was dark, stormy and 7 degrees below zero. Now First Officer Rataczak's watch showed almost 8 p.m.

"Everything OK back there?" he asked on the intercom. "Anything we can do for you?"

Finally a light showed that the stairs were fully extended.

"No!" Cooper replied.

At 8:12 p.m., the nose of the plane curtsied, and its instruments showed a small bump in cabin pressure. This meant that the tail had suddenly gotten lighter and that the stairs had bounced up and into the plane and then dropped down again.

Dan Cooper had jumped.

Around the potbellied stove in Ariel, two airline employees marvel at D.B. Cooper's knowledge.

Phil Brooks, 34, of Speedway, Indiana, an aircraft dispatcher, thinks that Cooper either was involved with an airline or did his homework very well.

"He was intelligent and gutsy," Brooks says. "That tells me he had a good background, maybe Special Forces or intelligence. He didn't work down at the car wash. And he was a major stud; he had the guts to jump out of an airplane at night in the winter."

Brooks proudly shows off a Cooper Vane, a device named after D.B. Cooper, which locks aft air-stairs from the outside during flight. It was installed on all 727s after the hijacking to prevent further Cooper capers. Years later, Brooks found the hijacked jet in a Mississippi scrap yard. He recovered the Cooper Vane from the Cooper plane.

With Brooks is Dan Gradwohl, 30, a first officer on 727s for Ryan International Airlines, a charter service. "Cooper knew something about the 727," Gradwohl says, "or he had to have talked to somebody and learned about it.

"He beat the system," Gradwohl points out, and spectacularly so. "If D.B. Cooper would have simply robbed a bank, he wouldn't be a legend.

"But he robbed several banks, and then he parachuted out of a plane."

When Flight 305 landed in Reno, the FBI found two parachutes, the butts of eight filter-tip Raleighs and 66 fingerprints. None matched prints in the FBI files.

The next day in Seattle, the parachute rigger realized his mistake. Cooper had jumped with a good parachute and a backup that would not open.

At one point, a reporter for United Press International spotted FBI agents at the Portland police station and asked a clerk what they were doing.

"They're looking for a guy named Cooper," the clerk replied. "D.B. Cooper."

The reporter phoned in his information. Although it was a fact that agents were checking out a man named D.B. Cooper, they cleared him almost immediately.

But the initials stuck.

Dan Cooper entered history — and folklore — with the wrong name.

The only significant evidence that Ralph Himmelsbach ever processed was the $5,800, found on a Columbia River sandbar by Brian Ingram, 8, of Vancouver, Washington, while he was picnicking with his family. Himmelsbach matched the $20 bills to Cooper's loot.

Will D.B. Cooper ever be located?

"I doubt it," Himmelsbach says.

Officially, though, the FBI case against Dan Cooper is not closed. Ray Lauer, an agency spokesman in Seattle, says:

"We're still trying to find the guy."

Researchers Paul Singleton, Julia Franco and Steve Tice contributed to this story.

❖

Reaching Way Out

In the middle of the Mojave stands a phone booth. There's no reason to call — except to make a connection.

BY JOHN M. GLIONNA · SEPTEMBER 18, 1999

MOJAVE NATIONAL PRESERVE — With only the lazy Joshua trees and hovering buzzards out here to bear witness, this isolated expanse of high-desert plain could well be among the quietest places on the planet.

By day, the summer heat hammers hard and the dull whistle of the wind is the only discernible noise. Come nightfall, the eerie silence is often pierced by the woeful bleat of a wandering burro.

But wait. There's another sound.

Along a line of wooden power poles running to the horizon in both directions, 14 miles from the nearest paved road, a solitary pay phone beckons with the shrill sound of impatient civilization.

Then it rings again. And again. And yet again, often dozens of times a day.

The callers? A bored housewife from New Zealand. A German high school student. An on-the-job Seattle stockbroker. A long-distance trucker who dials in from the road. There's a proud skunk owner from Atlanta, a pizza deliveryman from San Bernardino and a bill collector from Denver given a bum steer while tracing a debt.

Receivers in hand, they're reaching out — at all hours of the day and night, from nearly every continent — to make contact with this forlorn desert outpost.

They're calling the Mojave Phone Booth.

Here comes a curious caller now:

"Hello? Hello? Is this the Mojave Phone Booth?" asks Pher Reinman, an unemployed South Carolina computer worker.

Told by a reporter answering the line that he has indeed reached what cult followers call the loneliest phone booth on Earth, he exclaims: "Oh my God, I can't believe it! Somebody answered! There's actually somebody out there!"

Like Reinman, callers everywhere are connecting with the innocuous little booth not far from the California-Nevada border, along a winding and treacherous dirt road accessible only by four-wheel-drive vehicle.

Out here, where summer temperatures soar to 115 degrees and cattle often wander by en route to a watering hole, there's rarely anyone on hand to answer the calls, but persistent phoners don't seem to care. If someone does pick up, of course, so much the better.

Some of those who do answer are previous callers who, for unknowable reasons that make sense only to them, also feel compelled to visit the booth.

"For us," wrote screenwriter Chuck Atkins of his recent trek to the booth, "it was about driving into nowhere for no good reason, meeting fellow Netizens who shared our sense of childish glee at the coolness of a phone booth in the middle of nowhere."

Indeed, this public phone, first installed in the 1960s and operated with a hand crank by nearby volcanic cinder miners and other desert denizens, has been popularized by the globe's most advanced communications system: the Internet.

The craze began two years ago after a high-desert wanderer noticed a telephone icon on a Mojave road map. Curious, he drove out from Los Angeles to investigate, and wrote a letter to a counterculture magazine describing his exploits and including the phone number. After spotting the letter, computer entrepreneur Godfrey Daniels became so captivated by the idea he created the first of several Web sites dedicated solely to the battered booth.

Since then, word of the phone has been beamed to computers virtually everywhere.

It has evolved into a worldwide listening post straight from the mind of a Rod Serling or a David Lynch, captivating countless callers.

There's Preston Lunn of San Bernardino, whose wife reluctantly let him take a long-distance shot at reaching someone at the phone, a call he made "just for the hell of it, just to see what happens."

There's Debbie, the 20-year-old baby-sitter from Boston whose older sister, "the one who goes to college," told her about the phone. Bored, with her infant wards asleep, Debbie decided to take a chance and telephone the desert.

"So, what's out there?" she asked tentatively. "Just, like, cactuses and a dirt road and stuff?"

And there's Atlantan Jim Shanton, who heard about the phone "from one of the ladies on our pet skunk e-mail list." Added Shanton: "And I was just crazy enough to call. For me, this is like calling Mars. It's that far away from everything I know."

What callers reach is just a shell of a phone booth, actually, its windows long ago blasted out by desert gunslingers desperate for something to shoot at, its coin box deactivated so that only incoming calls and outgoing credit-card calls are possible.

But fans have taken the neglected old booth under their wing. Outside, they've posted a sign that reads, "Mojave Phone Booth — you could shoot it, but why would you want to?" Next to that is another placard reading: "If you call it, they will come."

On top of the pay phone perches a nude Barbie doll. Scratched into the booth's metal frame are its longitude and latitude coordinates. Inside, along with plastic-coated children's magnets spelling out "Mojave Phone Booth," are mementos such as candles and license plates. Visitors have covered the booth's bullet holes with Band-Aids.

Nearby, fist-sized stones form the phone's number along with a huge arrow pointing to the booth. The message can be seen from the air so, as one Mojave phone fan put it, "even aliens can find it."

The booth-oriented Web sites multiplied when their creators saw the phone on other sites and, after calling numerous times, decided to document their own pilgrimages to the desert phone.

There's the lighting designer from New York who was so thrilled to finally reach the Mojave phone that she stripped naked "and ran around like a giddy little girl."

And two L.A. writers, who later chronicled their trek to the Mojave, headed out just to return the receiver to its cradle after learning the phone was off the hook. They arrived to find the phone temporarily out of order.

Rick Karr, a 51-year-old spiritual wanderer, has no Web site, but says he was instructed by the Holy Spirit to travel to the desert and answer the phone. The Texas native recently spent 32 days camping out at the booth, fielding more than 500 calls from people like Bubba in Phoenix and Ian in Newfoundland and repeated contacts from a caller who identified himself as "Sgt. Zeno from the Pentagon."

"This phone," he said with a weary sigh, "never stops ringing."

Although she would not provide statistics, a Pacific Bell spokeswoman said the phone experienced "very low outgoing usage."

Still, the booth is sometimes used by locals to conduct business or check messages.

"I've passed that old phone booth just about every day for more than 20 years now and I've never given it as much as a second thought," said Charlie Wilcox, a sun-wrinkled 63-year-old tow-truck driver who has become the booth's unofficial tour guide. "And I'll be damned. Now it's a celebrity."

Phone booth callers, Web site creators and Internet intellectuals alike are trying to figure out just why this far-flung phone has gripped the imagination of those who come across it.

Some say calls to the booth are an attempt to create community in a disconnected world. Others view the calls as pure phone fetish, a sort of long-distance voyeurism.

"It's the kick of reaching out and touching a perfect stranger in a completely anonymous and indiscriminate way," said Mark Thomas, a New York City concert pianist who created a Web site listing the numbers of thousands of public pay phones worldwide, including the Mojave Desert phone.

Many of the phones on his list are in urban areas, such as the one at the top observation deck of the Eiffel Tower, and Thomas said the Mojave Phone Booth may attract so many callers because of its exotic isolation.

"You could make a chance contact at any pay phone, but the odds of reaching someone out in the desert are incredibly remote," he said. "That's why people call."

Others say calls to the phone are made out of sheer boredom.

"It's the get-a-life factor," said UCLA sociologist Warren TenHouten. "Some people just have nothing to do, so they pursue shreds of information that have no value. It amuses me, but there's something pitiful about it too. I mean, what's the most interesting thing that could happen by being so mischievous as to call a public pay phone?

"Someone answers, a person you have absolutely no connection with. You exchange names and talk about the weather. What a thrill."

One of the 60 callers greeted by a reporter on a recent visit acknowledged that he was shocked anyone was there to answer.

"I thought I'd just call and wake up the coyotes," said a purchasing agent from San Bernardino County who buzzed the phone from work. "Modern times are passing us by and it's just sort of romantic — just the idea that it's out there."

Computer entrepreneur Daniels, a Tempe, Arizona, resident, is considered the father of the phone booth. He was hooked in the spring of 1997 after reading of the Mojave phone in the cryptic letter to the magazine Wig Out.

The 36-year-old, who once ran for the Arizona Legislature and tried to start a country called Oceania, had discovered a new adventure: He began calling the booth every day. And he forced friends to call whenever they visited him.

After weeks of long-distance dialing, someone picked up.

"I was probably more surprised than he was that we were having a conversation on that phone," said Lorene Caffee, a local miner who answered the Mojave line in 1997.

Daniels transcribed the conversation on his new Web site. Later, after making several trips to the phone, he included such features as a 360-degree view of the surrounding desert from atop the phone and pictures of a bust of composer Richard Wagner, which he carries with him on his travels, inside the booth.

Soon came the call blitz. On one two-day trip to the booth, Daniels answered 200 of them, including a confused connection from Albania during the war in Kosovo.

Daniels plans to return on New Year's Eve to take Y2K reports from around the globe.

"I like the fact that you can have people who have never met or never will meet and they have this little intersection," he said. "Two people who have no business talking to one another."

Since most callers don't expect an answer, they gasp when a visitor actually picks up, many quickly hanging up like teenage telephone pranksters.

One call answered by a reporter came from 17-year-old Jan Spuehamer of Hamburg, Germany. "This is costing me a lot of money, but I think it is very funny," Spuehamer said. "One magazine article said you have to be very lucky to have someone pick up this line. Because this is the loneliest phone in the world, no?"

And so people keep calling the Mojave Phone Booth. And visiting.

On a drive home from Las Vegas, Wade Burrows and Brian Burkland impulsively decided to visit the booth. They walked around for 10 minutes scratching their heads, finally leaving behind their own memento: a car license plate they both autographed.

Said the 21-year-old Burkland: "Dude, this is, like, so cool!"

Then Burrows, a San Bernardino pizza deliveryman, placed a call from his favorite desert phone booth.

"Hey, Mom," he said, holding a cigarette burned down to the filter. "You'll never guess where I'm calling from — a phone booth in the middle of nowhere."

He paused, listening.

"Why am I out here? Well, Mom, that's a long story."

Editor's note: The lonesome phone booth was removed in 2000, but a few Web sites still pay homage to it:

> http://www.deuceofclubs.com/moj/mojave.html
> http://www.illuminatrix.com/mojave
> http://www.deadpan.net/mpb/why.htm

❖

Collecting Dialect:
It's No Fahdoodle

Frederic Cassidy, 84, has been cataloging juicy colloquialisms for 26 years, and his dictionary has reached the Hs. But don't be a dinkeldorf. It's 'not a rapid science,' he warns.

By Bob Secter · September 18, 1999

MADISON, Wisconsin — In his own words, not the ones he speaks but the deliciously rich variety he hunts and hordes like precious boodle, Frederic Cassidy at 84 is far from being a washed-up old foozle.

Sure, he's been cataloging uniquely American sayings since the hogs ate my brother up, and, sure, after 26 years he's only made it through those that start with the letter H.

But don't be a dinkeldorf. Cassidy can still whip his weight in wildcats, and any suggestion that he somehow won't make it to Z is pure fahdoodle. After all, crafting a work as intricate as the nation's first truly thorough and authoritative compendium of its varied dialects is something that's got to be well fogged out. To do it right, it's bound to take from here to Gypep.

"Lexicography is not a rapid science," deadpanned Cassidy, uttering the sort of fancy term for dictionary writing more suited to a blue nose trying to put on the dogs.

Such $10 expressions are definitely not the stuff of Cassidy's work: The Dictionary of American Regional English, an ambitious, groundbreaking and anything but expeditiously put together examination into the nooks and crannies of American speech.

DARE — the apt acronym for the project headquartered at the University of Wisconsin here — is not only a major work of American scholarship, it clearly is a major work in progress as well.

Conceived more than a century ago by the American Dialect Society, DARE didn't get off the ground until the elite fraternity of linguists recruited Cassidy, a professor of English at the Madison campus, to direct the monumental task.

Fueled over the years by millions of dollars in federal and private foundation grants, research began in 1965 when an army of fieldworkers fanned across the 50 states. Armed with tape recorders and an elaborate list of 1,847 questions about what people called things, they searched for juicy colloquialisms that have spiced conversations in many locales for generations. Under the original timetable, the research was supposed to take five years, and the collating and writing another five.

Instead, the mass of material was so great that Volume 1 — which scratches a path merely from A (as in "acknowledge the corn," an admission of drinking by someone in the nation's midlands) to C (as in "Cupid's cramp," a Westernism for an infatuation) — offers up 14,000 entries by itself and wasn't ready for publication until 1985. Volume 2, inching the genre from the likes of "dingclicker" (New Englandese for a fine person or thing) to "huggle-de-buck" (hurry up to a good ol' boy from Texas) debuted only this autumn.

DARE, declared Allan Metcalf, the executive secretary of the Dialect Society, is the most sweeping scholarly effort ever devised to comprehend the richness of American English.

"Standard dictionaries don't begin to scratch the surface of our language," Metcalf explained. "Because of commercial and time limitations they, of necessity, must limit themselves to the most widespread forms of words ... but [DARE] is providing a mine of materials to help us study language variation and language development. It's like mapping the stars. We're mapping the U.S., and until we do that, our understanding of our language will be very superficial."

There are, in essence, two forms of American English. There's the refined version of most conventional dictionaries, drawn in great measure from literature. To many, it's the language of the kind of stuffy poops who always seem to know which is proper, "who" or "whom," and like to preface their thoughts with snooty sounding things like "indeed," "to be sure" and "thus."

And then there's the casual kind that most of the rest of us speak, the real-world language ignored to a surprising degree by most dictionaries. "Most people who write take a different tone than when they speak, and people who speak most colorfully don't write at all," explained Joan Hall, DARE's associate editor.

In DARE, it's the speakers who get their say. A trip through its pages is part Trivial Pursuit, part scholarship and part treasure hunt. For instance, Volume 2 reveals that a synonym for a pregnant woman in Connecticut is someone who is "fat as God's pocket." If she were in the South, her midwife might be a "baby catcher."

A "cow county" is the sticks to some in California and Nevada. In the Ozarks, a staggerer is someone who "antigoddles." Nonsense can be "flumaddiddle" or "flummydiddle" or "fummaddiddle" in New England, while in Alabama it's "flurriddidle."

In the Southeast, it's said "there's a dead cat on the line" to describe a sense that something's wrong. Also in the South, a slippery person is one who shouldn't be trusted "behind a thin dime standing edgewise." A "dime-a-dip dinner" is a Nevada fundraiser. A "dime on the counter" could be the unbuttoned fly of a California man.

Smooth operators in many parts of the country might try to "honeyfuggle" (sweet talk) a pretty girl. Depending on the locale, someone eager to get married might be "anxious for the noose," "out on the carpet," "dying to jump the broom" or even "window-shopping." Or, it might be said that "bugs hit him" or that his "comb's getting red."

Women of the Ozarks and Appalachians who remain single even when younger sisters marry are "dancing in the hog trough." And those who married poorly in the South and midlands have been said to have "driven their ducks to a poor market."

Speaking of ducks, a sudden blast of anger or excitement in the South is sometimes called a "duck fit." Adolescent Kentucky boys whose voices are changing are said to be going through their "gosling age." In Pennsylvania, poor people have sometimes been identified as those who "crawled under the dog's belly." Eating light to a North Carolinian is to "drink some water and suck one's thumb."

On occasion, phrases get better as they migrate from place to place, especially put-downs. Someone without common sense in the Ozarks "doesn't know enough to pour piss out of a boot with a hole in the toe." In Texas, where everything is always grander, the same goofus "doesn't know enough to pour piss out of a boot with a hole in the toe and directions on the heel."

As DARE detectives scoured the country, they uncovered scores of different words for the same plants, animals and objects. Dust balls conjured up 176 phrases ("dust bunnies," "dust puppies," "dust tigers" and "collywobbles," just to name a few).

More than two decades after they were completed, the foundation of DARE still remains those original interviews carried out between 1965 and 1970. During that time, researchers quizzed natives of more than 1,000 American communities about the words they used to describe everything from a rain shower ("drizzle-fizzle" in Missouri) to a flighty person ("flippy-wippet" to some in New York).

The result was more than 2.5 million different responses, each of which must be computerized, collated, cross-referenced and researched. The process was complicated by a search for even more words in thousands of books, diaries and newspapers. "We all thought this would be done a whole lot faster than it has been," confessed Hall. "But the more we investigated, the more we found."

Without a doubt, the Dialect Society doyens didn't pick Cassidy to edit their masterpiece because of his reputation for speed. Before DARE, his best-known work was a single-volume dictionary of Jamaican Creole English. He started it in 1951 and finished 16 years later.

But the Jamaican work helped build Cassidy's reputation as perhaps the country's leading lexicographer. "He's the very top," said Virginia McDavid, president of the Dictionary Society of North America. "… A number of scholars got their start with him … a lot of [important] people in the study of American English and English historical linguistics today are former students of Fred's."

And so the work on DARE has dared to stretch on into its fourth decade. The tardiness doesn't seem to bother Cassidy a wit. "It's a careful, slow deliberate process," he explained. "You can't whip those things off overnight…. The first part of the Oxford Dictionary was published in 1884 and it wasn't finished until 1932."

With two volumes under his belt, Cassidy thinks his team of 20 full- and part-time researchers can pick up the pace a bit. The next volume, I through O, could be ready by as soon as 1994, he predicted. The real killer comes with S, which could take up a whole volume unto itself.

"It's going to take the rest of the century to finish it," Cassidy said of the entire project. "We'll get there, though."

But, at 84, will he?

"I have something to live for," he continued. "Lots of old people don't. They're just pattering along the last of it. Between discipline and luck I can probably make it to 100. We're planning on it."

In Virginia and Maryland, that's what they'd call "finger-nosing" at old age.

Times researcher Tracy Shryer also contributed to this story.

From the Dictionary of American Regional English:

Absquatulate: A Midwesterner who departs hastily or furtively.
Aggie forties: A stiff drink in the South.
Air one's lungs: Swearing or arguing at length in Illinois.
Alight and look at one's saddle: A Texan's invitation to stop, talk and perhaps share a meal.
Alphabet slinger: A Georgia schoolteacher.
Ankle express: Walking in the South and West.
Astor's pet horse: A Northerner's catty referral to an overdressed female.
Aunt Dinah's picking her geese: Acknowledgment of a huge feathery snowfall in Kentucky.

Barnyard golf: Horseshoes in the North.

Pleased as a basketful of possum-heads: Exceedingly happy in Arkansas.

Between hay and grass: A Northeastern male between youth and adulthood.

Blow your horn if you don't sell a fish: Said to a Cape Codder who blows his nose vigorously.

Bone orchard: A cemetery.

California prayer book: A deck of cards, especially during Gold Rush.

Calluses on one's feet: An Ozark baby born before its parents have been married nine months.

Cat beer: Milk in Minnesota.

Coffee strainer: A bushy mustache in Illinois

Cumfluttered: A Tennessean when flustered or excited.

Eat a pumpkin to a hollow through a crack in a board fence: Buck teeth in Florida.

Drench one's gizzard: Drinking to excess in Virginia.

Elephant year: A bad luck year in black folklore.

Flang-dang: A Texas party with music.

Fluff duff: Anything fancy from food to finery.

Goin' jesse: Full of energy in Illinois.

Ho-dad with a shufflin' rod: A made-up item in New Mexico.

Raisins with the mumps: Great Lakes lumberjack's prune.

Very close veins: varicose veins.

❖

The Poignant Puzzles of Lives

**In New York and around the country, scores of experts have embarked
on the enormous task of matching bodies with names, part of
the grim aftermath of 9/11.**

BY ROBERT LEE HOTZ • SEPTEMBER 25, 2001

NEW YORK — Identity — the first thing each infant learns — is the first thing
death erases, leaving the body a riddle that only a name can resolve.

With a name, a family can bury a loved one. With a name, an estate can be settled; a headstone can be etched; an end can be made.

Restoring the proper name to each scrap of bone and flesh found in the rubble of
the September 11 attacks on the World Trade Center here is expected to require what
experts in the field say will be the largest forensic identification effort ever conducted in this country. So crushing was the collapse of the twin 110-story towers, so caus-
tic the chemicals unleashed, and so fierce the fires, that few intact bodies are being
found.

Since the attacks, scores of medical examiners, dental experts, molecular biolo-
gists and pathologists at laboratories in New York, Utah and Maryland have been
struggling to identify the remains.

In the end, a million fragments of human body parts — many burned or torn
beyond recognition — may be found in the wreckage, several forensic experts said.
Each fragment will be bagged, tagged with a bar code, entered into a computer database, and its every characteristic — down to its DNA — studied intently in the months
to come.

There are other teams studying the remains of those who died at the Pentagon in
Virginia and in the crash of United Airlines Flight 93 near Shanksville, Pennsylvania.
But the problems facing forensic experts in New York are especially daunting.

The Pentagon has military identification tags and DNA banks to assist in identifying victims. Airlines have passenger manifests. Workers at the trade center began
with only an uncertain list of thousands of missing people, including residents of 60
nations, that fluctuates faster than they can recover remains.

Of the 276 confirmed dead so far, 206 have been identified.

Identifying the rest "is an enormous task," said forensic anthropologist Clyde

Snow, who pioneered many of the identification techniques now being put to the task.

"The challenges to the recovery people and the forensic scientists are going to be immeasurably greater than we have ever faced before in any disasters in this country," Snow said.

No one knows how long it will take, how much it will cost, or the emotional toll it will exact from the forensic experts now working in three shifts, 24 hours a day, seven days a week.

As best they can, morgue teams inventory the remains. They note any identifying detail that friends and families of the missing can provide: a spider-web tattoo on a woman from the 100th floor; a red medical alert bracelet worn by a 6-year-old boy visiting his mother on the 107th; a woman's name tattooed on the arm of a man from the 93rd floor; the half-circle of freckles on the broad shoulder of a broker last seen on the 89th floor.

Forensic specialists have a remarkable array of tools to match fragmentary remains with a name. Since fingerprints were first introduced as evidence of identity in a 1911 burglary trial, analysts have bolstered their diagnostic skills with techniques for facial reconstruction, chemical tests, computerized dental comparisons, X-ray dispersion and DNA analysis.

They can peel fingerprints from charred hands and rebuild burned faces.

They can analyze as many as 70 enzymes in blood, bone marrow and body fluids to put together a distinctive biochemical profile.

From the long bones of arms and legs, scientists can gauge someone's age, weight, sex, race and muscularity. With enough material, they can even tell if a person was right- or left-handed.

From a single strand of hair, some forensic experts can glean estimates of race, sex and other characteristics. Researchers at the National Institute of Standards and Technology are testing a way to use sophisticated techniques for chemical analysis known as gas chromatography and mass spectrometry to develop a chemical profile from hair samples that can be used like a fingerprint.

But for thousands of the missing, whose photographs are taped to Manhattan's walls and street poles, smiles may be all that survive.

Teeth could endure in the hellish heat that melted the World Trade Center's steel beams even when all other human remains were consumed. Dental enamel can withstand temperatures as high as 1,800 degrees Fahrenheit, forensic odontologists said.

As an almost indestructible marker of identity, teeth long have been a mainstay for forensic pathologists.

At the New York City medical examiner's office, 100 dentists have been working in shifts around the clock to assemble the needed X-rays and patient notes to match against teeth recovered from the rubble. They scrutinize each tooth with the intensity of a diamond cutter.

"For us, a tooth stands out like a beacon," said Jeffrey Burkes, the city's chief forensic odontologist. He would not discuss the specifics of any case but said the numbers of dead and missing are overwhelming.

"It is a staggering task. Without computers we would be lost."

When medical files are handed over by relatives, the identifying dental details are entered into a rapidly growing database of the dead. Teeth recovered from the ruins then can be matched quickly against the computerized files.

A single tooth can be enough to restore a name to one of the dead, said forensic expert Tom Glass, who supervised the dental identification of the 168 people killed in the 1995 Oklahoma City bombing.

"You need the right tooth or the right part of the tooth," Glass said. "Having a piece of the root may be enough, if it has enough unique characteristics."

Even the fillings in teeth can be revealing. An international team of forensic experts in 1985 identified the remains of fugitive Nazi war criminal Dr. Josef Mengele in part by analyzing the distinctive alloys from dental fillings in six teeth exhumed from a grave.

For many of the missing, however, only DNA — the molecule that binds all people into one human family and yet singles out each person with a unique chemical code — holds the key to identity.

Any tissue that survived the heat and blast should harbor viable DNA.

Under the most extreme conditions, DNA can survive intact inside teeth, protected from heat, moisture and corrosion by the tough enamel, Glass said. "All you need is a few cells with intact DNA."

Laboratory technicians can take even minute DNA traces and reproduce enough to create a sample that can be analyzed. They use an automated technique called a polymerase chain reaction, or PCR, that mimics nature's way of replicating DNA.

"Since we have this DNA technology, I am reasonably assured that everybody [whose remains can be found] will be identified," said Dr. Donald T. Reay, head of the forensic autopsy committee of the American College of Pathologists. "It is the pure volume that will be overwhelming. I shudder to think how you will do it."

Within hours of the disaster, the New York City medical examiner's office began collecting DNA samples from tissue discovered in the wreckage.

The city has perhaps the largest police DNA lab in the country. Even so, the scale of the required genetic testing is so big that New York officials looked for help. They reached out to the New York State Police forensic DNA laboratory in Albany, and two of the world's largest genetic sequencing companies: Myriad Genetic Laboratories Inc. in Salt Lake City, and Celera Genomics Inc. in Rockville, Maryland. A third company, Applied Biosystems Inc. in the San Francisco Bay Area, is providing equipment and other support to the identification effort.

Spread across four laboratories, the testing process is delicate, easily compromised, and must adhere to standards of evidence that can hold up in federal court, should any of the results be challenged or become part of a criminal proceeding.

Each DNA sample will take about 10 hours to extract, isolate, amplify and analyze.

So far, officials have collected 6,063 DNA samples that might help identify about 2,100 victims, New York City Police Commissioner Bernard B. Kerik said Monday. Dr. Robert S. Shaler, director of forensic biology for the medical examiner's office, is preparing to perform DNA testing on as many as 20,000 tissue samples at his laboratories. Forensic experts say that may only be the beginning.

"There are going to be a lot of unassigned parts," said Murray Marks, a forensic anthropologist at the University of Tennessee at Knoxville. "That will take a lot of DNA work, months and months of work. It's a huge effort."

Results from the four laboratories will be cross-checked continually to avoid any wrong identifications.

"There will always be double-check," said Ellen Borokove, a medical examiner's office spokeswoman. "If we don't have the same answers, we will have to go back and find out why."

Lab technicians at Myriad Genetics already have started analyzing DNA samples. Company officials estimate they could process 30,000 samples a month, if necessary. It is the pace of the recovery effort that will dictate the speed of the DNA testing, company President Dr. Gregory Critchfield said.

Myriad's automated genetic testing lines will search each sample for 13 distinctive stretches of DNA called short tandem repeats. These markers, arrayed along specific chromosomes, can be used as a characteristic profile that can "uniquely identify a person," said Brian Ward, Myriad's vice president of operations. "The chance that we would duplicate all 13 [in two people] is less than 1 in 250 trillion."

Once analyzed, a victim's DNA will be compared with hair and cell samples obtained from toothbrushes, clothing or hairbrushes the victim used.

If those are not available, it is still possible to identify people using DNA taken from blood samples of relatives, but this process is not as definitive. "They can extrapolate from that," said Norah Rudin, a private forensic DNA consultant based in

Berkeley.

Since the attacks, 500 families outside the New York area have come forward to offer DNA samples to identify missing relatives, said Dr. Marcia Eisenberg, senior director for forensic DNA testing at the Laboratory Corp. of America. The company, which has 900 DNA centers around the country, is coordinating genetic collections for the New York medical examiners.

Company officials have fielded calls from as far away as China and Australia.

Even as relatives of the missing pin their hopes on heredity, forensic experts are worried that conditions in the rubble may be so acidic and wet that after several months, some of the DNA may disintegrate before recovery workers can finish clearing all the debris.

"We are concerned about degradation of DNA over time," Ward said. So far, tissues are being recovered quickly enough that "we are fairly confident we can get DNA out of those samples."

The most severely damaged DNA samples may end up at Celera, a leading corporate research center that completed the first sequence of the entire human genome earlier this year.

Celera's scientists are expected to analyze tissue in which the DNA from the nucleus, usually used for analysis, has broken down. Instead of analyzing DNA from the nucleus, which lies at the center of the cell, they will seek genetic material contained in about 10,000 tiny cell structures called mitochondria. The mitochondria contain DNA sequences that are less definitive for identification but more plentiful, smaller and perhaps more robust.

For many families, hope rests on a cell sample swabbed from a relative's cheek on a cotton-tipped stick, tucked in a plain white envelope and turned over to a lab technician. Extracted from those cells, droplets of DNA are purified and poured into the tiny wells of a laboratory to be tested for a match.

Each well brims with expectation and fear.

New York City officials say they will conduct genetic tests on every piece of tissue recovered from the World Trade Center.

"We're talking thousands of samples," Rudin said. "It could take all year."

However long it takes, the effort is worthwhile, said Harrell Gill-King, a noted forensic anthropologist who runs the laboratory for human identification at the University of North Texas.

"We don't do forensic science for the dead," Gill-King said. "We do it for the living."

Times science writer Usha McFarling in Los Angeles contributed to this report.

❖

From the Attic, a Musty Document and a Load of Trouble

Deep in the Ozarks, the owner of a bed and breakfast discovered a county bond more than a century old. His effort to collect would produce more headaches than cash.

By Richard E. Meyer · March 24, 1982

GINGER BLUFF, Missouri — He had cleaned out the broken television sets and the old lamps and linen. About the only thing left, in a corner of the attic under the eaves, was a discarded pie chest. Had George Foster known the trouble it held, he might never have touched it.

It looked like an ordinary pie chest, the kind on counters in coffee shops. It had wooden sides, holes for ventilation and glass doors. But it lay on its face. "I'll hold it up and you open the doors," Foster told his bar manager. "We might find a suitcase of money."

"Just an old piece of paper," the bar manager reported.

Foster looked.

"It's a bond," he said.

He carried it downstairs to the dining room in Ginger Blue Lodge, a 67-year-old, rambling, two-story, gray-blue clapboard inn he had bought 10 years ago in this village of 54 inhabitants, deep in the Ozark Mountains of southwestern Missouri. Over lunch, Foster inspected his discovery.

Yellowed, a little water-stained and tattered at the corners, it proclaimed in green ink: "McDonald County Bond." In red ink, it promised "One Hundred Dollars," payable to two bondholders whose names were written in longhand — or payable to the bearer, who at the moment was George Foster. In black ink, the bond pledges interest at "10% per annum."

It had been issued in 1871.

Turning the years and percentage over in his mind, Foster figured it was worth about $600,000.

He grinned.

"Tell you what let's do," he told himself. "Let's go present it to the county."

When he made that decision, nine months ago, George Foster created a king-sized problem for McDonald County. The bond, it turned out, was worth more than five times what he had figured — and 31/2 times as much as the county's annual budget. Foster's effort to collect produced a drama the likes of which McDonald County had not seen since it tried to secede from Missouri in 1961, after the state left a McDonald County town off the map.

The bond sowed distrust that still ripples through McDonald County. And it raised troubling questions about old government debts everywhere — questions neither the county not the state of Missouri has been able to answer.

Must such debts be paid, no matter how old they are? Or can they be voided by a statute of limitation, like the kind that limits the time during which crimes can be prosecuted? Would such a statute of limitation be retroactive? Or does the Constitution forbid applying it to debts contracted before its passage? In instances where there is no specific mention of how the interest should be calculated, does simple interest apply? Or should it be compounded?

What happens if the government simply can't pay?

At his first opportunity, about three weeks after he cleaned out his attic, George Foster took his bond to town.

Tall, with graying blond hair and a quick sense of humor, Foster, 53, is a former contractor in Tulsa, Oklahoma, who moved to McDonald County in the late 1960s to get his kids away from dope and hippies.

After breakfast last June 25, he put on blue dress pants and a white shirt, climbed into his muddy, cream-and-tan Chevrolet pickup and drove six miles to Pineville, the county seat.

McDonald County totals 560 square miles but only 14,917 people. Foster's trip took him up hills and down hollows, called "hollers" and spelled that way on many maps — Reagan Holler, named for Owen, not Ronald; and Togi Holler, because it leads to Saratoga, called "Saratogi," or "Togi" for short. Foster drove through thick woods that hide ticks, chiggers, poison ivy and moonshine ($30 a gallon, delivered in plastic Clorox jugs).

The drive to Pineville can be accomplished at times without passing another person, but most often, Foster encounters other pickups. A number have gun racks, and many of the gun racks are full. The drivers almost always wave.

Foster pulled into the square in the middle of Pineville, with the News-Gazette on one corner, the stone sheriff's office on another, the McDonald County Bank on the third and Happy Valley Cafe on the fourth.

He parked on the gravel next to the new courthouse, strode past the flagpole, with its national and state banners flying, and walked in.

It's hard to keep a secret in McDonald County. George Foster had told only one or two people about his discovery, but when the county counsel spotted him in the hall, he shouted, 'Hello, George — got your bond with you?"

In a tiny room behind the clerk's office, the county's three most important people were meeting around a wooden table. The trio — county judges — listened to petitioners with problems for the county to solve.

In Missouri, county judges actually are county supervisors, policymakers who decide how the county should be run. They meet every Monday and Thursday morning, and run things with aplomb.

If something costs money, the answer most often is no.

For one thing, the county is usually broke. For another, it has a strong tradition against government doing what people can do themselves.

Any other approach to county affairs might bring the worst kind of government interference: higher taxes.

"Beware of strong drink," a sign in the courthouse warns. "It can make you shoot at tax collectors — and miss."

Foster stepped to the counter in the clerk's office.

The county clerk, Lou Harmon, 39, had heard that something was up. Harmon, whose forefathers had homesteaded McDonald County, is a careful man — and he had come up with some specifics: the face value of Foster's bond, the date of issue and its rate of interest. Harmon sat down at an adding machine and compounded the interest, year by year. When he finished, he had an adding machine tape 22 feet long. He knew that if Foster's bond was real, the county was in for a shock.

Harmon escorted George Foster into the judges' room.

At one corner of the table sat Stub Cantrell, the presiding county judge, born 62 years ago in the white house on his family's 976-acre ranch. He'd been out at 7 a.m. in overalls and a jacket, hauling hay to his cattle, but had changed into a long-sleeved white shirt and trousers for the meeting.

At another corner sat Fayette Crosby, 77, who had farmed, driven a delivery truck, worked as a grocery clerk and run a country store before retiring. He, too, had put on dress pants and a white shirt for the day's proceedings.

At the third corner sat Ted Bone, 48, lean and lanky, who lives with his brother on an old chicken ranch. "I'm helpin' my brother," he tells visitors. "And he ain't doin' nothin'." Bone usually wears a tractor cap, slightly askew and pulled down tightly over his head. He had left the cap at home, but he still was wearing bibbed overalls and an undershirt.

Foster sat down at the fourth corner. He laid his briefcase flat on the table, opened it and took out his bond. He closed the briefcase and placed the bond face-up on top of it.

The three judges eyed the bond. Foster explained what it was.

"I'm here to redeem it," he said.

There was a brief silence.

"Just what is this bond worth?" Crosby asked.

Lou Harmon unrolled his adding-machine tape: "$3,574,636.84," he said.

The entire McDonald budget for the year was less than a third of that — $1,005,102.63 and the county was currently overdrawn $5,000 to $6,000 at the bank.

To Foster, Crosby looked like he might have a stroke.

"We don't have that kind of money!" he said.

In his mind, Crosby envisioned a county he had heard about — he couldn't remember where — that had been sued for a huge amount. The plaintiff had won. It had caused taxes to climb out of sight.

To the three judges, George Foster was a newcomer. He hadn't lived in McDonald County much more than a dozen years. He thought and lived differently than most folks. He closed up his inn every winter, for instance, to take trips. He visited big cities and sailed and skied.

In McDonald County, that made him almost an outsider.

"Where did you get that bond?" Crosby demanded.

"I found it in the attic," Foster replied.

Crosby leaned forward and put his elbows on the table. Lou Harmon looked up. Crosby was staring through his dark-rimmed spectacles straight into Foster's eyes.

"What business," he snapped, "did you have in the attic?"

"Hell, I own it!" Foster shot back. "I own Ginger Blue. I own it."

Crosby realized his mistake — he thought Foster had been foraging around in the attic of the old county courthouse in the Pineville town square. It had been abandoned when the new courthouse was finished — and the townspeople had turned it into a museum and some arts-and-crafts shops. But it still had old county records stored upstairs.

Foster was half angry — the implication was that he had stolen the bond.

Crosby apologized. But he stayed on the edge of his chair.

The judges passed Foster's bond around the table.

Stub Cantrell stayed calm. If you do not have the money, he thought, you simply can't pay.

He handed the bond to Harmon.

The county clerk was chain-smoking Salems. He held the bond in his hand. It was indeed a bearer bond. Two coupons at the bottom had been clipped, then reattached when his counterpart had refused to pay the interest in 1875 and 1876 — because the county was broke then, too.

As the county budget officer, all Harmon could see were dollar signs. How long would it take to dig out if the county had to pay this thing?

Foster reminded the judges that they had a $1-million annual budget. "Just think," he said with a grin, "in three years you can almost have me paid off."

Nobody laughed.

Harmon handed the bond to Ted Bone.

Bone thought: Whatever fun Foster might be having, this isn't altogether a joke.

He handed the bond to Ben Hormel, 47, the county counsel. "Well," Hormel said dryly, "I advise we don't pay today."

The court asked Harmon to find out whether the bond was authentic and whether the county was legally bound to pay.

It told Foster he would have to wait.

"Take your time," Foster said. "The interest is costing you $1,000 a day."

He put the bond back into his briefcase and left.

It didn't take an hour for someone to scurry over to the old county courthouse and tell Jo Pearcy. A dark-haired woman with big brown eyes, an easy smile and granny glasses, Pearcy, 53, teaches seventh- and eighth-grade math at Pineville School. During the summer, she runs the museum and subleases space in the old courthouse to owners of the arts-and-crafts shops.

She listened to a description of Foster's bond.

"Hey, wait a minute!" she said. "We've got one of those."

She ran up to the empty second-floor courtroom. There, on the wall, just to the right of the judge's bench, in a cheap wooden frame, was another bond. She carried it downstairs and studied it.

Same three colors of ink. Same amount.

And it was No. 7 — well ahead of Foster's No. 19 in sequence of issue.

Her first concern was losing the museum. If Foster ended up collecting from the county, it might have to sell the old courthouse to pay him off. She sat down and wrote Lou Harmon a note:

"Tell George Foster not to put up his Foster County signs yet! Our museum has bond No. 7, issued June 10, 1871....

"Thank you (and thanks, Olin Armstrong, for the bond!)"

Over at the McDonald County Bank, Vice President Olin Armstrong groaned.

He had given the bond to the museum a year ago.

Before that, Armstrong, 59, one of the few men besides the undertaker who wears a tie, had the bond hanging on a nail in the maple paneling behind his desk. He had figured it was worthless.

Now people were calling him the banker who gave away $3.5 million.

He wasn't the only one who had given money away.

In the little green frame house behind the old stone high school in Noel, Louis Fiorito was watching television when the evening news had a story about George Foster and his bond.

Fiorito was shocked.

A soft-spoken man with mutton-chop sideburns, Fiorito, 49, works at a chicken-processing plant just outside of town. Twenty years ago, at an auction in Pineville, he had bought a box full of old papers. He had no idea what it contained. He paid $1 for it.

When he got it home, he found the bonds inside — 20 of them.

Certain their only value was antiquity, he gave several away — No. 19 to the owner of Ginger Blue Lodge before Foster bought it, and No. 7 to Armstrong, the banker.

But he still had two bonds tucked into a plastic folder in his bedroom.

"If Foster gets money for a bond," Fiorito said to himself, "I should too."

He sent his wife, Mary Jo, over to Pineville.

"By golly," she told the county judges, "if George Foster is going to get his money, we're going to get ours first — because we've got Nos. 1 and 2."

Foster, meanwhile, was hearing from Kansas City lawyers.

"Hey, I guarantee you we can collect that damn thing," one told him. "It's good. Hell, let's sue them. You'll get a judgment against the county and every time they get a dollar, you'll get a dollar."

Foster had T-shirts made. His employees and guests started wearing them. They said:

"I live in Foster County."

After days and nights of research in thick, red county ledgers, Lou Harmon found that Foster's bond was real.

During the Civil War, someone had burned the McDonald County courthouse. A replacement — the one that now contains Jo Pearcy's museum — was completed in 1869. Foster's bond was one of several issued to pay the builders.

The county had refused to redeem the bonds, and two bondholders sued.

The circuit court had ordered payment. But the bondholders were not the ones on

Foster's bond. Harmon could find no evidence that Foster's specific bond had been redeemed.

Ben Hormel, the county counsel, found no one who could tell him — not even the state attorney general — whether an old bond like Foster's should be considered a promissory note, which might have a limited lifespan, or a savings account, which could go on earning interest forever. He suspected it was like a savings account.

Nor could he find anyone who could tell him whether there was a statute of limitation that might void the bond, or whether it would be constitutional to apply such a statute retroactively if the bond had been issued before the statute was passed.

Nor could he find anyone who could tell him whether the return on a bond that does not specify otherwise should be calculated at simple interest or compound interest.

Finally, McDonald County logic took over.

Hormel told himself: "We're spending a great deal of effort here when, in fact, we aren't going to be able to pay the bond anyway. We ought to just refuse to pay it."

Seven days after Foster's first appearance, Lou Harmon got permission to use the circuit courtroom — larger and more comfortable than the little room the judges usually met in — and he summoned George Foster to sit down with the county judges once again.

When Foster walked in, he was amazed.

The 14 benches were filled with spectators. TV cameras were there from Joplin. Fayette Crosby's white shirt looked freshly pressed. Stub Cantrell had on a dress shirt with a white, brown and blue pattern. And Ted Bond had left his bib overalls and undershirt at home. He was wearing a maroon shirt with an Ivy League button-down collar and a western jacket.

"Well," Foster said, trying to keep a straight face, "at least I cleaned you guys up."

Nobody laughed.

Ben Hormel, wearing a navy blue suit for the occasion, looked hard at Foster — and decided to take the chance.

"I'm going to recommend," he told the court, "that we refuse payment of any sum on any of these bonds presented, including the one presented by Mr. Foster....

"It will be up to Mr. Foster and the other bondholders to decide whether or not to sue us. If they sue us, our first line of defense will be that the statute of limitation applies, and therefore any action to collect on these bonds will be barred. If that issue is decided against us in court, our second line of defense is going to be that the bonds have been paid. If that issue is decided against us, then our third line of defense will be that simple interest, not compound interest, applies on these bonds, which will put their worth at approximately $1,200 each, instead of $3.5 million."

Lou Harmon adjusted his tie against his Adam's apple and gave a lengthy description of how he had determined that Foster's bond was authentic. He closed by saying: "I would follow Mr. Hormel's recommendation that McDonald County pay nothing on Mr. Foster's bond or any subsequent bonds that have been presented."

Fayette Crosby didn't hesitate. "I'll go along with Mr. Hormel's recommendation."

"I will too," said Ted Bone.

Stub Cantrell made it unanimous.

If his bond had been paid, Foster asked, why wasn't it marked paid?

"I can't answer that," Harmon replied. "I don't know."

"Which I'm sure a legal person would bring up," Foster added, ominously.

Did he intend to pursue the matter further?

George Foster smiled and said: "We'll just have to wait and see."

In the nine months since Foster tried to redeem his $3.5-million bond, it has accrued enough interest to be worth nearly $4 million.

And McDonald County is uneasy.

Fayette Crosby hasn't talked to George Foster. "Don't have any desire to."

In fact, when Crosby's Republican Club met for lunch one afternoon at Ginger Blue Lodge, Crosby didn't go. "He wasn't gonna get any of my money."

Crosby still had doubts about where Foster's bond came from.

So does Ted Bone.

"It was county property once," Bone says. "It might have been pilfered."

Olin Armstrong says Jo Pearcy's bond belongs to him.

"I didn't give it," he says. "I loaned it to the museum over there. I just took it over there and left it with the ladies over there. I didn't tell 'em it was theirs. I just left it over there for display."

But Pearcy's bond, like Foster's, is a bearer bond. "At this time," she says, "I'm the bearer."

Foster says he was first in line for payment. "First come, first served."

But Louis Fiorito says: "Anybody collects, it's going to be me. That's why I kept Nos. 1 and 2."

The three county judges would like to think nobody can collect.

"No way. No way," says Fayette Crosby.

"It's dead," says Stub Cantrell.

"I'd say it's dead," says Ted Bone.

Ben Hormel, the country counsel, isn't so sure.

"I couldn't say it's been settled," he says. "You're talking about $3.5 million. People will do a lot of things for $3.5 million."

At Ginger Blue Lake, George Foster keeps his bond on a shelf in his office, tucked inside a March 1946 issue of Woman's Home Companion.

Isn't he afraid someone might steal it?

"Nah," he grins. "Whoever'd take it would have a hard time trying to cash No. 19. Ol' Fayette Crosby'd look at him real hard and ask, 'Where'd you git that? Whose attic you been in?' "

Foster laughs.

"I would love to collect it, or collect part of it," he says. "Money is money. So long as it wouldn't break the county."

Will he sue?

"Well, that's like suing your mother. I'm not a native here, but I've been here 13 years, and I've got to keep staying here, so what have I gained by bankrupting the county?"

But when Foster sees any of the county judges, he kids them.

"I just tell them, 'Save your money, boys. You're taxes are goin' up.'

"Of all the things I could find," he says, "why the hell didn't it say 'Standard Oil of New Jersey' on it or 'New York City' or something?

"Instead of McDonald County, U.S.A."

Character Studies

❖

The Only Sense Is of Loss

Michael Carneal can't explain why he shot his classmates five years ago. Missy Jenkins, now paralyzed, goes on with life but can't go back.

By Stephanie Simon · December 2, 2002

The flashbacks start, for Missy Jenkins, with "Amen."

She is holding hands with friends in the lobby of her high school, praying. It is the Monday after Thanksgiving. She skipped church the day before to see a movie. But she never misses morning prayer circle.

"Amen."

The three dozen students drop hands.

Then Missy sees a girl, a friend, crumple. She hears a pop. Nicole is on the floor, limp, bloody. Missy can't make sense of it. A prank, she thinks. Man, she thinks, man, is someone going to be in trouble. She hears screams. She sees students whirling, a blur of motion. Another pop.

Missy feels herself sliding to the floor. Her twin sister, Mandy, dives on top of her. The screaming is so loud. She can't think. And then, she can. And then, she knows.

"Mandy," she says. "I can't feel my stomach.

"I can't feel my stomach! What does that mean?"

The flashbacks start, for Michael Carneal, with chipped plaster.

He can't make sense of it.

He remembers, as through a mist, loading two shotguns, two semiautomatic rifles and 700 rounds of ammunition in the trunk of his sister's car that morning, the whole arsenal wrapped in blankets. An English project, he had explained. He remembers lugging the bundle into school. He remembers chatting about nothing with his friends. He remembers pulling a fifth gun, a revolver, out of his backpack as morning prayer circle broke up.

And now he's staring at this gouge in the wall, at plaster knocked loose by a bullet.

Michael looks around. He sees kids on the floor, crying, screaming. His friend Nicole is down there. She's still. Then he sees another student walking toward him, a

219

boy, approaching slowly through the noise.

"What are you doing?" the boy asks, calm.

"Shooting people," Michael hears himself answer.

"What for?" the boy asks. He draws closer.

Michael answers: "I don't know."

The flashbacks come again and again and again.

Five years ago, Michael Carneal, a skinny freshman, opened fire at Heath High School in West Paducah, Kentucky. He killed three classmates: Nicole Hadley, 14, who marched with him in band, 15-year-old Kayce Steger, and 17-year-old Jessica James. He also wounded five. Most of the injuries were minor. Missy Jenkins' was not.

The bullet entered just below her left collarbone, slammed through her — nicking her lung, her spinal cord — and came out by her right shoulder blade. She is paralyzed from the chest down.

The bloodshed in the working-class river town — the young girls gunned down in the Bible Belt as they prayed — rattled the nation. Exactly two months earlier, a 16-year-old boy had stabbed his mother to death, then killed two classmates at his high school in Pearl, Mississippi. But that tragedy had not grabbed national attention the way the shootings in western Kentucky did.

Carnage in other schoolyards would follow, all too often: in Jonesboro, Arkansas, and Springfield, Oregon, in Conyers, Georgia, and Fort Gibson, Oklahoma, at Santana High School near San Diego and at Columbine High in Littleton, Colorado, where two students killed 12 classmates and a teacher before turning their guns on themselves.

Michael Carneal would hold himself responsible for inspiring such rampages. Missy Jenkins would make it her mission to prevent them.

He would feel guilt ripping at him through the flashbacks. She would shake off each nightmare with fresh resolve.

Neither one wants that shattering morning to define them. But it has.

. . .

"I think about it all the time," Michael Carneal says.

He slouches into his chair in a conference room at the Kentucky State Reformatory in LaGrange. He is 19 years old now — tall, pudgy, pasty, with a scraggly beard and clunky square glasses. It's hard to see in him the scrawny, skittish freshman who pulled out a .22-caliber Ruger, pressed foam plugs in his ears and opened fire that Monday morning.

It's hard even for Carneal.

He knows he shot his friends. He remembers planning it. He remembers thinking the night before, after a game of chess with his dad: "Tomorrow, I go to prison." And now he is in prison, told when to shower, what to wear, his biggest treat the microwave popcorn he earns by keeping his cell tidy. It still does not feel real.

"I know it was me," he says, "but it doesn't fit my character. I'm not a violent person. A lot of people think I'm evil because of what happened. That's not true. I made a mistake. A big mistake."

He is on the psychiatric ward at the reformatory, mellowed by 11 pills a day. The medications push away the monsters he used to see leering at his windows.

The monsters came often in the months before the shooting. Carneal would cover up the vents in the bathroom so the bad guys could not grab him. At night, he felt them clutching his legs. He lived in terror. Yet he told no one. He played baritone in band. He played pranks on his friends. His parents noticed nothing.

Carneal told several classmates before Thanksgiving that "something big" was going to happen in school. He warned them the "day of reckoning" was near. But he was always goofing around — passing off parsley as pot, wearing the mat from a Twister game to school as a cape — and no one paid much attention. He felt always alone.

"I thought I might as well go to prison because I didn't have anything to lose," he says.

That doesn't explain why he murdered, though. Michael Carneal has spent five years searching for an answer.

He doesn't have one.

"That makes it all that much worse," he says.

He watches news of other kids killing kids in other schools, and he feels helpless to stop the spasms of violence, the awful trend he believes he touched off that awful morning. "If I don't understand my own motivation," he says, "how can I understand theirs?"

He says he's sorry. He says it often. His voice is flat. His eyes are blank.

In a sagging brown jumpsuit and high-top sneakers, Carneal spends his days in the medium-security prison playing crazy eights or shooting pool, reading, writing, talking to psychologists. He is locked in his cell only at night. It's a single cell, with a TV and a radio. His parents come to visit every weekend. They bring him cash, now and then, to buy oatmeal cream pies at the canteen.

Carneal was given a life sentence but will be eligible for parole in 20 years. He does not allow himself to think what he might do if he gets out. He really has no idea.

He never thought much about the future, back when he had one.

. . .

Missy Jenkins, three weeks shy of her 20th birthday, wheels through the holiday clutter of her apartment in Murray, Kentucky, dodging poinsettias as she maneuvers to the VCR. She picks through the tapes: "Scent of a Woman." "Young Guns." Then she finds what she's looking for and pops it in.

Her own image fills the screen: a slight teenager with long blond hair seated at a pink vanity table, putting on makeup. "My name is Missy Jenkins," she says in voice-over. "I had a GPA of 3.3. I was homecoming queen runner-up. I was vice president of my junior class. I was shot by a classmate."

The camera pans to show her black wheelchair, her long, thin, useless legs. "I'm one of the lucky ones."

It's a public service announcement she filmed this year for a national anti-violence campaign in the schools.

She has been lending her voice to similar efforts since the day after the shooting, when she answered questions from her hospital bed on national TV. She has taken her message to the White House and on MTV, has spoken before tens of thousands of students across the country.

All the while, she has pushed through a grueling rehabilitation, learning first to live using a wheelchair and then to walk short distances with special braces. Three years ago, Mandy as always at her side, she walked across the stage at Heath High to claim her diploma. The next year, she shuffled the first quarter-mile of the Los Angeles Marathon, in pouring rain, just to prove she could.

Her efforts have earned her acclaim: She won a federal crime-prevention award. She appeared on stage at the 2000 Democratic National Convention, in a tribute to heroes.

But Missy Jenkins does not want to be a hero.

She wants to be exactly what she is: a college junior at Murray State University in western Kentucky, majoring in social work.

She wants to get to her manicure appointment on time, persuade her sister to help her write a play for drama class, gossip with a roommate about the guy she hopes will ask her out. She wants to raise money for arthritis research with her sorority.

She wants to marry. She wants to be a mom. She wants to get an agent, to act in L.A.

She wants to do everything she would have done had Carneal not squeezed that trigger. She wants to be the same person she would have been.

"I think I am the same person," she says, "the exact same person."

And yet, now and then, loss shadows Jenkins' bright, open face. She wonders how she will be able to lift a crying baby from a crib. She wonders how she will be able to grocery shop for a family.

She misses dancing.

She wonders when she should tell her boyfriends all the embarrassing truths about her body. When she should show them her catheter. Or the 16 pills she takes each day to ward off muscle spasms and bladder infections.

She hates to be alone, because sometimes she falls as she hoists herself from wheelchair to bed and finds herself stuck on the floor, needing rescue.

Missy Jenkins may be the exact same person. But she is forever changed.

"I think about it every day," she says.

Missy and Michael knew each other in high school. It would have been surprising if they hadn't, in a school with just 486 students. They marched together in band. They teased each other.

One day, as one of his practical jokes, Michael wore a button he had made with a picture of the blond-streaked twins. The next day, Missy and Mandy countered with their own homemade Michael buttons. "He was a fun guy," Missy says. "Not creepy. The class clown. I try to picture him with the gun, but it's hard, because I knew him."

A year after the shooting, Michael tried to reach out to Missy. He wrote several letters. He called. Finally, Missy's father contacted an attorney. Michael was ordered to stop.

Looking back, he says he's not sure what he so urgently wanted to tell her. That he was sorry? That he could not explain?

Missy did not want to hear from him. She had confronted him once, in court. She wheeled up to him and, holding his gaze, told him about her catheter and muscle spasms, about her fears, her loss, her determination to make her pain mean something.

"I told him I forgave him, not to make him feel better, but so I could move on," she recalls. "I told him I would miss out on a lot, but I would not miss out on life." He listened to her in silence.

He falls silent now, thinking of what he would say to Missy if he saw her. The silence stretches a long moment. He gives up. "There's nothing you can say."

.   .   .

Students walking into Heath High this morning will see a wreath on the memorial stone in the school courtyard. No public ceremony is planned. There is no need. Reminders are everywhere in West Paducah.

Teachers stand each morning at the high school's door. They search book bags. But they also talk, and listen, trying to win students' trust, to counsel and console, to reach out to anyone who seems edgy. Almost all the teachers who were on staff during the shooting remain at Heath. Not one asked to transfer.

The Carneal family is still in town too. Michael's sister graduated from Heath High seven months after the shooting, as class valedictorian. His father, an attorney, still works downtown. His mother waves back at the neighbors, as always.

The Steger and James families remain in West Paducah as well, near the gravestones of their girls. The Hadleys moved to Chicago. Former Principal Bill Bond saw every student touched by the tragedy through graduation. Then he took a job as a national school safety consultant. He starts to say that life is back to normal now. Then he corrects himself: "It will never return to normal. Those 12 seconds changed everything for everyone involved."

Christmas decorations twinkled in West Paducah this weekend. But through the cheer, on this devastating anniversary, many will mourn. Many will remember.

❖

Anguish Turns to a Song of Joy

For years, Japanese novelist Kenzaburo Oe wrote the words his brain-damaged child could not speak. Now a gift for music has given the Nobel winner's son his own voice.

BY TERESA WATANABE · APRIL 12, 1995

TOKYO — It should have been a crowning moment in the life of Kenzaburo Oe, Japan's brilliant, brooding novelist who won last year's Nobel Prize in literature: June 13, 1963, the day his first son was born.

Except that the baby did not look like a son. Or even a human. A monster. A two-headed monster with half his brains spilling out, Oe thought as he took his first look at the baby with the red, pinched face, mouth agape in a soundless scream, the tiny head swaddled in bloodied bandages.

Oe's reaction was expressed through Bird, the hero of his celebrated 1969 novel, "A Personal Matter." The book mirrors his life — in particular, the hellish week when he faced the choice between death and life for his son, freedom or bondage for himself:

Like Apollinaire, my son was wounded on a dark and lonely battlefield that I

224

have never seen, and he has arrived with his head in bandages. I'll have to bury him like a soldier who died at war.

But the boy did not die.

No longer would the sweet, easy tears of mourning melt it away as if it were a simple jelly. Swaddled in skin as red as shrimp that gleamed with the luster of scar tissue, the baby was beginning ferociously to live.

The baby was still alive when Oe returned from a short writing assignment in Hiroshima, where the astonishing bravery of the atomic bomb survivors filled him with shame about his attitudes. When the agonized victims had every reason to commit suicide but did not, when the doctors had every reason to give up but never faltered in trying to heal and comfort their patients, how could he deny the tiny life struggling to survive, his very own son?

Oe chose life — an operation to cut away the protruding brain mass and cover the hole in the skull with a plastic plate. He named his son Hikari: light.

Hikari is now 31. He is epileptic and knock-kneed. He is nearsighted and cross-eyed. He understands only simple conversations.

But from the depths of a damaged brain, he hears the melodies of an inner music. He has learned to transfer those chords to paper. Hikari has become a composer of classical music.

In the last three years, he has released two CDs — short, simple compositions for flute, piano and guitar. Even before his father won the Nobel Prize, both CDs turned gold, with average sales of 160,000, a smash in Japan's classical recording industry, which considers 10,000 in sales a hit. In January, his CDs were released in the United States by Denon Records.

And Hikari is bound for further fame. His uncle, noted filmmaker Juzo Itami ("Tampopo," "A Taxing Woman"), has launched a project based on Oe's novel about a family's disabled son, "A Quiet Life."

Hikari's success as an artist marks a new passage for father and son. For three decades, Oe has served as Hikari's alter ego, expressing through his works what his son could not articulate for himself. The mission consumed him, changed his writing and, some say, drew his focus away from the broad social issues that earned his original celebrity as the voice of Japan's disenchanted postwar generation.

Now, at 60, Oe says that mission is over.

"Hikari has learned to communicate directly with society himself," Oe says with a satisfied smile.

This man whose prose pounds with the power of vivid metaphor and intricate ideals quickly came to terms with a fate that gave him a son incapable of speaking complex sentences. Since then, father and son have forged a symbiosis that has nourished and challenged both.

Hikari has expanded Oe and inspired him, fed his dreams and filled his life. He has changed Oe's very concept of manhood, says the writer, who revealed his own transformation in "A Personal Matter."

The protagonist, Bird, begins the novel with a brawl — one way men have proved their worth through the ages — and ends it with a far more exacting measure of manhood: All I want is to stop being a man who continually runs away from responsibility.

It was thus for Oe.

On a recent evening, he stood sauteing onions that Hikari had minced as they made curry, an occasional ritual to give Oe's wife, Yukari, a break. As Oe stirred the onions in the blackened wok, he recalled his days as Japan's *enfant terrible*. With his unapologetically leftist works, he stunned the literary world by winning the coveted Akutagawa Prize while still in college in 1958.

But the success oppressed him. He says he was immature and dangerously unstable, staggering under his fame and the fearsome burden of being the spokesman for a generation set adrift by the destruction of their values after World War II. And then his creative juices ran dry. He had nothing to write. He says he felt doomed.

Oe felt his son's birth personified his life's dead end. But as he anguished in a Dante's hell of indecision over what to do, he was forced into an inescapable showdown with himself and his fears.

What was he trying to protect from that monster of a baby that he must run so hard and so shamelessly? What was it in himself that he was so frantic to defend? The answer was horrifying: Nothing! Zero!

Admitting his emptiness, Oe chose to fill himself with the lifelong responsibility to cherish and nurture a brain-damaged son. His choice replenished him, giving him new power and creative direction and even a sort of spiritual meaning for a confirmed agnostic.

"I felt I was reborn," Oe said. "My creed became: 'If we can live through our difficulties, we can find a new dimension in life.' Without this accident, my life would have been doomed as a decadent writer who lived desperately and died early. I would have stopped writing and possibly committed suicide."

Oe thought he was saving Hikari that summer day when he decided on the operation. But in fact, he says, Hikari saved him.

The family calls Hikari "Pooh-chan," a term of endearment coined when he was a baby and resembled Winnie the Pooh. Now tall and heavyset, he still is the center of an adoring family: his parents, sister Natsumiko, 27, and brother Sakurao, 25.

They live in a handsome two-story home opening onto a garden of potted pansies and camellia trees in Seijo Gakuen, a tony Tokyo neighborhood peopled by the likes of Seiji Ozawa, the Boston Symphony conductor. Hikari and Ozawa frequent the same noodle shop, where they swap musical ideas and are collaborating on a piece for the conductor's birthday this summer.

On the recent curry night, Oe protectively held Hikari's arm as he guided him through the spotless neighborhood streets on a trip to the supermarket. "Pooh-chan, what do we need for curry? Onions, right? Carrots, right? You go find a good curry powder and buy it, OK? Understand? Understand?"

Hikari listens intently and nods, his eyes glued straight ahead. Off he goes, stopping only at intersections he knows he must not cross alone. "Once he has his objective, he moves very quickly," Oe says.

Hikari's attentive mother has carefully shaped her son's objectives. Noticing his keen ear for sound when he was a baby, she filled their home with Mozart, Chopin and Beethoven, and sang him lullabies. His father bought recordings of birdcalls after he saw Hikari perk up whenever he heard birds outside.

The breakthrough came when Hikari was 6. Strolling with his father along a path near the family's summer home, Hikari heard chirping. Imitating the narrator he had heard so many times, the boy gravely intoned: "This is a water rail." They were the first words he ever spoke.

Prodded by his parents, he memorized all 70 birdcalls on the record, although he lost interest in them a year after starting school. He showed a ferocious interest in classical music instead. His mother began teaching him piano when he was 9 and hired a teacher two years later when his vision problems and hand-eye coordination made the going rough.

At 15, Hikari developed epilepsy and lost what skill he had. But his instructor, Kumiko Tamura, had begun to teach him to write down what he was playing.

One day, Hikari presented Tamura with the scrawlings of a simple score. She thought it was a snippet of Beethoven or Mozart he had memorized. But it was Hikari's first composition; he was 13.

Blessed with what Oe calls "an absolute sense of music," Hikari composes in his head, without a piano, drawing upon the vast array of notes stored in the depths of his memory. He can hear a song, even the first few notes, and immediately name the chord and key, a skill he shyly showed visitors by cupping his hand to indicate the song in question was written in C.

Hikari continued to write: a composition for a school event at 18, a collection published by his family at 20, works for small concerts around town.

His big break came in 1991, when he was "discovered" by Hiroyuki Okano, head of Western music for the Nippon Columbia record company. Okano had been fascinated by drawings of Hikari's musical compositions in one of Oe's books and proposed a collaboration. The result, "The Music of Hikari Oe," was released in 1992 and became the biggest classical music seller in Nippon Columbia's history, Okano says.

He says the smashing sales cannot be explained merely by the father's fame or by curiosity about Hikari's disabilities. "Hikari's music is very fresh," Okano says. "Before Hikari, most classical CDs were geared toward commercialism or the scholarly extreme. But Hikari created a new music approachable by a broader audience."

Some critics call his music pure and beautiful and say that's why it sells so well. Others deem it unremarkable. Musician Ryuichi Sakamoto says in the January issue of Eureka, a Japanese arts magazine, "There should be a line between the artistic merit of music and the issue of the handicapped. Should all the music created by the handicapped be given credit?"

Oe says Hikari's first CD expressed a freshness and innocence, a joy and a lightness. But he detected something different in his son's second disc, released last year: "a dark soul screaming."

When Hikari was small, Oe tried to awaken the spark of imagination by coaching him to dream with tales of kangaroos at the foot of his bed. But his son showed irritation with the entire business of dreams and declared: "I don't believe there are kangaroos."

The matter was closed until Hikari composed a song, now on his second CD, called "Dreams." It conveyed an agony that shocked Oe. "I wondered if Hikari had this kind of dream," Oe says. "Or if he doesn't, I wondered if this scream comes through his soul."

Asked why his son's soul would be crying, what darkness he might be fighting through, the novelist shrugs helplessly. "I don't know."

Hikari does not cry. But he laughs. On this day, he is languidly wheezing out a tune on his accordion during a music class at his public vocational center. Suddenly, he emits a loud noise that did not come from his instrument. His teachers and classmates turn to him in glee. He turns pink and giggles.

He commutes to the center daily, usually delivered by his brother in the morning into the care of Shizue Ito, director of the Karasuyama Welfare Workplace in western Tokyo. Ito is a small, dynamic woman who flutters about in incessant motion and clucks warmth to her charges like a mother hen.

Hikari is one of 50 workers, all mentally disabled by conditions ranging from

Down's syndrome to autism. They generally spend their mornings in simple labor — weaving scarves, cleaning the parks — and are paid accordingly. In the afternoons, they learn activities from cooking to music.

Hikari's specialty is assembling clothespins and packaging them in plastic. He is skilled but slow, Ito says with an affectionate laugh. His colleagues average $90 a month; Hikari usually brings in $11 or so.

The reason may be the inner music he hears. While his cohorts package their clothespins one after another, Hikari spends much time laying his out on the table in intricate, beautiful patterns. He seems to be arranging notes to a musical masterpiece, his teachers say.

"He doesn't make much money, but his patterns are beautiful!" Ito says.

He loves to watch sumo wrestling but gets depressed when his heroes lose. He doesn't get angry easily. But he becomes visibly upset when his colleagues at the center don't do as they are told, or when in another setting he sees scenes suggestive of sexuality.

Ito says the Oe family has had an immeasurable impact on public attitudes toward the disabled by encouraging Hikari's high-profile career and opening their home to media interviews. Although gains have been made here in the past 10 years — the disabled now are guaranteed a public education, for instance — facilities are still widely lacking, and many families hide their children away for fear of social ridicule, Ito says.

Not everyone approves of Hikari's prominence. A magazine recently featured a survey: "Does Oe flaunt his disabled son too much?" Most refrained from clear answers, with some pointing out that the media, not Oe, initiate pieces about the pair. But such grumbles were apparent when the writer brought his son to the Nobel ceremony in Stockholm last year and allowed TV cameras to record his disco dancing.

It is not likely that Hikari sees himself as a crusader to heal society's misunderstanding of the disabled. But as he steadfastly meets life head-on — battling epilepsy, a weakening memory and a gradual slowdown in his musical output — those around him find strength and healing.

When he was 15, Hikari suffered his first epileptic seizure. Oe was burned out, crushed by the death of his mentor professor and thrashing around for a new direction in his work.

The family agonized over treatments and whether they would be able to manage this frightful development. But Hikari's condition stabilized and he proved resilient. His comeback, Oe says, propelled the writer to make his own breakthrough: He discovered the works of the English poet William Blake, which inspired him in a different literary direction: a series of short stories.

In 1996, Oe plans to move to the United States for a year to study at Princeton in search of a new literary form for the final work of his life: a healing message to bring about the "deep reconciliation of human beings," Oe says.

Hikari will be with him, as his muse and touchstone.

"By the guidance of Hikari, I have continued to live and to write," Oe says. "Sometimes I am afraid of the possibility that there is a God who gave him to me."

Tokyo bureau researcher Chiaki Kitada contributed to this report.

⁖

David Souter: A Life Rooted in the Law

The Supreme Court nominee's world is deliberately narrow, with few interests. But his mind is broad and deep and, to everyone but himself, largely unknown.

By John M. Broder · July 27, 1990

WEARE, New Hampshire — At the foot of a dirt dead-end road sits the Souter family farmhouse, an unkempt old pile under a siege of waist-high weeds. The brown paint is peeling and moss spreads on the bare wood, windows sag under years of dirt, cobwebs cling to the door and an ancient bird's nest perches above the porch light. There are five lightning rods along the roof, no television antenna.

Inside, no piece of furniture is less than half a century old. The ancient refrigerator is powered by an electric motor on the top, and the antique stove has white cast-iron handles. Boxes are piled to the ceiling, and the study is a warren of magazines, phonograph albums and books — reference books, novels, oversized art books, books on foreign lands and long-ago battles, books of laws, books about laws and books about the men who make laws.

It's hard to believe anyone lives in this creaking museum, except perhaps an aged hermit counting out his days rummaging through faded numbers of Collier's and the Saturday Evening Post. Yet this wreck of a house raised and still shelters U.S. 1st

Circuit Court of Appeals Judge David Hackett Souter, President Bush's 50-year-old nominee for the Supreme Court.

The house and its study give some clues to this man who may sit the rest of his life on the nation's highest tribunal. According to longtime friends and neighbors, Souter is a highly disciplined man who has kept a daily diary for 40 years but who cares little for earthly goods, for travel, for restaurants or receptions. Mundane matters — like cutting the grass — move him not at all. When he is not reading case law at work, he is reading at home. He relaxes by hiking the 4,000-foot granite peaks of New Hampshire's mountains. He wondered aloud the other day why anyone would want to leave New Hampshire.

Souter's life is deliberately narrow, encompassing only work, church, the historical society and a hospital board.

But his mind is broad and deep and, to everyone but himself, largely unknown.

He eats a hearty breakfast but takes the same lunch to work every day — an apple and a carton of yogurt. He buys the yogurt in bulk and washes out his luncheon container every evening to use again. He drives unwashed Volkswagens. He appears not to own a topcoat, wearing only a suit and a scarf even in the frigid New Hampshire winter.

Souter isn't merely frugal, his best friend says, he's cheap. "He'll squeeze a nickel until the buffalo groans," said fellow New Hampshire attorney Tom Rath.

He is a devout Episcopalian with broad tastes in literature, art and music. He is a devoted son who visits his mother weekly at a nursing home in nearby Concord. His social life is nonexistent, according to a close friend. He is a lifelong bachelor who in the past maintained relationships with women, but his interest in dating appears to have faded over the years as he has become more consumed by the law.

He says he's still looking for the right woman, said Nellie Perrigo, a neighbor and self-described second mother to the nominee, but "he wants all his time untouched for his job. I don't think he'll marry now."

. . .

According to all who know him, Souter is as austere in his approach to the law as he is in his personal life. In this, both liberals and conservatives find hope. Liberals see in him a strong streak of Yankee libertarianism, a "live free or die" philosophy that firmly opposes judges who dictate morality. Conservatives are hopeful that Souter will remain the restrained jurist he has been for a decade and will not seek to use the court as an instrument of social engineering.

He has excelled nearly everywhere he's been, and yet he has never lost his unassuming, almost shy mien. He embodies perfectly the reserved New Englander who, when he first meets you, just stands there staring at his shoes and, when he really gets to know you, stares at your shoes.

Souter was born September 17, 1939, in Melrose, Massachusetts, the only child of Joseph and Helen Hackett Souter. He spent his summers as a young boy at his maternal grandparents' farm in Weare.

After the Hacketts died, Joseph and Helen moved up to the farm when David was 11 years old, trading the faster pace of the Boston area for the solitude of the north.

Joseph Souter worked as a mid-level loan officer at the New Hampshire Savings Bank in Concord, which is 11 miles down the old Concord Stage Road from the Souter farm. Neighbor Howard Ineson, who has known the family since the Souters moved to Weare 40 years ago, recalled Souter senior as "very quiet, reserved, conservative; a perfect gentleman."

The father was not particularly prominent in town nor as wealthy as most bankers. The bulk of the family money apparently went into savings for college for young David.

Teachers at the Weare school immediately recognized the sixth-grader's promise. Nellie Perrigo, who taught there, said the small school obviously could not contain David's bounding intelligence. Because the town high school had no college preparatory classes, the village paid his tuition to the much larger Concord High School, where he was described in the yearbook as "very hard working and studious." Souter was voted "most sophisticated" and "most likely to succeed" in the class of 1957.

The yearbook also said Souter liked "giving and attending scandalous parties," but everyone says that was meant with tongue in cheek.

Like all 16-year-olds, he ached to get his driver's license. When he finally got his permit, he used the family car chiefly to take Perrigo's elderly mother on outings searching for antiques for her shop.

He was bookish, churchgoing and unathletic — what kids today would probably call a nerd or a dweeb — but "never prissy," Perrigo said. He carried a leather briefcase to high school, and legend has it that the only time he ever got in trouble was staying past closing time at the local historical society.

One summer in high school, Souter worked at Les and Barbara Knox's farm, about a mile away from his family's place across Sugar Hill Road. One day, Les Knox sent him out with an old farmhand to clear some woods. At the end of the day, Knox asked how young Souter had fared.

"Well," the hand replied, "he don't know much, but he's willin'."

In high school, Souter dated Ann Grant, daughter of a local state court judge, and the relationship continued after Souter left to attend Harvard in Cambridge, Massachusetts. It is unclear whether the two were ever engaged, but friends say the romance eventually faded after Souter graduated from Harvard and headed for Oxford University in England on a prestigious Rhodes scholarship.

As an undergraduate, Souter majored in philosophy, but his interest in the law was already evident. His senior thesis was on the judicial philosophy of Justice Oliver Wendell Holmes, and some friends, detecting Souter's unspoken ambition, used to jokingly call him Mr. Justice Souter.

At Oxford's Magdalen College, Souter lightened up a bit, according to fellow Rhodes Scholar and law school classmate William Bardel, now with the Wall Street investment house Shearson Lehman Hutton.

"He had a wry sense of humor, he enjoyed a party, having a pint of beer. He was very sociable even if he was wearing a three-piece suit," Bardel said.

"What I remember is David courtly, very gentlemanly, with his hands in the pockets, telling stories and especially doing imitations with his New England accent," he added. "I'm pretty sure also that he climbed in a few windows with me after midnight when they locked the college gates."

Souter did not serve in the military because his Rhodes scholarship extended his student deferment when his draft call would have come in 1961 or 1962. An Army official noted that draft quotas in those years were relatively low and usually filled by 18- and 19-year-olds without deferments, so Souter's case was not unusual.

He returned to Cambridge in 1963 to attend Harvard Law School, where classmates said he was not argumentative and seldom volunteered to speak in class. A member of Souter's class of 1966, Kent Bishop of Atlanta, remembered him as "a very serious, intense person" whose few outside activities included membership in a non-exclusive dining club called Lincoln's Inn.

Others remembered that Souter was one of only a handful of classmates who regularly attended religious services, and none could recall Souter's talking of traveling anywhere other than back to New Hampshire during breaks.

By contrast with his Rhodes scholarship and his Phi Beta Kappa standing as an undergraduate, Souter was a relatively undistinguished law student.

Souter was not chosen for the Law Review — the school's most eagerly sought-after honor — and in a class where nearly one in four students graduated cum laude or better, Souter did not.

"If there had been a list made of likely Supreme Court nominees, he would not have been on it," one classmate said. "He was just a quiet brain sitting there," another said.

After graduating from law school, Souter returned to Concord and signed on with the law firm of Orr & Reno. Malcolm McLane, a partner at the firm who had helped Souter secure his Rhodes scholarship, said the firm was delighted to land him.

Charles Leahy, another partner at Orr & Reno, said Souter soon chafed at the scut work of the "small country law firm," which chiefly handled tax matters, business disputes and some family law.

"He wanted to break out, to be in charge of something, to be responsible for his own outcomes," Leahy said.

When Warren B. Rudman, then the No. 2 man at the New Hampshire attorney general's office, offered Souter a job as a deputy attorney general, he jumped at it.

"Rudman recognized within a week that he had someone of superior abilities," Leahy said. Within a year, Souter was head of the department's criminal division and shortly afterward was named deputy attorney general when Rudman was elevated to the top spot.

When Rudman left in 1976 to enter private practice, he lobbied for his protege to fill his unexpired term. Arch-conservative Gov. Meldrim Thomson happily complied, said Rudman, now a U.S. senator who was instrumental in getting Souter named to the high court.

Working for Thomson forced Souter into defending some extreme stands, such as the governor's order that state flags be flown at half-staff on Good Friday in honor of Christ's crucifixion. The state, under Souter, also unsuccessfully tried to prosecute a man who defaced the words "live free or die" on his New Hampshire license plate, saying the words conflicted with his religious beliefs.

Leahy said Souter privately disagreed with both positions, but he articulated them in court because he was obligated to as the governor's lawyer.

"Given our ultra-conservative politics, he was pushed into a lot of fake issues and red herrings. He had to defend this business about flying the flag at half-staff and some other damn-fool right-wing causes.

"He privately felt that a lot of these things were not of such importance that they should consume court time. But he was also aware of his role in our political system," Leahy said.

But on the most contentious issue of the decade in New Hampshire — the Seabrook nuclear power station — Souter stood foursquare behind the state's conservative leaders.

Rowdy bands of demonstrators repeatedly tried to stop construction on the plant in 1977 through a variety of civil disobedience tactics. During several of these demonstrations, which were well planned and publicized long in advance, Souter set up a command post in the plant manager's office and personally supervised arrests.

He took it upon himself also to argue before a local magistrate that demonstrators should be sentenced to jail rather than be given suspended sentences.

"He didn't like to delegate important cases," said an attorney who worked with Souter in the attorney general's office. "He insisted on being on the scene himself [at Seabrook] while the protesters howled outside."

In a pattern that would be repeated later on other issues, he did not address the merits of nuclear power, only the more narrow issue of whether protesters were justified in breaking the law to challenge it. Souter felt strongly that they were not.

Leahy said that to this day he does not know whether Souter approves or disapproves of nuclear power. "But he feels strongly about public safety and orderly political protest. This was a deliberate and active violation of the law. David finds that type of thing deeply disturbing," Leahy said.

Despite his central role in quashing the Seabrook protests, the short, gray-suited attorney general never became a lightning rod for the anti-nuclear forces. Nor did he acquire a reputation as a harsh law-and-order official.

Perhaps in another state he would have become a conservative icon or a liberal bogeyman. But not in flinty New Hampshire. In New Hampshire, David Souter is a moderate.

That explains the elaborate praise he wins from Democrats and liberals in the state. "He is clearly an intellectual giant," said Concord attorney Kate Hanna, a former clerk for one of Souter's fellow justices on the state Supreme Court. "He stands out among all the other human beings I know. He is just a splendid, splendid jurist."

State Sen. Susan McLane, a Democrat and a leader of the state's abortion rights movement, also was unstinting in her admiration. She and her husband, Malcolm McLane, are friends as well as colleagues of the nominee.

"He is one of the most brilliant people I know. A fine, fine person," she said. The McLanes occasionally have Souter over for dinner, and she described him as a droll, if low-key, conversationalist. He enjoys food and wine, she said, and always sends a graceful thank-you note.

Again, Souter never revealed to his friends his views on a central issue — this time abortion. "I kick myself that I never asked him," Susan McLane said.

Souter's rare critics detect a lack of compassion in this cerebral, compulsively disciplined man. They say he has exhibited little concern for minorities, the poor and the disabled, both on the court and off. His extracurricular work has associated him with hospitals, historical societies, art galleries and a hiking club.

But George Langwasser, a Hopkinton, New Hampshire, banker who served on the vestry of St. Andrew's Episcopal Church with fellow parishioner Souter, called him a "very caring person." He escorts an elderly woman in a wheelchair to and from Sunday-morning services every week and has been generous with his time on church boards and committees.

Langwasser said Souter brought his judicial qualities to church meetings, sitting quietly as opinions were aired and then rendering his opinion. "He had the ability to cut through everything that was said and offer a solution," he said.

"If they're looking for a skeleton in his closet or a smoking pistol, they won't find it. He's above reproach," Langwasser added. "The only thing they can question is his judicial philosophy. He's not going to bring liberal ideas or social change to the court. He'll bring logic."

· · ·

His most ardent backers compare Souter with another reclusive, monk-like bachelor who achieved fame for his legal brilliance: Benjamin Nathan Cardozo, the "hermit philosopher" of the court from 1932 until 1938 — who lived most of his life with his unmarried sister and was eulogized when he died as a "reticent, sensitive and almost mystical personality."

Although Souter's admirers mean the parallel to be a compliment, the comparison between the two serves also to illustrate the rather narrow range of issues on which Souter has written in his career so far.

By the time Cardozo reached the Supreme Court, he had produced several books on legal theory and, from his seat on New York's high court, had written decisions that shaped the law nationally.

By contrast, Souter, as a member of the Supreme Court of a small, relatively homogeneous state, has had virtually no impact on the law outside New Hampshire. He has written more than 200 published opinions on the New Hampshire court, but little else, not even a law review article, except for a short piece commemorating a former state judge. Although he currently sits on the federal appeals court in New England, he was only confirmed this spring, has heard just one day of arguments and has not yet written a decision.

On the New Hampshire Supreme Court, to which Souter was named in 1983 by then-Gov. John H. Sununu, who is now President Bush's chief of staff, Souter was an "intense questioner" who "absolutely dominated oral arguments," said James E. Duggan, the state's chief appellate defender, who appeared often before the court representing criminal defendants.

Souter, Duggan said, was notably conservative but "not some crazy, right-wing law-and-order judge."

Former law clerks said that Souter's questions dominated debate in chambers among the court's five members, and that his line of reasoning often shaped opinions that were written by his colleagues. After hearing all the arguments on a case, Souter would retire to the solitude of his office and work long hours crafting his decisions.

The style of those decisions is eloquent, although at times turgid because Souter felt compelled to tie up every strand of his reasoning and because they so often concern relatively mundane matters: zoning appeals, disputes over state benefit programs and routine criminal cases.

"About the only thing you can tell by reading New Hampshire Supreme Court opinions is that you wouldn't want to be a New Hampshire Supreme Court judge," quipped New York University law professor Burt Neuborne.

The opinions contain few flourishes. They bespeak a mind well versed in interpreting legal rules but little interested in finding new ways to adapt them to changed circumstances. In short, they are conservative.

Critics who say Souter's conservatism involves a lack of compassion include Bruce E. Friedman, who directs the civil practice clinic at Franklin Pierce Law Center in Concord and often represents needy plaintiffs in state courts.

In one case, in which Friedman was involved, for example, Souter ruled against two elderly brothers who sued the state after they were denied unemployment benefits.

New Hampshire rules allow unemployment benefits only for those who work full time. The two brothers argued that the rule unfairly discriminated against the old and the disabled, but Souter disagreed.

Women's organizations objected to a decision Souter wrote in a rape case. The decision allowed defense lawyers to question a rape victim about allegations that she had spent much of an afternoon making sexual advances to numerous men in a bar before leaving with one man whom she later accused of attacking her. Civil libertarians, however, supported that decision, saying the questions were needed to ensure the defendant a fair trial.

Abortion rights activists have spent many hours analyzing Souter's brief comments in a medical malpractice case involving abortion, finding that it sheds little light on his views of abortion.

Souter joined an opinion requiring doctors to test for birth defects in cases where a fetus may be at risk. The opinion acknowledged that abortions might result and noted that the Supreme Court has ruled that women have that right. Souter then wrote a brief separate opinion expressing concern for the plight of doctors who may have moral or religious qualms about abortion.

Other opinions indicate that if Souter had been on the high court for the past 25 years, he almost certainly would have voted against many of the precedent-setting decisions that were supported by Justice William J. Brennan Jr., whom he has been nominated to replace.

In one case, Souter wrote of the need to determine the meaning of a part of the state constitution "as it was understood when the framers proposed it and the people ratified it" in 1784, a sharp contrast with Brennan, who spoke often of the need to understand constitutional provisions with an eye to what "the words of the text mean in our time."

In another case, Souter wrote of the importance of "ensuring that the executive and judicial branches concede the Legislature's power to act within its constitutional purview," a sentiment often voiced by conservatives who have accused the federal courts of overrunning legislative powers.

But if the record indicates that Souter would not have supported many liberal decisions of the past, his writings give virtually no indication of whether he would now vote to overturn them.

"He is by temperament thoughtful and skeptical, a show-me type of guy. He is conservative in every sense of the word," said Leahy, who has followed Souter's career for 25 years.

"His approach is, 'I'm on a firm rock — the constitution, a statute, a precedent. If you want to move me off this rock, you have to show me why it should happen.' "

Times staff writers Robert L. Jackson, David Lauter, Don Shannon and Marlene Cimons contributed to this story.

∴

The 'Unknown Soldier' of the Gulf

The modest trajectory of a common man — one week, he was on an assembly line, the next, on the cusp of battle. His impersonal death from a stray missile made him less hero than victim.

By Stephen Braun · March 29, 1991

PARAGOULD, Arkansas — On a day that Steven Mason would have recognized as perfect for a deer hunt, six strangers carried him to rest. Bucking a stiff March wind, the six men, U.S. Army pallbearers, hauled his flag-draped coffin toward a hole in the cold, pliant loam. The mourners waited under a billowing canopy in the small country cemetery, hemmed in by the dense wilds that blur the state boundary between Arkansas and Missouri.

Steven Mason knew these woods intimately. They were his refuge, an enveloping and silent place where private disappointments faded away, where, with a rifle and a sack and his backwoodsman's stealth, he was a match for most any man.

At home, in school or on the assembly line, there was no escape from the confining tedium of his hard, ordinary life. But inside any tree line, his mother remembered later, it seemed as if nothing could harm him, a thought that seemed somehow fitting later on, after he died.

Steven Mason's death came thousands of miles away from his woods, in a land without forests. Mason, 23, an Army reservist truck driver, was one of 28 American soldiers killed February 25 in Dhahran, Saudi Arabia, when a Scud missile plunged out of the night sky and fell into a barracks where they prepared for sleep.

He died in a manner that parallels the accelerated, computer-driven pace of the gulf conflict. He was killed — like most of America's 124 war dead — not in direct action with the enemy, but in an impersonal, long-distance form of combat that saw soldiers succumb to rocket attacks, land mines and cluster bombs.

Yet unlike so many others who were eulogized and exalted as heroes in the aftermath, there is no neatness, no tidy sentimentality about Steven Mason's death — or the unassuming life that preceded it. One week, he was a machinist on an earsplitting assembly line. The next, he was a scared, out-of-shape reservist on the cusp of battle. The next, he was dead.

If the gulf conflict, with its meager American death toll so unlike the nation's past bloody wars, fails to produce an unknown soldier, Army Spc. Steven Mason might well suffice.

He is this war's Everyman, a cog in the military machine who perished before he had the chance to contribute to the war effort. A reluctant patriot, he feared the conflict's hellish technology yet could not fathom taking his mother's advice to flee to Mexico. He left behind no grieving widow, no unseen child, no prospects for a bright, shining life. Even his final communications home were paltry and vague. In the end, there were only a few cartons of personal effects and a collection of guns and fishing rods to hand down to his numbed family and friends.

In Paragould, a town of 18,000 farmers and factory workers west of the Mississippi River, the few yellow ribbons still on display have begun to fray. Strangers who never knew Steven Mason are already talking about him as local history, as if he belongs to the town, a faded 19th-century mill center that survives on soybean farms and auto accessory plants.

"I think we all want to touch greatness," said Elinor Campfield, a retired elementary schoolteacher. "Everyone wants to say they knew him. As long as people here remember the war, they'll remember him."

But all that those who knew Steven Mason can make out is the modest trajectory of a common man.

"The person they're talking about is someone else," said Kerry Spencer, 23, the fallen soldier's best friend. "This was an average guy. I mean, the person they talk about is somebody great and strong. If that's what a hero is, I'm sure Steve'd want to be one. He was just a good friend. Now he's gone."

Condolence cards, dinner hams and donations have been left at the Mason home, a brick ranch house with an exterior as black as a scorched hearth. There were notes from congressmen, the governor and the president. Veterans called with talk of a memorial and maybe a plaque at Steven Mason's high school. Even the United Parcel man from Jonesboro, 25 miles away, stopped by to tell the dead man's mother "how proud he was" of her boy.

Peggye Hambrick accepted this goodwill quietly. She spurned a 21-gun salute but had no quarrel when her surviving son, Jerald, 18, chose a military funeral. So Steve was given a silver casket and Army pallbearers. He was dressed in a parade-ground green uniform and, head still shaved, buried to a military bugler's lonesome rendition of taps.

The whole time, Peggye Hambrick thought: "That isn't him. His mustache is gone. His hair is wrong. It looked fine, but that's not how I'll remember him."

Amid the funeral's solemn ceremony, she found herself drawn back to a moment in

1987. Steve had wangled a pass from Ft. Leonard Wood, Missouri, where he was training as an Army truck driver. As their car left the base, he told her to "please stop at the first gas station." He ran into a restroom, tore off his uniform and came out grinning in jeans and T-shirt.

It was that "country" side that Kerry Spencer and his brother, Rob, 21, knew from a decade of hunting. The week after Steve was buried, the brothers drove out to Scattered Creek, one of their haunts, a warren of white oak shading patches of sweet clover. Winter had denuded the trees and hidden trails with brittle leaves. But the two hunters had no trouble finding the isolated dells where, with Steve, they had stalked squirrel, rabbit and deer.

"I don't think he wanted that much out of life," said Kerry Spencer. "A Monte Carlo XS, maybe. He liked that car's style, said it had flair. He wanted his own land, maybe 10, 20 acres for hunting. And a house."

Then, he remembered something Steve had told him during his last, liquor-soaked, sleepless week at home before shipping out to Ft. Dix, New Jersey, his first stop toward the gulf.

"The last night we were together, we were sitting there in front of the television," Kerry Spencer said. "And he says: 'If I make it back, this town owes me.' I wasn't sure if he meant a job or some kind of chance. He never said. Some ways, I wonder if he got a better payback from dying than he might've got if he lived."

. . .

Steven Mason had not always been so resentful. He came into the world on equal footing with many northern Arkansas boys: barely middle class but well provided with necessities. His mother was a nurse and his father, Glen Mason, a science teacher, a job that brought a measure of renown to the family name, renown the son did not share.

Steve inherited Glen Mason's love for hunting, a passion handed down from fathers to sons in these parts like a birthright. When Steve was 3, his father bought him a BB gun, his first weapon. An independent child, Steve graduated to a pellet gun, then to a .22 rifle.

"He never did play soldier much," Peggye Hambrick recalled. "Cowboys and Indians, mostly. Backwoods games."

At school he was a science-fair winner, but withdrawn, with "the saddest brown eyes you ever saw," said teacher Elinor Campfield. There were hard reasons. By junior high, his parents had separated. And in his first year of high school, his father was killed on his motorcycle, run down by a car driven by a drunken classmate of Steve's.

The woods provided an escape. Sullen at home, he was unburdened in the forest. Steve and the Spencers swaggered like Southern gentry, with guns, chewing tobacco and Swisher Sweet Thins cigars. Sometimes, they brought a bottle of whiskey or marijuana that grows wild along the marshy banks of the St. Francis River, a Mississippi tributary.

"I think he wished he could spend his whole life back in those woods," his mother said. Lacking college or job prospects, Steve Mason turned in June 1987 to the Army. He was one among dozens from Paragould who enlisted over the last decade, part of a generation of jobless white kids from the Sun Belt drawn to the military because of financial hardship. Along with urban blacks, Southerners now form the backbone of the nation's volunteer fighting force.

"Either they can't find jobs or they don't know what else to do," said Sgt. James Parks, an Arkansas national guardsman who acted as an Army liaison for the Mason family in the days after Steve's death.

Pvt. Steven Mason arrived for basic training at Ft. Jackson, South Carolina, a likable youth with a penchant for talking big about his future. "He had problems with pushups, but he always said how he was going to be a paratrooper," said his bunkmate, David Swoboda.

One night near the end of basic training, Swoboda recalled, the recruits, who called themselves "Mad Dogs," sat in their humid brick barracks and talked about their plans. One man said that if he died in the line of duty, he wanted the others to hoist a drink in his honor. One by one, the other "Mad Dogs" joined in. Steve Mason chimed in with the rest.

But he never made airborne, training instead as a truck driver. He was assigned to Ft. Hunter Liggett, California, attached to the Army's Combat Experimentation Battalion, a testing unit, said his battalion commander, Lt. Col. Paul Trahan.

Settling into a supply man's numbing routine, Steve drove troop trucks, laser-carrying flatbeds, tankers brimming with fuel. It was 18 months of boredom, he told Rob Spencer. His weight problem revived. His superiors wanted him to lose 20 pounds. In April 1990, three months before his enlistment was up, he was discharged honorably — dropped, he told his mother, because of his paunch.

Before he left, Steve told Trahan he hoped to parlay his training into a trucking career. "He said he talked to a company back East," Trahan said. "It sounded like he had plans."

But from his $823 monthly paycheck, Steve had saved only $1,200. Home in Paragould, he took what he could get — a night job at Monroe Auto Equipment, punching holes in shock absorbers.

Civilian tedium replaced Army routine. His nightly quota was 5,800 shock absorbers. In a cavernous hall that stank of forklift fuel, workers wadded green plugs in their ears to mute the thunderous hiss of stamping machines. Steve kept sane, he told a co-worker, by mentally replaying songs by AC/DC, his favorite heavy-metal rock group. Shocks clanked by to the internal throb of "Highway to Hell" and "Those About to Rock (We Salute You)."

By day, Steve lived for the hunt. He could tell a deer's distance by the faint scrape of antlers against tree trunks, and decipher tracks in the soft mud. Among his friends, it was Steve who bagged a deer first, a seven-point buck. He was so excited, Kerry Spencer recalled, that he tripped on his overalls, pitching face-first into a pasture as he ran to claim his kill.

The last summer was an idyll. News that a force of 100,000 Iraqi Republican Guard troops had stormed into Kuwait on August 2 was someone else's concern, an item to discard like day-old baseball scores. There were more pressing matters: Squirrels were afoot at Scattered Creek. The catfish were biting in the muddy St. Francis.

It was not until November, when the first of his co-workers vanished from their jobs, called to duty, that Steve realized the gravity of the nation's situation — and his own. He had made an eight-year commitment to the Army. As an inactive duty reservist until 1995, he could be called up any moment.

An instinctive patriot who had a "love it or leave it" sticker on his truck, he supported the buildup in Saudi Arabia. "He just thought we should go in there and get rid of Saddam," Jerald Mason said.

But by Christmas, the growing likelihood that he, too, might have to fight clearly scared him. He took to his cramped bedroom, its walls lined with heavy-metal posters, and brooded under Ozzy Osbourne's bloodshot stare. He made gloomy references to his own death. When his mother gave him a new fishing rod for Christmas, he muttered to his aunt, Rosetta Jones: "I'll probably never get to use it."

Notice came January 20. He was at work. Jerald, home from school, saw the letter and ripped it open. Steve was to report to Ft. Eustis, Virginia, in a week. Jerald grew pale and paced around their small kitchen.

"What if he doesn't get the letter?" Jerald asked. "Does he have to go?"

"They'll find him," Peggye Hambrick said, trembling. That night, when Steven showed up, she tried to stay calm. "You got that letter you been waiting on," she said.

Steve cursed. There was little else to say. He sat poker-faced at the dinner table, reading the letter over. Peggye Hambrick had decided on a course of action. She wanted him to go to Mexico.

"I said: 'You don't have to do this. You can go down there, you can live for nothing, I'll send you money,' " she recalled. "I told him that all week. And he would say: 'Oh, Mom, be serious.' But anybody looking at him could see he was afraid to go."

Steve's deepest fear was chemical weapons. He had lived with guns and bullets all his life, but lethal as they were, he told Jerald, they seemed tame compared with the rumored Iraqi stockpiles of poison gas.

In public, Steve masked his fear with bravado. At the plant, he told personnel director Harold E. Diggs that he already had one medal, his Spearhead of Logistics, awarded for truck duty. He told Diggs: "I guess I'll have to get another."

At home, Steve prepared like an automaton. He made Jerald his legal guardian. He bought six cans of Skoal, stuffing them in a tube sock to hide from Army inspectors. He visited with grandparents. He considered buying a flea collar to ward off desert insects, then shaved his legs instead.

He stayed up for a week. He slugged whiskey in long gulps, bleary-eyed in front of the television at Kerry Spencer's place. Long into the morning, the two friends watched gulf news, speaking up only to talk about old times in the woods. They talked of one last hunt. But Steven Mason was sleepwalking, slouching towards the gulf.

"It's like he wasn't there," Spencer recalled. "His head was already in Saudi, I guess."

The day of Steve's departure, Peggye Hambrick made one last plea. On the way to the Memphis airport, they passed a billboard advertising a sunny holiday in Rio. She said: "I can get enough money. We can go there." He waved her off glumly.

At the security gate, she stood with Jerald and Jennifer, her 11-year-old daughter, as Steve shuffled through with his duffel bag. They hugged and shut their eyes tight to ward off tears. As she walked off, she turned to see Steve standing near the X-ray machine, watching.

He called every night from Ft. Dix, New Jersey, his processing camp. Peggye Hambrick heard the coughs of other soldiers in line for the phone. She wondered if they were as scared as Steve. They were all kept in their street clothes, he told her, confined to the crowded barracks "so they wouldn't run off."

Two short letters came. In hers, Steve was reassuring: "I will probably go to Saudi Arabia, but only in the rear. I won't see any action, so don't worry about me, OK?" To Jerald, he wrote: "Keep your fingers crosset [sic]. I could stay in the U.S.A. or go overseas. Well, I have to go."

His last call came at 6:30 one night, two days after Valentine's Day. His mother did most of the talking, reliving "how much I'd enjoyed him as a son. I guess it was a way of saying goodbye, but I didn't know it at the time. I told him about funny things he did when he was little, like the time we dressed him up in a big old cowboy hat and these ugly, plaid '70s pants. Things like that. I told him I thought he'd turned his life around."

. . .

The next week blurred by: The ground war started. A Scud missile fell on a barracks in Dhahran. The cease-fire came and went, with still no word from Steve. With the war over, his mother was elated. She drove into Jonesboro to buy poster board and packages of balloons and streamers for his homecoming.

When she watched replays of the Scud attack, Peggye Hambrick sometimes cried — but for other people's sons, not her own. "I could not imagine him being in a building," she said. "I figured he was out in the desert."

But at 8:30 that night in Dhahran, Steven Mason was somewhere in the central sleeping quarters of a newly built corrugated metal barracks. At that hour, soldiers were readying for bed, said Capt. Gregory Rich, commander of the 14th Quartermaster Detachment, a Greensboro, Pennsylvania, reserve unit that specializes in water purification.

Although Army officials told Peggye Hambrick that her son had been assigned as a "filler" — a temporary replacement — with the water detachment, Rich was not familiar with Steven Mason's name.

"At that point, truck drivers were in short supply in-country," Rich said. "They were taking soldiers from the front and training them to become drivers. He was definitely a needed man."

But if he was not with Rich's unit, Steve Mason was clearly no longer with his own, Army officials told his mother. And because he had just arrived in the gulf, Rich said, he was likely still "in orientation" and had not even begun his new assignment. "He was probably just reconning the area to get to know it," Rich said.

No one knows whether he was awake or asleep when the Scud struck. When the missile landed, according to Rich, it shredded the barracks, raining metal roof parts and shrapnel on those inside.

Peggye Hambrick prefers to believe Steve was sleeping. On the morning of March 2, when she went to view his open coffin at Heath Funeral Parlor in downtown Paragould, she first reacted like a nurse, not a mother. Steven's only wound was at the back of his head, she noticed. In the absence of details from the Army, she concluded that he was killed by a falling object.

"He always slept on his stomach," she said. "So I have to think something landed on him from above. I have to think he was asleep."

245

That morning, she took off the white gloves the Army had placed on Steven Mason's hands and slipped a white New Testament into his cold right fist. She put a nickel in his left pocket. He always kept the coin there, a private gesture whose meaning she had long ago forgotten.

Since then, Peggye Hambrick has driven out to her son's grave almost every day. She talks to him, weeping, "braying like a fool. I tell him I'm proud of him. I stand there bawling — God, I must look like an idiot — and I try not to think of him in his uniform. I pretend that he's out there in the woods."

Some mornings, caught in the stinging, cold rain that pelts northern Arkansas in March, it has been hard to make out the simple metal plate that marks Steve Mason's burial ground.

A headstone will soon take its place. It will be ready by summer, Peggye Hambrick hopes, a marble slab, simple and square, with just his name and his dates. And in a prominent place, somewhere where everybody can see, the head of a deer.

❖

Marion Barry Keeps D.C. Guessing

Media scapegoat? Target of a racist plot? Victim of his own excesses? The mayor not only weathers unending controversy, at times he also seems to court it.

BY BELLA STUMBO · JANUARY 7, 1990

WASHINGTON — Inside an elementary school auditorium, in a run-down part of town that tourists never see, Mayor Marion Barry is lecturing 400 youngsters on the evils of drugs and the importance of staying clean.

As mayor of one of the nation's most drug-plagued cities, Barry visits three or four schools a week with his message. It is his way, he says, of helping motivate the children.

His style is relaxed, warm, captivating.

"How many y'all know somebody in your family using drugs?" he asks gently. Nearly every tiny hand in the auditorium rises.

Barry counsels by personal example. "From time to time," he tells them, he is accustomed to "having a glass of wine." But when his 9-year-old son once asked him why he drinks it, it made a lasting impression. So, he advises the children, whenever someone in the family uses drugs, "ask them why ... and ask them to get some help."

It is a good speech. After leading the youngsters in a Jesse Jacksonesque chant — "Keep myself ... drug-free! Drug-Free! DRUG-FREE!!!!" — Barry opens the floor to questions.

For moments, no one moves. Finally, a solemn-faced little boy marches up the aisle to the microphone, looks up at Barry with steady eyes and, in his small child's voice, asks:

"Do people believe you when you say you don't use drugs?"

A hush falls over the auditorium. No one even snickers. The silence is complete, the scene indelible:

Here stands the mayor of the Free World's capital city, a tall, nice-looking, balding man of 53 in a dark business suit, trying to explain to 400 kids whose lives are being ravaged daily by drugs that he himself is not an addict, a hypocrite, a criminal.

He does it quickly, quietly, in an odd, backhanded way. The news media always focus on the negatives, he says. But he is a trained chemist, he knows what drugs can do. And "I know that you can't be a good mayor high on drugs and alcohol, and I want to be a good mayor. I know that you have to keep your body drug-free so that your mind will function well. And I'm going to continue to fight for a drug-free D.C."

A different man might surrender, call it quits, retire, anything to avoid such punishing moments as these. A different man, his reputation already in shreds over his own whispered drug habit, might at least avoid kamikaze runs into neighborhood schools.

Marion Barry's answer is to speed away in his big chauffeur-driven Lincoln to do it again, this time to a group of third-graders.

From yesterday's civil rights hero to today's TV talk show joke, Marion Barry is ridiculed, mocked, disgraced. "Mayor Barely," the pundits call him. "Jerk in the Box," blares a local magazine cover. "King Nightowl," hoots an Oliphant cartoon. "Know what the mayor's answer is to a paralyzing snowstorm?" cackles a comic. "Quick, gimme a straw!"

Barry's much-rumored drug use has never been proved and he denies it, but it no longer matters. Years of investigations and allegations, the continual gossip about pending indictments, the nonstop headlines blaring luridly of the mayor's personal life have all added up: Innocent or guilty, Barry is a man permanently branded, victim of that old saw — where there's smoke, there must be fire.

Some of his oldest friends and political advisers have lately jumped ship, publicly urging him not to seek a fourth term, for the city's sake and for his own. Five candidates have already announced for next fall's mayoral race, attacking not only Barry's image but his leadership too. On Capitol Hill, critics say Barry has set back the District of Columbia's quest for statehood by 20 years.

And all about town, beyond the nation's monuments and shrines, throughout this curious no man's land where some 600,000 Americans, most of them black, live under supervision of the U.S. Congress, the debate goes on: Is Marion Barry the victim of trial by press, of a racist plot against black home rule or of his own excesses? Is he a sick addict, a brazen rake or a martyr? Is this a Greek tragedy or a bad joke?

Washingtonians have been asking themselves these questions virtually every day since they elected Barry in 1978.

A Mississippi sharecropper's son with a master's degree in chemistry, Barry was among the most important voices of the 1960s civil rights campaign, a founder and first national chairman of the Student Nonviolent Coordinating Committee and prime mover in the Free D.C. Movement, one of the militant, dashiki-clad symbols of an era. Then, as now, he held special appeal for the poor and the elderly. Then, as now, D.C.'s affluent black establishment was unimpressed, finding his street language especially vulgar. A 'Bama, they call him behind his back — lowborn, country bumpkin, hick.

Barry has never been a low-profile politician. He can't stay out of the news for his life — whether he's getting caught in the Caribbean with a woman not his wife, or in a sleazy topless bar in downtown D.C. where cocaine was allegedly sold openly.

One day, it's the taint of City Hall corruption: People close to Barry keep going to jail for pilfering the public coffers, his ex-wife and two deputy mayors among them. Next day, it's yet another unverifiable rumor that Barry's been hospitalized for overdosing, or titillating grand jury leaks, or gossip about his friends with drug connections and city contracts.

Regardie's, the tony local business magazine, once even excerpted torrid passages from the diary of an alleged girlfriend, a convicted drug dealer, who described Barry's sexual performance for the world: "Very verbal in bed … great!"

But last November came the greatest Barry sensation of all: The government produced its first-ever alleged eyewitness against him. A former friend and city employee, Charles Lewis, testified in federal court that he sold Barry crack cocaine on several occasions in 1988 in a downtown hotel room. Barry insists that his visits were innocent social calls and dismisses his old pal as a cornered man trying to cut a deal for himself in exchange for helping the feds hook Washington's biggest fish.

Amid this clutter of scandal, Barry's mayoral record is also under unprecedented assault. Critics accuse him of losing focus, of bloating the bureaucracy for political purposes at the expense of deteriorating city services. His supporters — who reelected him to his third term in a landslide — credit him with creating one of the nation's most prosperous black middle classes.

Adding to Barry's headaches, his old civil rights chum, the Rev. Jesse Jackson, has moved to town, where he sits in coy silence, focusing even more national attention on Barry's problems by refusing to flatly rule out his own eventual mayoral candidacy. In a remark Barry called outrageous, Jackson once commented that he was praying for the mayor's health.

Nowadays, there are even places in his own backyard where Marion Barry dares not go for fear of being heckled. He doesn't handle it well. When a band of rowdies jeered him at a street festival in September, Barry's response was spontaneous and unequivocal: He flashed his antagonists one of his dazzling smiles and an obscene gesture.

"I'm gonna be like that lion the Romans had," Barry chuckles softly. "They can just keep throwin' stuff at me, you know? But I'll be kickin' their asses, every time! In the end, I be sittin' there, lickin' my paws!"

Barry is sitting in one of his favorite late-night bars, a dim, noisy, upscale place in an all-black part of town, drumming the table top to the blaring jukebox, dancing in his chair, sipping his wine, restless, eyes roaming the room, raw energy barely bridled. "I'd run now even if I didn't want to," he says, smiling sulkily through the gloom. "And I'll get 65 percent of the vote — at least. Isn't anybody in this town can beat me. I'm invincible."

That includes Jackson. "Hah, Jesse don't wanna be no mayor," he snaps. "Jesse don't wanna run nothing but his mouth. Besides, he'd be the laughingstock of America! He'd be run outta town if he ran against me. Even my enemies don't appreciate him coming in here saying: 'This is mine to take.' "

So much for the understated man on the elementary school stage. Even Barry's speech changes in private, now a soft, mumbled patter of dropped words and careless grammar, calling for an acquired ear. And no way is he understated. He is Pride itself, holding hard to tattered garb.

"Co-caaaane? How folks use that stuff, anyhow?" he asks, mockingly, coy, flaunting it all.

"You put it up your nooose? No! Ooooooooeeeeeee!" And with a mock shudder he dances off to the men's room, returning 10 minutes later to wonder, laughingly, sardonically, how much a Marion Barry urine specimen might be worth to the media or the feds — interchangeable elements, in his mind, in the racist conspiracy against him.

Barry ascribes all his difficulties to a venal, calculated smear campaign orchestrated by the white media to humiliate and unseat a popular black mayor for trying to spread the wealth.

This notion is not frivolous, not in this black city. The concept of a racist conspiracy to undermine black self-government is so prevalent that it is known simply as The Plan, and it is one reason nobody thinks Marion Barry can be easily defeated, drug rumors or not, unless Jackson runs, and maybe not even then. Whether the mayor uses cocaine may be less of a factor in the upcoming election than race and class polarization.

Barry promotes The Plan daily, in ways subtle and flagrant. "I'm innocent of all these things. The [Washington] Post has decided my time's up, that's all," he says matter-of-factly of his principal antagonist.

"But it's not unusual," he adds. "I guess some people find it hard to believe, but historically, those who do good sometimes suffer the most. Jesus is an example. Or Gandhi, in India … he was put in jail and eventually killed."

Then, like some exuberant, stormy teenager trapped in an early autumn body, the mayor's mind is suddenly prowling the rich realms of sex. "All this slander, about me chasing women — I'm innocent," he protests, silky and sly. He wonders if his second wife still loves him, then concludes that the poor woman must — she never had it so good in bed. "I was good then, I'm even better now," he proclaims. The mayor, now remarried with one son, is an expert in creative obscenities relative to sex, even more so when he's discussing how many ways he's been violated by the press.

He frowns. It does Barry no good whatsoever, dwelling on his enemies. "Father, forgive them," he says sarcastically, slugging back a wine, "for they know not what they do." Grin.

What galls Barry most is the insult of it all. "I'm not stupid enough to have done the things they accuse me of! God gave me a good brain. What I have done nobody knows about because I don't get caught," he hoots.

His mind flashes next to the defectors, some of them friends for 30 years, now abandoning him, even talking about him to the media.

"Chickens, goats and Judases," he hisses, scalded, vowing vengeance. Come victory day, "I'm gonna cut 'em off at the kneecaps!"

"Jews too!" he says, referring to two of the chief Judases, both former fund-raisers. "Jews should be the last to spread rumors, they've been persecuted themselves. You'd think they'd know better."

But, "truth crushed to the earth," he purrs, "shall rise again. Martin Luther King said that."

He did?

"I dunno. I think so. I just say whatever sounds good."

. . .

From early morning till the midnight hour, Marion Barry stays in the streets, among the people who can redeem him. From the glamour regions of downtown to the roughest drug zones of Southeast he goes, from schools to homeless shelters to neighborhood meetings, trolling nonstop in his big Lincoln with the bodyguard up front, the telephone in back. From here, city business is conducted, interviews granted, journalists charmed, as Barry hurtles through his day, demonstrating to the world that the mayor of D.C. is A-OK, above all this nonsense, the incumbent taking care of business.

This day begins at 8 a.m. on the public tennis courts where the "Night Owl," as Barry has always called himself, displays if not a great game, at least a proper regard for physical fitness.

"Don't look like no drug addict, do I?" he mumbles self-consciously, plopping into a chair, drenched with sweat, patting his paunch. In first encounters, Marion Barry is shy.

"I'm the most scrutinized politician in this country," he sighs, sounding more resigned than resentful. "It's always open season on black mayors — look at L.A. and New York. But it's been open season on me for 10 years. Barry bashing's the biggest thing in town."

Mornings turn out to be Barry's most passive hours. He even makes a half-hearted effort to explain why he thinks the white power structure is after him.

"Take my attitude about minority businesses," he says. "We go from 3 percent to 38 percent [in city contracts] ... between $150 and $175 million. That threatened a lot of people.... They [investigators] went after this contract business from the start," he says, shrugging, disgusted, dropping the topic.

It will be the only time all day that Barry bothers with a serious discussion of his leadership. While his supporters work overtime, trying to turn attention from drugs to his achievements, he seems too jaded, too preoccupied, too proud — or maybe just too media-wary — to waste his breath making his own case, even when pressed. Instead, Barry's day is one long fascinating act of determination and defiance.

Here, at midday, two school stops later, for example, is the mayor of D.C. suddenly, comically and inexplicably darting into an elegant lingerie shop near the White House — where he prowls about for five minutes in solemn inspection of frilly, flimsy items of women's underwear, while three young clerks hover from a respectful distance and his bodyguards cover the doors.

He didn't want to buy anything; he apparently only wanted to make another of his points: If he wants to peer at red satin brassieres, he by-damn will.

"That's part of their plan — to make me scared of my own shadow, to immobilize me, get me actin' different all of a sudden," he says, flouncing into the Lincoln. "So then they can go around saying I'm some sort of sick addict, sick in the head! Have people all saying, 'Oh, poor Marion! Poooooor Marion.' " Jeer him, laugh at him, despise him — but whatever you do, don't pity Mayor Marion Shepilov Barry Jr.

"Poor Marion nothing — poor them," he snaps, eyes on fire. "This isn't any Greek tragedy! I'm not gonna meet my demise at my own hand. I quit a two-pack-a-day [cigarette] habit. Cold turkey! I'm a workaholic — I don't need any crutches!"

Out of the car. Now he is sauntering through a brand-new city office building, home of public assistance, where he is greeted with adoring hugs and shy smiles. A jolly, fat woman with gold-sprayed hair and nails, sitting at the front desk, regards him like a naughty son.

"Marion Barry!" she shrieks, waving bejeweled arms at the roomful of worried people before her. "We need help here, we need more people!" she lectures. "We got burnout, things moving too slow! People getting evicted, the gas getting turned off before the damn assistance gets approved!"

Barry is magic in rooms like these. Unaffected, full of easy grace, he strolls among his employees, chatting, joking, taking personal interest in how things are going. Then he flows into the crowded waiting room. People flock to him, telling him their troubles. Barry gives advice, takes names, sympathizes. One woman with a baby on her hip and sores on her face tells him she can't afford Pampers, and he hands her a $10 bill.

"Hey, the Man's looking out for his people," cries one young fellow in dreadlocks, happy as if he himself had been personally blessed.

"I feel good, I helped them." Barry says, beaming, back in the Lincoln, high on public love. Then he's nudging his visitor, pointing out the window at a city construction crew cutting a curb. "See, we're at work," he murmurs with satisfaction. This goes on all day. "Hang in there, baby!" cries the driver of a passing car. "See," Barry giggles. "I'm invincible!"

Never has federal D.C. seemed so removed, so irrelevant to what goes on in the city streets around it. A day with Barry is an adventure in island fever, like touring some small kingdom with its soft-spoken, charismatic ruler, quelling unrest.

Then, in the next moment, Barry is looking as confused, as vulnerable as he ever does. "I'm the same as I always was. I didn't change any, they changed the rules in the middle of the game," he complains. "I'm supposed to be the political leader of this city, not the moral leader...." His voice trails off, but his point is apparent: It's not fair.

. . .

Nothing in Barry's history — a straight, steely, charmed march to the top — has prepared him for this.

He fought his way out of an impoverished childhood in the delta shacks of tiny Itta Bina, Mississippi.; he graduated from Fisk University in Nashville, then battled his way with top grades into the all-white graduate programs at the universities of Tennessee and later Kansas, where he began his doctorate in chemistry. But then came the siren call of the '60s. And the SNCC preempted chemistry forevermore.

He organized, protested and went to jails throughout the South, then moved to D.C. in 1965 to lead the SNCC's statehood drive. A calming voice during the 1968 riots, he also co-founded Pride Inc., a multimillion-dollar, federally funded youth training program that later became a national model in the War on Poverty. When home rule came in 1973, he was already a local star, primed for politics, elected first to the school board, then to a term on the City Council before running for mayor — endorsed, not incidentally, by the Washington Post, which once hailed him as "A Man for All Stormy Seasons."

"I was only 42 when I was elected," he reminds. And he's only 53 now — "most mayors are older than that." Marion Barry is, in short, still too young to tame. "But I'm trying to adjust to this new game," he finishes sarcastically. "I don't go to topless bars anymore, only to family-rated places."

Whereupon, in yet another exclusively Marion Barry moment, a solemn discussion is had about the mayor's views on toplessness — "Isn't my thing, I just go to visit with people" — and precisely why he was hanging around a seedy downtown hotel with a drug dealer to get himself into this latest mess in the first place.

"I didn't know he [Lewis] had changed his lifestyle," protests Barry, sincere, burdened, beleaguered. But not repentant. Even with indictment rumors flying, Marion Barry accepts no responsibility for the scrapes he gets into.

"Chuck Lewis came from a distinguished family, he'd never been arrested in his life. I thought he was the same man. They were innocent visits. I might do something improper by some people's lights — but I'd never knowingly do anything illegal."

One thing for sure, if Marion Barry is lying, he's got more gall than any 10 men. "I'm not lying!" he cries, laughing, boyish. "Here, see my eyes, they ain't hiding no lies." Big brown eyes, pretty grin.

And, if he's innocent, he's got the courage of a saint as he wades into one public gathering after another, inviting curious eyes to inspect him for themselves.

"There are two kinds of evidence, indirect — what you read in the Post and on TV — and direct. That's me, Marion Barry," he tells a crowd of maybe 60 people, all black, at an informal neighborhood meeting in the home of a city employee. Barry attends one, sometimes two of these grass-roots "socials" nightly. They are the spine of his reelection strategy. Indeed, if racial resentments don't get Barry reelected, his network of public employees may. In a city of about 270,000 voters, 52,000 are on his payroll. (Los Angeles, by comparison, with a population five times larger, has 14,000 fewer.)

In adult crowds, Barry doesn't wait for the drug question to be asked, he brings it up himself: "I'm not going to tolerate this innuendo. I know about myself. I was trained as a scientist, and I know how dangerous this stuff is to your body. Plus, you can't be a good mayor high on alcohol or anything, so we're gonna continue waging war."

The rest of his talk is brief, reassuring. He blames the drug infestation on the federal government's failure to intercept narcotics at the border, promises more police, more rehabilitation centers. Afterward, he does the usual chatting, mingling, caring.

"That's how you organize," he says, trotting buoyantly down the steps with a handful of chicken wings. "Every one of 'em going to go home and tell five or six people the mayor cares."

From there, the mayor pauses to "get my hair done" at the J.W. Marriott hotel (he dyes it). "See, no lint," he chortles later, patting his freshly fragrant head. "Nobody can say I been laying out all night."

Then to dinner, on a reporter's tab, at one of the most expensive restaurants in town, where Barry turns his notorious charm on a pretty young waitress. "You're looking beautiful, as usual," he coos. He asks her about everything from her school studies to where she lives. "You married?" he asks. No, she says, flustered, flattered.

"You see how she flirted with me, how she just sashayed right up?" Barry asks, grinning, as she departs. "Why you think that is?" he wonders aloud.

Well, his reputation, maybe? His charm?

"No!" he cries, laughing out loud. "Because I'm the mayor. Power!"

He calls for a doggie bag and trots out the door, $100 in mangled haute cuisine in a tinfoil wad under his arm, late for his next appearance.

The day ends about midnight at the Redskins game. Defensive end Dexter Manley has just been banned for cocaine use. "Just another tragedy of this war," says

Barry. "It's unfortunate that people think it's just a matter of willpower. Addiction is a disease, we should get these people some help.

"See this," he says, stepping into the front-row-center mayor's box. "It's the best one there is." He laughs. "They can't accuse me of getting no drugs or sex under the table here." He is as full of nervous energy as he was on the tennis court 15 hours earlier. He drinks wine, glad-hands, gossips, cheers. But, mainly, Mayor Barry is being seen, a man of dignity, unruffled, presiding as he should be over the affairs of his people.

Notably lacking in this 16-hour day with Marion Barry is much attention to affairs of governance. Late in the afternoon, he makes a two-hour visit to his office in the District Building, an ornate, pastel confection of marble and grand stairways reminiscent of some lazy Latin palace, not far from the White House.

He signs a stack of papers, then presides over a large interagency meeting on the city's drug crisis. Drugs. Drug rumors. Drug denials. Drug wars. For Marion Barry, there no longer is any other topic. Hunks of his city are being ravaged by drugs and related violence. D.C. now leads the nation in per capita murders and infant mortality. Jails are overflowing, courts backlogged, hospitals jammed with drug cases. There are a few neighborhoods now where cabbies won't go even in the daytime.

Barry is a picture of intent, informed leadership, as stubbornly heedless here as in the elementary schools to the bizarre credibility problem his image now poses, innocent or not. Rumors abound that morale in D.C. city government is at an all-time low. This crowd of about 30 agency leaders looks mostly self-conscious to find yet another reporter present, tracking their controversial mayor. Afterward, they flee the media.

Barry seems oblivious to all but the need to hit the streets again. "I've got credibility. I'm the mayor," he later says dismissively.

Nearly everyone agrees that Barry's first term in office was dynamic. He promoted a downtown development and revitalization boom, restored the city's financial credibility on Wall Street, built roads, improved services, poured resources into poor neighborhoods — and, not least, turned D.C. into a black city managed by the blacks who live in it, from top-level executive positions on down. Also, he mostly managed to keep his personal habits out of the headlines.

Whether Barry has done as well since depends on whom you ask.

The huge Hotel and Restaurant Workers Union, for instance, has already endorsed him — "unanimously and enthusiastically," declares Secretary Ron Richardson. The thriving downtown business community is nervous but not backing off yet. "The mayor has always cooperated with us, and we don't think it's our role to be judge and jury, or the media's," says William Sinclair, president of the Greater Washington Board of Trade. Minority contractors are happy. So are welfare recipients.

Unhappiest are middle-class Washingtonians without direct reliance on the city, who complain that their taxes are among the highest in the United States. Yet they are receiving steadily deteriorating city services — in everything from police protection to housing and schools. The city is under court order to correct prison and mental health facilities. Nearly half of all public housing sits idle for lack of repairs. Bureaucrats are so incompetent, arrogant and slothful, critics say, that even 911 calls go unanswered and ambulances may not arrive until tomorrow.

Blame is widely traced to the city's vast bureaucracy — which has grown by about 10,000 employees since Barry took office. Forty-seven percent of the annual city budget goes to payroll alone. One in 12 Washingtonians is a city employee, and they are among the nation's highest paid: The average D.C. secretary makes about $1,000 more annually than her equivalent in federal offices across the street.

"Every time something goes wrong in this town, people start talking about racism, they're always talking about The Plan," says veteran City Councilman John Wilson, disgusted. "Well, this government has done more to get people out of the city, with its taxing policies and housing policies, than any Plan could have ever dreamed of accomplishing."

Another former SNCC militant who has known Barry for 25 years, Wilson, 46, is one of Barry's most articulate critics, widely respected, blunt and cynical. His district includes Georgetown as well as a third of the city's public housing. Barry accuses him of treachery, of carrying water for the white man.

"The mayor has bloated the bureaucracy for his own political purposes," says Wilson. "We can't afford basic services, so the middle class is moving to the suburbs. We're turning into a city of the very rich and the very poor, and [the poor] don't pay any taxes. We're losing our tax base. Right now, 27 percent of the people pay 75 percent of the taxes. Marion governs as if there is no tomorrow."

Like many, Wilson is also worried that Congress might take away D.C. home rule, which gives the city limited autonomy subject to congressional veto. Relations with Capitol Hill have sunk to an all-time low. The federal payment to the district, about $400 million annually, hasn't been increased in four years, and Congress has been overriding district legislation as never before. Never fond of the idea of statehood for D.C., with its almost guaranteed addition of two Democratic U.S. senators, Republicans are riding the Barry issue with open glee.

"Forget statehood for 30 years at least — it'll take them that long to recover from this, and there's not going to be any [appropriations] increase," says Mark Robertson, aide to Rep. Stan Parris (R-Va.), ranking Republican on the District Committee.

"We're not going to pour more money down a rat hole, that government is an absolutely incompetent mess. It's Third World down there. He's Baby Doc. Those people have got to enter the 20th century," Robertson says.

This sort of talk stirs people up "down there."

"The capital of a white nation was not designed for blacks to be in control," thunders Calvin Rolark, a crusty, silvery-haired activist with the Black United Fund. "We call it a South African colony. Marion Barry is a victim [of the white Plan] to let the nation know we just aren't ready for home rule."

Rolark, who also publishes the black weekly the Washington Informer, is a good measure of the passions evoked by Marion Barry's troubles in parts of this town. "Black people understand the nature of the beast! It's the media, period. But the Post does not vote in this town. The people vote.

"And the masses of black people in this town respect Marion Barry! It's history that he's history. He's alerted kids that you can come from public housing and rise to mayor of the nation's capital, he's been an excellent mayor! I don't know any other U.S. city with more blacks in policy-making positions. He don't just talk it, he lives it!"

Barry justifies the size of his bureaucracy on the grounds that D.C. government is more complex than any other city, combining local, county and state functions. "The mayor of Alexandria doesn't have to worry about building freeways," he tells a neighborhood group. "Being mayor of D.C. is harder than maybe any other job except president." Otherwise, he blames Ronald Reagan administration cutbacks, Republicans and congressional meddling for most of the city's problems.

Beyond that, Barry is as defiant and blameless about governing as he is about drugs.

Why is the city under four court orders to clean up everything from mental hospitals to jails? "Mealy-mouthed liberal judges." Why is so much of the city's public housing still boarded up? "Bureaucrats, you know how bureaucrats are."

Why does he send his son to a private school? "Personal and religious reasons." Why does he even want this job? "A mission! Mission!"

Barry only scoffs at the idea that he is hurting statehood chances for D.C. "That's just another red herring. They didn't have statehood [before he became mayor] in '78, did they?" he asks. "But, if I thought it would bring statehood, I'd resign tomorrow — and run for governor."

From the sidelines, some of Marion Barry's oldest, closest friends from the

SNCC days watch silently with varying degrees of anger and sadness. None seem surprised at the corner Barry has gotten himself into. It would have happened before, they say, if he hadn't originally been surrounded by some tough-minded SNCC lieutenants who kept him in line.

"Marion is in trouble today for the very same qualities that made his charisma for this town 15 years ago," says one friend, wistfully. "The movement was a fast time. It spoiled a lot of us for all time. In those days, nothing was impossible. You always had a group of buddies and a fight, and all the optimism of youth. Now, they're all gone. He's alone. It's such a hell of a beating he's putting himself through."

"Marion's always been a free spirit, he likes the ladies' man image," says Ivanhoe Donaldson, a former deputy mayor who was widely regarded as a dynamic force in Barry's first term, until he went to prison for stealing $190,000 from the city. "But we'd get on his case, say: 'Hey, Marion, we got work to do.' Get him interested in other stuff. But now, we're gone, he's only got yes men around him, so...."

Donaldson defends Barry's record as mayor but doesn't think he should run again. "I think Marion's bored," he says. "And image is image. You don't have to be a user to connect with the image. It's bad for the city, for the youngsters. That's reality."

Given the standards Marion Barry is now imposing on himself, this has been a triumphant day — apart from lunch.

Barry chooses to dine at a downtown restaurant called Duke Ziebert's, where the white establishment — bankers, lawyers, consultants, businessmen — go to be seen, do business and glad-hand.

As he enters, a sea of pink faces glances up — then, almost as one, bobs back to the soup bowls as he passes by. Manicured male heads suddenly deep into conversations. Peeping at him over their shoulders when he isn't looking. Smiling at each other. Whispering. Nobody in this florid, pinstriped frieze comes over to say hello to the mayor.

"See how quick they cleared this table for us?" Barry asks, confused, eyes darting about the room in search of at least one friendly face. "This is my regular table, I come here once a week," he says gaily.

"Everybody in this room, all of them, makin' money, 'cause of me," he says, snatching up a glass of wine. "Now, just look at 'em. All just waitin' to see what's gonna happen."

A band of small, rotund men in brown suits, most with shining pates, marches to the door, without so much as a glance in Barry's direction. He watches them with interest. "They all look alike, don't they," he asks with a soft chuckle. They do.

"Republicans. All wanting to embarrass one black mayor. Ain't that something?" he asks, a genuine note of curiosity somewhere there, amid the usual seething resentments. "Mayor Marion Barry," he says softly, almost to himself. "I really must be something."

❖

Mary Pickford Speaks From Another Age

The reclusive silent-film star hasn't been seen in public in nearly a decade. Will a visitor to her fabled Pickfair mansion get to see her?

BY JOAN ZYDA · MARCH, 3 1974

"Just let me go tell her you're here."

Former matinee idol Buddy Rogers bounded by the winding staircase to the third floor of his Beverly Hills mansion and called to his wife of 37 years: "Mary, darling. You have a visitor, pet."

There were murmurs upstairs. Then Rogers walked slowly down the white steps to his visitor beneath the portrait of Mary Pickford in the spacious living room.

He shrugged and shook his head. "Mrs. Rogers would like to see you, darling, but she's in the shower, dear."

The scene is usually the same these days when anyone calls on the admired queen of the silent films. She is either sleeping or in the shower, always "unavailable."

Hundreds have been party guests of Buddy Rogers at fabled Pickfair in the last decade, but none has ever seen Miss Pickford. Even her stepson, Douglas Fairbanks Jr., doesn't see her when he spends an occasional week in the guest cottage.

One of her last interviews was in 1965 — with an English silent-film historian who has tried many times to see or phone her. But she is unavailable.

Mary Pickford, who will be 80 in April, is upstairs in her bedroom in a self-imposed seclusion that has lasted nearly two decades.

She was the first real movie star, a pioneer of the movie colony, coming to Hollywood when it was no more than a country village. She was America's Sweetheart of the early 20th century — famous for her golden Mary-Jane curls, dimpled chin and simple charm. They called her Goldilocks.

Rogers — tanned, athletic and manicured at 68 — shook his head affectionately. "She just doesn't go out. But she's doing great, darling. I took her out for a drive last week, but she said it made her nervous and she wanted to go home."

Pickfair, 1974, is a museum — once called the "White House of Hollywood" — where U.S. presidents, foreign heads of state, financiers and famous authors paid court to Miss Pickford.

Contemporary accounts of those gleaming parties come so vividly to mind while in the mansion that one can almost hear music and laughter, faint and incessant, from the garden and the cars going up and down the heart-shaped drive.

In the old days, guests at Pickfair could ride horses through the mountains to the Pacific Ocean and pass only one house along the way.

But time and progress have taken their toll on Pickfair. Only five of the original 15 acres remain. Five $150,000 homes were built on what used to be her vegetable garden.

A china set that Napoleon gave Josephine in 1807 is locked inside a glass cabinet. The mansion property and artistic contents are valued at $2 million.

The big rooms and high hallways are full of Frederic Remington paintings, early 18th-century antiques from Europe, Chippendale chairs and mirrors and Victorian tables. A sterling silver urn, given to Miss Pickford by the queen of Siam, is also in a glass case.

Film awards — including the first Oscar for the best performance by an actress in sound — are scattered around.

In almost every room are portraits of Miss Pickford staring down from the walls — at stages of her life from 18 to 59.

Rogers points out every detail eagerly. "Look here, darling!"

He leads the visitor into the small "Rodin Room," named after Auguste Rodin, father of modern sculpture. There are his rare sketches of nude dancing women, which Miss Pickford bought almost half a century ago.

Ultimately, Rogers confided, the visitor would get her audience with Miss Pickford after all — after a fashion.

He dialed his wife on a house phone on a small table.

"Yes, darling, she's here," he said. "She's a young one, dear."

He handed over the phone. "Mrs. Rogers wants to talk to you, sweet. She's so happy you're here, darling."

Gusty Santa Ana winds slapped hard against Pickfair, howling loudly, rattling closed windows.

"Boy! If I were outside right now I'd feel like a hen caught in a tornado," Miss Pickford laughed. It was fresh and spontaneous laughter.

It was the kind of voice that the ear follows up and down as if each syllable were an arrangement of notes that would never be played again. Her voice was sad and lovely and grandmotherly, but with bright things in it.

"I just hopped out of the tub," Miss Pickford said. "I'd come down and chat with you but my hair isn't fixed. I'm afraid I'd have to get all dressed up for you."

She said she enjoys the privacy and rest long denied her after all the busy years in the public eye as one of the world's wealthiest and most beautiful women.

"Yes, I miss my career, certainly," Miss Pickford said. "But I feel I've earned this rest. I used to work from 6 in the morning until midnight — the actress by day, the producer by night! It was a struggle. I never had time to myself.

"This is the first time in my life that I've been able to do things without constantly being interrupted."

She did not specify what has intruded on her solitude for the last decade or more, but she said she now goes nowhere — not to movies, nor to shows, nor out to dinner, nor even shopping. "I've chosen this way of life for myself," she said. "I like my privacy."

She said she reads mysteries and newspapers, dictates, looks out of her bedroom windows at Los Angeles and Beverly Hills, listens to records and watches television.

"I'm reading all about the devil," Miss Pickford confessed. "I think all this exorcism business is a hoax. Buddy says the movie is scary and I don't like to be scared."

Rogers sat slumped in a nearby armchair watching, amused.

Miss Pickford is aware she is different from other silent stars who have kept busy and still earn honors on stage and screen despite their ages.

(Lillian Gish, a close friend of 75, often appears in comedies as a little old lady. Gloria Swanson, the same age, is on Broadway and TV. Marlene Dietrich still does her famous songs at nightclubs and theaters at 74.

(Mae West, 83, likes to stay public and recently judged a UCLA kissing contest. And Helen Hayes is starring in a new, prime-time TV series called "Snoop Sisters." She's 73.)

"It's been so long since I met the public," she said. "People are so nervous these days. I don't think people would have the patience to listen to me....

"I played little girls, you know. Actresses can't go on and on forever doing that type of role. I can't imagine Jack Benny being 80, can you? And yet he's kicking around all the time on TV. Women can't get away with that like men can.

"Although I often dream I am before the cameras again. The other night, I imagined myself in a long shot and wondered if I should not redo my hair for it...."

She paused, then said musingly, "I have several pretty house dresses. I could throw one on and come down and talk to you ... but I'm too lazy."

Damn....

Some who have not seen Miss Pickford for years guess that time has not been kind to her. But her business manager, Matty Kemp, 64, describes her as having the "beautiful skin of a baby." She's 5 foot 1 and very slim.

"She keeps her hair blonde and has that same winsome smile that everyone remembers," Kemp said. "You can't detect a wrinkle on her face."

Two favorite friends of Miss Pickford are Miss Gish and Mildred Loew (producer Adolph Zukor's daughter). They visit Miss Pickford once a year when they are in town.

Miss Pickford has not viewed her films for 25 years. They have been shown only twice in the United States since they were locked up in the vaults at Bekins and Producers Film Center in Hollywood in 1933.

There they have sat, deteriorating with time. Miss Pickford wanted it that way. She is one of the few stars who owns and controls her films.

Just recently she was persuaded not to order her films burned at her death. She had not wanted to be compared with today's actresses.

"I always thought of myself as an entertainer for my own generation," she explained. "That was all that counted. It was Lillian Gish who convinced me that the films belong to the public and that I had no right to destroy them."

So the Mary Pickford Foundation, run by Kemp, has spent about $260,000 to preserve and restore the films. (Some foreign countries have copies of her movies and show them at special screenings.)

Some will be shown this month at film festivals honoring Miss Pickford throughout Europe. Her managers want to test the reaction of other countries before they consider showing them in the United States.

She wants to attend the Paris tribute.

"I'm longing to see Paris again. I got my warmest reception there long ago. I wonder if their reactions to me would be the same. Did you know that I can speak straight French for a half an hour?"

If she goes, it will be her first public appearance since 1965, when she visited Europe.

In the early 1970s, England and France had film tributes to Miss Pickford. There were parades in London and Paris, and thousands of people lined the streets to get a glimpse of her. They shouted for her autograph and locks of her hair.

But Miss Pickford was not there. At the last minute, she stayed at Pickfair. Rogers went alone and waved to the crowds for her.

She still misses producer D.W. Griffith.

"No one came close to him," she said. "He mastered the close-up, the fade-out. No one ever called him David because everyone had the greatest respect for him. He was always Mr. Griffith."

Miss Pickford also spoke of Douglas Fairbanks Sr., her second husband. They were considered the world's most romantic couple.

In films, Fairbanks was the dashing hero who could dispose of 20 adversaries in a running fight. According to Miss Pickford, he was exuberant and often did handstands or leapt over sofas to amuse friends.

"Because he had never outgrown a small boy's penchant for showing off, he was rarely referred to as Douglas or Mr. Fairbanks," she said. "It was always Doug."

Miss Pickford laughed about a call she had made to producer Adolph Zukor on his 101st birthday recently.

She sighed and her voice became sad.

"I just got word that my beloved cameraman Charles Rosher died in Portugal. He was a master, too."

Another pause.

"He once said, 'I'm not going to shoot this film because there's a shadow on Miss Pickford's face.' I said, 'Charlie, what does it matter?' But he insisted. He was so loyal. I don't know where to send word to his wife."

Miss Pickford said she was appalled by Watergate.

"I can't see any individuals destroying this glorious country," she said vehemently. "The United States is supposed to be the leader of the world and some punks are letting it go into the ashcan. We obviously need some housecleaning."

(She was a big contributor to President Nixon's reelection campaign, according to Kemp. During World War I, she also sold $48 million worth of Liberty Bonds for the United States.

(The government wanted her to make war propaganda films then, but she would make only humorous ones. One showed her riding a horse down San Francisco's Market Street, her golden curls flying in the breeze, leading the 143rd Field Artillery shipward to France.)

Of today's stars, Miss Pickford said she is most impressed with Katharine Hepburn and Liza Minnelli.

But her favorite remains Shirley Temple. "Oh, she was the cutest baby," she said. "She had more talent than anyone. Too bad she had to retire, but she left us with a lot of beautiful memories."

She added that there were no actors she was particularly fond of. "Nope. None since Gable," she said.

There was another deep sigh. Rogers seized on the silence to draw the conversation to a close. "She's doing great, darling, but I don't want to tire her out," he said.

Miss Pickford's voice started to trail away.

"It was nice talking to you," she said. "Maybe I'll see you someday...."

❖

Arthur Miller's Undying 'Salesman'

As the ambivalent playwright prepares to endure 50th-anniversary celebrations, the drama still has a grip on the American psyche.

BY PAUL LIEBERMAN · FEBRUARY 5, 1999

NEW YORK — Arthur Miller toyed with calling his play "The Inside of His Head" and staging it inside an enormous skull. After he decided those notions were "simply pointless" and came up with a new name, the producer tried to talk him out of it — "Death" in the title, the man warned, meant death at the box office.

Yet from the evening of February 10, 1949, when the play opened at the Morosco Theatre and the last eulogies were said over the grave of Willy Loman, and the audience paused in grief and then erupted in applause, "Death of a Salesman" has occupied a special place in the American theater.

"Salesman" burst forth not only as a work of art but also as a measure of a country and its people: its economy, families, values and dreams.

Willy Loman, who could no longer sell whatever was in those suitcases he carried on stage, became the symbol of American bluster, false pride and self-deception. Still, everyone's heart went out to this sagging man who felt so temporary.

Some took it literally and debated the plight of aging salesmen — companies even asked Miller to speak to their road crews. The highbrow crowd on campus, meanwhile, debated whether only the mighty could be tragic figures or whether a common man, like Willy, could join their ranks. Psychoanalysts pondered how the past haunted Willy's present, and fathers and sons reconsidered their expectations of each other.

Over the years, the play has sunk into the everyday culture by hard measures (11 million copies of the book version sold) and soft ones (quipped about on "Seinfeld").

A half century after the curtain went up, "Death of a Salesman" still seems to have a grip on the American psyche — even if it is required reading in high school.

The 50th anniversary will arrive with considerable pomp on Wednesday, as a new revival has its official opening night on Broadway, featuring a new score (edgy jazz), a new set (it revolves) and a new Willy (hulking Brian Dennehy).

But the words are the same ones Miller wrote as a young man in a 10-by-12-foot shed he built with his own hands on a knoll in Connecticut. And during the last two weeks, preview audiences have squirmed just like the ones of 1949 as Willy sits across from the son of his old boss, hat in hand, to plead for a break — and the pip-squeak-in-a-suit shines him on, wanting only to get him out of there. Downsizing, they call it these days.

Of course, not every line stings in 1999 like it did in 1949. In an era when credit cards come in the mail, unsolicited, it may be hard for some to understand Willy's despair at owing a few bucks on his fridge.

Night after night in previews, though, you still hear sobbing in the audience — men sobbing — as Willy embraces his son Biff, who may be a failure, a thief and a "dime a dozen" like his dad, but the boy loves him, he loves him! Minutes later, Willy is dead, his wife, Linda, is sprawled on his grave, and the audience is on its feet, just like in '49.

Whatever it is that "Salesman" is selling, folks still are buying.

. . .

Why, then, as acclaim awaits him anew at 83, is Arthur Miller … ambivalent?

We find America's most renowned living playwright in early January with his bags packed. Not Willy's strapped, stuffed sample carriers, but the modern ones — you yank up the handle and pull them along.

As rehearsals begin a few miles away, at the Eugene O'Neill Theatre on 49th Street, Miller is preparing to fly to Ireland. He's visiting his daughter, Rebecca, and her husband, actor Daniel Day-Lewis, and their 7-month-old, Miller's new grandson. He's also eager to get away, at least for 10 days, from everyone tugging at his sleeve, wanting him to size up his "Salesman" once more.

"I'm tired," he says. "I could spend the rest of my life talking about this."

Miller offers up that "it's not my most produced play" — that's "The Crucible" — and that some don't view it as his best, either.

It can be unsettling for any artist to have to talk about his work. He does what he does; it speaks for itself. It can be especially difficult when you're still churning out plays — three in the '90s — and they want you to talk about one you wrote 50 years ago.

Two nights earlier, 900 people packed the concert hall at the 92nd Street Y to hear Miller in one of those interviews-on-a-stage: only the playwright and British scholar Christopher Bigsby. The session dealt with Miller's work since the '60s, but when questions were allowed, someone quickly asked about his inspiration for "Salesman."

In his autobiography, "Timebends," Miller wrote about how he drew from his Uncle Manny, a salesman whose mind — up to the day he killed himself — was drugged by competitiveness, always boasting about the big things in store for his sons, Buddy and Abby. Manny would spout out comments that seemed comical, having nothing to do with what came before. Approached with a simple greeting, he'd reply, "Buddy is doing very well."

At the Y, Miller gave the short version. "I had a character before I wrote it," he told the audience. "I just knew that he would die."

Elia Kazan, who directed the original "Salesman," saw a mixed blessing in how Miller connected on so many levels with "Salesman." "I don't know any other play … that does all these things at the same time," he wrote in his autobiography. "But Arthur Miller did them all — that one time and never again."

Kazan noted that life was never the same for the principals in the 1949 triumph, not for him or Lee J. Cobb, the actor who was Willy Loman, or for Miller, most of all. "Truth was soon out of sight," Kazan wrote. "We all puffed up."

Miller has himself partly to blame for all the analysis of "Salesman." Two weeks after it opened, he came out with his essay "Tragedy and the Common Man," arguing against the notion that the genre had to involve the fall of a great figure, like a king.

Still, how could he anticipate all the attempts to psych out his character's name (Loman? Low-Man!) when he actually took it from a 1933 Fritz Lang movie (a young detective, desperate to reach his boss, whispers into a phone, "Hello? Hello! Lohmann? Lohmann!"). Or the exegeses on whether the fountain pen stolen by Biff was a phallic symbol?

"This [New York] psychiatrist … came up with a talk. I was curious to see if he could add some psychological insight," Miller recalls. "All he did is read pieces of scenes. He performed my play!"

According to the Modern Language Association, the organization of English professors, Miller — or "Salesman" — has been the subject of 413 scholarly books, articles and PhD dissertations since 1963. "Salesman" has been picked apart by "feminists, universalists … social constructionists, Jungians, Marxists …," says Georgia

State University's Matthew D. Roudane, who edited the association's guide for teaching what a survey found to be the American play "most studied at the university level."

The original debate did not envision feminist interpretations of Willy's marriage, of course. Most everything then revolved around the postwar era's explosive politics, the brewing Cold War. The day "Salesman" opened, the big news was: 11 Reds on trial in New York and President Truman resists U.N. demands for atomic weapons data.

One right-wing publication branded "Salesman" a "time bomb expertly placed under the edifice of Americanism." When Hollywood began preparing a film version, timid studio executives wanted to add a disclaimer saying that salesmen were no longer treated like Willy. To Miller, that was like "urging people to get up out of the theater ... if 'Death of a Salesman' is so outmoded."

Today, we can see the Miller of 1949 as quite moderate, almost a believer in the system. Yes, Willy indicts the American dream, to the degree he buys into the credo of the conquerors, exemplified by his ghostly brother Ben, "a great man!" In an apparition, Ben reminds Willy that he walked into the jungle at 17, "and when I was 21, I walked out. And by God I was rich!"

Miller's voice, though, is heard in the neighbor, Charlie, who cautions Willy, "You take it too hard." When the boss makes promises across the table — there'll always be a place for you — be wary.

Miller acknowledges that audiences today, despite our overall prosperity, have fewer illusions about their jobs — and exhibit less loyalty in return. Aren't the young now instructed that they will have several careers? But look where that leaves them.

"Any Monday morning you can be told you are no longer needed, the company is moving to Guatemala. This is something that goes very deep down. In a very primitive way, you just can't tell somebody to just get lost." He quotes Willy: "You can't eat the orange and throw the peel away — a man is not a piece of fruit!"

Miller hardly dislikes money. He recently replaced his longtime Connecticut country place with a 400-acre upgrade and stands to make a mint from the new Broadway run. He figures that if he wrote the stuff, "why not me?"

But he's still the man who was made so uneasy by his first success, with 1947's "All My Sons," that he signed up to do manual labor. And he remembers well the opening of "Salesman," when the owner of the theater gave a white-tablecloth feast for his tuxedoed friends — not for the creative crew — right on the famous set depicting the Lomans' bare-bones Brooklyn home. The "pain and love and protest in my play," he wrote later, were "transformed into mere champagne."

A product of the New York streets, he still feels a need to mix with "those on the bottom." In January, before he packed his bags, Miller went to an East Harlem settlement house to assist a literacy program that teaches new immigrants English using literature.

"Their need is right on the skin, these people," he said. "I don't mean their financial need — their need to understand what you're saying. What are you up to? Are you with me or against me? Can I lean on you or are you going to bite me? They're listening that way. I like that."

He, too, feels a bit like an outsider. How many in his position still relish, like Willy, working with their hands, in his case with wood? Miller recently finished the unpainted coffee table in his apartment's sparse living room. Although there's a small TV on the far wall, he can hardly watch the nonsense that "disperses itself into the room, under the rug, into the furniture." Movies? Look how Americans embraced that feel-good "Forrest Gump." He hated it.

"He's always triumphant," Miller says of the Oscar-winning Tom Hanks character. People today "want to participate in a victory. They don't want to participate in a defeat. Which is interesting, my saying that in view of 'Death of a Salesman.' "

He knows the time has passed since audiences — American ones, at least — looked at the serious theater as their great shared experience. Only splashy musicals now fill enough seats to meet the bottom line on Broadway.

Miller's "Broken Glass" got mixed reviews here in 1994, and the play — set in 1938 and dealing with anti-Semitism — ran only two months on Broadway. Then it opened in London, at the National Theatre and, boom — box office and renown, Britain's Laurence Olivier Award. The National Theatre stages more plays by Miller than any other playwright except Shakespeare. "They have a theater," is how Miller puts it. "We have show business."

"In America, he tends to get treated like a Smithsonian Institution figure. 'Oh, is he still around?' " says Bigsby, the English scholar, who heads the Arthur Miller Centre — which focuses on American studies — at the University of East Anglia in Norwich, England. "Or else, it's Marilyn [Monroe]. He's been married to Inge [photographer Inge Morath] since 1962, and he still gets asked about the marriage to Marilyn."

That old bout with celebrity frenzy may be one reason Miller craves his privacy. But he seems reluctant, as well, to see what happens to his works: Few productions produce the music he hears with his own ears. One group did "Salesman" with a car on the stage facing the audience, shining its brights at them. He laughs now at that inane bid to be different, then observes, "You have to face the fact that when you're dead, they'll do whatever they want with your plays."

The front foyer of his apartment is decorated with posters advertising his plays all over the globe. "Salesman" has been done from Scandinavia to Communist China, where the audience had no concept of salesmanship but identified with Willy's frenzy to leave a thumbprint on the world. "We also want to be No. 1," one man said on opening night.

Miller sees that part of the magic of "Salesman" is how audiences view Willy, and the play, their own way. People his age, for instance, tend to connect with "the part that deals with his disorientation."

"I tend to side with Willy more and more," he says, "with his devotion. I think I understood it when I wrote it, but I wasn't taking sides. Now I am."

Forget the politics. These days he views "Salesman" as "basically a love story."

"Everyone loves Willy," Miller explains, "except Willy doesn't realize it."

A tragedy, indeed. One that begs a question as it's time to leave: When the anniversary arrives, will Miller be ready to accept love, namely America's love for the play that he didn't so much write 50 years ago but, as Kazan put it, "released."

. . .

From the first moment, you're told this is a new production. The original's haunting flute music is replaced by the jarring noise of traffic, then the first chords of a Richard Woodbury jazz score. The legendary "reality-condensation" set of Jo Mielziner — with its 6-foot bedroom, tiny kitchen table and lone appliance, the fridge — is replaced by platforms and boxcars and a turntable and moving sidewalks. They allow others in his life, and his memory, to literally come to Willy or revolve around him in a near-dizzying blur of past and present, reality and fantasy. We're back, in a sense, to Miller's original concept, "The Inside of His Head."

The production isn't ignoring the social comment but takes pains to avoid one trap of "Salesman," which is to beg for pity. There's none of that in Dennehy's Willy Loman — no sense that he's hopelessly weighted down with those bags when he arrives home, having been unable to make it past Yonkers.

Dennehy follows quite a lineup of Willies: Cobb on stage and in a TV version in the '60s, Fredric March in the film, George C. Scott in the '70s and Dustin Hoffman in the last Broadway production, in 1984.

Uncle Manny, the inspiration for Willy, was a small man, like Hoffman. But the burly Cobb convinced Miller that it was done best as a big man's part, like Lear. Dennehy, 60, a former Columbia University football lineman, sets a new standard in that regard, though he only once rises to full size, like a grizzly, to bellow from the front of the stage, "I am not a dime a dozen! I am Willy Loman."

This is Dennehy's fourth partnership with director Robert Falls, 44, the artistic head of Chicago's Goodman Theatre, which worked up this "Salesman" in the fall. After one of the first previews, a Saturday matinee, they walk across 49th Street from the O'Neill Theatre to gulp down dinner before the evening show and to talk about, among other things, their fathers.

Falls goes first: "While I was working on this play, my father" — in his 70s — "had a little car accident. He had no idea how it happened. He just was going the wrong way at the wrong time and got broadsided. It shook him to the core, and he had this tremendous fear and anger in him that I had never seen. In his eyes. And that look, I knew, was Willy Loman coming in the door. How did this happen to me? How did I get old? He's not going gently into that night."

Dennehy, drained from the matinee, gulps down water. Willy and son Biff are always fighting, he notes, but when Biff heads off, "all of a sudden Willy says [to his wife], 'Remember that Ebbets Field game?' " — the city football championship, at which Biff was the star — "It's when he leaves the room that Willy expresses his love." The actor then says: "My father and I would fight all the time — and his friends would say, 'But you really ought to hear how your father talks about you.' And I'm saying to myself, 'Why doesn't he say it to me?' "

Dennehy says that when he's on stage and collapses in his son's arms, he looks into the audience at the men, crying. "I got to tell you there are 50 people out there living their own lives. It has nothing to do with us — it's them."

That's how it goes, even in 1999. Sure, "Salesman" may have "accumulated a little bit of dust over 50 years," Falls says. That's why he wanted to stop paying homage to the original look and "rethink the piece as if I was handed the manuscript for the very first time, doing a new play by a young writer named Arthur Miller."

It's an 83-year-old Miller, though, back from Ireland, who is coming to see their evening show.

"I do hope he's ready to accept what's going to happen," Dennehy says. "You know, the 'Thanks.' 'Congratulations.' 'We appreciate it.' I hope he's ready to have that peace. There's always the problem of people thinking it's all over — and he shouldn't think that way. But at the same time, there's no reason he can't say, 'You know, you're right. I did a hell of a job.' "

They're planning panels and parties and other festivities around the Wednesday anniversary.

The Saturday-night preview gave Miller a dose of what will unfold. Outside the theater, a "gang" — that's what he called it — spotted him leaving and surrounded him. Translation? A hundred theatergoers would not stop applauding until he drove off.

He had notes, naturally, to give to Falls in the morning. The first act needed a little work. Biff needed some more arc.

But overall? He loved it. The last 10 minutes? Perfect. Everything about Dennehy's Willy. And Elizabeth Franz as Linda, playing the woman as angry, fighting for Willy's dignity. The sets and music too. Miller once thought "Salesman" was riveted to the original look. "This is a revelation," he said. "I learned one thing: Thank God, there is more than one viable way to do this play."

The way the audience was riveted? It didn't seem like nostalgia to him.

He still wasn't sure about the fuss outside the theater. "The producer had the car waiting, thank God. We could get out of there."

On Wednesday, when they are certain to drag him on stage?

"I have strong teeth, and I'll grit it out. At the same time, I'd just as soon stay home."

But he won't.

"I suppose they'll do it, and I suppose they'll get me up, and I suppose I'll put up with it. And I suppose," Arthur Miller confesses, "I'll enjoy it."

❖❖

A Good Cop's Long Slide to Disgrace

In Merced, the ex-lawman of the year was convicted of stealing cocaine in a betrayal of his badge and family, including the cousin who helped bring him down.

BY MARK ARAX · JUNE 6, 1996

MERCED, California — Growing up in the peach orchards of the San Joaquin Valley, Jim Slate was a bit too innocent and coddled for his cousin Larry's taste.

Larry, six months older and wiser to the world, did what he could to educate him. It was Larry who introduced Jim to his first fistfight, his first beer and his first romance.

They played side by side in Pony League: Larry a catcher, all guts and tattered uniform, and Jim a meticulous outfielder with a line-drive swing. They shared a dream to become police officers and graduated from the same class at the academy in 1976. True to form, Larry became a motorcycle patrolman and Jim a 16-hour-a-day, by-the-book detective.

Jim went on to be celebrated as one of the finest officers Merced ever had — tough, fearless, a workaholic on behalf of the law. He didn't blink an eye at the pressure to let old teammates and buddies off easy. The armed robber in his first felony arrest was his best friend from grammar school.

But the Jim Slate who waddled into the federal courthouse in Fresno in May 1995 was a different man, a wheezing, 420-pound disgrace with two bad knees and the nickname "Tiny." The former Merced lawman of the year pleaded guilty to stealing 15 kilograms of cocaine from a bust that he and Larry had worked together. Last month, he left Merced to begin a 10-year sentence in federal prison.

It was an unthinkable betrayal of his badge and hometown and the foursquare values that the large Slate family had always stood for, and it stunned this farming town. Suddenly the texture of life seemed frayed.

Jim Slate gone bad? No way.

His secret might have remained safe from his cousin and everyone else, except that he peddled the dope through a local dealer who was every officer's snitch. Larry Slate refused to believe it. When state narcotics agents, now his co-workers, first related their suspicions, he told them to go to hell. Finally, confronted with the undeniable, he turned cop on his cousin and helped the investigation.

"He insulted me. The SOB insulted our family and town and my profession," Larry said. "We were partners. We were cops. We put guys in jail who did what he did…. I turned on him, you bet. And if the situation was reversed, I'd expect the same from him."

Jim offered no reason for raiding the evidence locker entrusted to his care. Although his guilty plea spared the Slate family from the grimy details of his crime, it also robbed this community of a trial and a possible explanation, however self-serving, from Jim.

The questions still echo.

How could a model police detective, a man who seemed to take special pride in busting dirty cops, take such a plunge? He was the son of decent, hard-working parents in a tightknit community of farmers, housewives, police, coaches, hunters and fishermen. There were so many places he could have gone for help.

Maybe it was the obesity — his weight had doubled over the last decade. Or the longtime girlfriend who dumped him, and his attempt to find a replacement in a police groupie half his age. After all, Jim spent only a fraction of the cocaine proceeds on himself. Most of it went to this new woman and a cousin who was jobless.

Just before he left for prison, the 42-year-old Slate sat in the small, spare bedroom of his parents' home — his self-imposed jail cell for two years — and talked for the first time about his downfall. He had used his voice so little since his arrest that he went hoarse after two hours.

He was still recovering from radical surgery to seal much of his stomach in an attempt to lose weight. He had lost 160 pounds. He was learning to walk — without the shuffle — and he paced back and forth, washed and dried his hands what seemed like a hundred times, and drank constantly from a half-frozen bottle of Crystal Geyser water. His now-tiny stomach kept gurgling.

"It's funny," he said, smiling beneath a Fu Manchu mustache. "Here I am freeing myself of all this weight that's imprisoned me for years, and I'm headed off to prison.

"I've done nothing but lay in this bedroom for two years and think, 'When did I let go? When did I make that fatal mistake and go over the line?' You know, I can sit here and say something snapped. But I didn't hear something snap."

If he tended to overdo things as a cop, meeting snitches at 2 a.m. or refusing to take a sick day in 11 years, he knew no other way. The whole Slate clan, refugees from the Dust Bowl, worked hard. His father, J.B., ran Del Monte's 4,000-acre peach ranch by day and a turkey insemination business by night.

Jim tried to help with the turkeys but had a deep fear of birds. Larry had to catch and pry open the hens. "Larry wasn't afraid of anything and he couldn't understand my fear of birds," Jim said. "He used to tease me. 'How can you be as tough as you are and be afraid of a little old bird?' "

The oldest of three children, Jim grew up on the peach ranch and attended Merced schools. Larry's house was 10 minutes down the road in a rough little town called Planada, where his father served as constable. The cousins, so close in age, were like brothers, and they competed fiercely in baseball whenever the extended family got together for barbecues at the ranch.

Home plate was the shade of a mulberry tree, left field the bunkhouse where the migrant farm workers slept, right field the tin equipment shed. Off the pecan tree was a homer, an easy swat for the tall, broad-shouldered Jim. The game would just get going when Jim's mother would shout, "You can run, Jim, but I don't want you sweating." Larry thought that was the most ridiculous thing, proof that his cousin could use a little dirtying up.

One summer night before their sophomore year of high school, the cousins were hanging out in the park in Planada when four guys jumped them. They nearly got their throats cut but Jim held his own, never leaving Larry's side. He finally proved himself in the eyes of his fearless cousin.

Family and friends recall that Jim had a hard time fitting in when Larry wasn't around. At Merced Junior College, baseball coach Butch Hughes was impressed with Jim's versatility on the field but noticed he was awkward socially. Even so, Jim managed to get elected student body vice president.

"Jim had this deep need to please people, and yet he turned them off with an attitude that seemed arrogant," Hughes said. "Then he would overcompensate and try to buy their friendship. He was such a good person and he didn't need to do that."

After helping Merced win a state championship in 1973, Jim received a scholarship to Idaho State University. He led the Big Sky conference with a .396 batting average and might have had a chance at the pros but his girlfriend back home got pregnant and he returned to Merced. They married and he signed up for the Police Academy — the same class Larry was in. Jim's marriage lasted five years.

"All I cared about was being ... the best detective and the longest-running detective this city had ever seen," he said. "I'd work my normal shift, come home, eat, and then go back out and ride with someone else and work six to eight more hours for free. Seven days a week. I didn't care about anything else. Nothing."

His reputation for giving no quarter made life uncomfortable for his mother at the Ragu tomato plant where she worked: He kept busting the children of her co-workers. With equal fervor, he pursued killers and cops-turned-petty-thieves. Praise poured in from the district attorney's office, victims, businessmen and housewives in this fast-growing town with its share of drugs and bad guys. His glowing evaluations each year recommended only one thing: Slow down and lose a little weight. He looked in the mirror. At 6 feet 2, he managed to wear his 280 pounds pretty well.

He began dating Mary Papageorge, a mother of four who was 10 years older, and they rented an apartment near headquarters. Always the workaholic, he let his cases — junkies and informants — invade their bedroom hours. She could never figure out what drove him.

"There's a lot about Jim I'm still totally in the dark about," Papageorge said. "He was slowly killing himself, working morning to morning, and eating fast-food hamburgers and cookies. He tried all kinds of diets. One friend gave him a diet where you make this big pot of vegetable soup and you're supposed to eat a bowl whenever you get hungry. I think he lasted a day."

When the state formed a local drug task force in 1986, the cousins were among the first hired. Jim was named custodian of the evidence locker and a backup supervisor. Even though he now weighed close to 350 pounds, he closed twice as many cases as the next officer and insisted on being the first to burst through the stash house door.

He trained everyone in the unit, then watched his cousin and the others promoted to the state Bureau of Narcotic Enforcement office in Fresno. The state would have taken him too if not for his weight. "This new batch of youngsters replaces the old batch, and he's having to train them too," Larry said. "They're drinking and chasing women, all the things young guys do, and here's Tiny, by himself, plugging along, almost a father figure. It was sad."

One year he went to the 80-member department's annual Christmas party in a mood to drink tequila. He asked the bartender what the record was for straight shots in a single sitting. Seventeen, he was told. "Well, put out 20," he said. "Jose Cuervo Gold."

"He polished off all 20 shots in about 30 minutes," said Police Chief Patrick Lunney. "That's a quart of tequila, enough to literally kill some men. But he got off the bar stool and was in pretty good shape."

In late 1992, after waiting years for him to change, his girlfriend decided she had enough and left. Jim was devastated. He looked in the mirror and saw a 40-year-old man who weighed 400 pounds with bad knees and gout in his ankles. On his own again, he tried running with the youngsters in his unit. Tiny's place became a clubhouse. All the beer and cold cuts were on him.

"He invited me to a card game, and I walked in and there were all these young cops and young girls," Larry said. "They were drinking his beer and using his apartment to hit and run. They were playing him for a chump and he didn't even see it."

Unknown to Larry, talk on the street was that Jim was spending thousands of dollars on one of these women, money possibly lifted from the evidence vault. Larry got a call from a state investigator who wanted to meet. It was hot and the investigator was standing too close, wearing a leather jacket. Larry figured he was being recorded.

"We were bumping guns, talking, and there was no way I was going to believe him," Larry recalled. "I told him: You show me some evidence before I believe my cousin's gone sideways. Talk is cheap."

That night he called Jim to his house and confronted him in the driveway. Jim was cool as could be and denied any wrongdoing. Larry wanted to believe that the spending spree was nothing more than his cousin finally parting with all of his overtime money. "If he would have owned up to anything criminal, I would have beat the hell out of him right there in the driveway, and he knows it," Larry said.

The young woman, a mother on welfare, told investigators that Jim had spent more than $200,000 in recent months, much of it in an effort to woo her to bed. Except for a new truck, little of the money was spent on himself. She said he made a game of it — hiding $100 bills under the sofa and making her crawl until she found them, handing her $7,000 and telling her she had 20 minutes to spend as much as she could at the mall.

A six-week search of task force records — books that Jim had kept — unmasked his first crimes. He lied to people who sought to reclaim cash seized in busts, saying the money had been forfeited under the law. He later doctored the paperwork and pocketed the cash.

It was a perfect crime except for one slip. The doctoring was done with a slightly different blue ballpoint pen. "We were doing this with a magnifying glass and a flashlight. The Sherlock Holmes thing," said Vince Jura, the state investigator who headed the internal probe. "We were able to account for $10,000 this way. This was his pocket change. The money he was blowing in bars. But where was the big score? We still didn't know."

Investigators discovered that a destruction order for cocaine had been falsified. The order was signed by a judge and dated, but the amount of drugs to be destroyed — 31 kilos, worth nearly $400,000 — was added after the judge's signature. Investigators knew this because Jim used two typewriters whose fonts differed ever so slightly.

"Narcs just don't sell 31 kilos of cocaine. No one would trust them," Jura said. "So I figure he's got to be working with someone. Who is his king informant? Who's the guy he protects, the guy he's been working with all these years?"

The answer was easy. Every officer in town knew Chato, the heroin addict who had a special relationship with Jim. But Chato wasn't talking. By this time, Larry had heard enough to know that his cousin had irrevocably crossed the line. He confronted him a second time, and once more Jim denied any wrongdoing.

Larry passed the details of the conversation back to Jura, but they were hardly needed. Chato got caught with heroin and was talking. He told investigators that Jim had given him a few ounces of cocaine, then 5 kilos and then 9. Thirty-one kilos in all. Jim was so foolish. He gave a hefty chunk to Chato and got back $13,000 a kilo. But much of this money he gave away — to the mother on welfare, to a cousin who was unemployed.

And Chato had one more bewildering detail. After each dirty deal was done, they would sit in the car and Jim would play a cassette of Eric Clapton's "Cocaine."

From there, the case was a matter of piecing together bank deposits, dates, telephone toll calls and hotel registrations — all leading back to Jim. Police Chief Lunney blamed himself for not insisting years earlier that Jim change beats and leave the task force. But no one else was willing to do his job.

The task force supervisor, Jim Pell, also second-guessed himself. "What really upsets me is not the big rip-off but the … everyday stuff," Pell said. "He buffooned me the whole time."

The cocaine came from a high-profile bust that Jim and his cousin and most of his former colleagues — cops now working for the state narcotics office — participated in. That was a little too much paradox for Larry.

"He boosted money out of the cases I did, my cases," he said. "He was a good cop, smart, tenacious, incredibly hard-working. He was 400 pounds and the biggest slob in town, but by God he was the best cop Merced ever saw.

"He thought he was bulletproof," Larry said, shaking his head. "He got stupid about it."

The cousins haven't spoken in three years. They doubt they ever will. "I feel bad that I did this and let Larry down, but I feel equally bad that he stuck his nose where it shouldn't have been," Jim said. "They never got anything from Larry that they could use against me. All they did was cause the family to go off in splinters."

So why did you do it?

"I was hurt, physically down," he said, sitting on a worn sofa surrounded by old baseball trophies. "I was emotionally drained from the job. I carried the workload of too many officers for too many years. I lost Papageorge. She was my stability. I weighed 400 pounds. Then all of a sudden I start getting pimped by this girl and my ego shoots through the roof. She used me like no sugar daddy's ever been used. I started drinking again.

"Do you think this is what I wanted out of life? I didn't do this for myself. I didn't have some second home in Bullhead, Arizona. I didn't have a bank account hidden somewhere. I didn't get the money the dirty cops in New York got."

He said the case against him was embellished, many details made up by informants. He offered more than once to take a polygraph test, but he said his ex-colleagues refused. He said he stole 15 kilos, not 31.

He caught himself sounding contrite and defiant at the same time, and his hoarse voice became a whisper. "I betrayed everything I ever stood for. God, I don't know why. It wasn't me. It just wasn't me."

❖

Stock Cars — an Also-Ran Is Also Driven

In this sport, it takes money to win. But to land a sponsor who'll put out the cash, you have to win first. One driver hopes this is the year he can beat the system.

BY RUDY ABRAMSON · APRIL 1, 1979

NORTH WILKESBORO, North Carolina — This is a story about a young man named Smut Means and all the trouble he's had pursuing his dream of joining the great American middle class.

You've never heard of him unless you habitually read deep into the agate type of the sports pages. That's where the also-rans are enshrined in the kind of tiny letters they use to print help-wanted ads — down there with the pitchers who have lost their fastball, the quarterbacks who have lost their nerve and the fighters who have answered too many bells.

Smut Means is a stock-car driver. That's all he's ever been. He's an also-ran on the fried-chicken circuit, the big leagues of stock-car racing where on Sunday afternoons the spiritual heirs of the South's moonshine haulers rocket down straightaways at better than 200 mph, sending the good ol' boys and the good ol' girls into an ecstasy reserved for those who love strong preaching, cold beer, greasy chicken, the smell of motor oil and the sight of Richard "The King" Petty in his Day-Glo orange and blue Chevy daring the Almighty and making enough noise to bring back the dead.

The difference between being broke and being rich is 7 or 8 mph. If Smut could run that much faster, he'd be up there in front, hard-changing with the wealthy — Petty, Cale Yarborough, Bobby Allison, Darrell Waltrip, Benny Parsons and folks like that. The people down in the infield at Darlington, North Wilkesboro, Bristol, Daytona and Talledega would shell out $5 to get a ball cap with his name on it and put Smut Means bumper stickers on their vans. Like Richard and Cale and Bobby, he'd be a bigger hero than George Wallace and Willie Nelson put together.

But now he's getting old, looking for that 7 or 8 mph.

Before he even needed a shave, when he was still called Jimmy, the name his mother gave him, he bought a motor out of a Huntsville, Alabama, junkyard, gratefully accepted the gift of a rear end and some sheet metal from a man in Birmingham, and built a racing car — with the help of friends who have stuck with him from that day to this, as though his dream were their own.

It didn't take him long on the short tracks at Huntsville, Nashville and Birmingham — bullrings, they call them — to establish himself as a man with a steady hand, a heavy foot and grit. Nearly four years ago, he decided to try the big time, the NASCAR — the National Association of Stock Car Automobile Racing — grand national circuit.

He didn't have any illusion that he was going to be one of the immortals of Southern racetracks.

What he really had in mind was making a good living. He grew up poor in a section of Huntsville where residential areas were being overtaken by gas stations and fast-food parlors and building-supply outfits.

His father repaired refrigeration equipment and his mother worked for the Army. They didn't own an automobile. They didn't own much of anything. Jimmy Means' first job was sweeping up in a garage when he was 14.

It was natural for him to see the automobile as his way toward a piece of the great American dream. He grew up in a time and place where the automobile was worshiped as much as it ever was before or has been since.

It was manhood, affluence, equality, independence. It was identity. Question: "You know Jimmy Means?" Answer: "What does he drive?"

Jimmy Means' generation down in the tail end of Appalachia was preoccupied with four-barrel carburetors and glass-packed mufflers and spinner hubcaps. It didn't matter if you lived in a tar-paper shack if you drove a Rocket 88. It didn't matter if your car was old if it was loud. It didn't matter if you couldn't read if you could drive.

Jimmy Means was a kid without a car. That was why he was poor. That is where he came from, and that is why he is the way he is.

He became Smut instead of Jimmy when he grew so enraptured with the motion of racing cars that he went about incessantly quoting one Smokey Yunick, whom he considered the world's preeminent and uncontestable authority on any facet of stock racing, especially engines. "Boy," said one of his elders, "you ain't no Smokey. You're not even a Smut" (soot).

So far the road to success has been rougher than growing up poor.

There have been times when it seemed Smut would have to give it up and go to Huntsville and work in a garage. There have been times when he was scared and sick.

In one race, he hit the wall in Talledega so hard that when they pulled him out of the car and took his shoes off, his feet were solid purple. Bruised.

One night in Birmingham, he T-boned a driver named Denny Rewis. That is to say he hit him in the side at a 90-degree angle, traveling at a speed that would get you arrested on any interstate highway in the United States. Rewis was unconscious for a week. Smut kept calling the hospital day and night and couldn't sleep a wink until Dennis came to and Smut had a chance to apologize.

Then there was the time on his home track in Huntsville six years ago when, during a lonely practice session, he ran through a guardrail at 100 mph, just missed a Church of God billboard, crashed through a corrugated metal fence and descended through the tops of two trees outside the track. He was not hurt.

During his first year of racing, his weight fell to 115 pounds although he's nearly 6 feet tall. That was fortunate, he thinks in retrospect, because when he crashed he usually didn't hurt anything but his knees and elbows. "I was," he says, "about as big around as a crankshaft."

Smut Means in the last four years has been frustrated like tens or hundreds of thousands of other people, those who gamble everything they have, even their lives, to break into the middle-class world of color televisions, 40-hour workweeks and automatic garage-door openers. He wants his wife, Marsha, to have the Means family's first food processor, and he wants his children, Brad and Lori, to be the first to go to college.

The trouble is that he finds himself shut out by the system. He could have as much talent as the immortal Junior Johnson, the onetime whisky hauler who did more than anybody to make stock-car racing an industry, and he would still be an also-ran. Smut Means competes like the mom-and-pop grocery store competes with a Safeway across the street.

He is a man with little money in what a banker would call a capital-intensive business.

He still lives in the neighborhood where he grew up. After living expenses, he puts every penny of the $220,000 he has earned back into his business. He has come more than ever to look at racing as a business rather than a sport.

He has to be a skinflint because he hasn't won a big race; he hasn't run at the head of the pack. The producers of motor-oil additives, the hamburger chains, the garbage-truck manufacturers, the breweries and the car dealers who sponsor drivers haven't seen enough promise in Smut Means to take a big gamble with him.

When he wins, he will find a sponsor easily. But without a financial sponsor, it's nearly impossible to win. He is in the predicament of the first-time job hunter who finds experience the only prerequisite.

So he stretches his engines; he races on "scuffs," the tires the big shots take off when they stop for gas; he has a different pit crew for every race; he doesn't take chances in the turns.

Smut's dream is being held together by his friends.

They are people like Shelly Black, an electrical engineer who has dug into his own pocket when times are hardest, and Jim Williams, who bought a van to ferry pit crews to races, and Bill Gray, who quit his job and drew unemployment compensation while he worked on Smut's engines.

There were also others, like J.D. Smith and J.P. Roberts and Joe Woods, who have worked on his cars into the wee hours of the morning, even through winters when there wasn't a heater in the old cinder-block garage in Huntsville.

Then there are the out-of-town friends like Billy Joe Potts in Daytona, who shelters and feeds Smut and his crew during the Daytona 500. Taylor "Mousey" Brown, an old drag-racer, lives in North Wilkesboro and joins the pit crew when the grand national racers come here to run on Junior Johnson's home track — a sacred place in the stockers' minds — in the foothills of the Blue Ridge Mountains.

This was supposed to be the year when Smut made his move.

He spent $14,000 getting ready for the Daytona 500, the beginning of the season, one of the momentous occasions of stock-car racing, when 100,000 fans turn out and live television carries the race across the country.

He bought a new tubular steel frame from Banjo Mathews, an Asheville, North Carolina, expert who builds the special lightweight frames for Petty and Yarborough. He had a spanking new engine.

To cap the stack, he got a call from Mr. Transmission, a chain of transmission service shops, offering to put up $1,500. For the first time in memory he would start a race on new tires.

But that was not to be. His new engine didn't run as fast as the old; he switched back to his old engine, and it blew up in the time trials. He was back home in Huntsville when Richard Petty took first place in the run for $600,000 in prize money.

In the following weeks, he started in Atlanta, and Rockingham, North Carolina, and Richmond, and didn't get close to finishing a single time. He broke an axle in Richmond minutes after he had ordered two new tires at $80 apiece. And he damaged a wheel and dropped out in Rockingham just after the eight front-runners had crashed, giving him a splendid opportunity to move up to the money.

When he arrived here for last Sunday's 400-lap event, he had not finished a race this year, and he had spent more on tires than he had earned. His only consolation was that he finished in the top 20 in the drivers' point standings last year — 20th, as a matter of fact. That meant that he would get a payday just for showing up at tracks this year.

After he had turned the five-eighths of a mile track at better than 103 mph Saturday afternoon, qualifying him to start in 22nd position Sunday, Smut worked on his car until nearly dark and then went to Mousey Brown's house for dinner. Later he talked with an old friend who had shared his dream from the beginning.

He was $10,000 in the hole. He still owed Banjo Mathews some money on the new frame, and he owed Bobby Allison money on a truck he had bought from Allison to haul his car to races. He hadn't heard any more from the man at Mr. Transmission.

"The dream is slipping away," he said. "I've got to do something by the time I'm 30, and I'm going to be 29 this year.

"I've got to start saving some money. I've just got to start taking the first $100 I get and put it in the bank or something."

Sunday morning he was at the track early. An icy wind was blowing snow across the empty Junior Johnson Memorial Bleachers while he and Sandy Jones worked on the car in pit row. It was his short-track car — a yellow and black Chevy, with a frame that had belonged to Junior Johnson himself when it was new.

Junior Johnson, the man who made lawmen feel foolish by the way he handled his car on the back roads of the Carolina hills; who perfected the about-face, a way of turning 180 degrees without ever stopping. Junior Johnson, the man who revolution-ized stock-car racing with the discovery of drafting, the phenomenon that lets a driv-er get on the bumper of a high-speed car in front of him, let up on the accelerator and still keep up because the front car has cleared out the wind resistance.

Junior Johnson, as Smut worked on the old Chevy, was 200 yards down pit row in a Bush Beer jumpsuit setting up a shiny racing machine for Cale Yarborough, who won $500,000 last year.

Smut didn't even leave his car to go to the drivers' meeting before the race, or to the church service where a preacher with an enormous belly and a cowboy hat spoke to a congregation seated on racing tires near the finish line.

He did fine when the race first started.

One straightaway at the North Wilkesboro speedway goes downhill, and the other goes uphill, straight toward the Blue Ridge Mountains way out beyond town.

Smut's Chevy tore it up, going both ways. He passed five cars and was in a bunch of squawling Chevys, Fords and Dodges up toward the front after a dozen laps.

On the 14th lap, Petty was in front, and the old boys with the "Petty Power" ball caps were rocking the Junior Johnson Memorial grandstands.

Not many of them noticed when Smut went into the pits on the 14th lap with oil pouring out of his engine.

He changed clothes and watched the last 385 laps from behind his truck.

When it was over, Bobby Allison won, boosting his earnings for the first half-dozen races of the year to more than $100,000.

Petty, working on the fourth million dollars of his career, finished second by nine seconds.

It was 2 a.m. Monday when Smut and Sandy rolled back into Huntsville.

Later in the day, they took the blown engine apart to see what was wrong, and started getting another ready to put in the Chevy for today's race in Bristol, Tennessee.

While they worked on it, the radio in the garage kept playing a Kenny Rogers song, "The Gambler." It was popular last winter when they started getting ready for Smut's winning season:

> *You gotta know when to walk away, and know when to run.*
> *You never count your money while your sittin' at the table.*
> *There'll be time enough for countin' when the dealin's done.*

❖❖

A Tax Reformer on a Crusade

Howard Jarvis, one of the men behind Proposition 13, takes his movement to the nation. Whether they cheer or boo, by God, he'll still tell them a thing or two.

BY AL MARTINEZ · SEPTEMBER 30, 1978

Watch the politicians scamper. I've got a blowtorch to their butts.
—Howard Jarvis

Here is Howard Jarvis, flame-throwing his way across America, bellowing at an auditorium full of students that they're too stupid to understand what he's saying — as they walk out on him.

Here is Howard Jarvis in the back seat of a limousine streaking through a rainy Kentucky night, near tears as he remembers the death of his second wife, saying softly, "I didn't think I would ever stop crying…."

Here is Jarvis in Atlanta and Louisville and Fort Wayne and Baltimore, "a crusty old rhino in the last 20 minutes of life trying to do something for the people" — and possibly a little something for the rhino.

Jarvis. Suddenly a messiah. The Muhammad Ali of tax reform. A combination of Don Rickles and Billy Graham. A thunder out of California, gone national.

He is traveling America on the second of three tours to ignite what he hopes will be a national tax revolt, peddling a mixed bag full of cotton candy dreams and sweet reform.

He is chairman of the American Tax Reduction Movement that was born on the night Proposition 13 won, and because that victory has shaken the nation, no one is laughing at Jarvis — unless he wants them to.

"This is the end of apathy and stupidity," he is thundering from coast to coast. "This is the end of staying home…."

They're listening — at airport press conferences, in speeches to chambers of commerce, in private debates, on radio and television talk shows, in jets, in bars, at universities.

Jarvis gives 'em hell. He tells his listeners that he is going to do for America what he (and Paul Gann) did for California.

He is going to take his crusade "to those damned fools in Washington" and force them to put money back in the pockets of America's hard working people.

"The government is practicing grand theft on our wages," he bellows, "and we've had it!"

Sometimes they stand and cheer when he says that. Sometimes they hug him and thank him. Sometimes they just sigh and walk out and think he's an unrealistic old fool.

One listener, unimpressed, left a Jarvis session muttering sourly, "From those wonderful folks who gave you Dick Nixon…."

Jarvis. At 76, he is America's newest tax commando, an unlikely folk hero "with a lot of arrows in my ass" who tells both Republicans and Democrats what boobs they are.

"They're all crazy," the old rhino roars. "The only difference is, the Democrats don't know it!"

When they boo, he batters them down. When they shout, back he shrugs and grins, "This ain't new. I've always been in trouble."

Love him or hate him, one simply does not ignore Howard Jarvis anymore. Proposition 13 glows over him like a halo.

"The press said for a long time I was nothing but a kook," he gloats in Indiana. "But they said the same thing about Edison until somebody pushed a button and the lights went on."

He takes on Jerry Brown — "the world's greatest tap-dancer" — wherever he goes.

"The governor went full-bang against 13 until 30 minutes after the polls closed," he tells his audiences, "and then it was hi-ho Silver and a double U-turn."

This is no nickel-and-dime crusade Jarvis is on. He's out to balance the federal budget and cut everybody's income taxes by 25 percent in the next four years.

To do so, he committed his American Tax Reduction Movement to a $600,000 debt for a 30-minute television special shown in prime time on 130 stations across the country last Tuesday.

With that and a mail appeal to 7 million households soon to follow, he hopes to raise $20 million for his crusade.

The classy (and not inexpensive) Butcher-Forde consulting agency has been hired to shepherd Jarvis and the ATRM into the national limelight, and according to Jarvis they will make $160,000 out of the telecast alone.

The old rhino himself stands to make a few bucks. He has hired the William Morris Agency to set up his speaking engagements, for which he is paid anywhere from $2,500 to $5,000 — and he's got about 30 of them lined up already.

"But hell," he says in private moments, "I'm not in this for the money. I'm worth half a million bucks. I don't have to struggle. Maybe I'll donate a lot of this for tax research. I'm thinking about that…."

Then what, the question is often asked, is in it for Howard Jarvis?

"Nothing," he says in Atlanta, peering over the top of his gold-rimmed glasses, perspiring under the hot lights of television.

"I want to prove that one old man can change the attitude of the people. I'm too old to run for president."

At Georgetown University, needled by a student, he answers a similar question another way: "I'm an American citizen," he roars, "and I have the same right to speak as you have to sit down, so please do!"

Georgetown, not far from the nation's Capitol, is where Jarvis began his national crusade on a steamy Washington night, and they may never get over it.

Slightly hunched over the speaker's dais, double chin thrust forward, he talks tax reduction and the American way to about 600 students, quoting Robert Browning, Abraham Lincoln, Jesus and Woodrow Wilson.

The speech at Georgetown in an auditorium with no air conditioning sets the tone of the tax revolt. You reward your friends and punish your enemies.

"Ask your candidate, whatever he's running for, if he's for our program, and if he is, vote for him. If he isn't, vote against him. Don't give him a chance to say another word."

That kind of talk would later win standing applause at conservative Western Kentucky University and the Fort Wayne Chamber of Commerce.

At Georgetown, there is some clapping when Jarvis talks tax reduction, but then comes the question-and-answer period.

Was Proposition 13, someone asks, racist?

The old rhino bristles. "[Sen.] George McGovern was the first to say that, and I told David Hartman on 'Good Morning America' what I'll tell you. George McGovern is a boob, he always has been a boob and he always will be a boob!"

"So will Howard Jarvis!" a student shouts, and the fun begins.

"Go ahead," Jarvis bellows, shaking his fist, "shout out in stupidity!"

"You need mental health treatment!" he hollers at someone trying to ask a question.

"If you want to make a speech, rent another hall!" he tells another.

The end comes when a student pleads, "Will you start answering questions and stop calling us asses?"

The young man receives a standing ovation, over which Jarvis thunders: "If you have a question to ask, ask it and stop talking like a girl!" About half the audience gets up shouting and walks out, as Jarvis hollers after them, "I've been insulted by smarter people than you!"

On a corner of the stage, Harvey Englander, traveling with Jarvis for Butcher-Forde, slowly removes his tie and says wearily, "Well, no reason to look nice anymore."

Later, leaving the scene of bedlam, Jarvis would light his pipe and say, "That went pretty well." Englander didn't know whether to laugh or cry.

Jarvis is an enigma, the common man risen to heights of power who still clings stubbornly to that element in him that remains common.

He has been called both crude and arrogant, and sometimes he is both. He sees himself as an international savior ("This is worldwide!") and power broker whose influence extends beyond the bounds of his Proposition 13 victory.

"I'm the one man who did more for the people of California than anyone in history!" he tells the people.

"There's no one else in the world like me," he says.

But at the same time, his voice chokes with emotion and his eyes fill when he tries to explain how he feels about what has happened and what is happening to him.

"When someone comes up to me and tells me I saved their home, I just … why hell…." He pauses and shakes his head. "In what better condition can a man go to

Forest Lawn?"

His language is waterfront, and it takes towering self-restraint for the old man to limit his public expletives to "That's a lot of compost" and "He's full of manure" and "That's a bucket of steam."

Offstage or off-camera, he does more goddamning per airline mile in a few days than most political candidates do in a whole campaign.

Applying the goddamns in the proper places, Jarvis variously observes that:

— Columnist Jack Anderson is a liar.

— Public employees are a menace.

— American business is stupid and cowardly.

— The Post Office department is a boondoggle.

— Summer school is (was) a rip-off.

— The Los Angeles Times is dumb.

When it comes to his Proposition 13 coauthor, Paul Gann, Jarvis — who says he "created" Gann — is slightly more restrained.

Rumors persist that the two have had a falling out. Gann preceded Jarvis to Fort Wayne and supposedly said of Jarvis that "he ought to be swinging by his tail from a chandelier."

Jarvis grins tightly at the comment and says, "Jealousy and revenge are man's two worst diseases." Then he adds, "As the whore said, I'm not prone to argue."

There are times when one Howard Jarvis gives way to another Howard Jarvis — to the one who is not belligerent or arrogant, who does not gloat or insult.

It is that Jarvis who arrives in a storm at a one-shed airport in Bowling Green, Kentucky.

Lightning flashes and thunder rolls as the old man meets the press in Causey Field's crowded Air Kentucky office. By then, his delivery has become a litany:

Cut federal spending by $100 billion, lop $50 billion off the federal income tax, reduce the capital gains tax….

Even then, however, it is broken by flashes. "Why are you leading the national revolt?" a reporter asks argumentatively. "Because you didn't," Jarvis snaps.

He hurries on from there in a drenching rain to Western Kentucky University and gives his standard speech with variations to 350 students — but it isn't the speech that isolates an important part of Jarvis.

For a brief period before the formal talk, he sits with a dozen students over coffee and sandwiches and gives them a lesson in civics they could never get in a classroom.

He tells them that one person can make a difference and that change is possible in the fabric of American government. He says, "Look at me."

He tells them how he has weathered defeat and recrimination for 15 years, but has held to his commitment and has won. He says to them, "You can do it."

Here, more than anywhere on the tour, there is a kind of glory to that old man hunched over a cup of coffee or striding bareheaded through the rain, by his presence enhancing the nobility of individual effort in a mass society.

The moment in Bowling Green is special, unmatched even by the standing ovations he would win later.

At his worst, Jarvis is impossible.

At his best, he is funny: "You get the feeling sometimes that God created the world as a tax loss."

Wry: "No politicians bothered about tax cuts at first. But now they're all riding the horse in the direction that it's going."

And challenging: "I don't care if you're different. But I care deeply if you're indifferent."

Wherever he goes, there is a curiosity about the old man from California who bucked big government, big names and big newspapers — and won.

Jarvis gladly answers any questions, including those about his health.

"Well," he says to one startled young female television interviewer, "I had a little trouble with the front plumbing for a while, but I've been drinking fruit juice every day, and the plumbing's just fine."

Prudence suggests she not pursue the subject, and she doesn't.

To others, he says that a little vodka and honey helps too, and possibly a little vodka without the honey.

There are quiet moments for Jarvis, and one of them comes in his hired limousine, riding through the night, when he talks about his father, "a tough old Mormon," who died at 93.

It was his father, Jarvis says, who taught him not to give up, not to lie to anyone and not to be ashamed to take 49 percent of a deal, because "the 49 percents can add up fast."

"I'll never forget that old man," he says, the trumpeting voice now almost a whisper. "The last time I saw him, he had throat cancer and couldn't talk. But he still made a V-for-victory sign. You couldn't beat him."

Later, in Cleveland, Jarvis meets New York Yankees superstar Reggie Jackson by chance in the lobby of a downtown hotel.

It is the day the California Supreme Court has declared Proposition 13 constitutional.

The right fielder, in town for a game against the Cleveland Indians, shakes the old man's hand and says, "You're a winner, Howard."

Later, hunched over a drink, Jarvis says he will remember that moment always, because Reggie is a winner too.

That night, Jackson doubled in two runs. The Yankees lost by one.

My Story, Myself

❖❖

'He Loved Those Towers'

Timothy Gerard Byrne worked on the 104th floor of the World Trade Center. Since his father died in 1986, he had been a dad to his nine siblings. Now he's gone too.

BY J.R. MOEHRINGER · OCTOBER 1, 2001

HUNTINGTON, New York — He wanted to remind them that laughter is a form of bravery, an act of defiance, a family tradition. He wanted to say that in hard times, laughing is the best thing you can do, and when all is lost, it's the only thing.

But he couldn't find the words.

He rolled his shoulders, shifted his weight, bounced on the balls of his feet like a prizefighter in a black tuxedo. He made jokes, trying to stall, breaking up the crowd. No one in the family could be funnier than Tim, especially when the occasion was serious.

But this wedding toast needed to be more than funny. As best man for his younger brother Sean, he wanted to say publicly that Sean had stayed strong when their father died. He wanted to tell everyone that Sean didn't fold when the family found itself alone and adrift: 10 kids with $27 in the bank and their heroic young father gone.

Finally, after bantering with the drummer, after fussing with the microphone, Tim's trademark deadpan dissolved, and he looked straight into Sean's eyes. "Life has a way of throwing things at us, good and bad," he said, his voice catching. "It's important to have a sense of humor."

A few more words, and then he couldn't go on.

But the point was made: We must.

Last week, the videotape of that 1998 toast became more than just a family memento. It became a message in a bottle. Watching the tape over and over, Tim's family couldn't help feeling that he was speaking to them from afar, raising his glass once more and trying to deliver one last piece of advice. It would have been just like Tim — to keep leading, keep coaching, keep urging his family forward, no matter what.

Timothy Gerard Byrne, my cousin, worked on the 104th floor of the south tower of the World Trade Center, a bond trader at Sandler O'Neill. He was one of the thousands who never got out, one of the thousands presumed dead, one of the thousands whose stories ended when the building's 110 stories collapsed before the nation's eyes.

He was 36, unmarried, though that's misleading. He was the head of a huge family. When his father died in 1986, Tim was just 21 years old, the third son, but he "stepped up," as his nine siblings are so fond of saying. He became the father to his eight brothers and one sister, the financial and emotional support for his mother, my Aunt Charlene. He became the family's center, their tower, as seemingly indestructible as the World Trade Center towers, and every bit as irreplaceable.

Just after the attacks, his siblings had hope. If anyone could walk out of a burning skyscraper, brushing dust off his wide shoulders, it would be Tim. He was the closest thing to a superhero they ever saw. Able to leap tall buildings. It seemed impossible that he could survive, but making the Syracuse University football team as an undersized walk-on seemed impossible too, and Tim did it anyway.

After a week, the family was forced to face the truth. "We'll have a memorial Mass," Aunt Charlene told the priests. "And if he comes home, we'll have a massive party."

The family scheduled Tim's memorial Mass for Sept. 22, the anniversary of the death of Tim's father. It would have been Tim's wish. It would have been his father's wish. It would have been an astonishing coincidence, almost as astonishing as the fact that his father's birthday was Sept. 11.

The church, however, said no. Two weddings were booked that day. So the memorial was reset for Sept. 21, and I phoned Aunt Charlene to say I'd be there. In fact, I'd try to come a few days early.

She wept. She protested, lightly. But it was clear, even with her sons all around her, there would be things to do, ways to help. The days leading up to the memorial would be filled with chores and details and emotional trials. She would need all the family she could get.

Aunt Charlene isn't really my aunt. She's my mother's first cousin, and her children are my second cousins. Still, I've called her Aunt Charlene forever, and as a boy I spent long summer days at her house, down the road from my hometown, Manhasset. I attended her husband's funeral, and I can still close my eyes and see the five oldest Byrne brothers carrying their father's coffin.

I played marathon games of whiffle ball with those brothers. Pat, Joe, Tim, Sean, Chris, Kevin, Brian, Jim, Colin—they were ferocious competitors, with sharp elbows, and they reminded me as they got older of the movie-star Baldwins, that other numberless band of strapping Long Island brothers.

Then there was the daughter, Kathleen, the eighth child, a tomboy in ribbons and bows.

Eventually, I left Long Island, lost touch with the Byrnes. But the connection was never cut. It couldn't be. Our mothers were close. Our grandmothers were sisters. Our great-grandmother was an indomitable woman named Margaret O'Keefe, and we all inherited her mythology, drew inspiration from the story of her 19th century journey: Cork, Ireland, to Ellis Island to Long Island. We all grew up hearing again and again how tragedy couldn't defeat Maggie O'Keefe, though tragedy tried and tried.

The Byrnes were always my people. We had a bond that withstood distance and time, a bond of shared blood, which now includes shed blood. The same could be said of all Americans. Shed blood makes cousins of us all.

I drove to Aunt Charlene's from Denver, arriving late Sept. 18. Sean met me in the frontyard. The fourth son, 35, a shipping broker, he hugged me and introduced me to his wife and brought me inside.

Four brothers lined up to embrace me — Chris and Brian and Jim and Colin. Next came Kathleen, followed by her 7-year-old daughter, Laurelle, then Aunt Charlene, eyes swollen from crying, but still beautiful. She put her arms around my neck, and we didn't say anything, because we couldn't.

We gathered in the living room, in the house Tim helped Aunt Charlene buy, on the furniture he gave her last Christmas, and Aunt Charlene described how Tim had phoned her when the first plane hit. He said he was fine. The plane hit the other tower; he didn't want her to worry.

Mom, he said, I wish I had a camera, because I'm looking at an airplane sticking out of the World Trade Center.

Stop admiring the view and get out of there, she yelled.

Security is giving us the all clear, he said. They're telling people to return to their desks, everything is fine.

Get out, she pleaded.

He promised he would, then hung up. Minutes later, Aunt Charlene watched on TV as the second plane hit Tim's tower.

"He loved those towers," said Sean, sitting at the piano, which was covered with candles and photos of Tim: Tim golfing. Tim hugging. Tim laughing.

Sean loved the towers too. That's why he proposed to his wife at the top of one. That's why he gave Tim a framed black-and-white photo of the towers as a Christmas present last year. "He loved being up high, looking out on the world," Sean said, snapping his fingers, rapid-fire, to mean that his brother loved being a mover, a doer, a man who sat astride the clouds. It took years to reach the top, years of struggle and scrimping and sacrifice, and Tim was learning to enjoy his time.

Sean talked about his reaction to the news of Tim's death. He walked into his daughter's room and sank onto her bed. "I looked at all her dolls lined up," he said. "I set 10 dolls in a row, and I thought: 'Look at them all. That's us. That's my family.' Ten kids. How can 10 kids come out of one person?"

(Each brother's middle name is Gerard; St. Gerard is the patron saint of pregnant women.)

Now, Sean shot a look of disbelief at his mother, who gave him a weak smile in return. We all fell silent, and one of the brothers suggested watching home movies.

Aunt Charlene's big-screen high-definition TV seemed like a time machine. It made Tim so vivid, so present. Here he was, walking around the basement, bare-chested, close enough to slap on the back. Here he was, about to graduate from St. John's Business School, strutting around the backyard in his scarlet robe. Here he was, teasing his younger brother Chris, his arm hooked around Chris' neck, his face set in that devastating deadpan.

Chris tried not to smile and couldn't help smiling. He was getting the Tim treatment, the business, but it was OK, because for Tim, all laughter was a type of love.

The next morning, while Aunt Charlene was at church, Brian and Jim and Colin gathered on the porch, bracing themselves for what lay ahead. With only 48 hours before the memorial, there would be an onslaught of phone calls, errands, relatives, reporters. It fell to Chris, 32, the fifth son, a pharmaceutical salesman, to contend with one local reporter who asked, "If you could say anything to the terrorists, what would it be?"

Brian, 29, the seventh son, also a pharmaceutical salesman, told his brothers that the church was considering what to do with all the donations being made in Tim's name. Possibly a memorial wall on the football field where Tim was a high school star.

"That would be nice," said Jim, 24, the eighth son, an investment research salesman. "To throw the football around on a Sunday, in front of Tim's wall?"

"Yeah, yeah," Brian agreed, but he couldn't hide what he was really thinking: I'd rather throw the ball around with Tim.

Brian was hungry, which made him remember how Tim taught him to hide food when they were boys. With nine brothers under one roof, Brian said, you were quick, or you were out of luck. When their mother whipped up a new batch of brownies, for example, it was crucial to get there first, extract a hunk and stash it. Preferably on a high shelf, where the other boys wouldn't find it.

The other boys, Brian said, always found it.

Jim smiled and nodded.

Jim looked tired. He confessed that he'd been up all night watching home movies of Tim. "At 2:30," he said, "I couldn't find any more movies of Tim, so I watched my old football games."

He laughed, embarrassed, then looked away.

A former wide receiver at Cornell, Jim recalled the many times Tim drove all day to attend his games. Coming off the field, Jim would look for Tim in the stands and raise his helmet above his head in a special Tim salute. "He was father, brother, best friend, wrapped into one," Jim said.

I asked about girlfriends. Anyone serious in Tim's life?

No, Jim said, looking down. Because Tim already was patriarch to one family, "you wonder sometimes if he didn't want to make any long-term commitments." His eyes filled with tears, and he wiped a big hand across them. Next to him sat Colin, 18, the youngest, a sophomore at Notre Dame. He glanced at Jim, saw his brother's tears and bowed his head.

Days before the attacks, Jim had a long chat with Tim on the phone. They planned a trip to see Colin this month. They reviewed different career options Jim was weighing. Tim offered to put his younger brother in touch with colleagues, work the phones on his behalf, whatever Jim needed. As always, Tim was wise, shrewd, fatherly — a lifeline.

Finally, before hanging up, Tim reviewed the whole family, checking names off one by one, giving a status report.

"It was weird," Jim said, "how he just went down the list, how each of us were doing. And he was happy, because we were all doing really well."

Kathleen, 28, an art teacher, appeared on the porch. She said she was going to the library to photocopy FBI forms that needed to be filed with New York City to classify Tim as a crime victim. I went along, and we took Laurelle, who rode her scooter. On Main Street, we stopped at a stretch of sidewalk that was a mosaic of melted candles.

"What's this?" Laurelle asked.

"This," Kathleen told her, "is from a memorial service last night for all the people who are — umm — who they don't know where they are."

She looked at her daughter's confused face and put a hand on her head.

We bought Laurelle a smoothie, then ducked into a coffee shop, and while we were waiting in line, Kathleen's cell phone rang.

"How are you?" Kathleen whispered into the phone. "You're alive?"

She listened.

"My brother's not," she said. "Tim. Yeah. Thank you."

When Kathleen hung up, her face was pale. The friend who called was a firefighter who said he'd lost 30 fellow firefighters in the World Trade Center. His parents died recently, Kathleen said, and the firehouse had become his surrogate family. A huge band of brothers and surrogate fathers — Kathleen knew all about that.

We walked back, slowly, Kathleen telling me about her troubles as a young girl in Catholic school, when the nuns made her feel stupid. Tim would come home on weekends, from wherever he happened to be, and tutor her for hours. He explained that she had an intelligence nuns couldn't measure, an intelligence that made him proud.

She stopped walking.

"How many older brothers do you know who would say something like that?" she asked.

She recalled a long weekend Tim recently spent in the Bahamas. He happened to see Aaliyah, the singer, who was killed that same weekend in a plane crash. In fact, Tim was staying at the same hotel as Aaliyah, and his plane took off minutes after hers.

When Tim told Kathleen the story, she shuddered to think about her brother brushing up against death.

"Aw," he said. "If I died, don't you know your student loans would all be paid?"

She looked at him in horror.

"Don't you know," she said, "that I'd rather live a lifetime in debt than a day without you?"

She was grateful for that chance to tell Tim she loved him. But she was haunted that he'd had some sort of premonition. He seemed so knowing, so resigned.

We talked about Tim's love of stories, our family's love of stories, which was genetic, going back to our great-grandmother, at least. Kathleen smiled. "Stories are how we make meaning in this family," she said. "Everyone in this family invests everything with so much meaning. We're all little meaning-making machines."

It will take a lot of storytelling to make meaning of Tim's death. Kathleen vowed to get started right away, to write down the funny stories for Laurelle, for all the Tims to come. "I have to write them down," Kathleen said, sounding frantic. "I have to. Because you forget. You forget."

Her voice trailed away, and she stared at the sidewalk, until Laurelle zoomed past on the scooter.

I asked whether Kathleen had given any thought to what she'd tell Laurelle in the coming days.

"I'll tell her what I tell her about my father," she said. "My father is a spirit that's with us and guides us, and now Tim is with us, in our hearts, a source of strength that no one who didn't know him can have."

We both looked at Laurelle for a long time, then turned for home.

We found Aunt Charlene in the dining room, sifting through some of Tim's bills and papers. Credit cards. Car payments. She could only think for so long before she had to lie down on the couch. Laurelle went to her grandmother and asked whether she could watch an Uncle Tim movie. She liked the one of Uncle Tim in his scarlet robe best.

"I don't think I can see the graduation movie again," Aunt Charlene told her. "Makes me too sad. Everyone wishing him luck in the future."

Laurelle frowned.

"Let's watch Sean's wedding," Aunt Charlene told her, "when Tim's being so funny."

Tim gave his toast again, and I sat with Aunt Charlene, talking about her husband, Pat. All his life, she said, Uncle Pat was prone to seizures. Then, one night, after a big meal with the whole family, he went upstairs to bed, and while Aunt Charlene was washing the dishes, he suffered a seizure from which he never awoke.

He was 47 years old; the children at the time ranged from 24 to 3.

"I sat down on one of the kids' beds and I couldn't move," Aunt Charlene recalled. "But I felt this voice say: 'Get up. You have all these people depending on you. You have to go on.'"

Now, Brian walked into the room and kissed his mother. Soon, friends of Tim began arriving — schoolmates, old buddies. The house was filling with people, and one woman brought an enormous dish of lasagna.

"I forgot all about dinner!" Charlene said, kissing the woman. "I thought it was the middle of the afternoon. Oh, thank you."

We ate, then gathered in the living room and flipped back and forth between the news and home movies. A few of the brothers drifted out to the porch, to get some air. It was turning cool. Autumn was hours away, which made them sadder. Football season was Tim's favorite.

"I was doing OK," said Chris, who lives with his wife just around the corner. "Then this afternoon I was hanging the flag at my house, and I started thinking about Tim never coming over again, and I kind of lost it."

The brothers leaned forward, listening.

"When Tim used to come stay with us," Chris said, "my wife and I would get all excited. We'd make sure to have some special dessert. We'd put clean sheets on the bed. He was like the kid we never had yet."

Brian talked about the way Tim would arrive at his house, a one-man band, arms full of food and presents. "He'd walk in the door and say, 'I wanted to bring some chips, but I didn't know what kind you liked, so I got them all: sour cream and onion, barbecue, vinegar, extra whatever.' "

In hoarse whispers, the brothers discussed Tim's final minutes in the tower. They wondered what he knew and when he knew it. They prayed that he didn't know anything, and they took some comfort in the fact that he didn't phone home a second time.

"Those people who got goodbye phone calls," Brian said, shaking his head. "How horrible is that? Thank God my mother didn't get a second call. I don't think we could've handled that."

I asked whether anyone had seen Sean lately. The brothers looked at each other and laughed. Sean was undoubtedly home, they said, having an anxiety attack about his eulogy. If they knew Sean, he'd be up all night.

"This is like a best man speech times 10," Jim said.

The next morning, the phone rang. Kevin, 31, the sixth son, was calling from California. Like Pat, 39, the oldest son, Kevin is estranged from the family, and the call got the day off to an emotional start.

Soon, the doorbell rang, and the woman from the funeral parlor arrived. Kathleen presented her with a framed photo of Tim, to be set on an easel near the altar. A lovely photo, taken Labor Day weekend, it showed Tim seated on his mother's couch, arms spread wide, about to laugh.

Aunt Charlene took one look and covered her mouth.

"He was just here," she sobbed. "Look at him — he was just here!"

Chris rushed over and maneuvered her slowly away from the photo.

Sean came through the door with his eulogy. His eyes were bloodshot. Took me all night, he said sheepishly. He passed out copies, and everyone sat down to read. The brothers laughed when they reached the part about "fireside chats," which Tim initiated after their father died.

Every Sunday night, the siblings and their mother would gather in the basement, and Tim would hand out Lotus spreadsheets of the family's finances. "This is the net net," he'd tell them. Then he'd solve everyone's problems with school, work, love. Then he'd praise individual achievements. The reason for the meetings was often serious and scary: The family was on the financial brink. But the siblings remember the basement ringing with laughter.

Jim was the first to finish reading Sean's eulogy. He walked across the room to hug his brother.

"Great job," he said, sniffling.

Sean's shoulders slumped with relief. Then he made an announcement: "I'm OK today," he said. "I had myself a good cry this morning, and I'm OK. I'm ready to go."

The day promised to be frantic. There were haircuts to be had, neckties to be bought, last-minute details to be settled before the memorial. Who was carrying the flag? Who was in charge of lapel ribbons? Sean set out a battle plan for the afternoon. He and Chris would go into Manhattan and check on Tim's apartment. Jim and his girlfriend, Elizabeth, would pick up Joe, 38, the second son.

Kathleen and I would go to make copies of family photos.

We drove through Huntington, then Cold Spring Harbor, an idyllic village with sailboats wobbling peacefully at anchor off the main road, and a marker commemorating an early resident who divulged an assassination plot against George Washington. An old church was draped in bunting. Shop windows held flags and pictures of residents still among the missing. Funerals and memorials were taking place all day, and a bagpiper could occasionally be heard.

Kathleen pointed to a fancy restaurant and laughed.

"That's where Tim took my mother to break the news that he was moving out."

It was 1991. Upon graduating from business school, Tim had moved back home, to watch over his brothers and to pay rent each month to the "Byrne Corporation," as he called it. Once he'd put the family's finances on an even footing, however, he wanted privacy again, his own place.

"My mother started crying," Kathleen said, "and everyone was looking over at their table, like Tim was breaking up with this woman."

At the copy store, the clerk knew somehow that Kathleen was connected to the World Trade Center. Something about the way she carried herself. He asked, so she told him. An hour later, when we picked up the photos, we found a note attached: "NO CHARGE. Please say a prayer for two friends, Jim Haran, Kevin Frawley, Cantor Fitzgerald."

Back at the house, Sean and Chris had returned from Tim's apartment. Seeing all of Tim's stuff, inhaling his scent, was hard, they said. To calm themselves, to honor Tim, they raided his humidor and smoked two of his fattest Cuban cigars.

They also raided his stash of family memorabilia, bringing back shoe boxes full of photos. Aunt Charlene sifted through them, lingering over one portrait: her husband leaning against a tree, seven young Byrne boys in the branches or on his shoulder. "Look how this photo is fading," she said, touching the faces with her fingers. "Why is it fading like that?"

We watched home movies again. A family trip to one of Jim's football games.

Tim was behind the camera, doing a hilarious running commentary. At one point, he zoomed in crazily on Colin, who couldn't stop laughing. Even when Tim aimed the humor at him, along with the camera, Colin only laughed harder. There was nothing like the feel of Tim's focus.

As Thursday night wore on, as the memorial loomed the next morning, the mood in the house grew darker. Aunt Charlene's sister Edith arrived from Vermont, with her husband, Don. Aunt Charlene wept and clung to them, and Sean thanked them for coming. "We'll get past this," he told them in the front hallway. "There's only one direction to go, and that's forward, and this family will move forward."

They studied him. The transformation was already underway.

Friday, the black limousines arrived at 9 a.m. sharp. The family rode slowly to the church where Tim had been an altar boy, a favorite of the priests, and where he would've been married one day.

Two brothers were assigned readings. Jim read from the New Testament, the first letter of Paul the apostle to Timothy. Brian read from Ecclesiastes.

"I have seen the business that God has given to everyone to be busy with," Brian read, his voice raw. "He has made everything suitable for its time; moreover, He has put a sense of past and future into their minds, yet they cannot find out what God has done from the beginning to the end."

Dan Driscoll, one of Tim's best friends, delivered a staggering tribute, clenching his jaw as he spoke, refusing to break. He described Tim as "a prince — the prince of his family."

Tim was tireless, Driscoll said. He never buckled under the weight of his responsibility.

"I would call him at his desk," Driscoll recalled with a laugh. "And I'd say, 'How's it goin' Byrnesy?' And he'd say, 'Gettin' it done, Dan-O. Gettin' it done. I'm in the trenches, gettin' it done.' "

The mourners roared with laughter.

In the future, Driscoll said, he would most remember Tim's laughter. "Laughing, laughing, laughing," he said. "I was friends 20 years with Tim, and we never had a conversation without laughing."

Recently, Driscoll said, a priest helped him see death differently. Picture Tim on a boat sailing into the distance, the priest said. While watching him disappear, you say, "There he goes, there he goes." But realize that the boat is sailing to another shore, and on that shore are people waiting for him, saying, "Here he comes, here he comes."

Among those people, Driscoll said, will surely be Tim's father. "And when Tim steps on that shore," Driscoll said, trembling, "his father's going to be the first to greet him."

He looked down at the long row of Byrnes in the front pew, lined up like the dolls of Sean's daughter.

"And his father's going to shake Tim's hand and say, 'Son, I am so proud of you.' "

Nearly 1,000 mourners filed outside into a light rain. A bagpiper played a dirge as the Byrne family got into the limousines. They went to a brief reception, then home to Aunt Charlene's house, which now felt desolate.

Aunt Charlene sat on the couch, watching friends with fruit baskets come through the front door. Glancing down, she spotted the framed photo of Tim, which someone had propped against the coffee table. She picked it up and held it on her lap.

"This is right where you were sitting, Tim," she whispered, looking into his eyes. "Right here on this couch."

She smiled.

"You look so relaxed," she said tenderly, as though he were a boy and she were tucking him in for the night.

She ran her fingers across the glass, once lightly across his smiling face.

"It just shows," she said. "We have no idea what lies ahead."

❖

A Loss of Innocence…a Flight to Freedom

'I should've died that day. I should have been one of the 37,000 Americans to perish in that strange and awful war.'

BY AL MARTINEZ • JUNE 24, 2000

I remember you.

You were the big guy with "Cornhusker" scrawled on the back of your dungaree jacket, ahead of me in the long, thin line of Marines that trudged up the mountainside.

You grumbled as we bent into the effort, 40 pounds of gear on our backs, as darkness deepened and our anxiety grew. We could hear the unfamiliar boom of artillery from far off and the odd, muted drift of voices from the high ground.

It was a strange and scary time.

We'd been Korea only two days and already they were leading us up to the main line of resistance, the MLR, and you kept complaining that we weren't "acclimatated" yet. It was the biggest word you knew, Cornhusker, and it was wrong.

That was in April 1951. I'm in Korea now, near a place called Wonju, standing on a hillside looking for that MLR, an imaginary stretch across the north-central part of the peninsula. We called it the Quantico Line.

I'm here to resurrect memories of a war begun a half-century ago Sunday, because that kind of anniversary just can't go unnoticed. The fact that the war itself went pretty much unnoticed continues to rest uneasily on the national conscience. It wasn't a real war back then. It was a conflict. A police action.

Even though it killed 4 million human beings on both sides, military and civilian, it just didn't seem right calling it a war only five years after the Big One had ended. Euphemisms prevailed in the 1950s as the young men marched away.

And now I'm back in this ancient land at a time when the presidents of North and South Korea are talking peace, shaking hands and laughing as though all that pain never existed and all that blood never flowed.

The fighting ended in 1953, Cornhusker, but the war, that element of hostility that keeps hatreds alive, never has ceased. Even detente won't erase memories.

You'll always be a part of the inner me, Cornhusker. You're one of those guys who continue to haunt my dreams all these years later. I remember you because we were so close for a while, and a sniper killed you with a single bullet just a few weeks after we'd arrived. You died without a word, and I looked at violent death for the first time in my life.

Oh, I remember you.

. . .

I'm here seeking old battlefields. The driver tells me we've covered about 900 kilometers from Seoul to Taegu to the Hwachon Reservoir. We did it in two days. Back then, mountain by mountain, it took us nine bloody months.

I have a diary kept through most of my time in Korea. Much of it is in pencil, watermarked and hard to read. But I can make out sentences here and there. For instance on April 3, a Tuesday, I wrote, "I'm beginning to feel detached from myself, as though it is someone else here, doing these things...."

The feeling prevailed from the day our troopship landed at Pusan until the day I left Seoul. I lived in a world reduced to essentials. Happiness was a beer ration. Grief was the sniper's mark on a guy like Cornhusker.

One minute alive, the next minute dead. Existence snapped in and out of focus that quickly.

We took the days as they came and moved on from one hill to the next, bearing down on our emotions, keeping them in check. Something within perishes in war. An internal dead zone allows a soldier to face terror that might otherwise break him. Fear abates at the cost of involvement. You come home a different person than the one who left.

These thoughts come to mind as I follow the route of the 2nd Battalion, 7th Marines, on a drive called Operation Killer. And the dread that returns from the past still chills me.

. . .

I remember you.

You were the old man on the porch of a home somewhere in the Yongso Valley, a stretch between high mountains devastated by war. Artillery had left your small house a battered shell, but as we passed I noticed you sweeping.

Slowly, methodically, using a handmade broom, you swept your porch clean as troops and tanks forged north. Operation Killer was the first major offensive after Inchon's glory and Chosin's icy ordeal, an assault geared to finding our way back into the war against a massive influx of Chinese soldiers.

But war and peace have passed this way many times before through Korea's troubled history, and you continued to sweep, despite the destruction of your home and the agony at your doorstep.

The shell-pocked rice paddies around you were thriving once, but in war they are simply annoyances in combat's path, something we had to slosh through, ankle deep in water and mud, often dodging fire from distant hills.

But still you swept, old man, clinging to that fragile element of the quiet life you once knew.

The rice paddies are still here this spring of the year 2000. The war has long since passed and the fields are green with new life. Another old man works the ground now. His name is Sam Joon Byun, and, at 79, he remembers when his village lay in ruins. "There was nothing left," he says through an interpreter. "Nothing but ashes."

He is thin and bearded, with skin the texture of parchment. "We lived in holes in the hills," he says, pointing toward a ridge line. "The Communists found some of us. Many were killed, others taken to the North and never seen again. We were afraid and hungry."

In my diary for April 21 I wrote: "The civilians we passed huddled together around fires near their burned-out houses. A man stood with his hands behind him, straight up, almost proudly, wearing rags. And I heard myself saying bitterly, 'Behold, the glories of war.' "

A morning fog lifts as we talk, the old man and me. It is a gray and unsettling mist, and I'm glad when it's gone. It reminds me of the shrouded dawns when the cry "Saddle up!" roused us from our foxholes to move through valleys like this toward objectives that rose abruptly from the shallow floor.

There was peril at every step. Mortars from the ridges, mines in the lowlands. As I walk along the roadside today, a scene flashes into memory: There's a Marine not 20 feet in front of me. He glances back. I see his face. An explosion. A cloud of smoke. Silence.

There were no screams. There was no time to scream as he stepped on a mine and was shredded by the blast. I still see his face. There and gone. We move on.

. . .

I remember you.

Your name was Pete Mamaril. You were small for a Marine, barely 5 foot 5, a 20-year-old born in the Philippines who had come to America in search of a future.

For a little guy, you had a laugh that could fill a barracks and a smile that faced any situation. It's the smile I remember most about you, Pete. You loved the corps, and nothing they did to us could change that.

We went through boot camp and advanced training together, and ended up on the same fire team in combat, comrades in arms. I remember you as we fought for the high ground east of Hongchon, the most mountainous section of Korea. Here, the peaks tower over the low valleys, disappearing back into fading shades of blue as far as the eye can see.

Today, the high ground is thick with pine and fir trees, and with maples whose leaves turn to glory when autumn comes. Back then, it had been bombed and scorched with such ferocity that the trees were almost nonexistent. Those that remained were torn and leafless, their branches reaching like claws to the lowering skies.

Napalm blackens everything, including human beings. I remember us, Pete, going up one of those nameless hills after the Corsairs had brought thunder down onto it. We saw humans who were charred figures, their bodies still smoking, caught by napalm in the posture of their flight. One died as he reached forward, seeking a haven beyond his grasp.

And that night when we dug in, sickened by the sights and smells of what we'd seen, we heard a woman wildly crying, her sounds carried up from the valley to our hillside foxholes, intensified by the evening's silence.

It was a wail that lasted for hours, and we wondered, Pete, why she was crying. For a dead husband? A lost child? "Maybe," you said, "she's just crying for all of us." I remember the look on your face, and it wasn't a smile.

We moved out the next day, assigned to different units to fill spaces left by the dead and wounded. I was halfway down the hillside when enemy mortars flew in, hissing out of nowhere, few but deadly, a quick wharumph! and then silence.

I didn't look back, Pete. We were a company in assault, and hesitation could mean the destruction of our drive to something called Objective Able. We leaned into our fears.

In my diary I wrote: "Once I was a small child and I was afraid of things, so I ran from them. Now I'm a man in war and the things I fear could mean my death, but I don't run. Oh, foolish travesty of intelligence, where is your reason?"

It was only later, after we had secured our objective, that someone said to me, "You know your friend? The little Filipino guy? He's dead."

Yes. I remember.

. . .

The villages are towns now and the towns are cities. South Korea is a prosperous nation, and that is reflected in the countryside. Chunchon, Yanggu and Inje bustle with commerce. The streets are full and traffic heavy on superhighways that were once dirt roads packed down by the tread of tanks.

This part of Korea is a tourist mecca today that covers almost 17,000 square kilometers and includes a population of 1.5 million. Children pedal brightly colored paddleboats on lakes so clear that you can almost see the bottom. Families camp on mountains we took at the point of a bayonet.

One brochure offers tours of an old battlefield above Chorwon called the Iron Triangle, another of that region around Yanggu we knew as the Punchbowl.

I remember the Punchbowl.

We were on a ridge line that bordered its singular shape, moving deliberately toward an enemy hill, our energy sapped by a numbing heat wave. It was at the start of July. Soon the rain would come, as it always did in July and August, but this day seemed years away from any kind of cooling comfort.

Often, because we moved so fast, our supply trains couldn't keep up. We scrounged for water where we could, once drinking from a pond that, we discovered to our horror, contained a human leg at the bottom. We dropped extra purification tablets into our canteens, closed our eyes and drank it anyhow.

307

This day shadows my memory. As we trudged along the ridge line, enemy fire blasted through our ranks. It was a flat-trajectory, 76-millimeter artillery piece firing down on us from high ground across the valley.

We scattered and sought shelter on the reverse slope, listening to the boom of ignition, the evil hiss of the shell and the almost instantaneous explosion as it hit. They fired many. One was meant for me.

I lay with my head down on the steep reverse slope, feet propped against a dead tree. I heard the 76 fire … and the tree that I leaned against shattered into wild fragments, its trunk and branches strewn over the ridge line.

And then I realized. The missile had hit the tree but hadn't exploded. It was a dud. I lay there long after our own artillery had silenced the enemy weapon.

I should've died that day. I should have been one of the 37,000 Americans to perish in that strange and awful war. Why am I still alive? "Let's go," a platoon sergeant said softly, knowing what had happened, knowing what I was thinking. "Let's just go," he said.

And I moved on, leaving a part of me by that tree, and the rest of me still wondering what it all meant.

· · ·

I remember you.

Your name was Joe Citera. You were a rangy kid with big ears from Greenpoint, Brooklyn, whose raspy imitation of Jimmy Durante somehow kept us going through the worst of times.

I remember us lying flat in a rice paddy, half buried in mud, incoming mortars exploding around us … and you rising and asking, in that Durante rasp, "I wonder what the poor people are doing?"

We called you the luck of Fox Company because with you around, we often managed to be where the danger wasn't and, well, because you made us laugh.

But there was a serious side to you too, Joe. You confided once that at 19 you'd never had a girlfriend because of your protruding ears. "Look at them," you said, pushing them out even farther. "They're like elephant ears. When I get out, I'm having them cut down and pinned back. They can do that now. And then wait'll you see me." The Durante rasp: "Step aside, Errol Flynn, and let this beautiful guy through."

You were a beautiful guy, Joe. Gentle, generous and without a hostile bone in your gangly body. You gave your chocolate rations to kids and your food to refugees along the road. The villagers I've talked to on this trip, and there were many, remember guys like you for those simple, humanitarian gestures. They remember you as bright moments on very dark days. I heard "Thank you" many times in the week I was here. So many of those thanks were meant for you.

Destiny should never have led you to Hill 749.

September. The rainy season had passed and the chill of autumn was setting in. The leaves of the maple trees normally turn brilliant at that time of year, but there were no trees around us on 749.

We were just grateful that it was dry, having survived sleeping in holes filled with water, drenched to the bone, and crossing rivers turned swollen and murderous by storms that rolled in one after another.

Hill 749 was waiting for us on the far side of one of those rivers. It was the first U.N. night attack of the war. We'd climbed in silence to surprise the enemy, but he knew we were coming. As we neared the knoll, he opened up from both flanks.

Machine gun tracers streaked the night, mortars blew around us. And then they came at us. Somehow, firing wildly into the gathering darkness at shapes that slipped in and out of the shadows, we managed to build a perimeter around the knoll.

I heard someone shout, "Citera's been hit!" and a coldness beyond the exterior chill filled me. But he hadn't abandoned us. As waves of North Koreans stormed up the hill, screaming threats and shouts in English, one enemy voice seemed to rise above the others. It said with deadly intent, "All Marines from California go home tonight!"

It would not go unanswered. Another voice, the Durante rasp of Joe Citera, filled the night when it asked, "What about Brooklyn?"

I don't know if I'll ever be able to adequately explain what that did to the company. I know this: We held off five vicious charges that were complete with bullhorns and bugles. We dug into a hill that was almost granite and held our ground throughout the hellish ordeal. And as long as he was able, Citera's voice urged us on.

Joe died just before sunrise from shock and loss of blood, his legs shredded by machine gun bullets. We were consumed with a sadness too deep to measure. But at least we could acknowledge his gift. We wrote a message on the side of a cardboard C-ration box and affixed it to a tree trunk. It said, "To Joe Citera, Hill 749. You held our luck as long as we needed it."

I remember you, Joe. We all do. We always will.

• • •

I stand by the Hwachon Reservoir looking toward the northeast, at a jumble of hills where 749 sits. We lost half a battalion here and won a Presidential Unit Citation "for extraordinary heroism, superb professional performance in battle and outstanding devotion to duty."

"One man killed today from a booby trap," I wrote less heroically in my diary for October 10. "One wounded from our own artillery. There are a million ways to die around here. Pick a way, any way...."

"You saved Korea," a retired college professor said to me in Seoul last week. Horace Underwood is from a third-generation American missionary family in Korea. His grandfather founded Yonsei University, where Underwood is now a member of the board of directors. During the war, he was a Marine translator.

"You could feel the turnaround from the first day of the war to the day the Americans came," he said. "You saved Korea in every sense."

The price we paid was heavy. From a June 4 diary entry as we prepared to leave a rest area to return to battle: "I knew all this couldn't last forever, but in war, the impossible is what a man clings to; the inevitable is what he scorns. Even now as I write, the men are out in the warm evening playing baseball, football or cards. And tomorrow night, the guy who's dealing out the blackjacks may be spread all over the front lines by a 120 mortar. The one who's pitching the curves may be sucking in blood from a bullet hole. And the one who's writing this diary may be cannon fodder too."

It was a possibility none of us ever ignored. We asked for just one more day as we crouched alone at night in foxholes dug along forward mountain slopes, entrenchments long since filled in by time's relentless mechanisms. Just one more day of life.

The constant presence of death created a terrible loneliness. There were empty places in our soul. I had a wife waiting for me and a daughter born two months after I'd been sent off to war. I knew her only from pictures. It was an ache beyond any physical pain I have ever experienced.

I remember realizing that the 38th parallel we crossed twice in combat was the same line in its reach around the globe that passed just north of San Francisco, my home at the time. It was a strange awareness, and it filled me with a desperation to live, to survive, to exist.

Just one more day.

· · ·

I remember you.

You were the thin young man aged by war, too old too soon, that they came for in the night, saying you'd been transferred to the rear. They had checked your records and discovered your interests and talents, and wanted you as a regimental combat correspondent.

You stared dumbly from your foxhole at the messengers who brought the news. "On your way," your platoon leader said, a first lieutenant just out of college. "Your war is over."

But how could you leave? How could you abandon those with whom you had shared such peril, those to whom you owed your life? Friendships are forged in combat that are closer than brothers, built around a mantra that says no Marine is ever abandoned; we bring out our dead, our wounded, our shattered lives.

"This isn't an invitation," the lieutenant said. "You've been ordered. Pack your gear and get the hell out of here."

So you left the front lines in the night, riding a jeep through the darkness to a place of tents and cots and hot food, far beyond the range of artillery.

But one never really leaves a war.

It stays with you down the years, hovering just beyond trills of laughter and times of happiness. Its sounds and images appear at unexpected moments: while holding a small child, or caught in a traffic jam, or alone in a garden.

But physically, at least, you spent the last few months of your war in relative safety and you left Korea aboard a troopship looking back at the land that lay in a mist of dreams and moments long since past.

I thought about those moments as I boarded a 747 last week that would bring me home. I thought about you, the boy you had been and the man you had become, wounded by war but moving on.

I remember you, Al Martinez. You were so young then, and so old.

❖

To Be a Jew

An American reporter based in Israel makes peace with her faith and her heritage even as she covers the conflicts of the region.

BY MARJORIE MILLER • JANUARY 23, 1999

JERUSALEM — As I waited to board a flight from Ben Gurion International Airport to New York, I felt an impatient shove from behind and turned to flash a bothered look at the offender, a rotund man who wore the sidelocks, black hat and frock coat of a devout Jew.

"You got a problem, lady?" he asked in a heavy Brooklyn accent.

"Yes," I answered. "I don't like to be pushed."

"Well, maybe you can deal with that problem when you get home," he said.

Mustering my most indignant voice, I fired back, "Mister, I am home."

This quieted the jostler as abruptly as I knew it would. For a religious Jew, immigrating to Israel is considered a mitzvah, the fulfillment of a biblical commandment. He had referred to the United States as "home," so I knew that he did not live in Israel. I did, which granted me the moral high ground. What clever repartee, I thought.

Too bad I had lied.

Well, technically it was not a lie: I am Jewish, and I had moved to Israel. But it was not as I had led him to believe. I had not immigrated or made *aliyah* — ascended, as Israelis would say — and was not committed to staying in the country that Jews call the homeland. In fact, from the day I had arrived two years before, I had never felt at home in Israel.

I am an assimilated Jew: I am not religious and not affiliated with any Jewish group beyond my family. I am married to a Roman Catholic and might never have visited Israel if I had not been sent on assignment for The Times.

Like most American journalists, I think of myself as a fair and impartial observer. Arriving in Israel in 1995, I felt I had no more stake in the Middle East conflict than I had had in the civil wars of Central America, which I had covered in the 1980s. I did not see myself as a participant in the Arab-Israeli tug of war, or in the religious-secular battles that were breaking out among Jews.

And yet I could not help but wonder if I would find that I had anything in common with Israelis by virtue of having been born Jewish. Would I recognize myself in these people, or them in me? For the first time ever, I asked myself why I had become so assimilated. Why had I rejected Judaism? Or, why did I still think of myself as Jewish when I had not practiced a religious rite since leaving my parents' home more than 20 years before? Would a few years of living in Israel alter the way I saw myself?

I am descended from Midwestern Jews whose original surname was lost in the last century somewhere between a Polish village that no longer exists and the pen of an immigration agent who signed my great-grandfather into America as Isaac Miller. We were offspring of the Enlightenment, Jewish at home and American in the street. We belonged to a Reform temple in Iowa and moved in a small world of a few hundred Jews.

My parents migrated to California in the 1960s to what seemed like a state of people who had cut ties to the past. We joined a Reform synagogue where my older sister finished religious school and my brother had his bar mitzvah. But after a year of religious school, I refused to go back, and our membership eventually lapsed. My mother made sure that we celebrated Jewish holidays three times a year — Passover, the High Holy Days of Rosh Hashana and Yom Kippur, and Hanukkah — and we did not celebrate Christmas, as did many of our new Jewish friends in California.

Mine was not a particularly Zionist household. I vaguely recall that my parents thought something wonderful had happened in June 1967 when Israel won the Mideast War, conquering the Golan Heights, Gaza Strip, Sinai Peninsula, West Bank and East Jerusalem. I believe that they contributed to the United Jewish Appeal and sent their dollars to plant trees. But Israel was not idealized at home, and my parents, who were not travelers, had not been to Jerusalem or Tel Aviv any more than they had been to Paris or Rome.

So it was that I arrived in Israel with very few expectations. And my first encounter provided little of the familiar. On one of our first days, my husband and I found ourselves driving through a funeral procession for a revered scholar of Jewish law. Hundreds of thousands of men in black hats and frock coats had converged on Jerusalem in February 1995 to pay their last respects to one of the giants of Torah study of this generation.

As our car inched through the streets, parting a sea of black, I was overwhelmed by this procession of Orthodox Jews in 16th century dress; I felt transported to a time and place I had seen only in photographs of Eastern Europe before World War II.

Growing up in America, I did not experience deep anti-Semitism or a sense of exile that many Jews describe feeling in the Diaspora, but I did have a sense of being different. I was a brunette in the blond, beachy California of the late 1960s and early 1970s. Although I was frequently told by Jews and non-Jews alike that I "didn't look Jewish," I did not conform to the California Girl stereotype. And I was not a Christian. I identified with Woody Allen's Jewish humor — that is, with Jewish jokes told by Jews. I thought of myself as outside the mainstream.

Now, here I was in Jerusalem, the soul of Jewish identity, and it was utterly foreign. There was nothing of me in this spontaneous outpouring of men in black who rejected modernity, revered a rabbi and embraced the Bible as the literal word of God.

Nor, I realized, did I identify with the Holy Land itself. We drove to the Promenade, a high point in Jerusalem that offers a panoramic view of the walled Old City. For the first time, I stood before the site that is holy to half the world, where the Jews built their First and Second Temple, Jesus walked to his crucifixion, and Mohammed rose to the heavens. I waited for an emotional pull, a kind of spiritual gravity, but felt none. I felt a tremendous sense of history but no tug on my soul.

In fact, as spring gave way to a summer of white heat, I began to hate the desert

313

landscape that everyone around me found so compelling. I recoiled from the gnarled branches of ancient olive trees like a young child stands back from the arthritic hug of a great-grandparent. What were those silver-gray leaves trying to pass for greenery? The famed cypress trees had none of the swirls and soft curves of a Van Gogh; to me, they were dark daggers jutting into a merciless sky.

Friends spoke of the beauty of Jerusalem, but I was blinded by sunlight blasting off hard stone and high walls. I was forever lost in narrow streets without grid or logic. I was hot and trapped among mottled apartment buildings that looked like giant sheets of matzo. I was quite miserable at times.

Like all journalists covering the Middle East, I immediately confronted the irreconcilable Israeli and Palestinian historical narratives and their dueling claims to the land. That is "the story" we are sent to cover.

The Israeli view is that a Jewish presence in the Holy Land dates back to the first Jew, Abraham, more than 3,600 years ago, and that the right of Jews to make their home here is derived from the Bible. Forced to live in exile for some 2,000 years, Jews decided at the end of the 19th century to rebuild their nation in the land of Israel, the land of their ancestors.

The Arabs who had lived here for hundreds of years were "newcomers" who rejected the Jews and their offer to partition the land called Palestine in 1947 and to live in peace as neighbors. The Arabs attacked. Jews fought back, won the war and statehood; the Arabs lost and left.

The Palestinian view is quite another. It is that Jews are colonialists from Europe and other parts who violently occupied their land in Palestine. The Arabs were living here when Jews immigrated en masse with the intention of usurping all the land for themselves and not, as Israelis tell it, to live together in peace. The Arabs of Palestine tried to defend themselves against the onslaught, lost and were evicted by the Jews. That is why, I quickly learned, Palestinians rarely use the word "Israeli," which legitimizes a citizen of a state that should not exist. Israelis are "the Jews." Jews had besieged them, and Jews were their historic enemy.

In fact, half a century and five wars later, most Palestinians accept that the state of Israel is here to stay. They are willing to negotiate for a smaller state of their own in the land Israel captured in 1967. And most Israelis recognize that they must give up some of that land in exchange for peace. They want to negotiate the price: how much land for how much security.

I had arrived to witness that negotiation, which was launched with a handshake between Israeli Prime Minister Yitzhak Rabin and Palestinian leader Yasser Arafat in September 1993, and is still uncompleted today. But while I saw myself as a spectator to the epic story of peacemaking in the Middle East, I quickly learned that neither side saw me that way.

Palestinians viewed the American press as wholesale suppliers of the Israeli government line. A dead Jew was front-page news in the U.S., but how many Palestinians had to die to make Page 1?

Israelis, on the other hand, generally felt that the U.S. press was in the Palestinian camp, portraying Israelis in the poorest possible light. Yet they would try to figure out where I stood personally.

"Are you Jewish?" Israelis asked me time and again.

"*Rak Ketzat* — only a little bit," I would answer humorously, knowing that to them, being a little bit Jewish is like being a little pregnant.

Yet the question confused and annoyed me. It had never come up in previous assignments. It seemed too personal and probing from perfect strangers. What difference did it make?

"It's a matter of trust," Hebrew University sociologist Stephen Cohen explained. "Clubbiness. Tribalism. Since they don't know by looking, they want to know, 'How do we treat you? As a member of the tribe or an outsider?' "

Well, clearly I'm not an insider, I thought. I'm a journalist, a perennial outsider. It was, however, a perspective that I also regarded as quintessentially Jewish.

I knew little of Jewish history. When I was a teenager, my father bought two copies of "Jews, God and History" by Max Dimont and said we would read the book together.

I said I wasn't interested. He responded that I had better get interested: I was a Jew under Jewish law — and Hitler's too.

That may have been "the law," but it was not my reality. I was American, a citizen of a country that allowed me to be as Jewish or non-Jewish as I pleased. At the time, I wanted to be a writer, maybe a zoologist. But Jewish?

What little I had learned of Judaism had made it seem like a religion of crises and conquests. Jews were always getting clobbered, forced into slavery or exile. Sure, they overcame, but that was not the message that stuck with me. I saw a persecuted people who broke a glass even during a wedding ceremony to remember the destruction of the Second Temple, recalling tragedy at a moment of unfettered joy.

It caught me by surprise, then, when a tragedy provided my first emotional link to the Jews: the assassination of Yitzhak Rabin.

Rabin was shot dead November 4, 1995, by a religious nationalist who believed that the prime minister was a traitor for giving up "Jewish" land to the Palestinians. It was a horrifying moment that plunged the country into gut-wrenching grief and self-examination.

Many Israelis agreed with the aims of the assassin, Yigal Amir, although not with a murder. They were convinced that the Palestinians could not be trusted. They wanted the peace process halted.

Others believed that Rabin was a hero for sitting down with the enemy and felt sure that Israel's only chance for peace had died with him. Devastated, they blamed his death on all religious and right-wing people, who lashed back in anger.

The mourning and mutual recrimination awoke a deep-seated fear in Israelis, who are taught in school that infighting among Jews was partly responsible for the fall of the holy Second Temple in AD 70 to the Romans. Division was dangerous. Now the assassination had revealed just how bitterly divided the Jews were again.

For decades, modern Israelis had suffered attack and inflicted occupation, even death, on others, be they Palestinians or Lebanese; they had accepted this as a necessity for the survival of a state of God's "Chosen People." Now, the leader of Israel had been killed by one of its own, and young Israelis in particular were forced to confront the fact that the Chosen People were a lot like everyone else. Israel, which had wanted to be "a light unto nations," was no more a beacon than India or the United States, which also assassinated its leaders.

In this time of naked soul-searching, many of the Israelis' usual defenses came down. And so did mine. Bold and blustery Israelis were humbled and exposed, and because of that I felt more intimate with them. Maybe I was an outsider, but I had been allowed into the living room at a time of family tragedy.

Life would be neater if I could say that my first encounter with my Jewish identity in Israel took place at the Western Wall of the Second Temple, or at least in a synagogue. But it was at the supermarket, next to the olives.

Israel's many varied olives are sold from open vats. A shopper spoons the desired quantity into a plastic bag, to be weighed and priced at the checkout counter.

One day, unconsciously, I began to taste olives right out of the vats. I had eaten about half a dozen before I realized that not only was the man next to me doing exactly the same, but also that a container had been set aside for the pits. The supermarket clearly expected such behavior.

I looked around to see another man munching on some nuts that he had grabbed out of a bin down the aisle. He had some more in his right hand and was shaking them like dice, just the way I had seen my dad shake nuts many times. Suddenly, between the olives and the nuts, I felt familiar with these people who behaved like me, noshing and making themselves at home in a supermarket.

Another flash of recognition occurred during a visit to the dentist.

"Hi, how are you?" I asked upon arriving.

"Oh, can't complain," he answered.

"Really, what's wrong?" I said.

We laughed together at a joke we both understood: If a Jew can't complain, something must be wrong.

I felt at ease and a sense of camaraderie, so much so that I decided to celebrate Passover for the first time since leaving my mother's home. I had a Seder with our closest friends in Israel, American Jews. But as we read the Haggada, the story of the Jews' enslavement in Egypt and later liberation, I could not help but revert to my outsider role.

"Do we know the Jews were enslaved in Egypt?" I asked. "Is there any archeological proof?"

"If it weren't true, I think we would have heard," answered my friend's father, a judge.

"It doesn't matter if it's true," Rabbi David Hartman answered when I put the question to him later at the Shalom Hartman Institute. "To me, the important issue is the narrative story that shaped my people's identity.... It symbolizes the belief that you can move from slavery to freedom."

That is why Jews end the Passover Seder with the words, "Next year in Jerusalem," even if they are in Jerusalem.

Belief was foreign to me, but I was beginning to feel more Jewish. I was starting to identify myself as a cultural Jew who shared a history with other Jews when I learned in the course of reporting on Israel's religious-secular divide that devout Jews did not see people like me as Jewish.

Although Jewish law says the child of a Jewish woman is Jewish, many observant Jews had decided otherwise: A Jew who did not keep to Jewish law and commandments was no longer Jewish.

This often-expressed view was succinctly put by Gen. Yaacov Amidror, one of the Israeli army's highest-ranking religious Jews, in the daily newspaper Yediot Aharonot: "There is much wisdom in the assertion that the secular are nothing more than Hebrew-speaking goyim" or Gentiles.

I didn't even speak Hebrew.

Woody Allen, paraphrasing Groucho Marx, said he wouldn't join a club that would have him. I hadn't wanted to join the club until some members said I didn't belong. Suddenly I was offended.

"What do you mean, I'm not Jewish?" I huffed.

After Rabin and the brief reign of his Labor Party successor, Shimon Peres,

Israelis elected Prime Minister Benjamin Netanyahu, the Likud Party leader who promised to slow down peacemaking with the Palestinians in response to a wave of suicide bombings that took scores of Israeli lives in a matter of days. He did.

The delays prompted both sides to retrench. Israelis stepped up construction in the occupied West Bank, and Palestinians started killing land dealers suspected of selling property to Israelis and withholding security cooperation. Chronic fears and habitual mistrust were reawakened.

As the Netanyahu government negotiated a hand-over of the West Bank city of Hebron to Palestinians in January 1997, I witnessed the inability of either side to recognize the rights and humanity of the other. I heard fundamentalist Jews who live in Hebron describe Palestinians living across the street from them as "animals." Then I crossed the street to hear the same thing about Jews from Palestinians. Blind hatred prevented both sides from seeing the ugly mirror image they presented.

I recoiled. I did not belong to this us-versus-them world. Maybe I was beginning to feel Jewish, but I did not regard the Palestinians as my enemy.

As the Israeli government debated a Palestinian prisoner release under the peace agreement, I heard some Israelis protest: "Don't release prisoners with Jewish blood on their hands."

What made Jewish blood so much more valuable than another's? I wondered.

Then one day I saw something that made my own blood boil. At a fashionable optical shop in Jerusalem, I was being attended by the owner, a hip, secular Israeli, when an elderly Palestinian woman in traditional embroidered dress sat down on the sidewalk in front to sell fruit. The owner went outside, shouted at her to move and swatted her on her covered head much as one might shoo away a stray dog.

Certainly, worse acts have been committed against Palestinians. Even now, perhaps on a daily basis, Palestinians are mistreated at army checkpoints in worse ways. Yet this image is engraved in my mind. That woman was somebody's grandmother, I thought. She deserved respect, even though she was forced by poverty to sell fruit on the sidewalk. The shop owner had treated her no better than anti-Semites had treated Jews in the Diaspora for centuries.

I became aware of an important subtext to the Israeli-Palestinian conflict. There was a competition to be the biggest victim. Israelis insisted that no evil as great as the Holocaust had ever been visited on human beings. They were determined that the Palestinians accept this — and all the centuries of Jewish suffering in the Diaspora — as justification for a Jewish state in Palestine.

Palestinians, who felt that they had been made to pay the price for the Holocaust with their land, often refused to acknowledge the Shoah — the Catastrophe — as

Jews call the Holocaust. The Palestinians said they had their own Catastrophe, the Nakba, which was the founding of the state of Israel in 1948.

This comparison drove Israelis crazy, and the competition, revived with every killing, drove me crazy. It also made me realize why I had turned away from being a Jew.

I was about 7 or 8 years old when I went to religious school. My teacher introduced me to the Hebrew alphabet, dreidels and the Holocaust — the story of the slaughter of Jews in Nazi Germany. Then one Sunday morning, she attempted to re-create the terror that Jews had experienced. Solemnly, in a scared voice, she called us to order and told us to pay close attention. Had we heard the radio? The government was telling the Jews that we had to convert or leave the country. This was the first step, she said, maybe the beginning of another Holocaust. What would we do?

Many children in the class began to cry. I began to calculate. How would they know I was Jewish? I didn't "look Jewish." No need to convert, I simply wouldn't admit to being Jewish.

Faced with so many tears, the teacher soon told the truth and explained that she had only meant to show us how it would feel. Many of the kids were relieved, but I was angry. Soon after, I refused to return to religious school.

I did not even remember this episode until I lived in Israel and considered what had happened. I had learned from it that to be Jewish was to be a victim. I didn't want to be a victim, so I wouldn't be Jewish. It was a choice that many Jews had made before me.

The peace process floundered for the next year and a half. Arabs and Jews continued to kill each other, with no apparent end in sight. It was a sad story and personally unenlightening; the fight over the land of Israel did not awaken a Jewish identity in me. But the Holocaust, the very history I had once fled, eventually, gradually, did.

I remembered my religious school "lesson" after meeting several Holocaust survivors. I saw the bruise-blue concentration camp numbers tattooed on their arms and heard the story of the Nazi terror from those who had lived through it.

Over coffee in her cozy living room, nursery-school teacher Aliza Landau recounted how she had hidden in the woods of Germany with her father until Wehrmacht soldiers found them in the final days of World War II.

She was a small girl holding on to her father's pant leg for life when they were lined up with dozens of other Jews at the edge of a freshly dug pit. The soldiers fired and Jews fell dead into the hole. Miraculously, the bullets missed the little girl, who lay still on her father's body until nightfall. Then, weak from hunger, she climbed over the corpses out of the death pit and crawled toward the sound of barking dogs — toward a farm — as her father had taught her to do if ever he was caught.

Driving home after hearing this story, I thought back to the time I had toured the wind-swept Nazi death camp at Buchenwald and seen ovens where the bodies of Jews had been burned. I had been horrified that the manufacturers were so proud of their product that they had put metal nameplates on the front of the ovens: Topf & Sohne. And it occurred to me that I had identified with Jews while standing before those ovens more than I had standing before the Western Wall in Jerusalem's Old City.

For many Jews, the two would be inseparable. Both symbolize the history of the Jewish people, their suffering and endurance. Like many secular Jews in Israel, however, I eventually found it easier to relate to the Holocaust. This was because of people like Landau and Daniel Chanoch, another of the 360,000 Holocaust survivors alive in Israel today.

Chanoch, 65, is a Lithuanian-born Jew who outlasted Dachau and Auschwitz and has dedicated himself to educating future generations about the Holocaust. His patient recounting of the horror, his black humor and beaming green eyes made me see him not as a victim but as a symbol of hope. He was a proud Jew who belonged to a tradition of survival and who laughingly called himself an "unrealistic optimist."

After three years in Israel, I had not become religious and was no more wedded to the country than I had been when I arrived. I was still an American reporter. Yet I had come to identify with Jewish history, and even to appreciate the beauty of Jerusalem: the way the evening light plays off the stones that I once found so hostile. I came to feel a part of the Jewish family, although, as often happens with family, part of me couldn't wait to escape.

I conveyed some of this to my parents when I called to tell them we would be moving to England.

"Well, Dad," I said on the telephone from Jerusalem. "Next year in London."

❖

Lessons in the Art of Dying — and Living

Talking of love, regrets, dreams and hard choices, 'students' in classes led by a former priest confront a reality often denied in our culture. Their goal: to craft a better death.

BY MARIA L. LA GANGA · DECEMBER 21, 1997

SAN FRANCISCO — This is Paul's dream of the perfect death: Retired math teacher, avid sailor, he circumnavigates the globe at age 99, is lost at sea and never seen again. His hands shake a little with Parkinson's disease as he tells this story in his soft, wheezy voice. Dapper in plaid shirt and neat jeans, Paul sounds as if he is talking about someone else. Lost at sea. Never seen again. Almost as if he will not be there when it happens. Lost at sea.

He repeats this story often in the neat apartment off Golden Gate Park where we meet for 10 successive Monday nights, September to November. Autumn deepens all around us. Leaves fall. Days shorten. We are here learning how to die.

We are not boning up on how to kill ourselves, although the topic does arise on occasion. Legislatures and courtrooms, talk shows and pundits may fixate on assisted dying, but it is somehow almost beside the point to the women and men who gather here hoping to craft a better death.

Pain is a far more important topic when we peer closely at the end of life. God, too. Love, regrets, family, paperwork, morphine. We have much to discuss and not much time — 20 hours in Richard Wagner's living room.

Through five weeks of talk — interspersed with five weeks of lecture and talk — we learn how to fill out documents that allow us to die without the aid of machines. We discover how our bodies will react, one week, one day, one hour before the end. We argue about the very best way to go: Renal failure wins hands down, with its dreamy drift from unconsciousness to death.

As traffic whizzes by outside, drowning out the occasional quiet confidence, we face each other in an intimate circle. We talk.

A lot happens from September to November. Paul and Sophia, both 80, sell off some property, celebrate 55 years of marriage and 55 years in this adopted city. Yet

321

another friend dies, No. 6 in the last year or so. They give most of their belongings to their children, apply for rooms in a home for seniors, argue about whether to go.

Famous architect Julia Morgan built the place. It is red brick and graceful. Close to the marina, Sophia says one day when Paul — again — brings up his final voyage. Paul does not want to move, not into this place, this hotel, this antithesis of home and comfort.

Adina travels further along in the process she refers to as "active dying." She is 43, has cystic fibrosis. Her oxygen tank soughs in the background. She coughs a lot. When we first meet, she is in danger of breaking her First Commandment: I will die with the lungs God gave me. She is freshly back from a trip to Stanford University Medical Center, an exploratory jaunt in search of a transplant.

By November, she is cleared for surgery, on the list and debating what to do. She wears (and forgets) and wears (and forgets) the beeper that links her with the medical center and the organs that could come at any time — or not in time. She looks at her prescriptions and credit cards; she will likely expire before they do. She laughs. Sometimes.

By the end of our discussions, Sandy will make love for the first time in a very, very long time. Well coiffed, perfectly made up, unable to stop smiling as she makes her announcement — Yes, I did it — she has come a long way.

In September, she was shy, maybe just a little dowdy, partway through radiation treatments, done with chemotherapy, at war with a body that betrayed her with breast cancer. A body that she was never all that comfortable in to begin with.

And once they start cutting around in your parts, she says, and her voice trails off. She cannot finish this sentence. Not in September. In September, she says I need to learn how to live as much as I need to learn how to die.

Which is precisely the point of this exclusive club. We are not just people who are going to die; if that were the case, you would all belong too. The eight women and three men know we are going to die. This is a big difference.

I am here in part to listen, but also to learn. I am healthy but an actuarial nightmare: practically the only member of my family not to have had cancer. At 38 years old, I am without a female relative who made it to 50. My mother died fast in 1973, one quick yank of a ventilator plug after rapid brain cancer and ineffective surgery. My father died slowly two years ago, as his body parts fell to age, disease, a lifetime of smoking. They left the ventilator on. He dwindled.

This is a real conversation-stopper at most polite dinner parties. There are very few places to say things like: What happens to my body on my last day? How can I make sure it doesn't hurt at the end? I'm lonely. I'm dying. Maybe I'm not dying. But

I'm afraid.

This is that place. It is not perfect. It is sometimes hard to bear. In most cities, finding something comparable is impossible. It is not for everyone. But it can be very helpful.

"What is magic about what happens here is that everyone is a self-identified mortal," Wagner says in October. A gay, defrocked Catholic priest who lost most of his friends to AIDS a decade ago, Wagner started this series of classes in 1995 for senior citizens and the terminally ill. At first, it was largely attended by gay men with the AIDS virus. Today, as AIDS treatment improves, it is largely women with cancer.

Wagner earned a PhD in clinical sexology while a practicing priest, but his doctoral research on the sexual attitudes and behavior of gay Catholic clergy knocked him out of favor with his church. While he has spent the last 14 years working with the dying, these days he is a sometime-therapist who pays the bills with a secretarial job.

He calls this group Paradigm: Enhancing Life Before Dying, a grand name for a worthwhile but shoestring operation. Lecturers donate their time. Wagner bakes the refreshments himself. Participants are asked to donate $10 per session if they can.

There is no money to advertise. Sandy heard about Paradigm in chemotherapy. Wagner gave Sophia, white-haired and charming, a brochure on the group as she got off a bus. He does this sometimes with people who look old and open-minded.

Some names have been changed to protect privacy. Wagner's is the only one unaltered. All stories — the heart of a process like this one — are true. "When I'm with you, what happens here, I can't manufacture with my friends," Wagner says. "They have not taken that important leap: 'Yes, I'm a mortal. I'm going to die.' "

Session I

What is your first remembrance of death?

This is how we begin our long conversation. For a group that ranges in age from the 20s to 80, whose youths spanned this century from World War I to the end of the Vietnam War, our responses are strangely uniform in tone. They are filled with pets and grandparents, silence and moments of inadvertent dark comedy, like Ellen's Depression-era tale of death and dinner:

"My father lost his job and went to raising chickens in the garage. And we got the chickens when they were little babies, and I named them all, and I loved them all, and then my father would take them and chop off their heads. And they would run around the yard, and I would cry, because I knew which chicken that was. And then I had to eat it."

Sandy's "first death" is more the norm. She is 7 years old, in Joplin, Missouri, when her grandmother dies of leukemia. She doesn't see it happen and doesn't hear much about it. "I remember them coming to me and saying, well, your grandmother won't be coming home. People just go away, and they don't come back."

Sandy remembers no funerals as a child, even the ones she attended. Even her father's when she was 16 and he was 39 and a salesman in the family cookie business when he died of a heart attack. Although she didn't realize it then, it changed her life. Yet she cannot even call forth an image of a coffin with her young self nearby.

She has introduced herself on this first night this way: My father died at 39 and I kind of thought I would too, so I didn't really make long-term goals. You don't know it while you're doing it.

All of a sudden she finds herself in her 40s. Stuck, really. Personal adventure seems to have ended. A set painter, she has shifted subtly from artist to craftswoman, from creativity to rote. When a love affair ends, she finds no substitute.

She is thinking that she wants to visit places one last time. "I wonder, in essence, how much I killed myself off. I always planned on having life be over at that point. So I sort of finished things."

By the time a routine mammogram comes back and she hears the chilling instruction — Find a surgeon — it is five days before Christmas in 1996, and she has outlived her own personal life expectancy by seven years. Four weeks later she is diagnosed with cancer. Twenty days after that, the lump is removed.

She cannot bring herself to ask for help, fights the dependence that comes from serious illness. The lumpectomy means she cannot raise her arm. Chemotherapy makes it hard to drive. She feels guilty, apologizes for her temporary helplessness. It is, she says on our sixth night, a horror — with one small, sweet exception.

Sandy had been estranged from her mother for years, separated by geography and difficult circumstances. Now "I happen to be one of her greatest supporters from the time that she washed my hair. In the process, I remembered being a little girl. You get soap in your eyes and you're fighting and all that. You never dream that you'll be sitting there at 47 years old with your mother washing your hair. And we're laughing about it."

Sessions II and III

The first several Mondays are filled with revelation. Ellen, 71, says she wants to be immortal, plans on being cryogenically frozen in a tank filled with nitrogen for "reanimation" at some future date, displays the MedicAlert necklace she is never without: Resuscitate-cool. No autopsy.

Adina, getting sicker, cautions calm if by some chance she coughs up blood. "It happens sometimes" is the nonchalant disclaimer from the petite woman with the oxygen tube that loops from tank to nose.

Paul is stunned by the recent wit's-end cry from the wife of an ailing friend — a man who has Parkinson's disease just like Paul. "It was his wife, a very loving wife, very caring, and she read a statement that said she wished Joe would die," he says. "That was a surprise to me."

Sophia announces her plans for their future with a cheerful "Paul and I are considering going into a retirement community, and one of the things we have to do is plan what to do about our bodies." Later, she is thrilled to find a low-ball bidder — a full-service cremation for just $395 per person, close by on Valencia Street.

We are learning the vocabulary of the end of life. We are practicing with our new-found voices to speak of longtime fears. We are given a list of 18 awful eventualities and pick our personal worst. We are confronting our fears. The top three: I'm afraid of being helpless and having to depend completely on others. I'm afraid of taking a long time to die. I'm afraid of losing control of my bodily functions.

Carolyn, in her 20s and infected with HIV, is most afraid of losing those she loves. "In thinking about dying, one of the things that makes me want to go on is that I love the people in my life. I'm stubborn. I really want to stick around. I want to have children and grandchildren. I want to have the length of life my parents had. I don't want to give it up before I'm 30." Carolyn has been married for just four months and leaves the group after just three meetings.

Session IV

There is little fear of post-death punishment in this small crowd of Unitarians, lapsed Catholics, lukewarm Methodists, sort-of Jews. But it is telling, as we speak of spirituality and death, that even those among us with a system of belief feel that it may not be enough.

Our search for spirituality seems as much a longing for community as it is for faith, as much for people with whom to celebrate ritual as it is for the ritual itself.

Still, the yearning for spiritual comfort is there. The answers are not. Question: Is it easier to die if you believe in God? Answer: Not necessarily. Who knows? Sometimes. And, sometimes, a resounding no.

David Pettee, hospice nurse, Unitarian minister, our guide through this slippery subject, believes that "thinking about large unanswerable mysteries in our lives as we're facing our mortality, that to me is what spiritual work is. And it tends to be better when done in relationship with other people."

As the flashier part of the national discourse on death — whether your doctor should help you kill yourself — threads its way into ballot initiatives and headlines, there is surprisingly little controversy or even discussion around the issues central to Paradigm: Is there a right way to die? Can you teach someone how to die? Should you teach someone how to die? If you can, if you should, who in their right mind would want to learn?

Of the hundreds of books on store shelves, of the thousands of Web sites that choke the Internet, of the countless support groups that lend a shoulder, very few are for people actually dying. Unless you reside here, you likely have little access to the small number of struggling organizations that make up the conscious dying movement.

Unless you are in a hospice program or are very, very lucky, your doctor likely views death as failure and does not want to talk about it. Even if you are fortunate enough to receive the ministrations of hospice workers, it may be too late for you to benefit much.

Hospice care, by legal definition, is for the terminally ill with six months or less to live. This is theoretically time enough to put your affairs in order, to reach out to your loved ones, to teach those around you about the kind of death you want — and don't want. But more than 15 percent of all hospice patients die within a week, because they, their doctors and their families cannot admit sooner that there is no hope.

What is lost by this denial? An opportunity to become more human, says Dr. Brad Stuart, medical director for VNA & Hospice of Northern California. "What I would call the basic spiritual message that dying brings us is that we move toward wholeness, and wholeness doesn't always feel good," he says. "When you become a truly whole human being, you assimilate the lightest parts of being human and also the darkest.... People who are dying and their families become more human, and that's what I'd call growth."

Americans, says Dr. Ira Byock, author of "Dying Well: The Prospect for Growth at the End of Life," are perhaps not ready for this discussion, not prepared to embrace an active role in their own deaths. Asking why there are not more services addressed specifically to the dying in 1997 is like asking why there were not more home births in 1966.

"We're five years too early," Byock says. "The generation of baby boomers, a

326

third of this country, is just now dealing with these issues in a way that is forcing them to rethink traditional approaches.… We're beginning to get there. The problem is that denial can really rob us of this opportunity."

Session V

If Americans cannot speak of death, imagine a conversation on sex and death, our biggest taboos twinned together. This is our topic tonight — sexuality, intimacy and death. Half the chairs in Wagner's living room remain empty, perhaps because of a scheduling mix-up, perhaps because of the subject.

It is a night full of loss and longing, of bodies that no longer function the same way, of scars and oxygen tanks and shortness of breath. Of rejection.

Adina's grief is perhaps the most palpable. I actually feel a lot closer to dying, was her somber beginning to our last meeting. Tonight she is feeling better after two weeks on prednisone. The steroid was prescribed to clear up a fungus in her lungs, an ailment that produces more labored breathing and could stand in the way of a lung transplant.

But improvement comes at some cost. Now she has steroid-induced diabetes, which means more medication and many blood tests. "In some ways it's worth it," says Adina, who is on her second trip through the Paradigm process, this time helping facilitate the group. "It's quality of life. I'm not going to worry about all the horrible things that can happen to you if you're on it for 10 years. I won't be on it for 10 years."

Adina has known from childhood that she would never be blessed with old age. Her friends joke that she's been dying for as long as they've known her, that they've been hearing about this death stuff forever. Two years ago, she was diagnosed with congestive heart failure, told she had 12 months to live.

Life is getting smaller and harder. Fearful, she cancels a long-planned vacation. "What if something really awful happens?" she asks. "What if I push myself so much that I take a turn I can't come back from?"

She plans her death: At home. No ventilator. Her carpenter friends build her casket, load it into her husband's van, head off to the cemetery. One afternoon she drives her dog to the park, feels the sun on her thin face and thinks, This is enough.

On this night, though, her life is not enough. Nowhere near enough. "Before I got on the prednisone, and I was having a hard time breathing, I was thinking, Oh my God, the last thing I could do is have any kind of sexual encounter. When I even ate something I was out of breath. So how can…." Her voice is pierced with longing.

327

Session VII

I am looking at the official form, having some trouble filling it out and wondering why. It's pretty self-explanatory, four pages long, handed out at the beginning of our session on legal affairs. Called the "durable power of attorney for health care decisions," it is the dying person's best friend.

The goal is simple: You write down how you want to die. You pick a person to be your champion when you are no longer able to communicate. You explain your wishes to your doctor, put a copy in your medical file, break the news to your family and the advocate you've chosen. Then, when the end comes, you can rest relatively safe in the knowledge that you have done what you can to die the way you want.

The California Medical Association, which distributes a widely used version of the form, even spells it out for you. All you have to do is initial the part that says: I do not want efforts made to prolong my life and I do not want life-sustaining treatment to be provided or continued.

I do not want to die like my father. Kidney failure had sentenced him to years of dialysis: four hours a day, three days a week, hooked up to a machine that cleansed his blood. A lifetime of Marlboro Reds, then Marlboro Lights, then low-tar-and-nicotine Nows had pretty well pulverized his lungs.

He had fought off cancer some 15 years before, but could not overcome the stroke and congestive heart failure that slammed him into a hospital bed in the spring of 1995.

Unable to breathe without a ventilator. Unable to endure the pain of the ventilator without morphine. Tied to the hospital bed so that he would not tear out the offending tubes. The doctors: He will never breathe unaided again unless we do something. "Something" is heart bypass surgery on a ravaged body barely clutching to life. He dies two days before.

I do not want to die like my father. But for the first time, I understand my stepmother and sister, who grasped at bypass surgery as a way to save his life. Let me control my end, I've always thought, let me go before I turn into something — not someone. But here I am, balking at this piece of paper and thinking: Maybe there could be a miracle. I sign the form.

Session IX

We come bearing homework. The assignment: What would you do in your last six weeks of life? The first five you would be ambulatory and relatively well. The last one you'd be in bed but lucid.

328

Ellen wants to rob a bank. Sandy wants to travel — to Greece or Egypt, then New York, then Florida, then she'll rent a red car and drive to Missouri. Jennifer, infected with HIV and newly 30, wants to ride her motorcycle up the Sonoma County coastline.

When was the last time you did that? asks Wagner. And why don't you do it now? Here, it seems, is the crux of our 10 weeks together: Why don't you do it now? Give yourself the gift of a conscious end, the calm of well-ordered affairs, the solace of reconciliation, the peace of knowing that you need not die in pain, the comfort of a life well lived. Why don't you do it now?

Paul is having none of it. What would he do with a six-week prognosis? Get a second opinion and then a third, he says, and we laugh. Then he'd take care of his paperwork. And then he'd go sailing. He wants to go back to Ohio, see old friends. Sophia doesn't want to go, but he will not go alone. "We'll work it out," Sophia tells us gently. They usually do.

She's the instigator, he says, and I'm the modifier. She is the healthy one. He is not. She is the one who is ready to go. He is not. It was Sophia's idea to join this group. Paul came along.

It was Sophia's idea to move to the retirement home. Paul wants to stay in their house. We'll do a three-month trial run, she says. It'll be like a cruise. We hear their back and forth every week as they go through the hurdles to gain admission. What if I pass the physical, and she doesn't? They both pass.

"We went to a memorial last Wednesday," Sophia says in early November, when we meet to talk one afternoon near the end of the sessions. "Two of our neighbors have died recently, and two are in nursing homes. One of the reasons we're going to Heritage House is because of the social stimulation. Everyone we know is dying."

The three of us sit in her family room, stripped of everything but a few chairs, a bookcase, family portraits painted in oils. If you want to see our things, she jokes, go to our children's houses. What's left here is what they didn't want. Sophia has stopped reading newspapers, doesn't watch television, announces that she's started disengaging, slowly stepping back from life. "I'm not going to call 911 for you anymore," she jokes to Paul. "I'll get a cell phone," he laughs.

We walk from their house to the No. 6 Parnassus bus stop. The air is cold, the memories warm. There's the house they could have bought for $14,000 in 1951, if only Paul had made more than $3,000 a year. It just sold for $1.1 million. And look, that's where Elsa used to live. She was a social worker just like Sophia. She died. Was it this summer?

Sophia, merry in a green beret and a plum-colored coat, helps Paul put on his windbreaker. "We've been debt-free since October 10, when we sold the house," he says. "It's a good feeling," she says. "It only took 80 years," he says. "So I guess we are getting ready for the end," she says.

We are all still around. Our final session has come and gone — an evaluation of the last nine weeks, quiet goodbyes, almost anticlimactic. We resume old lives equipped with new tools.

Jennifer has gone skydiving for the first time. "There I was, hanging out the door, attached to this guy," she recounts, breathless. "Then I was flipping. Ground. Sky. Ground. Sky. It was really remarkable."

Adina's beeper has not gone off, forcing her to decide whether to risk a transplant that may or may not help her live longer.

Paul and Sophia remain — so far — in their home of 52 years. They've made another visit to Heritage House, admired the Christmas ornaments in the graceful lobby. "We told them no," Paul says. "No, we didn't," smiles Sophia.

❖

The War, Up Close and Very Personal

For one reporter, embedding opens an exhilarating but terrifying window on the world of men in battle.

By David Zucchino · May 3, 2003

BAGHDAD — Our troop truck lost its way in a dust cloud at night, somewhere near the holy city of Karbala. It careened across a dirt causeway and plunged into the murky brown waters of a canal. Men pitched headfirst to the bottom, dragged under by the weight of their flak jackets. Heavy boxes of bottled water and rations tumbled down on them. Soldiers hacked away with bayonets at gear straps tangled around their necks.

After several terrifying minutes, 24 soldiers and one embedded reporter were pulled to safety, all accounted for. Some of the men vomited on the slick canal bank. Two had to be revived by medics. A few shivering young soldiers seemed ready to weep as their sergeants berated them for losing their night-vision goggles.

I felt like crying, too. My computer, satellite phones, clothes, tape recorder, cash, notebooks and everything else I carried was lost or ruined.

It was 5:30 a.m. on April 4. Journalistically speaking, I had become what the military calls "combat ineffective." My military embed, having brought me closer than I ever imagined to the perils of the front, seemed to have ended at the bottom of the canal.

Embedding — that awkward and ephemeral term for being in the Army but not of it — is a remarkable contrivance. It can be bent and manipulated by commander or reporter, often to the benefit of neither. It can also provide an exhilarating, if terrifying, window on the unscripted world of men under stress and fire.

Not since the Vietnam War have journalists worked so closely with soldiers in combat. The embed, in which reporters live 24 hours a day with their assigned units, was instituted on a limited basis in Afghanistan after the heaviest fighting had ended. Expanded, it was to be the grand journalistic experiment of the Iraq war, and a departure from the briefing coverage of the Persian Gulf War 12 years earlier. About 600 journalists volunteered.

During seven weeks spent with half a dozen units, I slept in fighting holes and armored vehicles, on a rooftop, a garage floor and in lumbering troop trucks. For days at a time, I didn't sleep. I ate with the troops, choking down processed meals of "meat, chunked and formed" that came out of brown plastic bags. I rode with them in loud, claustrophobic and disorienting Bradley fighting vehicles. I complained with them about the choking dust, the lack of water, our foul-smelling bodies and our scaly, rotting feet.

At 5:30 a.m. on April 7, precisely 72 hours after plummeting into the canal, I was in the belly of a Bradley, its 25-millimeter cannon pumping out rounds, as an armored column of the Army's 3rd Infantry Division rumbled under fire into downtown Baghdad. And 72 hours after that, I was sleeping on the marble floor of Saddam Hussein's Presidential Palace.

I saw what the soldiers saw. And, like most of them, I emerged filthy, exhausted and aware of what Winston Churchill meant when he said that "nothing in life is so exhilarating as to be shot at without effect."

Most important, I wrote stories I could not have produced had I not been embedded — on the pivotal battle for Baghdad; the performance of U.S. soldiers in combat; the crass opulence of Hussein's palaces; U.S. airstrikes on an office tower in central Baghdad; souvenir-hunting by soldiers and reporters; and the discovery of more than $750 million in cash in a neighborhood that had been the preserve of top Iraqi officials.

Yet that same access could be suffocating and blinding. Often I was too close or confined to comprehend the war's broad sweep. I could not interview survivors of Iraqi civilians killed by U.S. soldiers or speak to Iraqi fighters trying to kill Americans. I was not present when Americans died at the hands of fellow soldiers in what the military calls "frat," for fratricide. I had no idea what ordinary Iraqis were experiencing. I was ignorant of Iraqi government decisions and U.S. command strategy.

Embedded reporters were entirely dependent on the military for food, water, power and transportation. And ultimately, we depended on them for something more fundamental: access. We were placed in a potentially compromised position long before the fighting began, and we knew it.

Lt. Col. Patrick Fetterman, who commands an elite infantry battalion of the 101st Airborne Division, told me many times that the most lethal thing on the battlefield was his own forces.

For journalists, the greatest enemy was ourselves — our ingrained human tendency to identify with those beside us. Bombarded with drama and emotions, it was impossible to step back, or to report every story with absolute detachment. We didn't just cover the war — we were part of it.

This newspaper, like many, also assigned reporters and photographers to Iraq who were not embedded with U.S. troops. They covered what we could not — the Iraqi government, civilian casualties, humanitarian crises, military strategy, political fallout and everything else beyond our cloistered existence.

Reports from embedded reporters did not dominate newspaper war coverage. They were part of it, giving an intimate look at the 250,000 U.S. troops in the gulf. But the raw reporting emerging from embeds was weighed and balanced by editors against information from other reporters spread far and wide. In that context, embedding provided a valuable contribution.

In most cases, the officers and soldiers I accompanied were too busy or distracted to pay attention to what I was doing. There was no public affairs minder to keep me in line. Not a single soldier or officer I encountered refused to be interviewed. I attended countless intelligence briefings. I listened to radio communications crackle in the heat of battle. I walked through battle rehearsals that choreographed every angle of attack.

Some officers seemed to expect reporters to serve as boosters for their unit's exploits. A few pointed out that my presence in a Humvee or Bradley deprived them of one more fighting man.

Others strictly interpreted the ground rules all reporters signed, which prohibited us from identifying positions, revealing war plans or describing U.S. combat losses. For instance, I was ordered to withhold information about extensive damage to nearly three dozen Apache gunships in one battle, yet reporters with other units reported every detail.

I quickly learned to push the rules. Under combat conditions, the embed restrictions softened. Without official permission, I moved from unit to unit, trying to get closer to battle. I would stumble onto a unit, seek out the commander and get his permission to jump aboard. With my greasy jeans and sweat-stained shirt, I felt like a homeless man cadging a meal.

But if I had not abandoned my original unit, I would have sat out the war, in Kuwait, where that unit remained for the bulk of the fighting.

After my new battalion plunged me into the canal, I joined a brigade that took me to the core of the battle for Baghdad.

Along the way, I discovered it is not combat that men detest most. It is the tedium, the petty rules, the filth, and the common soldier's state of utter ignorance regarding where he is going, when or why.

With the troop truck submerged near Karbala on April 4, the soaked troops and I were dumped onto other trucks already packed with soldiers. Shivering and sleep-deprived, we bounced toward Baghdad for the next 20 hours.

Our convoy was ambushed south of the capital, then lost its way. We stumbled into an idyllic water garden of lilies and marble columns. Under fire and assaulted by mosquitoes, we were pinned down there much of the night, our second in a row with no sleep.

The men cursed and moaned and were ordered by their noncommissioned officers, in bursts of loud profanity, to shut up. But the NCOs also complained bitterly that no one higher up was telling them what was happening.

Just before dawn, the convoy snaked its way to a group of buildings. The troops slept inside on an oily floor for three hours, expecting to take part that morning in the fight to seize Baghdad's international airport, which they believed was several miles away. But when the men awoke, they discovered they had spent the night at the airport. It had been taken by the 3rd Infantry the day before. And the water gardens turned out to be one of Hussein's nearby palaces.

The battalion's commanders knew all this, of course. But word never leaked down to the fighting men.

Ordinary soldiers are constantly foraging for scraps of information beyond their platoon or company, hoarding any precious nuggets.

"What's the news, man?" was the constant greeting I received from soldiers, and it shamed me to have to confess, usually, that I didn't know any more than they did. Anyone in the United States reading a newspaper or watching TV had a far better understanding of the war. I was like a scientist squinting into a microscope, oblivious to anything else in the lab, much less the world beyond the door.

At the airport that morning, I walked out onto the tarmac and stumbled upon a convoy of bullet-riddled tanks and Bradleys of the 3rd Infantry rumbling across the runway. The tankers told me they had just completed a harrowing run through Baghdad, killing roughly 1,000 soldiers while losing one tank and an American tank commander.

I sought out the 2nd Brigade commander, Col. David Perkins, and asked to link up with his men. He pointed to the open door of an armored personnel carrier. "We leave in 30 minutes," he said.

I ended up at the brigade command post on Baghdad's southern outskirts. Until then, I had spent my time at the battalion level and lower. Now I was privy to the planning of the assault on Baghdad with a brigade about to descend on the capital. My battle fog lifted.

When I was thrown with soldiers into combat on April 7, I wasn't just a reporter covering a story. I was in effect a crew member of Lightning 28, a Bradley whose gunner was setting Iraqi pickup trucks afire and cutting men in half with ragged bursts from the Bradley's "co-ax," its clattering M-240 machine gun.

When Iraqis fired RPGs — rocket-propelled grenades — at the Bradley and peppered it with small-arms fire, they were trying to kill everyone inside, including me.

That is the subtle and insidious alchemy of the embed. The seven soldiers in the Bradley were much more than news subjects. They were fellow Americans fighting desperately to stay alive, and my fate was linked inexorably to theirs.

The strangers launching RPGs at us from bunkers weren't just Iraqi fighters. They were the enemy.

War is an intensely selfish and personal experience. When I scanned the smoky streets through the Bradley's tiny glass vision blocks, searching for "Iraqi dismounts," as the tankers called infantrymen, I wasn't just recording the scene for a story. I was searching for targets.

Placed in a soldier's seat, I had been asked by an officer to perform a soldier's job. He said, "Hey, watch that vision block."

I saw flaming trucks and shadowy figures in the thick haze, but nothing stationary enough to be targeted and killed. Yet if I had spotted an exposed Iraqi fighter with an RPG aimed at the Bradley, I believe I would have screamed, "Dismount at 9 o'clock!" like anyone else inside. I was relieved that I did not have to make that decision.

A Bradley under fire cannot be covered dispassionately, like a news conference or a political rally. The vehicle commander, setting off shattering booms with each cannon round fired into Iraqi bunkers, wasn't an anonymous soldier to me. He was crew-cut Mark Jewell, a garrulous Marine major, a father of two troubled about missing his wedding anniversary that week.

The Bradley fought its way to a traffic circle near a presidential palace that morning. We watched through the vision blocks as the big guns on the tanks and Bradleys of Cyclone Company ripped into half a dozen suicide drivers speeding across the 14th of July Bridge. They kept coming — wild-eyed men, some in uniform, some in civilian clothes, some firing AK-47s from passenger windows.

The gunners inside the tanks and Bradleys kept up a wall of fire, ripping open chunks of roadway with warning shots before pulverizing pickup trucks and sedans and human beings in flaming red explosions. Some vehicles exploded more than once as incendiary rounds set off ammunition or explosives stored inside.

"There's brains and guts all over that bridge," Staff Sgt. Anthony J. Smith said with the spare and brutal commentary typical of so many soldiers I encountered.

We sat buttoned up in the Bradley, all hatches locked, as stray RPG and small-arms fire spattered the roadway. Suddenly the main cannon jammed, and Maj. Jewell radioed another vehicle for a repair tool. Minutes later, someone was pounding on the heavy rear hatch. The door swung open to reveal the helmeted form of Geoffrey Mohan, my colleague at The Times, a wrench in his hand.

Mohan had been in the next armored vehicle for the entire battle and had volunteered to deliver the tool in order to step outside to use his satellite phone to call in his story to the newsroom in Los Angeles.

Mohan was a godsend. With my computer and phone lost to the canal, I had no way to send my story on the pivotal battle of the war. Mohan lent me his laptop and phone.

I climbed outside for the first time in two hours. I was overcome by the stench of cordite and the peculiar sour odor of scorched human flesh, the remains of an Iraqi soldier who had been blown apart. His AK-47 and helmet were still there, arranged in a messy still life. His face was contorted in a grimace, but I felt no pity. I wanted to feel compassion for a fellow human being who had been slaughtered, but I could not stop thinking that his RPG could have left me dead on the spot.

Lt. Matthew Hanks noticed an RPG launcher lying in the dirt in a small grassy park a few yards from the Bradley. Then he saw several bunkers.

The radioman, Marine Sgt. Dennis Parks, grabbed a flashlight and Jewell's 9-millimeter Beretta. He volunteered to be a "tunnel rat" and explore the bunkers. I watched him disappear into a hole that had been covered with a sheet of corrugated metal and camouflaged with palm fronds.

Inside the bunker, around a bend in a tunnel, Parks found Iraqi soldiers huddled in the dark, their arms raised, begging not to be shot. Parks cursed and shouted for help. As he put it later, "My heart hit my [spine] and I started yelling at them" to get out.

Only after the Cyclone crews had hogtied 15 prisoners and collected seven RPG launchers, 60 rockets, 40 grenades and 5,000 rounds of ammo did Parks fully comprehend the lethal threat. He was a compact, nimble young man from Michigan, a 21-year-old with uncommon maturity and decisiveness.

"They could have easily killed us all. They could have hit us before we even knew where they were," he said. He seemed more mystified than relieved.

I survived, but other reporters did not. More than a dozen have died covering the war in Iraq, including Washington Post columnist Michael Kelly, who drowned along with a soldier when their Army Humvee plunged into a canal similar to the one that claimed my troop truck a day later.

Embed access also claimed Julio Anguita Parrado, a gentle, boyish reporter from El Mundo in Spain.

Parrado and I had shared the unnerving experience of listening to Col. Perkins lay out for his staff the plan to smash into the heart of Baghdad with just three battalions consisting of about 970 fighting men, 74 tanks and 54 Bradleys, backed by air and artillery.

It was the night of April 6, just hours before the tanks and Bradleys would roll out from the brigade command post on Baghdad's southern cusp.

Parrado was disturbed by a chilling assessment from the brigade intelligence officer, Maj. Joffery Watson, of the firepower still in the hands of the Special Republican Guard units protecting the capital.

Parrado approached me afterward, confessing his fear that the mission was too dangerous. He asked whether anyone would consider him a coward if he decided not to go along. I told him that I was afraid, too, and so were most of the soldiers. No one would think poorly of him.

Later that night, Parrado told me that he and a colleague, German photographer Christian Liebig, had decided to stay behind. Aware that I had lost my notebooks and was writing on scraps of paper, Parrado offered me a notebook.

I respected their decision, but I was going into the city. I had come too far to turn back just as the war was reaching a climax.

Soon after I left in the armored convoy, an Iraqi missile screamed into the brigade headquarters. Parrado and Liebig were killed instantly. Three soldiers also died and

17 were wounded, some of them horribly burned by a fireball that engulfed the command post.

My first reaction was shock and grief. It did not seem possible that men I had seen hours earlier were gone, or that a missile had pierced what seemed to be a haven at the rear.

My second reaction — one that many soldiers admitted they also experienced when hearing of combat casualties — was: Thank God it wasn't me. I hated myself, but it was true.

For me, the deaths underscored what may be obvious from afar but is easy to overlook at the front: War is capricious. No decision in combat can be fully rational, and there is no safe place in a war zone.

That war turns men callous was driven home to me again later that day as I sought out Perkins for an assessment of the battle raging through the city center.

I rode to his command post with a medic, Staff Sgt. Luther Robinson, a free spirit from Atlantic, North Carolina, whose armored vehicle was transporting a wounded Iraqi fighter from one of the bunkers.

The Iraqi, who gave his name as Aziz, was ashen-faced and writhing in pain from a terrible wound to his foot. It hung grotesquely, attached only by ligaments and held fast by a bandage Robinson had applied.

Aziz seemed determined to carry on an idle conversation with me. I had spoken a few words of Arabic to him from my limited supply of phrases. Now I was trying to write my story on Mohan's laptop.

I found myself becoming irritated at Aziz as he jabbered through his pain. A bloodied, half-delirious stranger, certain to lose his foot and perhaps his life, was trying to make polite conversation in the middle of a battle — and I was absorbed in a laptop.

To shut Aziz up, I handed him a bottle of water and told myself it was an act of mercy.

At that moment, I noticed an Iraqi grenade resting next to me on the gurney where I sat. An American soldier apparently had taken it from a bunker and left it there. Aziz saw it, too, and he shrugged. I moved the grenade out of his reach.

Outside, a tremendous explosion made the Bradley shudder. Robinson, standing in the hatch, bent down and grinned at me, his face red and smeared with sweat. He hollered: "I love this stuff!"

I understood what he meant. We had been transported from the ordinary and the mundane, and every sound and sight and emotion was intense and brilliant. Each moment seemed infused with a meaning that was difficult to comprehend. And when the battle was over, I felt enormous relief, but also a sense of deflation and an elusive feeling of loss.

After the worst of it, I lived in the Presidential Palace for a week. I watched GIs feed live sheep to the lions and cheetahs in the palace's private zoo. I roamed the halls and climbed to the roof to inspect four enormous sculpted heads of Hussein mounted there.

I had hundreds of rooms to choose from and selected a sunny ground-floor room overlooking a small garden.

When I had stayed up to write the night before, I slipped upstairs in the afternoons to one of the luxurious bedrooms with marble balconies overlooking the palace gardens. There, with the spring breeze carrying the scent of honeysuckle, I found a king-size bed and slept like a thief.

The adrenaline had drained by then, and the soldiers turned anxious and distracted. I felt the same way. There was a void. The battle had focused everyone's mind on a clearly defined goal. Now we were in the dangerous twilight between war and reconstruction.

The chaplains had soldiers lining up for counseling. They poured out tales of eviscerating strangers with fat rounds from their .50-caliber machine guns.

It wasn't that the soldiers felt guilty, the chaplains told me later. They had done what they were trained to do but had never fully comprehended what was required to destroy the enemy. This realization troubled them deeply.

I had never seen an armored brigade in action. The destruction inflicted by the tanks and Bradleys was astonishing. But more remarkable was the thorough and businesslike way the gunners went about their work. They were anxious and afraid and stimulated, of course. But they also were focused, methodical and deadly efficient.

"We're in the business of managing violence," explained Maj. Mark Rasins, who fought in the city for the 4th Battalion, 64th Armored Regiment.

Embedding taught me much about the way the American military functions under combat pressure. The military loves meetings, and paperwork about meetings. It loves to do things at night, preferably late at night. It spends days planning complex missions, only to cancel them abruptly. It loves to have everyone sit in vehicles with the engines running for long, maddening stretches. It prefers orders to logic, rules to imagination.

Yet with overwhelming air power and just three battalions on the ground in central Baghdad on April 7, the military had ripped out the heart of a major Arab capital with alarming speed.

I did not encounter any soldiers who reveled in killing. In fact, many men told me beforehand that they hoped they would not have to kill. But some laughed and mugged every time they passed an Iraqi corpse whose head had been flattened by a tank, and many spoke in a clinical and detached way of killing other men.

When I asked one company commander about events of Tuesday, April 8, he replied casually: "Uh, Tuesday, yeah. Tuesday afternoon we spent killing enemy dismounts."

Soldiers wearing chemical suits joked endlessly about the effects of biological or chemical weapons. They laughed about "doing the funky chicken," referring to convulsions caused by exposure to nerve agents. They nominated one another for "least mission critical" — that hapless soldier who would be the first one ordered to take off his gas mask after a chemical or biological attack.

In a convoy south of Baghdad on April 4, several soldiers and I watched a pair of A-10 Warthogs destroy trucks full of Iraqi fighters in the hazy distance. My companions were thrilled by the low growl of the planes as they unleashed barrages from their 30-millimeter Vulcan cannons at 4,700 rounds a minute. They cheered and shouted: "Yeah, man! They're gettin' some!"

Staff Sgt. Richard Clinton, a muscular Army Ranger, listened to them and said: "Somebody just died right now."

Outside the city of Najaf one afternoon, I asked Lt. Col. Fetterman whether his soldiers admitted to fear before battle. He was preparing to lead his men on an air assault mission, his pistol on his hip and two letters from his wife in his helmet liner.

"Here's what I tell my soldiers: What makes a man is the counterbalance between pride and fear," he said. "You reach down and find your pride and overcome your fear."

Embedded reporters had their own fears — of being killed or maimed, of missing a story, of being compromised by their craving for access or manipulated by commanders.

Last week, I wrote about five soldiers from the 3rd Infantry who were suspected of stealing $12.3 million from hidden Iraqi caches totaling $768 million in $100 bills.

I knew one of the suspects. He had told me about his children and his quarrels with his wife and his conflicted feelings about living in strangers' homes and pawing through their bedrooms. His predicament pained me.

There was no question I would write the story. But a staff officer later confronted me, accusing me of tarnishing his unit's reputation. He told me I should not have reported the thefts, that I was abusing my embed access.

"We don't need this negative publicity right now," he said, and I realized that by "we," he was including me.

❖❖

Other Books by the Los Angeles Times

DRAWING THE LINE
by Paul Conrad
Two hundred drawings, spanning the period from the late 1960s to President Clinton's impeachment trial, from America's premier political cartoonist. $25.45

ETERNALLY YOURS
by Jack Smith
Who can forget Jack Smith, the Los Angeles Times' columnist for nearly 40 years? When he died in 1996, we all lost a treasure. But at least his words survived. Here, Jack's widow, Denise, and his sons, Curt and Doug, have collected some of their favorite columns. $16.95

CURBSIDE L.A.
An Offbeat Guide to the City of Angels
by Cecilia Rasmussen
Enjoy a truly eclectic tour of Los Angeles. Explore the L.A. you've not seen with enticing excursions into the city's peerless history and diversity. $19.45

DAY HIKERS' GUIDE TO SOUTHERN CALIFORNIA
by John McKinney
Walks in Southern California, from the simply scenic to the challenging, as described by *Los Angeles Times* hiking columnist and author John McKinney. $16.45

52 WEEKS IN THE CALIFORNIA GARDEN
by Robert Smaus
How to make the most of your garden by the foremost authority on gardening in Southern California. $17.45

ANSWERS FOR CALIFORNIA GARDENERS
by Robert Smaus
Expert advice in an easy-to-read Q&A format from the foremost authority on Southern California gardening. An excellent companion to Smaus' *52 Weeks in the California Garden*. $21.45

IMAGINING LOS ANGELES
Photographs of a 20th Century City
Foreword by Ray Bradbury
Collected here are some 175 photos from more than a dozen Southern California archives that tell the tale of men and women from all over the world who hoped and dared on a grand scale and who turned Los Angeles into the quintessential 20th century city. $28.95

L.A. UNCONVENTIONAL
by Cecilia Rasmussen
Where some people see roadblocks, others, such as the men and women in this volume, see possibility, opportunity and excitement. $30.95

THE SAN FERNANDO VALLEY
America's Suburb
by Kevin Roderick
Valley native Kevin Roderick recounts the area's vibrant past, from its Native American residents through the Spanish, Mexican and American settlers, spinning along the way the tales that give the Valley its unique history and culture. $26.45

SUNSET BOULEVARD
Cruising the Heart of Los Angeles
by Amy Dawes
A guide to the sights, experiences and lost legends of Los Angeles' most famous boulevard. Loaded with photos, maps and tips on where to dine, party and shop. $28.45

ICONIC L.A.
Stories of L.A.'s Most Memorable Buildings
by Gloria Koenig
The architecture and drama behind 13 of Los Angeles' most recognizable landmarks, including the Bradbury Building, the Getty Museum, Walt Disney Concert Hall and the LAX Theme Building. With an introduction by Frank O. Gehry. $29.95

DESERT REALTY
by Ed Freeman
This is the Southern California desert you've never seen. Photographer and computer artist Ed Freeman has digitally manipulated snapshots of ordinary buildings and turned then in spectacular works of art. $33.45

LAST OF THE BEST
90 Columns From the 1990s
by Jim Murray
The best of Jim's columns from the last decade of his life are included in this paperback volume compiled by *Los Angeles Times* Sports Editor Bill Dwyre and featuring a foreword by Dodger legend Tommy Lasorda. $19.45

THE GREAT ONES
by Jim Murray
The top men and women of the sports world written about as only this late, great sports columnist could. Foreword by Arnold Palmer. $24.45